THE AMERICAN TRAJECTORY

Divine or Demonic?

by

DAVID RAY GRIFFIN

Clarity Press, Inc

ISBN: 978-0-9986947-7-1

EBOOK ISBN: 978-0-9986947-8-8

In-house editor: Diana G. Collier

Cover: R. Jordan P. Santos

Photo credit: His 128th birthday / Keppler. Library of Congress http://www.loc.gov/pictures/item/2011645546/

Library of Congress Cataloging-in-Publication Data

Names: Griffin, David Ray, 1939- author.
Title: The American trajectory : divine or demonic? / by David Ray Griffin.
Description: Atlanta, GA : Clarity Press, [2018] | Includes bibliographical
references and index.
Identifiers: LCCN 2018004815 (print) | LCCN 2018017104 (ebook) | ISBN
9780999874707 | ISBN 9780998694795
Subjects: LCSH: United States--Foreign relations--20th century. | United
States--Foreign relations--Philosophy. | United
States--History--Philosophy. | United States--History--20th century. |
Exceptionalism--United States--History. | National characteristics,
American--History. | Imperialism--United States--History. | Christianity
and politics--United States. | Political ethics--United States.
Classification: LCC E713 (ebook) | LCC E713 .G75 2018 (print) | DDC
973.9--dc23
LC record available at https://lccn.loc.gov/2018004815

Clarity Press, Inc.
2625 Piedmont Rd. NE, Ste. 56
Atlanta, GA. 30324 , USA
http://www.claritypress.com

"David Ray Griffin is a master of the art of courageously, constructively and meticulously exposing and debunking dangerous myths, propaganda and disinformation. He is a therapeutic disinfectant for brainwashed minds. Just as his previous book, *Bush and Cheney: How They Ruined America and the World*, was essential reading to understand the world in which we now live, *The American Trajectory: Divine or Demonic?* is essential reading to understand the true nature of the 'exceptional' role of the United States in world affairs—past, present and future."

—John Whitbeck, International lawyer;
author of *The World According to Whitbeck*

"This new book by David Ray Griffin is essential reading for anybody who wants to understand the dark side of US Imperialism in its global context."

—Dr. Daniele Ganser, Director Swiss Institute for Peace and Energy Research; author of many books, including *NATO's Secret Armies.*

"David Ray Griffin has done it again. His new book should be read as a prequel to the seminal *Bush and Cheney: How They Ruined America and the World.* Supported by extensive research, Griffin thoroughly debunks the myth of an American Empire as a benign, exceptionalist, divinely ordained historical agent. Instead of Manifest Destiny, what reality-based Griffin charters is the 'malign'ways of US foreign policy since the 19th century; a trajectory founded by slavery and genocide of indigenous peoples and then imperially expanded, non-stop. 'Malign' happens to be a term currently very much in vogue across the Beltway—but always to designate US competitors Russia and China...

This sharp, concise history of the American Empire ultimately demonstrates, in Griffin's analysis, the 'fraud' of endorsing self-praising American Exceptionalism. A must read."

—Pepe Escobar, *Asia Times*/Hong Kong;
author of *2030* and *Empire of Chaos*

TABLE OF CONTENTS

ACKNOWLEDGMENTS

I was blessed with people willing and able to provide good advice on the various chapters: Daniel Athearn, John Whitbeck, and Elizabeth Woodworth.

As for content, the endnotes show my indebtedness to a wide range of scholars, especially Gar Alperovitz, Andrew Bacevich, William Blum, Noam Chomsky, Bruce Cumings, William Engdahl, Philip Foner, Daniele Ganser, Piero Gleijeses, Sylvester John Hemleben, Robert Hilderbrand, Chalmers Johnson, George McT. Kahin, Walter Karp, Stephen Kinzer, Gabriel Kolko, Walter LaFeber, Alfred McCoy, G.J. Meyer, Cornelius Murphy, F.S. Northedge, Diana Preston, David Schmitz, Michael Shafer, Stephen Sniegoski, Robert Stinnett, Paul Williams, Marilyn Young, and Howard Zinn.

As for bringing my long-gestating manuscript to the light of day, my thanks go to the always-easy-to-work-with Diana Collier of Clarity Press.

Finally, as always, I am primarily indebted to my wife, Ann Jaqua, *sine qua non.*

INTRODUCTION

Since its formation, US politicians have referred to America in divine terms. In some cases, this description has been literal—with the country being portrayed as having been especially inspired and guided by God. Sometimes America is treated as divine only metaphorically—as exceptionally good, which is what is usually meant by the phrase "American Exceptionalism."

1. America as Divinely Founded and Guided

Presidents of the United States have often described America as behaving in accord with divine providence. In his first Inaugural Address, George Washington said:

> No people can be bound to acknowledge and adore the Invisible Hand which conducts the affairs of men more than those of the United States. Every step by which they have advanced to the character of an independent nation seems to have been distinguished by some token of providential agency.[1]

John Adams, in his inaugural address, said that Americans

had been operating "under an overruling Providence which had so signally protected this country from the first."[2] In his Farewell Address, Andrew Jackson said to the people:

> Providence has showered on this favored land blessings without number, and has chosen you as the guardians of freedom, to preserve it for the benefit of the human race. May He who holds in His hands the destinies of nations, make you worthy of the favors He has bestowed.[3]

More recently, Ronald Reagan, prior to becoming president, said:

> You can call it mysticism if you want to, but I have always believed that there was some divine plan that placed this great continent between two oceans to be sought out by those who were possessed of an abiding love of freedom.[4]

Still more recently, President George W. Bush said:

> This young century will be liberty's century. By promoting liberty abroad, we will build a safer world. By encouraging liberty at home, we will build a more hopeful America. Like generations before us, we have a calling from beyond the stars to stand for freedom.[5]

In the formative years of the United States, there were many terms used to summarize the view of America as called by God to be the agent of special divine purposes. One of these terms was "God's New Israel." A sermon using this term described the hardships suffered by George Washington's troops in the Revolutionary War as parallel with those of the children of Israel in the wilderness.[6]

Then there was the term "Redeemer Nation," which was

extensively discussed in a book of this title.[7] "Almighty God," said Senator Albert J. Beveridge in a 1900 address entitled *In Support of an American Empire*, "has marked the American people as His chosen nation to finally lead in the redemption of the world."[8] In 1919, President Woodrow Wilson said that if America supports the League of Nations (see Chapter 7 below), the United States will lead in the "redemption of the world."[9]

Beveridge's statement also used a term that was more widely employed to characterize America—that it is God's "chosen nation," so that Americans are God's "chosen people."[10] More modestly, Abraham Lincoln referred to America as "God's Almost Chosen Nation."[11]

Perhaps the best known of the terms for characterizing America's divine mission was "manifest destiny," which—said famous sociologist Daniel Bell in 1975—"was the civil religion of 19th-century America." This phrase, said Bell, indicated "the conviction of a special virtue of the American people different from anything known in Europe."[12] This phrase was used in 1900, for example, by Senator Henry Cabot Lodge in a speech defending the taking of the Philippine Islands. Lodge said:

> I do not believe this nation was raised up for nothing. I have faith that it has a great mission for the world—a mission of good, a mission of freedom. I would have it fulfill what I think is its manifest destiny.[13]

The idea of manifest destiny is discussed more fully in Chapter 1.

Although statements describing God as especially concerned with America were more widespread in previous centuries than today, this belief is still held. In fact, surveys in recent years suggested that over half of the American people believe that God has a "special relationship" with the United States, or that God has assigned this county a "special role" in history.[14]

In 2016, talk-show host Michael Medved published a book entitled *The American Miracle: Divine Providence in the*

Rise of the Republic. Endorsing the "old idea that God shows special tenderness toward the American experiment," Medved said that the truth of this idea is proved by divine miracles that accompanied the founding of the country, such as the "intervention of supernatural forces" on the "the Glorious Fourth"—the fiftieth Fourth of July.[15]

This intervention, said Medved, was demonstrated by the fact that "the two titans who had played the most prominent roles in declaring independence," John Adams and Thomas Jefferson, both died on that day.[16] The fact that providence "selected the United States for special purposes" was also demonstrated by the "nation's illogically rapid rise to world dominance." Indeed, said Medved, "the story of America stakes its own powerful claim [alongside that of the Bible] as the greatest story ever told."[17]

To give one final example: In February 2017, just after Donald Trump had been elected president, David Brooks in *The New York Times* described America as a nation "assigned by providence to spread democracy and prosperity; to welcome the stranger; to be brother and sister to the whole human race."[18]

2. American Exceptionalism

Today, rather than using terms such as God's New Israel, Redeemer Nation, or Chosen Nation, many people simply describe America as *exceptional.* One way to express American Exceptionalism today is to call America the "indispensable nation." This phrase was coined by Bill Clinton's secretary of state, Madeline Albright, who said: "We are the indispensable nation. We stand tall and we see further than other countries into the future, and we see the danger here to all of us."[19]

However, although the idea of American Exceptionalism is generally used in a self-congratulatory way, at least by Americans, it evidently originated as a disparaging term. In 1929, Soviet leader Joseph Stalin reportedly condemned the "heresy of American exceptionalism." The heresy was the claim that American capitalism was an exception to Marxism's economic laws, held to be universal. Then in 1930, the Communist Party USA, indicating that the beginning of the Great Depression showed American capitalism not really to be an exception, said: "The storm of the economic crisis in the United States blew down the house of cards of American exceptionalism."[20]

In any case, even aside from Marxism's disparaging use of the term, the endorsement of American Exceptionalism does not necessarily indicate praise. For example, in *American Exceptionalism: A Double-Edged Sword*, sociologist Seymour Martin Lipset said that America's "organizing principles and founding political institutions" are "exceptional, qualitatively different from those of other Western nations." But these principles and institutions do not necessarily make America the best nation.

In speaking of American Exceptionalism as a "double-edged sword," Lipset meant that "the norms and behavior of an open democratic society that appear so admirable" are inherently linked to "many negative traits that currently characterize the society, such as income inequality, high crime rates, [and] low levels of electoral participation." In fact, far from calling America the best nation, Lipset said, "we are the worst as well as the best, depending on which quality is being addressed."[21]

However, most commentators in the United States who speak of American Exceptionalism mean that America is the best nation in the world. In a book entitled *The Myth of American Exceptionalism*, Godfrey Hodgson said that the idea generally means that, besides being the richest and most powerful nation in the world, America "is also politically and morally exceptional."[22]

Indeed, a Gallup poll in 2010 found that 80% of the American public believes America "has a unique character that makes it the greatest country in the world."[23] Because the self-congratulatory version of American Exceptionalism is so widespread in the country, it is virtually obligatory on US presidents to confess this creed. At a NATO meeting in 2009, President Obama, in response to a question as to whether he affirmed this belief, said:

> I believe in American exceptionalism, just as I suspect that the Brits believe in British exceptionalism and the Greeks believe in Greek exceptionalism.[24]

This response evoked an enormous amount of criticism. *National Review* portrayed Obama's answer as "The Bashing of American Exceptionalism." The author, Jonah Goldberg, said that criticisms of the idea of American Exceptionalism are based on the idea that it "is an artifact of right-wing jingoism, xenophobia, or ignorance." The truth, Goldberg said, is that "American exceptionalism has been a well-established notion among scholars for more than a century," as illustrated by thinkers such as Alexis de Tocqueville and Seymour Martin Lipset. However, ignoring the ways in which de Tocqueville and Lipset defined American Exceptionalism, Goldberg stated what *he* meant by the term: "America is the greatest country in the world."[25]

In other words, Obama was criticized for "bashing" American exceptionalism because he did not endorse it in an unqualified manner. Apparently in response, Obama in the future would say—as he did in his West Point speech in 2014—"I believe in American exceptionalism with every fiber of my being."[26]

More recently, in February 2017—before he had agreed to play by neocon rules—President Trump ran afoul of the exceptionalism police. During an interview on Fox News, Bill O'Reilly asked Trump why he respected a killer like Putin. Trump replied: "There are a lot of killers. We've got a lot of killers. What, you think our country's so innocent?" Aghast that Trump was "drawing a moral equivalency between the United States and Russia," the editorial board of *The New York Times* said: "Asserting the moral and political superiority of the United States over Russia has not traditionally been a difficult maneuver for American presidents."[27]

In an essay entitled "The Myth of American Exceptionalism," Stephen Walt laid out several versions of this myth. According to one of these versions, "The United States Behaves Better Than

Other Nations Do." According to another one, "The United States Is Responsible for Most of the Good in the World."[28] A third one repeats the point made in the previous section: "God Is on Our Side."[29]

One might suspect that the destructive results of the wars in Vietnam, Afghanistan, and Iraq would have made Americans less self-congratulatory. It did appear at the time that the disastrous Vietnam War might bring the America-is-the-greatest-nation-in-the-world version of American Exceptionalism to an end. Having said that the American Century "foundered on the shoals of Vietnam," Daniel Bell, in a 1975 essay entitled "The End of American Exceptionalism," declared:

> Today, the belief in American exceptionalism has vanished with the end of empire, the weakening of power, the loss of faith in the nation's future. . . . The American Century . . . foundered on the shoals of Vietnam. . . . There is no longer a Manifest Destiny of mission. We have not been immune to the corruption of power. We have not been the exception. . . . We are a nation like all other nations.[30]

However, self-praising American Exceptionalism did not vanish permanently. As pointed out in an article asking "Are We Coming to the End of 'American Exceptionalism?'" which was published by *Newsweek* in 2016, "the belief in exceptionalism came roaring back with Ronald Reagan's 'shining city on a hill' in the 1980s."[31]

This post-Vietnam recovery of American Exceptionalism has been surveyed by Trevor McCrisken in a book entitled *American Exceptionalism and the Legacy of Vietnam: U.S. Foreign Policy Since 1974.* In the chapters of that book, McCrisken explained how the American presidents for the remainder of the 20th century—Gerald Ford, Jimmy Carter, Ronald Reagan, George H. W. Bush, and Bill Clinton—tried to revive the public's faith in American Exceptionalism.[32] These efforts were eventually successful, providing support for the claim of an article entitled: "American Exceptionalism: An Idea That Will Not Die."[33]

In any case, the 21st century began with American Exceptionalism alive and well. The 9/11 attacks then made Americans even more patriotic, and the war on Afghanistan did not erode this faith. But then, the Iraq War was another matter.

Part of the reason for this loss of faith, said Stanley Hoffman, was the "new exceptionalism" of the Bush-Cheney administration, according to which "the most important of America's unique qualities was its military dominance," the belief that "the good the United States does for the world justifies all means," and "the claim that the U.S. Constitution allows no bowing to a superior law, such as international law."[34]

Besides the fact that the Iraq War led many Americans to reject the idea that America is exceptional in a positive sense,[35] it also led to a great increase in anti-Americanism around the world.[36]

However, there are citizens of this country for whom American Exceptionalism in the positive sense is still endorsed as strongly as before. One of those was former Vice President Dick Cheney (who was primarily responsible for the Iraq War[37]). A book entitled *Exceptional: Why the World Needs a Powerful America*, coauthored by Cheney and his daughter Liz Cheney, began by asserting: "Yes, We Are Exceptional." Spelling out their self-congratulatory beliefs, the Cheneys said:

> We have guaranteed freedom, security, and peace for a larger share of humanity than has any other nation in all of history. There is no other like us. . . . We are, as a matter of empirical fact and undeniable history, the greatest force for good the world has even known.

Our children need to know, they continued, "that they are citizens of the most powerful, good, and honorable nation in the history of mankind, *the* exceptional nation."[38] At the end of the book, they continued their praise of America by saying:

> [W]e have been the last, best hope of earth because we are freedom's defender, not just for ourselves, but also for millions around the world. We do it because it is right. . . . No nation has ever worked so successfully to extend freedom to others. No nation, in the history of mankind, has ever been such a force for good.[39]

In addition to pointing out, "It is not healthy to congratulate oneself," Godfrey Hodgson also expressed distaste for the tendency of Americans to demand "uncritical assertion of national superiority" and especially for "a new insistence that America be admired, almost worshiped."[40] Hodgson also found American Exceptionalism objectionable insofar as it constitutes "a myth that seems to justify, even demand," that Americans "rule others by superior force."[41]

Closely related, American Exceptionalism can become *exemptionalism*, meaning that the claim to be exceptional can lead a country to believe that it is exempt from the standards that apply to other countries. Discussing this issue in relation to North Korea's test of a nuclear weapon in 2013, Glenn Greenwald wrote:

> North Korea tested a nuclear weapon, and the US—the country with the world's largest stockpile of that weapon and the only one in history to use it—led the condemnation.

Greenwald was, of course, asking why America may have nuclear weapons but North Korea may not.

Charles Cooke, the editor of *National Review* Online, rejected the perspective of people like Greenwald, writing (evidently without tongue in cheek):

> I never understand the moral equivalence on this. We can have nuclear weapons because we're right. They can't because they're wrong. . . . Why should we condemn North Korea's test? Because they're a totalitarian nightmare state and this is the greatest country in history.

In other words, said Greenwald mockingly, because we are the greatest country ever, we are "entitled to do that which other countries are not."[42]

According to Russian policy expert James Carden, "the hubristic nature of American Exceptionalist ideology feeds delusions of innocence, which serve to prevent a critical rethinking of America's recent, mainly catastrophic adventures abroad. . . . In the end, the ideology of American Exceptionalism feeds delusions of American Innocence and prepares the ground for military intervention the world over."[43]

3. American Empire: Benign or Malign?

Whereas Americans tend to describe their country as exceptionally good, perhaps divine, other countries tend to disagree. Indeed, "Nothing is more vexing to foreigners," said Andrew Kohut and Bruce Stokes of the Pew Research Center, "than Americans' belief that America is a shining city on a hill."[44]

Some countries have even portrayed America as demonic, as when Iran's Ayatollah Khomeini in 1979 began referring to America as the Great Satan (while referring to the Soviet Union as the Lesser Satan).[45] Some critics of America speak of it as literally possessed by the devil or demons, but the term is usually employed metaphorically, to indicate that America is terribly evil and destructive.

Although treatments by Americans of their country as demonic had been given earlier—such as the criticisms by thinkers such as Mark Twain and William James of America's behavior in its war against the Philippines (see Chapter 1)—the highly negative view of America first became widespread among its citizens during the Vietnam War. It again became widespread because of America's attacks on Iraq and other countries in the so-called War on Terror.

The question of whether America is divine or demonic, exceptionally good or exceptionally bad, is now largely discussed in terms of the question of whether the *American Empire* is benign or malign, benevolent or malevolent.

Logically, of course, there is a third view, according to which the American Empire is neither benevolent nor malevolent but simply neutral. One might think that its policies neither help nor harm people, or that its helpful policies balance out its harmful ones. But most people who think about the issue seem to regard the American empire as either good or bad, benevolent or malevolent. The question this book addresses is which of these views is best supported by the historical evidence? That question presupposes, of course, that America has an empire.

American Empire

For most of the 20th century, talk of an "American Empire," and especially of "American imperialism," was virtually taboo. Almost the only writers to use such language were left-wing critics of American policy, such as Noam Chomsky, Richard Falk, Harry Magdoff, Michael Parenti, and Gore Vidal.[46] Accordingly, as Andrew Bacevich pointed out in his 2002 book, *American Empire*, "references to an American empire . . . were . . . fighting words." This was so because of what Bacevich called "the cherished American tradition according to which the United States is not and cannot be an empire."[47]

This tradition had been so cherished that those analysts of US foreign policy who violated it were marginalized, being either derisively dismissed or simply ignored by mainline commentators. It was simply not permissible to describe America as a burgeoning empire, at least in public discourse.

However, as Bacevich pointed out, all this changed early in the 21st century. American politicians still felt a need, to be sure, to avoid acknowledging reality. President Bush, in his speech at West Point in June of 2002, said: "We don't seek an empire." And when Secretary of Defense Donald Rumsfeld was asked by a correspondent if the Bush administration was bent on "empire-building," he replied (with or without tongue in cheek): "We don't seek empires. We're not imperialistic. We never have been. I can't imagine why you'd even ask the question."[48]

But American commentators on US foreign policy came in the 21st century to speak freely of American hegemony and empire. As neocon columnist Charles Krauthammer put it in 2002: "People are coming out of the closet on the word 'empire.'"[49] In that year, for example, Michael Ignatieff, after quoting Bush's statement "We don't seek an empire," asked rhetorically: "Yet what word but 'empire' describes the awesome thing that America is becoming?"[50]

This coming out of the closet often involved comparisons to Rome. "America is no mere international citizen," wrote Krauthammer. "It is the dominant power in the world, more dominant than any since Rome."[51] Andrew Bacevich made the point even more dramatically. With reference to the statement by the great American historian of the first part of the 20th century, Charles Beard, that "America is not to be Rome,"[52] Bacevich added that "most citizens still comforted themselves with the belief that as the sole superpower the United States was *nothing* like Rome." But in the 20th century, Bacevich said, "The reality that Beard feared has come to pass: like it or not, America today *is* Rome."[53]

As Krauthammer illustrated, the commentators who in this century came to use the E-word (empire) and the I-word (imperialism) for America were proudly at the opposite end of the spectrum from the left-wing critics, who in earlier decades were about the only ones to use these words. The political conservatives and neo-conservatives have even engaged in something of a public relations campaign to reverse the earlier conceit that America is not an empire.

For example, in 2000, Richard Haass, who was soon to

become the director of policy planning in Colin Powell's State Department, gave an address called "Imperial America," in which he called on Americans to "re-conceive their global role from one of a traditional nation-state to an imperial power."[54] Krauthammer, having made his coming-out-of-the-closet comment, added that this is a good thing, because Americans need to face up to responsibilities entailed by the fact that they are now undisputed masters of the world.[55]

In so arguing, Krauthammer was taking a line similar to that in British historian Niall Ferguson's *Empire,* a book widely acclaimed by American advocates of empire-building. Saying, "The United States is the empire that dare not speak its name," Ferguson said: "An empire that doesn't recognize its own power is a dangerous one."[56] In a later book, *Colossus: The Price of America's Empire*, Ferguson argued that the primary problem with the American empire is that it is "an empire in denial," which leads it to allocate insufficient time and resources to bring about political and economic transformations in the problematic countries it targets.[57]

The American Empire as Benign

Given the fact that "empire" and "imperialism" were widely considered antithetical to American ideals throughout the 20th century, most Americans probably found it startling to hear fellow Americans and their allies acknowledging that America has an empire and that it should exercise its imperial tasks more fully and openly. But these advocates of empire-building are picking up on the view, popular in the 18th and 19th centuries, that America was creating an empire, which was a good thing for the world, because it is a benign, even benevolent, empire. Thomas Jefferson spoke of the country as building an "empire of liberty"[58] or "empire for liberty."[59]

George Washington's protégé, David Humphreys, wrote a poem that included these lines:

> Our constitutions form'd on freedom's base,
> Which all the blessings of all lands embrace;

> Embrace humanity's extended cause,
> A world of our empire, for a world of our laws.[60]

America's cause, in other words, is identical with humanity's cause, which is freedom.

This school of thought was, in fact, expressed by a few thinkers prior to the collapse of the Soviet Union. For example, in a 1966 book entitled *Pax Americana*, Ronald Steel acknowledged that "by any conventional standards for judging such things," America is "an imperial power," having an empire "the scope of which the world has never seen."[61] However, America had been, Steel argued,

> engaged in a kind of welfare imperialism, empire building for noble ends rather than for such base motives as profit and influence. . . , permitting other nations to enjoy the benefits of freedom, democracy, and self-determination.[62]

When America intervenes, Steel said—at the time that the debate about the American role in Vietnam was heating up—it does so with "the most noble motives and with the most generous impulses."[63] In the same vein, Samuel Huntington in 1982 wrote:

> The overall effect of American power on other societies [has been] to further liberty, pluralism, and democracy. . . . The conflict between American power and American principles virtually disappears when it is applied to the American impact on other societies.[64]

Steel and Huntington later became more skeptical of American goodness,[65] but the earlier line they took became the leitmotif of those who, after the collapse of the Soviet Union, advocated imperialism.

In 1990, for example, Charles Krauthammer published an

essay entitled "The Unipolar Moment." Speaking, like Steel, of a *Pax Americana*, Krauthammer said that, although historically,

> the world recoils at the thought of a single dominant power for fear of what it will do with its power. . . [,] America is the exception to this rule [because] the world generally sees it as benign, [as a power that] acts not just out of self-interest but a sense of right.[66]

Another prominent representative of this point of view, neocon Robert Kagan, wrote an essay in 1998 entitled "The Benevolent Empire," in which he said:

> Ever since the United States emerged as a great power, the identification of the interests of others with its own has been the most striking quality of American foreign and defense policy. Americans seem to have internalized and made second nature a conviction held only since World War II: Namely, that their own well-being depends fundamentally on the well-being of others. . . ; that American freedom depends on the survival and spread of freedom elsewhere; that aggression anywhere threatens the danger of aggression everywhere.[67]

In the same vein, Canadian historian Michael Ignatieff, claiming that America's empire is devoted to replacing dictatorships with democracies, wrote:

> America's empire is not like empires of times past, built on . . . conquest. . . . [It] is a new invention . . . , an empire lite, a global hegemony whose grace notes are free markets, human rights and democracy. . . . It is the imperialism of . . . good intentions.[68]

One of the most extreme statements was made by Dinesh D'Souza, who notoriously was pardoned in 2018 by President Trump. In 2002, D'Souza had written: "America has become an empire," but happily "the most magnanimous imperial power ever."[69]

What the members of this school have in common is the idea that America acts in terms of ideals rather than interests, or at least that, as Bacevich described their position: "To the extent that interests [have] figured at all, . . . American interests and American ideals [have been] congruent."[70] Stated more simply, Hillary Clinton, during the 2016 presidential campaign, said: "America is already great. But we are great because we are good."[71]

From this point of view, the American Empire can only be a blessing for all. Whenever America triumphs, democracy triumphs.

The American Empire as Malign

The view of American imperialism as a benevolent enterprise devoted to the promotion of freedom, democracy, and human rights is strongly challenged by intellectuals of varying persuasions. Rejecting the portrait of a democracy-promoting American empire as a myth, they argue that the United States, like Rome and every other imperial power, has used its power to enrich and aggrandize itself, a goal that has often led it to rob, oppress, terrorize, and even slaughter other peoples. Several advocates of this view will be discussed:

Noam Chomsky: Whereas Colin Powell declared that the United States is now "the motive force for freedom and democracy in the world,"[72] Noam Chomsky entitled one of his books about US foreign policy *Deterring Democracy.*[73] While leaders of the Bush administration were proclaiming that they had intervened in Iraq to bring democracy to its people, Chomsky commented on the "implausibility of the belief that Washington is suddenly concerned with democracy and human rights in Iraq, or elsewhere."[74] He said, in fact, that the Bush-Cheney administration by early 2003 had shown "a display of contempt for democracy for which no parallel comes easily to mind, accompanied by professions of sincere dedication to human rights and democracy."[75]

Chomsky's 2003 book, *Hegemony or Survival,* expressed by its subtitle, *America's Quest for Global Dominance,* Chomsky's view of the Bush administration's real agenda. Chomsky's view as to the import of that quest was shown by the stark choice presented in the book's main title. Arguing that America's drive for military dominance now poses a threat to the very survival of the human race, Chomsky also argued that the US government's willingness to take this risk reflected its "value system," according to which "hegemony is more important than survival."[76]

Richard Falk: The goal of the Bush-Cheney administration was likewise seen by Richard Falk as global dominance, rather than global democracy. Explicitly taking issue with "the school of benign imperialists," which saw the American Empire as "a benevolent political configuration," Falk suggested instead that it involved a "global domination project," which posed the threat of "global fascism."

Saying that several features of 21st-century US foreign policy pointed in this direction, Falk especially referred to the Bush-Cheney administration's (1) use of the "mega-terrorism" of 9/11 as a pretext for attacks on countries that had no relationship to mega-terrorism; (2) aspiration to military preeminence in conjunction with the rejection of any constraints from international law and the United Nations; (3) movement to intensify state power at the expense of civil and political rights; and (4) "dangerous blend of religious and geopolitical zeal."[77]

Samuel Huntington: It is not surprising, of course, that such views are held by left-leaning thinkers such as Chomsky and Falk, who have been critical of American imperialism all along. It *is* surprising, however, to find that some well-informed conservatives also reject the portrayal of the American empire as benevolent, or at least benign. Samuel Huntington revealed his change of mind in a 1999 essay entitled "The Lonely Superpower." After citing some American officials who portray the United States as a "benign hegemon," Huntington commented: "Benign hegemony, however, is in the eye of the hegemon."[78]

Andrew Bacevich: In the aforementioned 2002 book by Bacevich, *American Empire,* Bacevich said that as a conservative, he was surprised to discover that those left-leaning radicals who had described the American project as a drive to create a global empire were right. Bacevich's revelation came in the 1990s when the US Government, having defeated the Soviet Empire, did not drastically slash its military budget, its weapons programs, and its overseas deployments. That was what should have happened if the American participation in the Cold War had been, as officially claimed, a purely defensive effort to contain Soviet expansionism. Instead, however,

> in the decade following the fall of the Berlin Wall, . . . [t]he United States employed military power not merely in response to a crisis. . . It did so to . . . anticipate, intimidate, preempt . . . . and control. And it did so routinely and continuously. In the age of globalization, the Department of Defense completed its transformation into a Department of Power Projection.[79]

These developments convinced Bacevich that his understanding of what had been going on had been false.

Looking for a key to understand what was really going on, Bacevich turned to William Appleman Williams, whose mentor had been Charles Beard and who himself had become the mentor of many of the historians who came to write of America as an empire.[80] Besides his most influential book, *The Tragedy of American Diplomacy*, which was first published in 1959,[81] Williams also published, among other works, *From Colony to Empire* (1972) and *Empire as a Way of Life* (1980).[82]

Although Williams had long been the *bête noire* of conservative and even liberal thinkers who rejected criticisms of America as an empire, Bacevich decided that Williams was basically correct about American foreign policy—that it reflected "a coherent grand strategy" that had remained essentially the same for many decades. "[T]he scope of [this] project," said Bacevich, "is nothing short of stupendous," because its goal is the creation of a military-political-economic-cultural empire of global scope.[83] By 1992, furthermore, America had come close to realizing this goal, having after "nearly a century of struggle . . . emerged victorious, becoming unarguably the greatest power in all recorded history."[84]

Besides accepting the reality of an American empire of global extent, Bacevich also rejected the central claims of those who regard it as benign. He dismissed, for example, what he called the "The Myth of the Reluctant Superpower," according to which "greatness was not sought; it just happened . . . as an unintended consequence of actions taken either in self-defense or on behalf of others." He also dismissed the conceit that "the United States [has] fought [in wars] for altruistic purposes, seeking to end war itself and to make the world safe for democracy."[85] He ridiculed the claim "that the promotion of peace, democracy, and human rights and the punishment of evil-doers—*not* the pursuit of self-interest—[has] defined the essence of American diplomacy." And as quoted above, he rejected the claim that, "[t]o the extent that interests [have] figured at all, . . . American interests and American ideals [have been] congruent."[86]

Bacevich rejected all of that rhetoric and spoke instead of "the unflagging self-interest and large ambitions underlying all U.S. policy" and of the aim of US forces "to achieve something approaching omnipotence: 'Full Spectrum Dominance.'" He mocked the claim that, whereas such power wielded by others would be threatening, "it is by definition benign" in America's hands, because the leader of the free world "does not exploit or dominate but acts on behalf of purposes that look beyond mere self-interest."[87]

Finally, whereas believers in America's benign imperialism claim that America intervenes in countries such as Iraq in order to promote peace and democracy, Bacevich pointed out that in previous countries in which America has intervened, such as Haiti and the Dominican Republic, "democracy [did not] flower as a result." The result of the US "war on terror," he added, is less likely to be a world genuinely at peace than "a Pax Americana . . . maintained by force of American arms." With regard to the US-led NATO intervention in Serbia in the Kosovo conflict, which President Clinton had described as a matter of doing "the right thing," Bacevich said that this war "had never actually been about doing the right thing in the right way. Its purpose had been to sustain American primacy."[88]

Chalmers Johnson: Bacevich was not the only conservative who wrote critically about the nature of American foreign policy after coming to reject prior assumptions about its benign nature. Chalmers Johnson was another. Unlike Bacevich, however, Johnson became an *erstwhile* conservative. His conclusions about the extent and non-benign character of the American empire led him to become a radical critic.

For most of his professional life, Johnson had been a conservative who, in his own words, was "a spear carrier for empire." But about a year before 9/11, he published *Blowback: The Costs and Consequences of American Empire.* In this book, Johnson argued that it is important for us "to grasp what the United States really is," namely, that "Washington is the headquarters of a global military-economic dominion."

The fact that Johnson did not consider this dominion benign was shown by his definition of "blowback": negative consequences for ordinary citizens of policies carried out by their government without their knowledge.[89] Explaining why most Americans do not know about these policies, he suggested that because Americans have had a self-image of championing liberty and democracy around the world, their leaders have exercised "stealth imperialism," meaning a kind that is invisible to the majority of the citizens. "Most Americans," Johnson said, "are probably unaware of how Washington exercises its global hegemony, since so much of this activity takes place either in relative secrecy or under comforting rubrics."[90]

Johnson developed his ideas at much greater length in a 2004 book, *The Sorrows of Empire.* In this book, Johnson repeated the central point of the earlier book, saying in the very first sentence that "most Americans do not recognize. . . that the United

States dominates the world through its military power."[91] But the primary emphasis of this book was on the distinctive nature of the American empire.

Accepting the simplest definition of imperialism—"the domination and exploitation of weaker states by stronger ones"—Johnson argued that no particular institution is essential to it except one: militarism: "Imperialism and militarism are inseparable."[92] Imperialism does not, for example, necessarily involve formal colonies, as shown by the fact that neocolonialism is the most formidable type of imperialism.[93] And with this point we come to Johnson's main emphasis: America has created "a new form of empire," which is "not an empire of colonies but an empire of bases."[94] Also new is the fact that this empire is not merely regional: "Its reach is global," with well over 700 military bases outside the United States.[95]

Johnson saw the creation of this empire as having occurred in several stages. The first stage ran throughout the 19th century, during which the American empire developed in the traditional way.[96] The second stage, creating the distinctive nature of the American empire, began when "a group of self-conscious imperialists" used the Spanish-American War of 1898 "to establish military and naval bases in the Caribbean and the Western Pacific."[97] The third stage consisted of World War II and the Cold War, during which the number of bases was increased exponentially.[98] The fourth stage began with the end of the Cold War. It was the fourth stage with which Johnson was primarily concerned, and to which he referred in the book's subtitle: *Militarism, Secrecy, and the End of the Republic.*

For Johnson, like Bacevich, the end of the Cold War had revelatory significance: As long as the Cold War lasted, America's empire of bases was "not recognized for what it was because the rationale of containing the Soviet Union disguised it."[99] But once the Soviet Union dissolved, America's refusal to cut back drastically on military spending, especially by reducing its system of overseas bases, revealed that this system existed for a different purpose.

For Johnson, however, the end of the Cold War, besides

revealing what had been true all along, also brought about a real change, initiating a new stage in the empire's development. No longer portraying itself as a purely defensive power, the United States started giving hints of "the openly—proudly—imperial role it would take on in the new century."[100] This change of behavior eventually became revolutionary:

> From 1989 to 2002, there was a revolution in America's relations with the rest of the world. At the beginning of that period, the conduct of foreign policy was still largely a civilian operation. . . . By 2002 . . . [t]he United States no longer had a "foreign policy." Instead it had a military empire.[101]

A crucial factor in this revolution was 9/11, which led some of our leaders "to see our republic as a genuine empire, a new Rome . . . no longer bound by international law."[102] For Johnson, therefore, the present stage of American imperialism was inaugurated by two events: the breakup of the Soviet Union and the attacks of 9/11.

The purpose of Johnson's book was to inspire Americans to do battle against this empire, especially in its present, most virulent, form. He recognized, to be sure, that some thinkers have argued that we should celebrate this more aggressive imperialism, because America is a "good empire," which uses its power to spread democracy.[103]

Like Bacevich, however, Johnson rejected this rationale. The United States, he said, has never, in its decisions to establish military alliances, given preferences to democracies; it has backed numerous military dictators; and it has even "undercut democracy whenever it was inconvenient."[104]

Far from promoting freedom and democracy, Johnson argued, the United States is "a military juggernaut intent on world domination."[105] Far from having good effects, this attempt will—as indicated by his book's title—bring nothing but sorrows: to Americans themselves as well as the rest of the world.[106]

Conclusion

The remainder of this book provides a historical argument supporting the view that the trajectory of American foreign policy has been more malign that benign, more demonic than divine. The evidence for this argument is continued in my 2017 book, *Bush and Cheney: How They Ruined America and the World.*[107]

Endnotes

1 Washington's Inaugural Address, 30 April 1789.

2 "Inaugural Address of John Adams," 4 March 1797.

3 President Andrew Jackson, Farewell Address, 4 March 1837.

4 Reagan's statement to the first Conservative Political Action Conference convention, 1974.

5 George W. Bush, "Remarks Accepting the Presidential Nomination at the Republican National Convention in New York City," 2 September 2004.

6 Conrad Cherry, ed., *God's New Israel: Religious Interpretations of American Destiny* (1971; University of North Carolina Press, 1998), 269.

7 Ernest Lee Tuveson, *Redeemer Nation: The Idea of America's Millennial Role* (University of Chicago Press, 1968); see also Orrin Schwab, *Redeemer Nation: American and the World in the Technocratic Age - 1914 to the Present* (American University & Colleges Press, 2004).

8 Senator Albert J. Beveridge, "The Philippine Question," Washington D.C., 9 January 1900.

9 John B. Judis, "The Chosen Nation: The Influence of Religion on U.S. Foreign Policy," *Carnegie Endowment for International Peace*, March 2005.

10 See Clifford Longley, *Chosen People: The Big Idea that Shapes England and America* (Hodder & Stoughton, 2003).

11 See Joseph Leconte, "My Take: An Almost Chosen Nation," Special to CNN, 19 January 2013.

12 Daniel Bell, "The End of American Exceptionalism," *National Affairs*, Fall 1975: 5.

13 Lodge's speech was reprinted in Julia Ward Howe, ed., *Masterpieces of American Eloquence* (Kessinger, 2011).

14 "Survey: Most Americans Still See God's Hand on America," ChristianNewsWire, 24 November 2010; "Survey: 53% of Americans Think God Has a 'Special Relationship' with the U.S.A.," Relevant, 6 July 2015.

15 Michael Medved, *The American Miracle: Divine Providence in the Rise of the Republic* (Crown Forum, 2016), 1.

16 Ibid., 2.

17 Ibid., 16, 24.

18 David Brooks, "A Return to National Greatness," *New York Times*, 3 February 2017.

19 Said on NBC's *Today Show*, 19 February 1998.

20 Terrence McCoy, "How Joseph Stalin Invented 'American Exceptionalism,'"*Atlantic,* 15 March 2012.

21 Seymour Martin Lipset, *American Exceptionalism: A Double-Edged Sword* (W. W. Norton, 1996), 13, 18.

22 Godfrey Hodgson, *The Myth of American Exceptionalism* (Yale University Press, 2009), 10.

23 Jeffrey M. Jones, "Americans See U.S. as Exceptional; 37% Doubt Obama Does," Gallup, 22 December 2010.

24 Michael Scherer, "Obama Too Is an American Exceptionalist," *Time*, 4 April 2009.

25 Jonah Goldberg, "The Bashing of American Exceptionalism," *National Review*, 10 November 2010.

26 "Remarks by the President at the United States Military Academy Commencement Ceremony," White House, 28 May 2014.

27 "Blaming America First," Editorial Board, *New York Times*, 7 February 2017.

28 Stephen M. Walt, "The Myth of American Exceptionalism" (*Foreign Policy,* 11 October 2011). Walt added: "Americans watching *Saving Private Ryan* or *Patton* may conclude that the United States played the central role in vanquishing Nazi Germany." Actually, however, "most of the fighting was in Eastern Europe and the main burden of defeating Hitler's war machine was borne by the Soviet Union."

29 Walt repeated Abraham Lincoln's admonition that we should be concerned about "whether we are on God's side" (ibid.).

30 Daniel Bell, "The End of American Exceptionalism," *National Affairs*, Fall 1975:4, 6, 16.

31 Hilde Eliassen Restad, "Are We Coming to the End of 'American Exceptionalism'?" *Newsweek,* 6 June 2016. (This essay was originally published in the *London School of Economics*, 4 March 2016, as "Donald Trump's Calls to 'Make America Great Again' Show that American Exceptionalism Is Still a Powerful Idea.")

32 Trevor McCrisken, *American Exceptionalism and the Legacy of Vietnam: U.S. Foreign Policy Since 1974* (Palgrave Macmillan, 2004).

33 Dale Carter, "American Exceptionalism: An Idea That Will Not Die," *American Studies in Scandinavia*, 29/2 (1997).

34 Stanley Hoffman, "The High and the Mighty: Bush's National-Security Strategy and the New American Hubris," *American Prospect*, 13 January 2003.

35 The Obama administration did little to change this situation, given Obama's extension of the Bush-Cheney wars, his starting of some new wars, and nonjudicial execution of people in various countries by means of drones. The Trump administration, moreover, has brought respect for America down still further.

36 See Andrew Kohut and Bruce Stokes, *America Against the World: How We Are Different and Why We Are Disliked* (Times Books, 2006).

37 See Chapters 2 and 4 of David Ray Griffin, *Bush and Cheney: How They Ruined America and the World* (Interlink Books, 2017).

38 Dick Cheney and Liz Cheney, *Exceptional: Why the World Needs a Powerful America* (Threshold Editions, 2015), 1, 5.

39 Ibid., 257, 259.

40 Hodgson, *The Myth of American Exceptionalism*, xii-xiii.

41 Ibid., xvii.

42 Glenn Greenwald, "The Premises and Purposes of American Exceptionalism," *Guardian*, 18 February 2013.

43 James Carden, "Getting the Left to Embrace US 'Exceptionalism,'" *Consortium News*, 24 October 2017.

44 Andrew Kohut and Bruce Stokes, "The Problem of American Exceptionalism," Pew Research Center, 9 May 2006.

45 Mark N. Katz, "Iran and Russia," in Robin B. Wright, *The Iran Primer: Power, Politics, and U.S. Policy* (United States Institute of Peace, 2010), 186.

46 See Noam Chomsky, *American Power and the New Mandarins* (1967; New York: Vintage Books, 1969), *Year 501: The Conquest Continues* (Boston: South End Press, 1993), and *Rogue States: The Rule of Force in World Affairs* (Cambridge: South End Press, 2000); Richard Falk, "Imperialism in Crisis," an introduction to Mansour Farhang, *U.S. Imperialism: From the Spanish-American War to the Iranian Revolution* (Boston: South End Press, 1981); Harry Magdoff, *The Age of Imperialism: The Economics of U.S. Foreign Policy*; Michael Parenti, *Against Empire* (San Francisco: City Lights, 1995); and Gore Vidal, *Empire: A Novel* (New York: Random House, 1987), and *The Last Empire* (New York: Vintage Books, 2002).

47 Andrew J. Bacevich, *American Empire: The Realities and*

Consequences of U.S. Diplomacy (Cambridge: Harvard University Press, 2002), 30, 218-19.

48 "Remarks by the President at 2002 Graduation Exercise of the United States Military Academy," 1 June 2002; Donald Rumsfeld, Department of Defense press conference, 23 April 2003, quoted in Rahul Mahajan, *Full Spectrum Dominance: U.S. Power in Iraq and Beyond* (New York: Seven Stories Press, 2003), 9.

49 Krauthammer's statements were quoted in Emily Eakin, "All Roads Lead to D.C.," *New York Times*, Week in Review, 31 March 2002.

50 Michael Ignatieff, "The Burden," *The New York Times Magazine*, 5 January 2003: 23-27 and 50-54, at 23. The quotation is from Bush's West Point speech in June of 2002.

51 Charles Krauthammer, "The Bush Doctrine," *Time*, 5 March 2001, quoted in Chalmers Johnson, *The Sorrows of Empire: Militarism, Secrecy, and the End of the Republic* (New York: Henry Holt [Metropolitan Books], 2004), 68.

52 Bacevich, *American Empire*, 242 (quoting Charles Beard, *Giddy Minds and Foreign Quarrels* [1939]), 87).

53 Ibid., 244.

54 Richard N. Haass, "Imperial America," 11 November 2000, quoted in Bacevich, *American Empire*, 219.

55 See Emily Eakin, "All Roads Lead to D.C."

56 The name of the British edition is simply *Empire: How Britain Made the Modern World* (London: Allen Lane, 2002). The full title of the American edition, meant to point to the lessons for America, is *Empire: The Rise and Demise of the British World Order and the Lessons for Global Power* (New York: Basic Books, 2003).

57 Niall Ferguson, *Colossus: The Price of America's Empire* (New York: Penguin, 2004), 294.

58 Gordon S. Wood, *Empire of Liberty: A History of the Early Republic, 1789-1815* (Oxford University Press, 2009).

59 Walter Nugent, *Habits of Empire: A History of American Expansion* (Knopf, 2008), vii, xiii.

60 Anders Stephanson, *Manifest Destiny: American Expansion and the Empire of Right* (New York: Hill and Wang, 1995), 19.

61 Ronald Steel, *Pax Americana* (New York: Viking Press, 1967), 15, 14.

62 Ibid., 16-17, 18.

63 Ibid., vii.

64 Samuel Huntington, "American Ideals versus American Institutions," *Political Science Quarterly*, Spring, 1982.

65 Ronald Steel, *Temptations of a Superpower* (Cambridge: Harvard University Press, 1995); Samuel Huntington, "The Lonely

Superpower," *Foreign Affairs*, March/April 1999: 35-49.

66 Charles Krauthammer, "The Unipolar Moment," in *Foreign Affairs* 70/1 (1990-91): 295-306, at 304-05. Krauthammer had earlier said that every president from FDR to LBJ had aimed at "promotion abroad of both freedom and world order" (*New Republic,* February, 1986).

67 Robert Kagan, "The Benevolent Empire," *Foreign Policy*, Summer 1998: 24-35.

68 Ignatieff, "The Burden," 24, 52.

69 Ruth Marcus, "Trump's Pardons Show His Twisted Brand of Mercy," *Washington Post*, 31 May 2018; Dinesh D'Souza,"In Praise of an American Empire," *Christian Science Monitor*, 26 April 2002.

70 Bacevich, *American Empire*, 46.

71 Dan Mangan, "Clinton Blasts Trump: 'We Are Great Because We Are Good,'" CNBC, 9 October 2016.

72 Colin L. Powell, "Remarks at Confirmation Hearing," Senate Foreign Relations Committee, Washington, D.C., 17 January 2001, quoted in Bacevich, *American Empire*, 216.

73 Noam Chomsky, *Deterring Democracy* (New York: Hill and Wang, 1992).

74 Noam Chomsky, *Hegemony or Survival: America's Quest for Global Dominance* (New York: Henry Holt [Metropolitan Books, 2003]), 140.

75 Ibid., 4.

76 Ibid., 231.

77 Richard Falk, "Will the Empire Be Fascist?" *Global Dialogues*, 2003; "Resisting the Global Domination Project: An Interview with Prof. Richard Falk," *Frontline*, 20/8 (12-25 April 2003).

78 Huntington, "The Lonely Superpower," 38, 42.

79 Bacevich, *American Empire*, 127.

80 See, for example, Walter LaFeber, *The New Empire: An Interpretation of American Expansion 1860-1898*, 35th Anniversary Edition (1963; Ithaca: Cornell University Press, 1998); Thomas J. McCormick, *China Market: America's Quest for Informal Empire, 1893-1901* (Chicago: Quadrangle Books, 1967); Marilyn Blatt Young, *The Rhetoric of Empire, 1895-1901* (1968); Carl P. Parrini, *Heir to Empire* (1969); Ernest A. Paolino, *The Foundations of the American Empire* (1973); Lloyd C. Gardner, Walter F. LaFeber, and Thomas J. McCormick, *Creation of the American Empire* (Chicago: Rand McNally, 1973).

81 Williams' *Tragedy of American Diplomacy* was extensively revised and expanded in the 1962 and 1972 editions, the latter of which was reissued in a 1988 Norton edition containing a retrospective essay by Bradford Perkins.

82 William Appleton Williams, *From Colony to Empire* (John Wiley,

1972); *Empire as a Way of Life: An Essay on the Causes and Character of America's Present Predicament with a Few Thoughts about an Alternative* (Oxford: Oxford University Press, 1980).

83 Bacevich, *American Empire*, ix, 6, 10-11, 30.

84 Ibid., 242.

85 Ibid., 7.

86 Ibid., 46.

87 Ibid., 4, 133, 52.

88 Ibid., 115, 242, 195-96.

89 Chalmers Johnson, *Blowback: The Costs and Consequences of American Empire* (New York: Henry Holt, 2000), 8, 9, 17, 223. "A Spear Carrier for Empire" is the title of the Prologue. Johnson's point was that he had been such first as a member of the navy and then in his work as an intellectual--until he came, he said, to "see clearly for the first time the shape of the empire that I had so long uncritically supported" (xii, xviii).

90 Ibid., 65.

91 Chalmers Johnson, *The Sorrows of Empire: Militarism, Secrecy, and the End of the Republic* (New York: Henry Holt [Metropolitan Books], 2004), 1.

92 Ibid., 23, 30.

93 Ibid., 30.

94 Ibid., 1, 23.

95 Ibid., 188, 4. With regard to the statement "well over 700," Johnson first pointed out that in September of 2001, the Department of Defense acknowledged the existence of 725 such bases, then added that there are "many more," since some bases were not acknowledged and more bases had been created in the meantime (ibid., 4).

96 Ibid., 2, 23.

97 Ibid., 2, 192.

98 Ibid., 2, 23, 193.

99 Ibid., 23.

100 Ibid., 21.

101 Ibid., 22.

102 Ibid., 3.

103 Ibid., 3, 70.

104 Ibid., 203-13, 33.

105 Ibid., 33, 4.

106 Ibid., 284-309.

107 Interlink Books, 2017.

| Chapter 1 |

FROM THE BEGINNING TO WORLD WAR I

American imperialism is often said to have begun in 1898, when Cuba and the Philippines were the main prizes.[1] What was new at this time, however, was only that America took control of countries beyond the North American continent. As John Bassett Moore, who had been an assistant secretary of state at that time, later wrote:

> It is true that the expansion of 1898 involved . . . the taking of a step geographically in advance of any that had been taken before; but so far as concerns the acquisition of new territory we were merely following a habit which had characterized our entire national existence.[2]

This statement is of utmost importance, because it points out that, already in 1898, imperial conquest was a long-standing habit of American policy makers. America had been engaged in expansionism from the outset.

1. The Creation of the American Empire

Maintaining that US imperialism began only in 1898 depends on an artificial distinction between "expansionism" and "imperialism," holding that conquests are imperialistic only if a sea has been crossed. If that distinction were otherwise enforced, the Mongol Empire created by Ghengis Khan and his sons, the most extensive empire created until that time, could not be called an empire.

Historians who reject this artificial distinction date the origin of America's empire much earlier. For example, in his important book *The Rising American Empire*, Richard Van Alstyne reported that "before the middle of the eighteenth century, the concept of an empire that would take in the whole continent was fully formed." The War for Independence, he added, was fought "under the spell of [the] imperial idea . . . that the continent of North America belonged, as of right, to the people of the thirteen colonies."[3]

The right referred to here was a *divine* right. One way of expressing this sense of divine authorization was to call America the "new Israel."[4] But the phrase that really caught on was "manifest destiny," which John O'Sullivan, urging the annexation of Texas, coined in 1845 to signify the mission of the United States "to overspread the continent allotted by Providence for the free development of our yearly multiplying millions."[5]

One problem with this assessment of the divine will, of course, was that "our" millions encountered the millions of people who were already here. Experts now estimate that at the time of the European invasion, the Native American population of the area that is now the continental United States was about 10,000,000. By 1890, that number had been reduced to about 228,000.[6] This means that in the interim, about 95 percent of the native population had been eliminated. Many of the deaths were, to be sure, due to the new diseases brought by the Europeans, to which the Native Americans had no resistance.

But the "American Holocaust," said David Stannard in his book of that title, was a result of "microbial pestilence *and* purposeful genocide."[7] Stannard's book dealt with South as well as North America, and the number of indigenous peoples exterminated was far greater in the southern hemisphere. Nevertheless, our own forebears made a significant contribution to what was, in Stannard's words, "the most massive act of genocide in the history of the world."[8]

This genocidal process was made all the more ignoble by a long series of lies and broken promises. The European Americans signed treaty after treaty with the Native Americans—some 400 in all—and broke almost every one[9]—a fact making the expression "Indian giver" one of the great ironies of history.

For example, Secretary of War Lewis Cass promised, in an 1825 treaty with the Shawnees and Cherokees, that if they would move to new lands west of the Mississippi,

> The United States will never ask for your land there. This I promise you in the name of your great father, the President. That country he assigns to his red people, to be held by them and their children's children forever.[10]

In perhaps the most famous of all the promises, President Andrew Jackson told his "Choctaw children" and his "Chickasaw children" that if only they would move beyond Alabama and Mississippi, they would be "in possession of land of their own, which they shall possess as long as Grass grows or water runs." Jackson's efforts resulted in the 1832 Treaty of Washington—which was broken within a few days.[11]

Breaking promises was, at least in some cases, premeditated. Treaties with Indians, a governor of Georgia said, "were expedients by which ignorant, intractable, and savage people were induced without bloodshed to yield up what civilized peoples had a right to possess."[12]

This sense of rightful ownership reflected the idea that the Native Americans were destined to disappear to make room for the new empire. That this idea was shared even by ordinary troops is suggested by a young soldier whose regiment had the task of destroying Iroquois villages on behalf of the State of New York, which was thereby violating a treaty it had recently forced the Iroquois to sign. "I really feel guilty," he said in a letter home, "as I applied the torch to huts that were Homes of Content until we ravagers came spreading desolation everywhere." But then, surmising that he might be serving a higher cause, he said: "Our mission here is ostensibly to destroy but may it not transpire that we pillagers are carelessly sowing the seeds of Empire?"[13]

For European Americans, their genocide of Native Americans did not necessarily conflict with the idea that they were fulfilling a divine plan; Anglo-Saxon white racism shielded them from any such realization. This dimension of the idea of manifest destiny was exemplified by a congressman who said:

> I take it for granted, that we . . . must march from ocean to ocean. . . . We must march from Texas straight to the Pacific ocean. . . . It is the destiny of the white race.[14]

An even more imperialistic version of Anglo-Saxonism was expressed by a senator from Virginia, who said:

> It is peculiar to the character of this Anglo-Saxon race of men to which we belong, that it has never been contented to live in the same country with any other distinct race, upon terms of equality; it has, invariably, . . . proceeded to exterminate or enslave the other race.[15]

The question today, of course, is whether this "race" is willing to live in the same *world* with any other people "upon terms of equality."

In any case, as this senator's brutally honest statement indicated, there was perceived to be only one alternative to extermination: enslavement. The other great crime against humanity perpetrated during that period of empire-building was the massive slave trade. In addition to all its unspeakable indignities and sufferings, this trade resulted in an enormous number of deaths during capture and transport, with the North

American part of the slave trade likely being responsible for about 10 million African deaths.[16]

Neither was the conviction of being divinely guided necessarily regarded as being in conflict with the act of military conquest. In the midst of the war with Mexico, one senator, explaining in what sense he subscribed to "the doctrine of 'manifest destiny,'" said:

> I believe we should be recreant to our noble mission, if we refused acquiescence in the high purposes of a wise Providence. War has its evils . . . but however inscrutable to us, it has also been made, by the Allwise Dispenser of events, the instrumentality of accomplishing the great end of human elevation.[17]

No matter how brutal the methods, Americans were instruments of divine purposes.

The expansion to the Pacific, in any case, led to a further expansion of the American sense of manifest destiny. In 1850, an editor named James DeBow wrote:

> We have a destiny to perform, a 'manifest destiny' over all Mexico, over South America, over the West Indies and Canada. The Sandwich [Hawaiian] Islands are as necessary to our eastern, as the isles of the gulf to our western commerce. The gates of the Chinese empire must be thrown down . . . and the haughty Japanese tramplers upon the cross be enlightened in the doctrines of republicanism . . . . The eagle of the republic shall poise itself over the field of Waterloo, after tracing its flight among the gorges of the Himalaya or the Ural mountains, and a successor of Washington ascend the chair of universal empire![18]

As DeBow's remarkable statement shows, Americans in those days spoke openly of the American empire, associated it with commerce as well as Christianity, and, at least in some cases, already had a vision of a *global* empire. One of the first steps in realizing this vision was taken four years later. Commodore Perry, using his heavily armed ships to force "the haughty Japanese" to open their country to American commerce, declared: "The World has assigned this duty to us."[19]

2. Going Abroad: Hawaii, Cuba, and the Philippines

As the use of force in Japan in 1854 illustrated, it is not strictly true that US imperialism did not go overseas until 1898. That date did, nevertheless, mark a new phase of American imperialism. Our intervention in Cuba initiated what is usually called "neo-colonialism" or "neo-imperialism," which--said Philip Foner in his great study *The Spanish-Cuban-American War and the Birth of American Imperialism*—became "the characteristic feature of American imperialism."[20]

In this form, the imperial power does not take formal control of the country, as Britain did in India and other parts of its empire. Rather, the country is *formally* independent. Its rulers, however, must obey US directives or suffer intervention and overthrow, so there is no *real* independence.

American historians have generally called the fighting of 1898-1902 "the Spanish-American War" or simply 'the war with Spain." But these names obscure the fact that the primary combatants against Spain were the Cuban and Filipino rebels, not the Americans. Even more important, those traditional names obscure the fact that US military action was directed more at Cubans and Filipinos than against Spanish troops. This latter fact is acknowledged with regard to the Filipino rebels by speaking of the war in the Philippines as "the Philippine-American War." Likewise, Philip Foner acknowledged the truth about the war in Cuba, as indicated above, by calling it "the Spanish-Cuban-American War."[21]

But although these names are improvements, they leave us without a label for the overall US thrust in the wars of 1898-1902, given the fact that the US took Puerto Rico and Guam as well as Cuba and the Philippines. The US actions of this period could be called "the wars to take Spanish colonies."

Annexing Hawaii

However, even that term is inadequate, because the United States also formally annexed Hawaii during this outburst of imperialist lust. There were several reasons for this lust, including the fact that Hawaii would be an ideal place to begin trade with China and to project military power across the Pacific. President McKinley said: "We need Hawaii as much and a good deal more than we did California. It is Manifest Destiny."[22] The bill to annex Hawaii was submitted by the most imperialist member of the Senate, Henry Cabot Lodge, who—in Stephen Kinzer's words—"wanted the United States to dominate the world."[23]

Lodge and his fellow imperialists—including Theodore Roosevelt, whom Lodge had groomed[24]—were confronted by a growing band of anti-imperialists, which included many of the nation's leaders. The debate between these two movements is recounted in Steven Kinzer's 2017 book, *The True Flag.*[25] One of the leaders of the anti-imperialists was Harvard professor Charles Eliot Norton, who said in a speech entitled "True Patriotism":

> A generation has grown up that has known nothing of war. The blessings of peace have been poured out upon us. We have congratulated ourselves that we were free from the misery and the burdens that war and standing armies have brought upon the nations of the Old World. And now of a sudden. . . , America has been compelled against the will of all her wisest and best to enter into a path of darkness and peril. Against their will she has been forced to turn back from the way of civilization to the way of barbarism.[26]

The annexation of Hawaii was also opposed by Senator Allen of Nebraska, who called the debate about it "the greatest question that has ever been presented to the American people. The taking of Hawaii, he correctly predicted, would be only "the first act in the drama of colonization."[27]

The War to Take Cuba

American policy makers and businessmen had long had an appetite for Cuba. In 1823, John Quincy Adams, explaining that there was a "law of political as well of physical gravitation," said US policy should continue to support Spanish sovereignty until such time that Cuba, when "forcibly disjoined from its own unnatural connection with Spain," would fall into US hands, just as "an apple severed by the tempest from its native tree cannot choose but to fall to the ground."[28] In 1825, after all Spain's colonies in this hemisphere had achieved independence except Cuba and Puerto Rico, the USA—which had accepted France's help for its own war of independence—followed Adams' "apple policy" by preventing Mexico and Venezuela from helping Cuba liberate itself.[29]

By the end of the century, the appetite for Cuba had become ravenous. In 1881, Secretary of State James Blaine said that this "rich island" is a crucial part of the American commercial system and "the key to the Gulf of Mexico." Accordingly, if it "ever ceas[es] to be Spanish, Cuba must necessarily become American."[30] In an 1895 symposium—entitled "Ought We to Annex Cuba?"—a leading Wall Street figure wrote: "It makes the water come to my mouth when I think of the state of Cuba as one in our family." Another writer said that we could wait for Canada and the rest of Mexico: "*But we want Cuba now.*"[31]

What the Cuban people wanted was, in this discussion, not a desideratum, although they had been making clear for some time that they wanted independence. In 1868, rebel forces began the First War for Independence. But the USA did not help. While it sold rifles to Spain, it withheld recognition from the rebels, partly because of America's "apple policy" and partly because giving recognition would have released Spain from its obligation to protect US property.[32] (This would be only one of hundreds of cases in which the American government's professed desire to promote freedom would take a back seat to the interests of the American economic elite.) Because this lack of recognition meant that the rebels could not borrow money or buy rifles, they had to give up their battle in 1878.

The Cubans' Second War for Independence began in 1895. Inspired by many Cuban intellectuals, especially José Martí, and led by many outstanding military strategists, especially Máximo Gómez and Antonio Maceo, the Cubans, without outside help, fought bravely and brilliantly.[33] By 1898, it was clear that the Spanish forces, in spite of being much better armed and outnumbering the Cuban forces six to one, were not going to defeat them.[34]

Although without US intervention the war might have dragged on for many more years, the rebels did not believe they needed, and certainly did not ask for, US intervention (in spite of claims to the contrary by the US administration at the time and by many US historians since).[35] The Cubans only wanted US recognition, which would have allowed them to borrow money and buy arms.[36] Having warned from the outset that Cuban freedom would be compromised if it was won through military intercession by any other country, Antonio Maceo wrote, in response to discussion in the USA as to whether it should intervene to shorten the war:

> [W]e do not need any intervention to obtain victory in more or less time. Do you really want to cut the war down? Bring Cuba 25,000 to 35,000 rifles and a million bullets. . . . We Cubans do not need any other help.[37]

Likewise, Máximo Gómez told President Grover Cleveland that the Cubans were confident of their strength and did not need others to do their fighting for them. Indeed, when the next president, William McKinley, decided to intervene while still refusing to give the Cubans recognition, one of the Cuban spokesmen said they would "regard such intervention as nothing less than a declaration of war by the United States against the Cuban revolutionists."[38] All the Cuban leaders reflected the view of José Martí, who asked, rhetorically and prophetically: "Once the United States is in Cuba, who will get her out?"[39]

There is no evidence, furthermore, that the USA entered the war because it thought that the Cubans could not win on their own. Instead, it evidently entered because it feared that they *would.* The written record suggested, said Foner, that the McKinley administration thought that "Spanish sovereignty in Cuba was collapsing" and that "if the United States waited too long, the Cuban revolutionary forces would emerge victorious, replacing the collapsing Spanish regime."[40]

This interpretation certainly fits with America's "apple policy" and with its behavior after intervening. It also fits with the fact that McKinley's secretary of state, John Sherman, advised him that US policy toward Cuba "must be controlled by commercial interests rather than by sympathy with a people struggling for liberty."[41]

The president was, in other words, to treat the Cubans as a means to our commercial ends, not as ends in themselves. But this view could not, of course, be publicly expressed: The loss of a humanitarian pretext for intervention would have undermined not only the USA's long-standing intention to catch this fruit when it was ripe but also its plan "to use the 'pacification of Cuba'" as the occasion for its twin goal of appropriating the Philippines.[42]

Like recent wars of conquest, the war to take Cuba was portrayed as a war of liberation. We were going in to liberate the Cubans from the Spanish, even though they did not want our help. The US military was able to enter Cuba after a battleship named the *Maine*—which President McKinley had stationed in Havana Harbor without invitation—exploded, killing 266 of the 350 men on board.

Although Theodore Roosevelt, then the assistant secretary of the navy, accused Spain of "an act of dirty treachery,"[43]

Washington knew that the last thing the Spanish wanted was for America to have an excuse to intervene. But US newspapers, led by William Randolph Hearst, inflamed the American public with the charge that Spain was responsible. The national slogan became "Remember the *Maine,* to hell with Spain." McKinley took advantage of this situation to get Congress to appropriate money for the war.[44]

After US forces had run the Spanish out, the McKinley administration's plan to annex Cuba was momentarily thwarted by Congress. The Senate had adopted an amendment proposed by Senator Henry Teller, which said:

> The people of the Island of Cuba are, and of right ought to be, free and independent. . . . The United States hereby disclaims any disposition or intention to exercise sovereignty, jurisdiction, or control over said Islands except for the pacification thereof, and asserts its determination, when that is accomplished, to leave the government and control of the Island to its people.[45]

But the administration got around the Teller Amendment by refusing to pull US troops out of Cuba until the Cuban leaders signed a bill submitted to the Senate by Senator Orville Platt (although it was actually written by Senator Henry Cabot Lodge, Secretary of War Elihu Root, and Theodore Roosevelt, who was then the vice president).[46] This Platt Amendment gave America the right in perpetuity to use Guantánamo Bay and to intervene whenever it wanted. Under this amendment, as one outraged Cuban politician put it:

> The only Cuban governments that would live would be those . . . more attentive to obtaining the blessings of the United States than to serving and defending the interests of Cuba.[47]

Probably a more accurate prediction has never been made.

In any case, American leaders fully understood that the Platt Amendment gave them complete control. General Leonard Wood, who was the military governor of Cuba at the time, said:

> There is little or no real independence left to Cuba under the Platt Amendment. . . . She is absolutely in our hands. . . . With the control we have over Cuba . . . we shall soon practically control the world sugar market.[48]

Besides showing that neo-colonialism was little different from colonialism,[49] Wood's statement, made in private, showed that the public statements, which were all about liberating the Cubans from tyranny, were pure propaganda.

Not all Americans were fooled. One congressman called the Platt Amendment a manifestation of "imperialism and commercial spirit." Moreover, some American newspapers in those days still told the truth about US foreign policy, with one paper's headline proclaiming: "Imperialism Now An Accomplished Fact."[50] As US business interests quickly took control of Cuba's natural resources, one historian wrote:

> The idea that we are in Cuba on a philanthropic and humane mission has gone to join the other misplaced, absurd and hypocritical pretexts which history has flung . . . into limbo near the moon.[51]

The War to Take the Philippines

Although the intervention in Cuba, especially after the imposition of the Platt Amendment, created considerable opposition, America's war in the Philippines enlightened an even larger portion of the American public as to the imperialistic nature of their government. From the perspective of American designs, furthermore, the Philippine Islands were actually more important than Cuba. What Senator Lodge called the "large policy" was to use the Cuban crisis to obtain a set of bases (including Hawaii, the Philippines, Guam, and Wake Island, all of which were also annexed in 1898) that would connect America to the fabled China market.[52]

As the first American wars to establish bases, the Wars to Take Spanish Colonies were the beginning of what Chalmers Johnson, as stated in the Introduction, considered the distinctive form of the American empire—that it is an empire of military bases.

In any case, the fundamental motive for the intervention was expressed by Senator Albert Beveridge, an indiscreet imperialist, who took the floor to say:

> American factories are making more than the American people can use; American soil is producing more than they can consume. Fate has written our policy for us; the trade of the world must and shall be ours. . . . We will build a navy to the measure of our greatness. . . . The Philippines are logically our first target.[53]

The American people would, of course, be told that the intervention was for humanitarian purposes.

In any case, as soon as war was declared against Spain because of Cuba, Commodore Dewey was sent to Manila's harbor, where his superior ships quickly destroyed the Spanish squadron, so that they could not come to Cuba to help Spain's war. Then, while Dewey and his men waited for army troops, the Filipino insurgents, led by Emilio Aguinaldo, came close to taking Manila. When the US army units finally arrived, their officers, to be allowed to share in the conquest, had to negotiate with Aguinaldo, who gave his consent. Aguinaldo hoped thereby to encourage US recognition of the Philippine Republic, which had recently declared its independence.[54]

The United States, however, not only withheld this recognition but also refused to allow the Filipinos to participate in the Paris Peace talks, even though the designated representative had personally pleaded with McKinley and had then gone to Paris, warning that any agreements reached without Filipino participation would be invalid.[55]

McKinley, however, had decided that he should not grant independence to the Philippines, because its people were "unfit for self-government." The idea that America should seize the Philippines came to McKinley, he said, while he was in prayer, asking "Almighty God for light and guidance." God, observed Steven Kinzer, "sounded remarkably like Theodore Roosevelt and Henry Cabot Lodge."[56]

Senator George Frisbie Hoar, evidently not believing that the president had actually received light and guidance from God, said: "If we take the Philippines under the treaty of peace, the downfall of the American Republic will date from the administration of William McKinley."[57]

In any case, although American troops had captured only part of Manila—the rest of Luzon and the other islands had all been won by the Filipinos—America demanded, to Spain's astonishment, that it be ceded all the islands. For the entire Philippine archipelago, consisting of 3,141 islands, the United States paid the token sum of $20 million while again congratulating itself for not engaging in theft.[58]

Back home, as soon as the Filipinos heard that the Paris treaty had ceded their islands to the USA, they vowed to "fight to the bitter end for their rights and freedom."[59] Although, as in the Mexican War, the US president claimed that the other side started this bitter war by shedding American blood, US soldiers had been told to provoke the incident, as later admitted by the military officer in charge, General Arthur MacArthur (father of Douglas MacArthur).[60]

This, the USA's first full-scale war in Asia, anticipated the later Asian wars in savagery, surely in part due to the racism involved. The correspondent for a Philadelphia paper reported:

> [O]ur men have been relentless, have killed to exterminate men, women, children, prisoners and captives, active insurgents and suspected people

> from lads of ten up, the idea prevailing that the Filipino as such was little better than a dog. . . . Our soldiers have . . . taken prisoners people who held up their hands and peacefully surrendered, and an hour later, without an atom of evidence to show that they were even *insurrectos*, stood them on a bridge and shot them.[61]

Such reports were denied by US officials. In this case, Secretary of State Elihu Root declared:

> The war in the Philippines has been conducted by the American army with scrupulous regard for the rules of civilized warfare . . . with self-restraint and with humanity never surpassed.[62]

By contrast, one of the American soldiers wrote in a letter home: "Caloocan was supposed to contain 17,000 inhabitants. The Twentieth Kansas swept through it, and now Caloocan contains not one living native."

Some supporters of the war, rather than denying that such atrocities occurred, simply justified them. Senator Beveridge, referring to the charge "that our conduct of the war has been cruel," told his fellow senators that they "must remember that we are not dealing with Americans or Europeans. We are dealing with Orientals."[63]

The reason for slaughtering civilians was the fact that the insurgents were supported by the common people, whose cause, after all, they were championing. This support was acknowledged by General MacArthur, who had previously assumed that Aguinaldo's troops represented only a faction. "I did not like to believe that the whole population of Luzon," he said, "was opposed to us," but he was "reluctantly compelled" to believe that this was indeed the case because the Filipino army's tactics "depended upon almost complete unity of action of the entire native population."[64]

The fact that the US forces were fighting the Filipino

people themselves, not just an armed band of unrepresentative radicals, explained both why the civilian deaths were so high and why the US forces adopted the policy of herding civilians into concentration camps, where many of them died from hunger and disease. (This policy created considerable outrage back home because the Spanish concentration camps in Cuba had provided the major basis for the claim that America had to intervene there for humanitarian reasons.[65])

The extreme difference in the number of deaths suffered by the two sides—about 4,000 Americans compared with about 250,000 Filipinos—was due not only to the US policy of killing unarmed civilians but also to the fact that America possessed overwhelming firepower. One British witness was led to say: "This is not war; it is simply massacre and murderous butchery."[66]

President McKinley, however, assured the American people that "the mission of the United States is one of benevolent assimilation, substituting the mild sway of justice and right for arbitrary rule."[67] Anticipating Secretary of Defense Donald Rumsfeld's declaration that "we don't do empire," McKinley said that imperialism is "foreign to the temper and genius of this free and generous people."[68]

> What American wants [McKinley clarified] is not territorial expansion, but expansion of civilization. We want, not to acquire the Philippines for ourselves, but to give the Philippines free schools, a free church, open courts, no caste, equal rights to all. This is for our interest.[69]

America's only interest, in other words, was our interest in freedom for everyone. If we were establishing an empire, it was, in Jefferson's phrase, "an empire for liberty."[70]

The Anti-Imperialist League

Some prominent Americans, not buying this propaganda, formed an Anti-Imperialist League. Although the League opposed US imperialism in Cuba and Puerto Rico as well as the Philippines, it focused primarily on the latter.[71] One member, the usually ironic William James, exclaimed: "God damn the U.S. for its vile conduct in the Philippine Isles."[72] He also said:

> [The United States is] now openly engaged in crushing out the sacredest thing in this great human world—the attempt of a people long enslaved to attain to the possession of itself, to organize its laws and government, to be free to follow its internal destinies according to its own ideals. . . . We are cold-bloodedly, wantonly, and abominably destroying the soul of a people who never did us an atom of harm.[73]

Another member of the League was former President Grover Cleveland, who gave a statement that expressed the original meaning of American Exceptionalism. He declared:

> Our government was formed with the express purpose of creating in a new world a new nation, the foundation of which should be man's self-government, whose safety and prosperity should be secured in its absolute freedom from Old World complications and in its renunciation of all schemes of foreign conquest.[74]

Still another member of the League was the richest man in America, Andrew Carnegie, who wrote:

> Is it possible that the Republic is to be placed in the position of the suppressor of the Philippine struggle for independence? Surely that is impossible. With what face shall we hang in the schoolhouses of the Philippines our own Declaration of Independence, and yet deny independence to them?[75]

The membership of the League also included Mark Twain, who said that creating a flag for the Philippines would be easy: "we can have just our usual flag, with the white stripes painted black and the stars replaced by the skull and cross-bones." Twain also rewrote "The Battle Hymn of the Republic," with the first line saying, "Mine eyes have seen the orgy of the launching of the Sword," and with the final line saying, "His lust is marching on." As one could imagine, Twain's writing and speeches "made him the anti-imperialist movement's highest profile star."[76]

After the Filipinos began to fight back, 24 prominent Americans, including former President Grover Cleveland and Charles William Eliot, the president of Harvard University, gave this statement to the Senate: "In accordance with the principles upon which our Republic was founded, we are in duty bound to recognize the right of the [Filipinos] to independence and self-government."[77]

The imperialists, however, said that the Filipinos (like the Cubans) had no such right. In the words of Senator Beveridge:

> The rule of liberty—that all just government derives its authority from the consent of the governed—applies only to those who are capable of self-government. We govern the Indians without their consent. . . . We govern our children without their consent.[78]

On the war against the Filipinos, Carnegie congratulated one of the signers of the Paris treaty, saying:

> [Y]ou seem to have finished your work of civilizing the Filipinos. It is thought that [so far] about 8,000 of them have been completely civilized and sent to Heaven.[79]

Although the Anti-Imperialist League failed to prevent the takeover of the Philippines, it succeeded in educating many

Americans. The League had meetings in 30 states, and by the middle of 1899 "its membership numbered in the hundreds of thousands."[80] Because of the activities of the Anti-Imperialist League, the wars to take Cuba and the Philippines constituted a revelation to many Americans—a revelation of the fact that American policy in relation to Cuba and the Philippines (along with Puerto Rico and Guam) was diametrically opposed to the American ideals of independence and self-government.

We can, in fact, think of the wars to seize Spanish colonies as providing the first revelation of this discrepancy to the American people (with the Vietnam War and America's post-Cold War imperialism constituting later revelations).

The day was, of course, carried by those who portrayed the war and the subsequent annexation of the Philippines as a full-fledged colony as part of America's manifest destiny.[81] As Ernest May said in his study, *Imperial Democracy*, the imperialist movement's "leaders had discerned that public opinion could be captured for an imperialist cause, if only that cause could be clothed in the rhetoric of piety."[82] So, although one of those leaders, Senator Beveridge, said that "candor" required us to acknowledge that American economic interests had to take priority over any moral qualms the war might evoke, he added that the war is also justified by "the mission of our race, trustee, under God, of the civilization of the world."[83]

But what *kind of God* were we under? One of the best theological critiques of the war in Cuba was provided by another member of the Anti-Imperialist League, Samuel Gompers, the president of the American Federation of Labor. Gompers said:

> There are some Americans—our money makers—whose only god is the almighty dollar, whose only human or divine trinity is dividend, interest and profit. They have come to the conclusion that if poor, suffering Cuba can be handed over to their tender mercies, their deity and their deviltry can hold full sway. To these gentlemen, when there is a question between liberty and profit. . . , liberty is thrown to the dogs.[84]

The statement by Gompers stated the basic contradiction between American ideals and American interests, which has characterized it from the beginning. On the one hand, America, born in a revolt against the leading imperialist power of the 18th century, created an ideology of freedom, self-determination, and democracy. It believed, in fact, that it had a divinely ordained role to spread liberty. But when the businessmen and their policy makers had to choose between liberty and profit, liberty always lost out.

Despite the negative reactions by Americans such as James, Twain, and Gompers, those who believed that America's destiny was to become the head of a global empire were elated. Brooks Adams, grandson of John Quincy Adams and brother of Henry Adams, referred to the wars of 1898-1902 as "the turning point in our history," providing the basis for America to "dominate the world."[85] Chauncey Depew, a Wall Street banker-turned-US Senator, said that, thanks to President McKinley, President Roosevelt, and God,

> [W]e have our markets in Cuba, in Porto Rico, in the Philippines, and we stand in the presence of 800,000,000 people, with the Pacific an American lake. . . . The world is ours.[86]

For these members of the elite class, the wars to seize Spanish colonies were revelations not of the gap between America's ideals and its behavior, but of what a great empire America could create by ignoring those ideals in practice while using them rhetorically for their propaganda value.

3. Using a Big Stick in America's Hemisphere

Believing the world to be theirs by divine right, American leaders began preparations to take it. Theodore Roosevelt—who became president after McKinley was assassinated in 1901—is famous for the maxim that America should "speak softly and carry a big stick." A "big stick" meant a powerful navy. Roosevelt's advisor, Brooks Adams, had pointed out that America "cannot have the earth for nothing." So, he said, if America is not willing to "pay for what she takes," which she clearly was not, she had to "fight for it." To do this, she would need superior force.[87] So Roosevelt proceeded to build a big modern navy.

The Open Door and the Monroe Doctrine

A major purpose of this navy was to convince other countries, beginning in Asia, to adopt the economic policy that American leaders wanted most of the world to adopt, which came to be known as the "open door" policy. The basic meaning of this policy was that in each country, all other countries would be able to compete economically on equal terms. This policy, in spite of its friendly name, was simply a recipe for American dominance. US leaders knew that, with their growing economic strength, this policy, which would prohibit tariffs or any other special privileges for other countries or their friends, would allow American business interests to gain control of the market.

Another problem with this insistence on open doors in the East was that it was diametrically opposed to American policy in the Western Hemisphere. This policy was summarized in the Monroe Doctrine, which expressed the belief, which Americans had held virtually from the outset, that they had the natural (perhaps God-given) right to control the Western hemisphere. This doctrine, first formulated by John Quincy Adams in 1823 (the same year he enunciated his apple-falling-into-US-hands policy), came to be widely employed in the 1840s, especially in relation to the drive to take Mexican territory. This doctrine explicitly declared that European powers were not to colonize or otherwise intervene in the Western hemisphere.[88]

But this doctrine implicitly meant that, in Van Alstyne's words, "the United States shall be the only colonizing power and the sole directing power in both North and South America."[89] The United States, in other words, enforced a decidedly *closed* door policy in the Western Hemisphere while insisting that no other major countries, such as China, have any such policies in their own neighborhoods. This double standard, along with the US willingness to use its economic and military power to enforce it, would become the main basis for the charge that the USA, besides being imperialistic, was hypocritical. Here, however, the focus is on America's use of its big stick in its own hemisphere.

Colombia and Panama

Roosevelt's advisors told him that, having taken Hawaii and the Philippines in order to move into Asia, we needed a canal through Central America. So he simply stole Panama from Colombia.[90] Roosevelt's action was a source of outrage in Latin America and in parts of the United States, with even the usually bellicose Hearst press calling it "a rough-riding assault upon another republic over the shattered wreckage of international law."[91]

As a result of the treaty imposed on Panama, it remained legally sovereign, but in practice it was treated as a colony. This was especially the case with the ten-mile-wide canal zone through the center of the country, which was subjected to a formal and direct colonial policy.[92] The treaty gave the United States all authority in the zone "as if it were the sovereign of the territory" and the right to intervene anywhere in Panama when it saw fit.[93]

This treaty allowed the USA to have complete control of Panama's foreign policy and its communication and financial systems.[94] Through the virtually unlimited powers allowed by this treaty, the United States came to dominate Panama's political and economic life—disbanding its army, determining who won elections, and, when "uncooperative" people got into office anyway, sanctioning coups.[95]

The "independence" given them by the treaty, Panamanians rightly complained, was empty. As a result, "Humiliation followed humiliation," the rights of Panamanians were not considered, and Panama became one of the most troubled places in the world for the remainder of the century.[96]

The Dominican Republic and the Roosevelt Corollary

That was in 1903. In 1904, Roosevelt had his navy ensure the success of a coup in the Dominican Republic (then called Santo Domingo) by a faction that promised to turn over the country's custom houses and naval bases to the United States. Roosevelt justified this intervention by promulgating what came to be known as the Roosevelt Corollary to the Monroe Doctrine, which declared:

> All that this country desires is that the other republics on this continent shall be happy and prosperous; and they cannot be happy and prosperous unless they maintain order within their boundaries and behave with a just regard for their obligations toward outsiders.[97]

The United States claimed that it had the right to help other countries become "stable, orderly, and prosperous." But this intervention achieved the opposite. Disorders beginning in 1911 led, after a political intervention in 1914, to a military occupation from 1916 to 1925.[98]

Haiti: From Riches to Rags

Another victim of US "humanitarian intervention" was Haiti. Having been one of the hemisphere's richest countries at the end of the 18th century,[99] Haiti became the poorest. Part of the responsibility for this decline belonged to France, which derived much of its wealth from Haiti. But much of the responsibility has belonged to the United States.

America invaded Haiti two dozen times between 1804, when it supposedly won its independence, and 1913.[100] Then in 1914, under President Woodrow Wilson, America asked for a treaty that would hand Haiti's vital interests over to US bankers. When Haiti refused, Wilson sent in the marines, who stole $500,000 from the Haitian treasury, causing the government to collapse. When the Haitians then refused the US demand that they hold elections, Wilson sent in more marines. This invasion, in which US troops "hunted the Cacos like pigs" (in the words of the later testimony of one officer), took perhaps 15,000 Haitian lives and "resembled a massacre," according to a Haitian historian.[101] Besides dissolving the National Assembly and imposing a constitution that gave America control of Haiti's financial and foreign affairs and the right to intervene at will, the US government began an occupation that lasted from 1914 until 1934.

Nicaragua and the Central American Court

Another frequent target of US intervention was Nicaragua, in which American intervened over a dozen times between 1840 and 1906. After that date, America's interventions in Nicaragua became even more fateful.

The background to these later interventions was the fact that in 1893, the Conservative government, which supported US interests, was replaced by José Santos Zelaya, who then tried to help his country develop, to decrease US influence, and to create a union among the five Central American states. Disapproving of these efforts, Roosevelt in 1906 intervened militarily and then organized a 1907 conference that led to the creation of a Central American Court of Justice, which was supposed to arbitrate all future disputes. The question would be whether it would be allowed to arbitrate disputes between Central American countries and the United States itself.

The background for the first test case was created by a US intervention in 1909, at which time Washington helped rebels backed by US businesses come to power. Discontent with this new government, which allowed New York banks to take control of much of the country, led to a revolution in 1912. When this revolution was put down by US troops, this intervention was condemned by the Central American Court. But although Roosevelt had helped create this court, "Washington simply ignored the ruling."[102]

Another test arose in 1916, when the Central American Court again condemned US meddling. By then, Woodrow Wilson was president. He and his secretary of state, William Jennings Bryan, were both famous for their anti-imperialistic rhetoric. But they refused to recognize the Court's decision.

These refusals in 1912 and 1916 destroyed the Court, illustrating how, in Walter LaFeber's words, "the Progressive faith in legal remedies was worthless when the dominant power in the area placed its own national interests over international legal institutions."[103] These episodes also illustrated the fact that legal remedies would never work as long as the ultimate enforcer is one of the interested parties, because it will invariably employ double standards, violating standards to which it seeks to hold others.

In any case, the US intervention of 1912 led to a 20-year occupation. Finally, public pressure—one coffee planter pointed out that Americans were despised because the marines would "hunt down and kill Nicaraguans in their own country"—forced President Hoover to pull them out in 1933, leading to developments that will be reported later.

Brooks Adams, having predicted that because of the 1898 war, the United States "may dominate the world," later said that the years from 1900 to 1914 would be "looked back upon as the grand time."[104] That surely depended, however, on which end of the Big Stick one was viewing matters from.

Ideals and Interests

Roosevelt's Corollary to the Monroe Doctrine, said LaFeber, "triggered the most ignoble chapter in United States-Latin American relations," part of which was that, within two decades, the United States "dominated at least fourteen of the twenty Latin American countries through either financial controls or military power—and, in some instances, through both."[105] At the same time, the US government, especially during the presidency of Woodrow Wilson, was advocating "self-determination" as a general principle for international relations.

America's double standard was sometimes employed unconsciously, a fact illustrated by an event reported by LaFeber:

> In June 1916, Wilson sent the draft of a message for Congress to Secretary of State Robert Lansing for perusal. "It shall not lie with American people," the president wrote, "to dictate to another people

> what their government shall be or what use they shall have of what persons they shall encourage or favor." Lansing wrote on the margin: "Haiti, S. Domingo, Nicaragua, Panama." Wilson never sent the message.[106]

In making his marginal comment, incidentally, Lansing was not being critical of US policy, merely pointing out the difference between it and Wilson's idealistic rhetoric. Lansing himself said:

> In its advocacy of the Monroe Doctrine the United States considers its own interests. The integrity of other American nations is an incident, not an end. While this may seem based on selfishness alone, the author of the Doctrine had no higher or more generous motive in its declaration.

While holding that it would be "impolitic" to state this interpretation openly, Wilson reportedly found it "unanswerable."[107]

The Contradiction between Ideals and Policies

The contradiction between Wilson's actual policies and his professed ideals illustrated the basic contradiction that ran throughout the history of America's relations to its southern neighbors. LaFeber's book, *Inevitable Revolutions,* is one long illustration, in his words, of the contradiction "between the principle of self-determination, whose value has been self-evident to the U.S. mind, and the expansion of their nation's power, whose value has also been self-evident."[108]

On the one hand, America has seen itself as the beacon of liberty, not only providing its own revolution as an example to others but actively helping them to achieve self-determination. This self-understanding was expressed in an essay by Arthur Schlesinger, Sr., entitled "America's 10 Gifts to Civilization," in which the first gift was said to be "the right of revolution."[109]

On the other hand, America believed that it had the right to dominate the Western Hemisphere for its own political and economic advantage. It followed Thomas Jefferson, the author of the Declaration, who within a decade, in LaFeber's words, "recognized that [the Declaration's] principles no longer necessarily served U.S. interests" and who believed that, in Jefferson's own words, "America has a hemisphere to itself."

The Monroe Doctrine became "the public announcement" of this belief.[110] The United States became, instead of the champion of democratic revolutions, the great anti-revolutionary power. As a result, LaFeber reported:

> With a single exception, all of the foreign revolutionary leaders, cited by Schlesinger, who referred to the United States as their example did so before 1850.[111]

Conclusion

Having begun the trajectory of its empire with both slavery and genocide and then continued it with unending expansionism and imperialism, America never in practice exemplified the virtues expressed in its paeans to American Exceptionalism.

Endnotes

1 See Philip S. Foner, *The Spanish-Cuban-American War and the Birth of American Imperialism*, 2 vols. (New York: Monthly Review, 1972).

2 John Bassett Moore, *Four Phases of American Development: Federalism, Democracy, Imperialism, Expansion* (Baltimore: 1912), 147-48; quoted in Foner, *The Spanish-Cuban-American War*, x.

3 Richard Van Alstyne, *The Rising American Empire* (1960; New York: Norton, 1974), vii, 78.

4 See Conrad Cherry, ed., *God's New Israel: Religious Interpretations of American Destiny*, revised and updated edition (Chapel Hill: University of North Carolina Press, 1997).

5 Anders Stephanson, *Manifest Destiny: American Expansion and the Empire of Right* (New York: Hill and Wang, 1995), xi. In his *Habits of Empire: A History of American Expansion* (Knopf, 2008), Walter Nugent said that "manifest destiny" provided the best term for the needed ideology of expansion (222).

6 David E. Stannard, *American Holocaust: The Conquest of the New World* (New York: Oxford University Press, 1992), 267-68; Francis Jennings, *The Founders of America: From the Earliest Migration to the Present* (New York: Norton, 1993), 395.

7 Stannard, *American Holocaust*, xii.

8 Ibid., x.

9 "Native American Indian and Western Expansion of the United States," Virginia Museum of Fine Arts; William A. Howe et al., *Becoming a Multicultural Educator: Developing Awareness, Gaining Skills, and Taking Action* (Sage Publications, 2003), 70.

10 Howard Zinn, *A People's History of the United States* (1980; New York: HarperPerennial, 1990), 132.

11 Ibid., 131-32, 140.

12 Stephanson, *Manifest Destiny*, 26.

13 Quoted in Noam Chomsky, *Hegemony or Survival: America's Quest for Global Dominance* (Macmillan, 2003), 102, from Max M. Mintz, *Seeds of Empire: The American Revolutionary Conquest of the Iroquois* (New York: New York University, 1999), 186.

14 Zinn, *A People's History*, 153.

15 Ibid., 27.

16 Stannard, *American Holocaust*, 317.

17 Zinn, *A People's History*, 153.

18 Van Alstyne, *The Rising American Empire*, 159.

19 Ibid., 173.

20 Foner, *The Spanish-Cuban-American War*, ix. Credit for coining the term "neo-colonialism" is usually given to Kwame Nkrumah, the first post-colonial president of Ghana, who wrote *Neo-Colonialism: The Last Stage of Imperialism* (London: Thomas Nelson, 1965).

21 Foner, *The Spanish-Cuban-American War*, viii. As Foner pointed out, he was thereby following the practice of Cuban scholars.

22 David Bell Mislan, *Enemies of the American Way: Identity and Presidential Foreign Policymaking* (Bloomsbury Academic 2014), 157.

23 Stephen Kinzer, *The True Flag: Theodore Roosevelt, Mark Twain, and the Birth of American Empire* (Henry Holt, 2017), 19.

24 Ibid., 21, 67, 214.

25 Ibid.

26 Ibid., 48.

27 Ibid., 59.

28 Walter LaFeber, *The American Age: U.S. Foreign Policy Since 1750*, 2nd ed. (New York: Norton, 1993), 83.

29 Foner, *The Spanish-Cuban-American War*, xv-xvi.

30 Ibid., xxviii.

31 Ibid., xxxii.

32 Ibid., 183; LaFeber, *The American Age*, 185.

33 Foner, *The Spanish-Cuban-American War*, 21, 155-59, 177.

34 Ibid., 213, 229, 248.

35 Ibid., 139-150, 247-48.

36 Ibid., 179-87.

37 Ibid., 145.

38 Ibid., 258.

39 Ibid., xxx.

40 Ibid., 229.

41 Ibid., 209.

42 Ibid., 310.

43 Walter LaFeber, *The American Age: U.S. Foreign Policy Since 1750*, 2nd ed. (Norton, 1993), 11, citing *San Francisco Call*, 17 February 1898.

44 Ibid., 237, 245-47. In 1976, reported Geoffrey Perret, a navy investigation concluded that the explosion was probably an accident resulting from ammunition stored too close to the engine. See *A Country Made by War: From the Revolution to Vietnam—the Story of America's Rise to Power* (Random House, 1989), 280n. However, Cubans have always said that the Americans blew up their own ship as a pretext to go to war (USS *Maine* [ACR-1]), Wikipedia, accessed February 2017).

45 Kinzer, *The True Flag,* 38.

46 Ibid., 191.

47 Foner, *The Spanish-Cuban-American War*, 605.

48 Saul Landau, *The Dangerous Doctrine: National Security and U.S. Foreign Policy* (Westview Press), 79; quoted from Peter Bourne, *Fidel: A Biography of Fidel Castro* (Dodd-Mead, 1986), 8-9.

49 As Ralph H. Parker put it (in "Imperialism and the Liberation of Cuba"): Cuba, by virtue of the Platt Amendment, became "a part of the new American empire. . . . A new imperialism had displaced the old. Spain, clinging to the old colonial imperialism of the seventeenth century, gave way to a new country whose imperial dreams were economic and financial" (quoted in Foner, *The Spanish-Cuban-American War*, 631).

50 Foner, *The Spanish-Cuban-American War*, 581-82, 585-89.

51 Ibid., 466-83.

52 Ibid., 304, 309; Van Alstyne, *The Rising American Empire*, 132, 188. See also Thomas McCormick, *China Market: America's Quest for Informal Empire, 1893-1901* (Quadrangle Books, 1967).

53 Van Alstyne, *The Rising American Empire*, 184.

54 Perret, *A Country Made By War*, 288-89; Foner, *The Spanish-Cuban-American War*, 409.

55 Foner, *The Spanish-Cuban-American War*, 409-10.

56 Kinzer, *The True Flag,* 87-88.

57 Ibid., 94.

58 Johnson, *Sorrows of Empire*, 42.

59 Foner, *The Spanish-Cuban-American War*, 431.

60 Zinn, *A People's History*, 307; Kinzer, *The True Flag,* 118-19.

61 Ibid., 308.

62 Ibid.

63 Ibid., 306.

64 Ibid., 309.

65 Foner, *The Spanish-Cuban-American War*, 110-18, 663-64.

66 Zinn, *A People's History,* 309.

67 Proclamation of December 21, 1898; quoted at the front of Stuart Creighton Miller, *Benevolent Assimilation: The American Conquest of the Philippines, 1899-1903* (Yale University Press, 1982).

68 Stephanson, *Manifest Destiny*, 90.

69 Ibid., 88.

70 Ibid., 22.

71 Foner, *The Spanish-Cuban-American War*, 419.

72 Robert Beisner, *Twelve Against Empire: The Anti-Imperialists, 1898-1902* (McGraw-Hill, 1968).

73 Kinzer, *The True Flag,* 133.

74 Ibid., 61.

75 Ibid., 68-69.

76 Ibid., 182, 184, 186. For Twain's writings, see Jim Zwick, ed., *Mark Twain's Weapons of Satire: Anti-Imperialist Writings on the Philippine-American War* (Syracuse University Press, 1992).

77 Foner, *The Spanish-Cuban-American War*, 415.

78 Kinzer, *The True Flag*, 81.

79 Ibid., 156.

80 Ibid., 142.

81 Michael H. Hunt, *Ideology and US Foreign Policy* (Yale University Press, 1988), 41-42.

82 Ernest R. May, *Imperial Democracy: The Emergence of America as a Great Power* (HarperCollins, 1961), 281.

83 Zinn, *A People's History*, 306.

84 Foner, *The Spanish-Cuban-American War*, 418.

85 Walter LaFeber, *Inevitable Revolutions: The United States in Central America* (Norton, 1984), 39.

86 Foner, *The Spanish-Cuban-American War*, 672.

87 Lloyd C. Gardner, Walter F. LaFeber, and Thomas J. McCormick, *Creation of the American Empire* (Rand McNally, 1973), 265.

88 On the origin of the Monroe doctrine and its later applications, see Dexter Perkins, *A History of the Monroe Doctrine* (Little, Brown, 1963 [a revision of a 1941 book entitled *Hands Off: A History of the Monroe Doctrine*]).

89 Van Alstyne, *The Rising American Empire*, 99. The USA's early plan to remove the British Empire from North America by absorbing Canada became increasingly unrealistic after the Canadian Federation, created in 1867, purchased the Hudson Bay Company and annexed British Columbia. But many US imperialists continued to nurture this idea (ibid., 176).

90 Walter LaFeber, *The Panama Canal: The Crisis in Historical Perspective* (Oxford University Press, 1978), 29-33.

91 Ibid., 39.

92 Ibid., x, 37-39, 66-67.

93 Ibid., 42.

94 Ibid., 74-77.

95 Ibid., 49, 68-73, 81-82, 97-98.

96 Ibid., 73-74.

97 LaFeber, *Inevitable Revolutions*, 38.

98 See Bruce Calder, *The Impact of Intervention* (University of Texas, 1984), and Jan Knippers Black, *The Dominican Republic* (Allen & Unwin, 1986).

99 Noam Chomsky, *Year 501: The Conquest Continues* (Boston: South End, 1993), 199.

100 Ibid., 199-200.

101 Ibid., 202.

102 LaFeber, *Inevitable Revolutions*, 48.

103 Ibid., 41.

104 Ibid., 39.

105 LaFeber, *The Panama Canal,* 52.

106 LaFeber, *Inevitable Revolutions*, 54. Some years later the list of exceptions would have also included Costa Rica, Guatemala, and El Salvador, with the last example involving a massacre in 1932 of perhaps 30,000 people. American leaders, far from intervening to prevent this massacre, watched with approval and then rewarded the

Salvadoran government for carrying it out; see ibid., 54-58, 74-77, and Noam Chomsky, *On Power and Ideology: The Managua Lectures* (South End, 1987), 75-76.

107 Chomsky, *Year 501*, 158.

108 LaFeber, *Inevitable Revolutions*, 22.

109 Cited in ibid., 22-23.

110 Ibid.

111 Ibid.

| Chapter 2 |

WORLD WAR I

Whereas Americans are seldom exposed to the sordid details of US behavior in its own hemisphere, American participation in the two world wars has been the subject of countless books, movies, and television shows. It is these accounts that have, in fact, impressed upon the American psyche the image of the United States as the selfless defender of freedom and democracy for other peoples. The truth behind the image, however, is somewhat different. US leaders used these wars as occasions for two quantum leaps in America's acquisition of the power to establish a universal empire.

World War I—which prior to World War II was simply the Great War—has been called "the war that launched the American Century."[1] It is often said that Woodrow Wilson's reason for taking America into this European war was to "make the world safe for democracy." And he genuinely did hope to put an end to war through the establishment of the League of Nations (see Chapter 7).

But part of what he meant by this slogan was a global system based on the principle of "openness," which in spite its fine-sounding name, was based purely on American self-interest. In his campaign for the presidency in 1912, Wilson said: "Our domestic markets no longer suffice, we need foreign markets."[2]

After insisting that the League of Nations must embody the "American principles" of self-determination and open markets, Wilson then insisted that these principles were *not* to be interpreted in a way that would undermine the Monroe Doctrine—now understood in terms of the Roosevelt Corollary, which extended the prohibition of European intervention in the Western Hemisphere from military and political intervention to *financial* intervention.[3] "American principles," it turned out, meant closed doors where this benefited America, open doors where this benefited America.

Open doors benefited America in countries where it did not already have a stranglehold, because open doors in those countries meant that their economies could be taken over by the strongest economic power, and at the beginning of the 20th century, the United States was emerging as just that. During the years in which America was still neutral in the Great War, it made loans to belligerents, with the result that America went from being one of the world's greatest debtors to being its greatest creditor—a reversal that "helped turn the United States into the world's economic superpower of the twentieth century."[4] Indeed, said G.J. Meyer in his 2016 book, *The World Remade: America in World War I*, while all the other countries involved in the war became impoverished, "the United States grew fabulously rich."[5]

The loans also, it is widely held, provided one of the major reasons for why America eventually entered the war on the side of Britain and its allies, because most of the loans had gone to them, giving America a huge stake in an Allied victory.[6]

After the victory, America, with its new status as the world's economic superpower, would be able to force its open door policy on the world. And Wilson was quite prepared to do this, having earlier said: "[E]ven if the sovereignty of unwilling nations be outraged in the process. . . the doors of the nations which are closed must be battered down."[7] Britain and France, realizing that the United States would be able to out-compete everyone else in an open-door system, were making plans for protected markets. Wilson knew this but did not protest because after the war, he said, "we can force [England and France] to our way of thinking, because by that time they will be financially in our hands."[8]

This seamier underside of what was going on behind the scenes of the Allied victory also had its military dimension. Being aware that the British navy, then the most powerful in the world, would be a deterrent to American freedom of action, Wilson said, during the war: "Let us build a navy bigger than [Great Britain's] and do what we please."[9]

1. Getting into the War

For the Great War to launch the American Century, it was necessary for America to get into the war. This happened because President Wilson, as well as Winston Churchill—who at the time was the head of Great Britain's Admiralty—deeply wanted it.

Churchill's Desire

Prior to America's entry into it, the war was between the Triple Entente, composed of Russia, France, and Britain, on the one hand, and the alliance of Germany and the Austro-Hungarian Empire, on the other—a war for land and natural resources. In addition, the British Empire was feeling threatened by the rising financial and technological power of Germany. Although Great Britain still ruled the seas, German's rising technological power, including its airplanes and submarines, was making it a serious threat. Churchill wanted America to enter the war in order to ensure the victory of Britain and its allies.

Wilson's Desire

Wilson wanted America to enter the war for reasons of his own, as explained by Walter Karp, who was described by Lewis Lapham as "an historian of the best kind." The greatest part of Karp's book, *The Politics of War,* said Lapham, was devoted to "the bottomless deceit of Woodrow Wilson."[10] Wilson's primary deceit, according to Karp, was to claim that he wanted to keep America out of the war while doing everything possible to get it into the war.

People who knew Wilson made severe criticisms of him as a person. A member of his cabinet described him as "a man of high ideals but no principles." Former President Glover Cleveland spoke of his lack of "intellectual integrity." Karp offered an even more damning assessment, writing:

> The decisive trait of Wilson's political character was vainglory: a hunger for glory so exclusively self-regarding, so indifferent to the concerns of others, that it would lead him to betray. . . the hopes of a war-torn world.[11]

For example, although Wilson was a Democrat, he praised the "large policy" enunciated by Republicans during the Spanish-American War. He liked it, said Wilson, because of the "greatly increased power and opportunity for constructive statesmanship given the President" by this policy. Karp commented:

> Americans are not in the habit of judging a national policy by its personal advantage to their president. Nor are they in the habit of considering themselves and their country as mere instruments in a president's quest for glory.[12]

We know something about Wilson's secret thoughts because Wilson's main advisor, Edward "Colonel" House, kept a detailed diary. Karp described House as a "wealthy, dapper little Texan with a passion for behind-the-scenes wirepulling." For example, the members of Wilson's cabinet were actually chosen by House.[13]

After Wilson was elected, he publicly claimed that he hoped that his administration would not need "to deal chiefly with foreign affairs." But House knew better. When war broke out in Europe, Wilson regarded it as the opportunity of a lifetime—"the greatest, perhaps, that has ever come to any man," said House.[14]

House then began discussing with the British ambassador the possibility of Wilson's playing a major role in the conference to be held at the end of the war. The plan was that, by presiding over a great postwar conference, Wilson would become the first person in history to bring about everlasting peace. "This," House told Wilson, "is the part I think you are destined to play in this world tragedy and it is the noblest part that has ever come to a son of man."[15] Of course, to have a chance of presiding over the postwar conference, Wilson would need to enter the war and help the Allies win it.[16] Accordingly, Karp said:

> From autumn 1914 onward, the diplomacy of the United States would be conducted by Wilson and House not in the interests of America. . . , not by the wish to avoid a horrendous war, but solely by the desire to secure by any means possible Wilson's opportunity to play "the noblest part that has ever come to a son of man."[17]

Could the sinking of the *Lusitania* have been intended to be one of those means?

2. The Sinking of the *Lusitania*

A British luxury liner named the *Lusitania* was launched in 1906. Built by Britain's Cunard Line, it was the biggest and most beautiful liner in the world (it was "more beautiful than Solomon's Temple and big enough to hold all his wives").[18] On May 7, 1915, this ship, which carried several important people (including Alfred Vanderbilt), was making a return cruise from New York to England. Near the end of this voyage, this remarkable ship sank in the Irish Sea after being hit by a torpedo fired by a German submarine known as a U-boat (Unterseeboot). The *Lusitania* sank in only 18 minutes, with the result that, of the 1,924 people aboard, 1,198 of them, including 128 Americans, were killed.

Why did this huge ship sink so fast? William Turner, the captain of the *Lusitania*, said that, shortly after the torpedo struck the ship, there was a second, much bigger, explosion.[19] Many of the surviving crew and passengers reported the same thing.[20] But the submarine commander said that he had fired only one torpedo, and this claim was supported by his logs.[21] The British Admiralty, led by Winston Churchill, also knew this to be true, although it would not admit it.[22] If there had been only one torpedo, the ship should have stayed up for over two hours before it sank, in which case everyone aboard could have been saved.[23]

The people could also have been saved by the cruiser *Juno*, which was only an hour away, and had plenty of room for all the passengers. But after she set out to rescue the passengers, she was called back to port.[24]

Another mystery was why this ship was even struck. Great Britain knew the German codes, so it knew where the German U-boats were. And when the *Lusitania* entered into a war zone, where it might be hit, it was to be escorted by torpedo boat destroyers. So why was the *Lusitania* struck? Considerable evidence suggests that Churchill played a central role.

Churchill's Role

Churchill was anxious to have America enter the war, as shown by his statement (to the president of Britain's Board of Trade) that it was "most important to attract neutral shipping to our shores, in the hopes especially of embroiling the United States with Germany."[25]

In addition, people in Churchill's circles had talked about the possibility that an attack on the *Lusitania* might bring America into the war. On May 7 itself, Colonel House was in London, where he visited with Edward Grey, Britain's foreign secretary. According to House, Grey asked: "What will America do if the Germans sink an ocean liner with American passengers on board?" House answered: "I believe that a flame of indignation would sweep the United States and that by itself would be sufficient to carry us into the war."[26]

That same day, House and Grey met with King George and, House continued, "We fell to talking, strangely enough, of the probability of Germany sinking a trans-Atlantic liner. . . . He [the king] said, 'Suppose they should sink the *Lusitania*, with American passengers on board?'"[27]

There are several reasons to believe that Churchill and his Admiralty engineered the probability that the *Lusitania* would be sunk:

- Churchill was overheard referring to the *Lusitania* as "livebait."[28]

- By virtue of knowing the German codes, Churchill knew that U-boats were in the Irish Sea, where the *Lusitania* was headed. Yet he had no warning sent to Captain Turner.[29]

- The *Lusitania* could have been sent around the north of Ireland, where Churchill knew no U-boats were operating. Captain Turner, in fact, had reportedly asked to be allowed to take this route. But if so, this proposal was rejected.[30]

- The *Lusitania* in previous trips had been escorted by two destroyers, and Captain Turner had been promised that this would be the case on this trip. But no escort was provided, even though four destroyers were lying idle in a nearby port. (After his ship was sunk, Captain Turner complained bitterly about this lack of the promised escort.)[31]

- After the disaster, the Admiralty sent instructions "to ensure that bodies selected for the inquest had not been killed or mutilated by means which we do not wish to be made public."[32]

- The director of the Admiralty's Trade Division wrote a note to Lord Mersey, who was to preside over the inquiry, saying: "I am directed by the Board of Admiralty to inform you that it is considered politically expedient that Captain Turner the master of the *Lusitania* be most prominently blamed for the disaster."[33]

- Many years later, as movements toward World War II

> had begun, Churchill wrote: "In spite of all its horror, we must regard the sinking of the *Lusitania* as an event most important and favourable to the Allies. . . . [T]he poor babies who perished in the ocean struck a blow at German power more deadly than could have been achieved by the sacrifice of a hundred thousand fighting men."[34]

Patrick Beesly, who was considered the leading authority on the history of British Naval Intelligence, wrote in his 1982 book, *Room 40*:

> Nothing, absolutely nothing was done to ensure the liner's safe arrival . . . . I am reluctantly driven to the conclusion that there was a conspiracy deliberately to put the *Lusitania* at risk in the hopes that even an abortive attack on her would bring the United States into the war. Such a conspiracy could not have been put into effect without Winston Churchill's express permission and approval.[35]

Although G. J. Meyer said that conspiracy theories "deserve to be met with the firmest skepticism," he did cite Beesly's opinion as expressed in an interview, in which Beesly said:

> On the basis of the considerable volume of information which is now available, I am reluctantly compelled to state that on balance, the most likely explanation is that there was indeed a plot, however imperfect, to endanger the Lusitania in order to involve the United States in the war. If that's unacceptable, will someone tell me another explanation to these very very curious circumstances?[36]

In quoting this statement, Meyer seemed to agree that it would be difficult to find another explanation.[37]

Other experts, moreover, have had the same idea. According to Colin Simpson, the failure to warn the *Lusitania* may have been "the pinnacle of Churchill's higher strategy of embroiling the U-boats with a neutral power." Likewise, Patrick O'Sullivan said that the failure to pass on vital information could be "another move in Churchill's game-plan to embroil the *Lusitania* with a German submarine and thus bring America into the war."[38]

As to how Churchill's Admiralty could have arranged for the second, extremely powerful, explosion, which brought the *Lusitania* down: Colin Simpson argued that the explosion was possibly caused by a type of guncotton named pyroxyline. Captain Guy Gaunt, the British naval attaché in Washington, had learned about pyroxyline from a chemist named Dr. Ritter von Rettegh. In an affidavit, Dr. von Rettegh said:

> [I]f sea water comes into contact with the guncotton immediately a chemical change takes place. The free sulphuric acid in the latter will be chemically attacked by the bromine and iodine salts and also common salts contained in the sea-water, raising the temperature and causing sudden explosion.

When Gaunt asked whether von Rettegh thought that pyroxyline caused the rapid sinking of two British ships, which had recently gone down, he said that it was possible. The day after his conversation with Dr. von Rettegh, Gaunt ordered 600 tons of pyroxyline, which was sent to the *Lusitania's* wharf.[39]

Wilson's Role

If Churchill and his Admiralty had indeed conspired to increase the chances that the *Lusitania* would be sunk, with much loss of life, there are reasons to believe that President Wilson, along with Colonel House, was part of the conspiracy.

- As stated above, Wilson fervently wanted to get America into the war, and was willing to use "any means possible" to achieve this goal.

- Five days before the *Lusitania* sank, Wilson's very pro-British ambassador to England, Walter Hines Page, had written to his son: "If a British liner full of American passengers be blown up, what will Uncle Sam do? That's what's going to happen."[40]

- A week before the *Lusitania* was to sail, the German government published a warning reminding people that Germany and Great Britain were in a state of war, so that people "sailing in the war zone on ships of Great Britain or her allies do so at their own risk."[41] However, the US Department of State did not publish the warning. Upon being asked by a German publisher why not, William Jennings Bryan, who was then the secretary of state, ordered the warning to be published. Bryan then urged Wilson to warn Americans not to travel on the *Lusitania*. However, "No such warning was issued by the President."[42] Surely partly because of this failure, the *Lusitania* was boarded by 159 Americans, only 35 of whom survived.

- This issue had arisen in a proposed bill in Congress. According to this bill, Americans would be warned about the dangers of traveling on ships owned by countries involved in the war. Wilson opposed this bill so strongly that it was withdrawn.[43]

It appears, therefore, that Wilson as well as Churchill wanted the *Lusitania* to sink, killing lots of Americans. If that was indeed their plan, it worked perfectly.

However, although British and American leaders assumed that the sinking of the *Lusitania* would mean an immediate declaration of war, Wilson discovered that most Americans were not yet ready for their country to enter the war.[44] After the sinking, 98 percent of Americans, "[Theodore] Roosevelt ruefully estimated," were still opposed to entering the war.[45] However, Wilson discovered that there was another way that the sinking of the *Lusitania* could provide a *casus belli*. Karp wrote:

> In Germany's submarine warfare against its enemies' shipping Wilson seized his chance— a slender chance but the only one he had—to force war upon the United States.[46]

This chance depended on Wilson's ignoring details about submarine warfare in relation to the *Lusitania.*

For one thing, when Germany started using U-boats to block British ports, this was in retaliation.

> From the start the British hoped to use their peerless navy to blockade Germany, deny it raw materials and foodstuffs, and thereby strangle its industrial economy and, as Winston Churchill candidly put it, "starve the whole population—men, women and children, old and young, wounded and sound—into submission."[47]

And the British blockade was extremely effective, reportedly causing almost 800,000 Germans to die of starvation.[48]

Wilson, however, imposed a double standard: While accepting Britain's starvation policy, Wilson condemned the German use of U-boats as immoral, refusing to agree that it was justified by Britain's starvation blockade, even though German's U-boat policy killed far fewer people than did Britain's starvation policy.[49] The irrationality of Wilson's position was, in fact, pointed out by Secretary of State Bryan, who asked: "Why be shocked by the drowning of a few people, if there is to be no objection to starving a nation?"[50]

Fully appreciating the hypocrisy of Wilson's position requires an understanding of how Churchill changed the accepted rules of submarine warfare in relation to merchant ships. According to these "cruiser rules," a submarine captain would board the ship in order to search it for munitions or other contraband. If contraband is found, the submarine captain, before sinking the ship, would allow all people on board to get into life boats.

However, Churchill's Admiralty unilaterally changed the rules by arming merchant ships and ordering them to ram any submarines that surfaced, tearing them in half, or else to fire on them. Churchill's new rules, pointed out Meyer, "made German observance of cruiser rules not just dangerous but impossible."[51]

In response to Britain's firing and ramming policy, Germany announced that it would strike British merchant ships in the war zone around the British Isles on sight.[52] Given the fact that Britain was no longer following the traditional rules, America could not reasonably have insisted that Germany follow those rules. But that is exactly what Wilson did.

Using the term "strict accountability," Wilson said that if a German submarine, failing to follow the visit-and-search rule, destroys an American vessel or the lives of American citizens:

> The Government of the United States would be constrained to hold the Imperial German Government to a strict accountability for such acts . . . and to take any steps it might be necessary to take to. . . secure to American citizens the full enjoyment of their acknowledged rights on the high seas.[53]

However, there are and were no such "acknowledged rights." Although Wilson said that the United States had a "sacred duty" to protect the right of its citizens to travel anywhere anytime, "there existed in law," said Meyer, "no such thing as the right to a guarantee of safety if one chose to travel on the ship of a nation at war."[54]

Nevertheless, insisting that the American government had a duty to protect the alleged right of Americans to sail on British ships, even though those ships may be carrying munitions, Wilson was risking war, said Karp, "in the name of a few hundred Americans who preferred to sail on a Cunard liner instead of a safe Dutch or Norwegian ship"—a position, in Bryan's view, "bordering on moral lunacy."[55]

However, Wilson knew what he was doing. In 1915, he told Colonel House that his policy of "strict accountability" was intended as a step toward war. In light of the fact that Americans were almost totally against entering the war, Wilson knew that he could be effective only if Americans believed that, although he wanted to keep the peace, Germany was forcing America to enter the war.[56]

Nevertheless, hoping that it could act so as to prevent America from entering the war, Germany agreed to return to cruiser rules. Having made this gigantic concession, German expected reciprocity—that America would use its influence to persuade Britain to give up, or at least alter, its blockade policy. But Wilson would do no such thing.[57]

In response, Germany, desperate to stop the starvation of its people, returned to unrestricted submarine warfare. On that basis, Wilson successfully, after U-boats had downed several more US ships, persuaded Congress to declare war on Germany.[58]

The *Lusitania* as Casus Belli

Although the sinking of the *Lusitania* did not lead to America's immediate entry into the war, it did eventually play an important role. After America declared war on Germany, "Remember the *Lusitania*" became a slogan used for recruitment posters. Another poster said, "Enlist and Avenge the *Lusitania.*" According to Diana Preston:

> Americans quickly forgot that nearly two years had elapsed between the sinking and their declaration of war. The myth grew, and it still persists today, that the United States entered the

> war as an immediate consequence of the sinking of the *Lusitania*.[59]

Be that as it may, the sinking of the *Lusitania* never created the unified nation that Wilson had so strongly desired. Unlike the attack on Pearl Harbor (see Chapter 5), the sinking of the *Lusitania* never convinced most Americans that World War I was a "good war." Large numbers of young people did not rush to enlist. Even after the declaration of war, Howard Zinn reported, "only 73,000 volunteered," although a million were needed.[60]

Government Recruitment Policies

Because Americans were not enthusiastic about the war, "The government," said Zinn, "had to work hard to create its consensus."[61] This work involved four measures.

First, the government engaged in a huge propaganda campaign, some of which was based around the "Remember the *Lusitania*" slogan. Also, 75,000 speakers were sent to some 5,000 cities and towns. However, these patriotic speeches were countered by socialist speakers, who denounced the declaration of war as "a crime against the people of the United States," and these speakers were more popular.[62]

Second, the government began a draft; but many of the men called for the draft claimed exception or otherwise dodged the draft.[63]

Third, because of the failure of the first two measures, the government decided to punish people who did not go along: It passed the Espionage and Sedition Acts, which were used to imprison people who spoke or wrote against the war. In other words, dissent was a felony. The most famous person arrested was Eugene Debs, who was sentenced to 10 years in prison (although he was released by the next president).[64]

Fourth, the government sponsored vigilante groups, who were to report any evidence of sedition, and the Post Office Department took away mailing privileges to any publications printing antiwar articles.[65]

These acts constituted severe violations of the First Amendment. Emma Goldman asked: "[P]oor as we are in democracy how can we give of it to the world?"[66]

3. The Path to World War II

Although Wilson's entry into the Great War turned out well for the United States economically, his expressed hope that it would be the war to end all wars was, of course, unfulfilled. In fact, only 20 years passed before World War II began. There were two reasons why this second world war came about.

The Treatment of Germany

Part of the reason for this second world war was the harsh treatment of Germany at the hands of the allies. As pointed out above, Britain and America employed a double standard, treating Germany's U-boat warfare as criminal while ignoring Britain's much more deadly warfare by starvation.

Also, Britain's starvation blockade was extremely cruel, killing close to a million German citizens—men, women, and children. As if this were not immoral enough, the British kept the blockade in place for seven and a half months after the Armistice—an act that has been called "the worst atrocity of the Great War." Wilson, moreover, supported this policy, declaring that "the existing blockade conditions set up by the Allies and Associated Powers are to remain unchanged."[67]

Even more important in leading to World War II were the punishments demanded by the Treaty of Versailles. It demanded that Germany pay a great amount of money for reparations. And it dictated that Germany lose 10 percent of its population and 13 percent of its territory, thereby losing a significant amount of its food sources. The German foreign minister said: "Those who will sign this letter will sign the death sentence for many millions of German men, women, and children."[68]

In addition to these physical punishments, the Treaty made a psychological demand that was extremely difficult for

Germany to swallow (because it was so far from the truth)—that it had to confess that it was solely responsible for the war.[69] Even Colonel House criticized the treatment of Germany at the Versailles conference, saying that it was "made as humiliating to the enemy as possible."[70]

The Failure to Ratify the League of Nations

The second major reason for the second world war was the failure of the League of Nations (to be discussed in Chapter 7). Part of the reason for the failure was the fact that the US Senate did not ratify the Treaty of Versailles and hence did not join the League—although students of this episode have said that the failure was due significantly to Wilson himself. For example, Walter Karp said that, after the conference in Versailles, Wilson returned to America so "mentally unhinged" that he could accept no changes in the treaty:

> Unless he acceded to some Republican demands for emendations and interpretative additions, the Treaty of Versailles (which included the League) faced defeat in the Senate. . . . Wilson stood adamant. He would accept no alterations.[71]

Meyer, agreeing with Karp on this issue, said that if Wilson had been willing to compromise, the Senate would have "approve[d] the treaty in a landslide."[72]

Be that as it may, the Senate's failure to ratify the treaty meant that the League of Nations had to try to maintain world peace without the nation that had become the world's greatest economic and military power. Accordingly, the League had no power to prevent Germany from trying to reverse the losses inflicted on it by the Treaty of Versailles.

Consequences

The rapid advent of a second world war has led many people to suspect that the world would have been better off if America had stayed out of the Great War. Michael Kazin, who in 2017 published *War Against War: The American Fight for Peace, 1914-1918,* has given this explanation:

> [America's] entry most likely foreclosed the possibility of a negotiated peace among belligerent powers that were exhausted from years mired in trench warfare. . . . [Without America, the] carnage might have continued for another year or two until citizens in the warring nations, who were already protesting the endless sacrifices required, forced their leaders to reach a settlement. If the Allies, led by France and Britain, had not won a total victory, there would have been no punitive peace treaty like that completed at Versailles, no stab-in-the-back allegations by resentful Germans, and thus no rise, much less triumph, of Hitler and the Nazis. The next world war, with its 50 million deaths, would probably not have occurred.[73]

From this perspective, far from being the country that brought victory over war, America was a primary contributor thereto.

Speaking of the formation of the League of Nations, Senator Philander Knox said: "God forbid that 'the war that was to end all wars' shall conclude with a peace that may end all peace."[74] But that is what happened. The Versailles Treaty and the League of Nations gave the victorious nations the power to restructure the Middle East because of the defeat of the Ottoman Empire, which had joined the war on the side of Germany and the Austrian-Hungarian Empire.

The Middle East was restructured by David Lloyd George (the British prime minister), Georges Clemenceau (the French prime minister), and President Wilson. Lord Balfour, the British foreign secretary—who had previously served as the prime minister—described them as "three all-powerful, all-ignorant men sitting there and partitioning continents."[75] Robert Lansing, Wilson's new secretary of state, said:

> I consider that the League of Nations is at present entirely useless. The great powers have simply gone ahead and arranged the world to suit themselves. England and France in particular have got out of the treaty everything that they wanted.[76]

The self-centeredness of the great powers resulted in enormous gaps between the treaty as written and Wilson's peace-seeking Fourteen Points, on which the treaty was supposed to be based. The treaty, said Meyer, "set in motion the tragedies that have continued to afflict the region down to the present day."[77] The history of the way in which the treaty led to tragedies in the Middle East was told by David Fromkin in a book with the title, *A Peace to End All Peace,* reminiscent of Senator Knox's worry: "God forbid that 'the war that was to end all wars' shall conclude with a peace that may end all peace."[78]

Conclusion

To enlarge on Michael Kazin's point: If America had not entered the Great War, there would have been no total victory, hence no possibility for "all-powerful, all-ignorant" politicians to divide the world up to suit themselves, thereby creating a peace to end all peace. If America had not entered World War I, there may have been no World War II.

Endnotes

1 "The War that Launched the American Century," *Telegraph*, 3 May 2014.

2 Howard Zinn, *A People's History of the United States* (HarperPerennial, 1998), 362.

3 Walter LaFeber, *Inevitable Revolutions: The United States in Central America* (Norton, 1984), 51, 58; Walter LaFeber, *The American Age: U.S. Foreign Policy Since 1750*, 2nd ed. (Norton, 1993), 284, 303.

4 LaFeber, *The American Age*, 273.

5 G.J. Meyer, *The World Remade: America in World War I* (Bantam Books, 2016).

6 Ibid., 272-73; Zinn, *A People's History of the United States*, 353.

7 Zinn, ibid., 353.

8 LaFeber, *The American Age*, 275, 297.

9 Ibid., 276. The point of this history is not that Washington was in the control of uniquely evil men, or even right-wing extremists. Woodrow Wilson was a liberal democrat. The point is that there is a logic to nationalism, which induces leaders to promote the interests of their own citizens, particularly those citizens to whom they are beholden, while being indifferent to the interests, or even the human rights, of citizens of other nations. And although we have a structure of international law, there is no power that exists for the purpose of enforcing it. It is only enforced, therefore, if the most powerful actor on the international scene wants to enforce it. It is not enforceable, therefore, against this most powerful actor itself. The creation of the United Nations, as discussed in Chapter 7, did nothing to change this.

10 Lewis H. Lapham, Introduction to Walter Karp's *The Politics of War* (see the next note), xiii.

11 Walter Karp, *The Politics of War: The Story of Two Wars Which Altered Forever the Political Life of the American Republic (1890-1920),* (Franklin Square Press, 2010) 151.

12 Ibid., 150.

13 Ibid., 175-76.

14 Ibid., 160, 172.

15 Ibid., 179; quoting House, *Intimate Papers* (see note 26, below) , vol. 2: 92.

16 Ibid., 180.

17 Ibid., 179.

18 Diana Preston, *Wilful Murder: The Sinking of the Lusitania* (Doubleday, 2002), 44 ("wilful" is an older spelling, still used outside of North America.)

19 Ibid., 444; Colin Simpson, *The Lusitania* (Little, Brown, 1972), 155.

20 Ibid., 191-95.

21 Patrick O'Sullivan, *The Sinking of the Lusitania: Unravelling the Mysteries* (Collins Press, 2004), 168; "Lusitania Online: The Home

Port of RMS Lusitania, Torpedo."
22 Preston, *Wilful Murder*, 304.
23 "Churchill and J.P. Morgan Sank Lusitania," Lies Your Teacher Taught You, 16 March 2012.
24 Meyer, *The World Remade*, 124.
25 Donald E. Schmidt, *The Folly of War: American Foreign Policy, 1898-2005* (NAlgora Publishing, 2005), 72.
26 Charles Seymour, ed., *The Intimate Papers of Colonel House*, Vol. 1 (Houghton Mifflin, 1926), 432.
27 Ibid.
28 Simpson, *The Lusitania,* 30.
29 Ibid., 131.
30 Ibid., 216-17.
31 Simpson, *The Lusitania,* 121, 130, 182; Preston, *Wilful Murder*, 399; Patrick Beesly, *Room 40: British Naval Intelligence 1914-1918* (Harcourt Brace Jovanovich, 1982), 105.
32 Simpson, *The Lusitania,* 180.
33 Ibid., 190.
34 Preston, *Wilful Murder*, 5.
35 Beesly, *Room 40*, 122.
36 Erik Larson, *Dead Wake: The Last Crossing of the Lusitania* (Broadway Books, 2016), 324.
37 Meyer, *The World Remade*, 126-27.
38 Simpson, *The Lusitania,* 130; O'Sullivan, *The Sinking of the Lusitania*, 152.
39 Simpson, *The Lusitania*, 95-97.
40 Burton J. Hendrick, *The Life and Letters of Walter H. Page,* Vol. 1 (Doubleday, Page & Co., 1923), 436.
41 Preston, *Wilful Murder*, 2.
42 Simpson, *The Lusitania*, 97.
43 Meyer, *The World Remade*, 130.
44 Ibid., 178; Preston, *Wilful Murder*, 272, 360, 366.
45 Karp, *The Politics of War,* 177, 207.
46 Ibid., 193.
47 Ibid., 180.
48 C. Paul Vincent, *The Politics of Hunger: The Allied Blockade of Germany, 1915–1919* (Ohio University Press, 1986).
49 Ibid., 198; George Dvorsky, "Was Britain's WWI Blockade the First Atrocity of the 20th Century?" (io9 Gizmodo, 1 December, 2014).
50 Meyer, *The World* Remade, 76.
51 Karp, *The Politics of War,* 202; Meyer, *The World* Remade, 63.
52 Ibid., 187.

53 Ibid., 191.
54 Meyer, *The World Remade,* 101.
55 Karp, *The Politics of War,* 204.
56 Ibid., 192-93, 194.
57 Meyer, *The World Remade,* 135-37.
58 Ibid., 249, 277; Preston, *Wilful Murder*, 366.
59 O'Sullivan, *The Sinking of the Lusitania,* 186; Preston, *Wilful Murder*, 445; 366, 367. (Thc text on page 366 of Preston's book had "198" instead of "128," but this was surely a typo.)
60 Howard Zinn, *The Twentieth Century: A People's History*, revised & updated ed. (HarperPerennial, 1998), 83.
61 Ibid., 85.
62 Ibid., 83.
63 Ibid., 83-84, 90.
64 Ibid., 88; Harry N. Scheiber, *The Wilson Administration and Civil Liberties, 1917-1921* (1960; Quid Pro, LLC, 2013).
65 Zinn, *The Twentieth Century,* 88-91.
66 Ibid., 93.
67 Meyer, *The World Remade*, 530, 474.
68 Ibid., 520-21.
69 Ibid., 520, 527.
70 Ibid., 529.
71 Karp, *The Politics of War*, 342.
72 Meyer, *The World Remade*, 557.
73 Michael Kazin, *War Against War: The American Fight for Peace, 1914-1918* (Simon & Schuster, 2017), xv-xvi.
74 Meyer, *The World Remade,* 525.
75 Ibid., 523.
76 Ibid., 548.
77 Ibid., 522.
78 David Fromkin, *A Peace to End All Peace: Creating the Modern Middle East, 1914-1922* (Henry Holt, 1989); Meyer, *The World Remade,* 525.

| Chapter 3 |

BETWEEN THE WARS

If one of the fateful consequences of World War I was the growth of US financial and military power, another was the rise of Communism as a global movement.[1]

1. The First Offensive Against Communism: From 1917 to World War II

Due to the emergence of the Soviet Union, America's interventions outside the Western Hemisphere increased considerably. Most of these were based on, or at least shaped and justified by, its post-1917 concern with checking the influence of "Communism" or "Bolshevism." Although this concern would be most pronounced during the Republican administrations of Warren Harding, Calvin Coolidge, and Herbert Hoover, which stretched from 1921 to 1933, this concern had already brought about a decisive reorientation of US policy in Wilson's administration, illustrated by his interventions in Russia and Hungary.

Russia and Hungary

Shortly after the Bolsheviks seized power in Russia, they began distributing land to peasants, nationalizing banks, and putting factories in the hands of workers.[2] Although Wilson had been advocating self-determination, he did not mean *this*. His administration, in fact, held that this was not a genuine case of self-determination, because the "present rulers of Russia do not rule by the will or the consent of any considerable portion of the Russian people."[3] Regarding Bolshevism as qualitatively worse than other forms of autocratic rule, Wilson called it "government by terror."[4]

Wilson for some time resisted the call to intervene militarily, partly because such intervention would violate one of the main points of his famous "fourteen point" peace plan—Russia's unhampered right "for the independent determination of her own political development."[5] Nevertheless, in 1918 Wilson sent thousands of troops into northern and eastern Russia, leaving them there until 1920.[6]

This violation of Wilson's own principles symbolized his post-1917 change of emphasis from promoting democracy to containing Communism. Although Wilson rejected the idea of trying to overthrow the new government in Russia, he said priority must be given to "keeping Bolshevism out of the rest of Europe."[7]

One such effort was made in 1919 in Hungary, where Bela Kun had established a Bolshevik regime. Wilson allowed his food administrator, Herbert Hoover, to use a food blockade to help topple this government. Washington then immediately supported the new claimants to power, even though Washington was somewhat uneasy about the truth in the Bolshevik claim that America was using its power to re-establish a "reactionary government."[8]

Wilson's change of emphasis was also reflected at home, where he helped foment the Red Scare of 1919-1920 by charging that "apostles of Lenin in our own midst" were spreading "the poison of disorder, the poison of revolt."[9] The importance of this Red Scare is incalculable, because it helped to usher in the twelve-year Harding-Coolidge-Hoover period, through which "the fear of revolution and radical thought became a fixture in American thought."[10]

Through this fearful thinking, American leaders would develop a justification for supporting right-wing dictators. This justification, David Schmitz pointed out, would first be developed in relation to Italian fascism.[11]

Italy

When Benito Mussolini violently overthrew Italy's democratically elected government in 1922, the US response was formulated primarily by the new Republican president, Warren Harding, his secretary of state, Charles Even Hughes, and his secretary of commerce, Herbert Hoover. Believing, in Harding's words, that "Bolshevism is a menace that must be destroyed" if Western society is to survive, this Republican triumvirate—Harding, Hughes, and Hoover—believed that US foreign policy should focus not on promoting Wilsonian "self-determination" but on preventing revolutions, especially Bolshevik revolutions.

Underlying this focus was this trio's belief that all progress rests on order or stability, which is to be promoted even if it means a "hateful autocracy," and on a free market, which would eventually lead to democratic institutions—so whether a nation has a free market was viewed as more important than whether its present form of government was democratic.[12] This trio also shared the more general assumption, of course, that US foreign policy should promote governments that cooperate with American business.

Given these convictions, the Harding administration responded positively to the fascist seizure of power under Mussolini. From the Harding-Hughes-Hoover point of view, the chief problem in Italy was widespread labor unrest, which threatened to lead to a Bolshevik takeover of the government and, in any case, created an unfavorable climate for American trade and investment. Mussolini solved this problem by preventing labor demonstrations and, more generally, all sources of public unrest, including free assembly and opposition newspapers.

American political and business leaders, savoring the benefits of this regime, ignored its destruction of Italy's constitutional democracy. They also either ignored the violence and brutality of the regime or else attributed it to "extremists" in the fascist movement while considering Mussolini himself a "moderate." All those opposing him were considered "communists, socialists, and anarchists."[13]

American investments in Italy, both governmental and private, soared. "Stability, economic recovery, and enlarged economic opportunities for American traders and investors were," Schmitz wrote, "advantages U.S. policymakers were unwilling to sacrifice to defend political democracy in Italy."[14] Mussolini, moreover, was widely perceived in US circles as "the man of the hour," the strong man who had saved Italy from Bolshevism.[15]

US political leaders would spend much of the rest of the century looking for similar men in other countries, based on their justification of right-wing dictators first worked out in relation to Mussolini. Central to this justification were the following ideas:

- Although a "Communist" government in the strict sense is one that is based on Marxist-Leninist ideas and related to the Soviet Union (or, later, Communist China), any government promoting leftist ideas, or economic nationalism, is *essentially* Communist.

- Communist governments are to be prevented or even overthrown whenever possible, because they are the greatest evil, involving a "totalitarianism" qualitatively worse than (right-wing) "authoritarianism."

- Communist governments never represent the will of the people, as they are either imposed by an extremist minority or else reflect the confused thinking of immature people who do not yet understand their true interests.

- Although the governments of such right wing dictators may have to use authoritarian means to prevent Communist infiltration, they can nonetheless be considered part of the "free world," because (a) such governments are part of the US-led alliance of the free world against international Communism, (b) such governments are protecting their people from Communist tyranny until they have sufficient maturity to be entrusted with self-government, and (c)

> the primary freedom, from which other freedoms are derived, is market freedom, so that a government that belongs to the capitalist world is, in its essentials, a free, democratic government, even if it does not yet have some of democracy's usual attributes.[16]

This justification for right-wing dictators would soon be applied in the Western Hemisphere as a way to protect US interests without sending in the marines, a practice that had become triply problematic: it was expensive, it increasingly evoked complaints about "US imperialism," and by 1933 it revealed the hypocrisy of the American complaint about Japan's imperialistic employment of its army in China under the guise of protecting its nationals.

Dictators in Nicaragua, the Dominican Republic, Haiti, and Cuba

Four of the most fateful applications of this Mussolini-inspired justification would be in Nicaragua, the Dominican Republic, Haiti, and Cuba.

Nicaragua: The search for Nicaragua's "man of the hour" was rooted in a civil war, which erupted in the midst of the almost continuous 20-year occupation by US marines that had begun with their intervention in 1912. Fighting began in 1925 when Emiliano Chamorro, who had lost the presidential election of 1924, forcibly overthrew the elected government. In line with the recently instituted US policy of promoting stability by not recognizing unelected governments, Calvin Coolidge (who had become president after Harding's death) replaced Chamorro in 1926 with another Conservative, Adolfo Díaz.

But then Juan Sacasa, claiming, as the deposed vice-president, that the presidency was rightly his, secured help from Mexico's revolutionary government, which in Washington's eyes was under Soviet influence. Coolidge sent the marines, which had been briefly withdrawn in 1925, back in to protect Diaz's hold on Nicaragua, claiming that it was about to be taken over by "Russian

Bolshevism," an eventuality that would jeopardize "American investments and business interests."[17]

Because of widespread criticism, however, Henry Stimson—who had earlier served as secretary of war and would later become Hoover's secretary of state—was sent to Nicaragua to find a way to maintain order while withdrawing the marines. Stimson's solution was that Diaz would remain president until an election to be held in 1928, that the marines would remain until a US-trained National Guard could maintain order, and that Sacasa's troops would lay down their arms.

Although most of Sacasa's generals agreed, Augusto Sandino, who was considered a Communist by Washington—although he was really simply an anti-colonialist who had been angered by the earlier interventions in Nicaragua and Mexico—vowed to continue the battle until US forces left. The task of creating the National Guard was given to General Frank McCoy, who was told that it was the "most vital feature of the [American] program." Although one newspaper said that McCoy had been made "the Mussolini of Nicaragua," that title would more fittingly belong to former latrine inspector[18] Anastasio Somoza, who was put in charge of the Guard.

With this Guard trained and the proper strong man installed at its head, Stimson and Hoover withdrew the last of the marines in 1933, confident that it could deal with Sandino. They were right. Sandino, having kept his promise to lay down arms after the marines had left, was granted amnesty by Sacasa (who had won the election in 1928) and invited to engage in talks. Following one of these talks in 1934, Sandino and his aides were seized and executed by Somoza's men.[19]

At his inaugural address in 1933, Franklin Delano Roosevelt (FDR) announced his Good Neighbor Policy, according to which the rights of others would be respected—which meant: no more unilateral interventions. One implication of this policy became evident in 1936. Chamorro, Sacasa, and Díaz, in response to the increasing brutality of Somoza's Guard, appealed to FDR's administration, saying that Nicaraguan civilians needed protection from this US-trained monster. "The State Department replied, apparently with a straight face, that it was contrary to U.S. policy to interfere in Nicaraguan affairs." [20]

Somoza, being thus assured that Washington would not interfere, illegally took over the presidency, beginning the 43-year dictatorship of the Somoza dynasty, the brutal practices of which were to be generously supported by US taxpayers.[21] FDR reportedly dismissed criticism of his support for Somoza with the now-famous remark that "he may be a son-of-a-bitch, but he's our son-of-a-bitch."[22] Washington, concludes LaFeber, "had found in the National Guard the answer to the perplexing problem of how to maintain an orderly, profitable system without having constantly to send in the marines."[23] This solution would soon be applied throughout the hemisphere.

The Dominican Republic: The military occupation of 1916-25 was followed by a series of obedient dictators, the most notorious being Rafael Trujillo, who took power in a coup in 1930. Although Trujillo was corrupt and barbaric, he behaved, in the words of the Roosevelt Corollary, "with a just regard for [his] obligations toward outsiders," so he was allowed to remain in power until he was assassinated in 1961. The Dominican Republic thus illustrated what would be true of every other country under US domination—that despite all the idealistic rhetoric, policy would be determined strictly in terms of US economic and geopolitical interests.

Haiti: After the 20-year military occupation from 1914 to 1934, control in Haiti was turned over to the US-trained National Guard.[24] This brutal period was followed by the even more brutal regimes of François ("Papa Doc") Duvalier and "Baby Doc" Duvalier from the 1950s through the 1970s. These regimes "were kept in power by a private army [that] may have killed as many as 100,000 people."[25] As elsewhere, the US corporations were enriched while the Haitian people, whose rights as ends in themselves were ignored, became increasingly impoverished.

Cuba: The same solution was used in Cuba. As a result of the imperialistic policies of 1898-1902, America had virtual control of Cuba's trade and its sugar, its sole export crop. By 1929, Cuba had become America's fourth best customer. By 1933, however, the Great Depression's effect on sugar prices led to the collapse of Cuba's economy and the regime of its dictator, Gerardo Machado, which Washington had supported.

Although US leaders had previously, using the Platt Amendment, sent marines in four times, FDR's administration, given its Good Neighbor Policy, did not want to prop up Machado's regime by invading again. At this point, some Cuban military officers, knowing the US desire for a new government, took charge. But they gave the reins to Ramón Grau San Martín, who pledged to "liquidate the colonial structure that has survived in Cuba since independence." He abrogated the Platt Amendment, interrupted America's monopoly on the Cuban market, and had workers take over sugar mills, all under the slogan "Cuba for Cubans"—which to US ears was a sure sign that he was a Communist.

The US State Department, describing Grau's government as "frankly Communistic" and as supported only by the "ignorant masses,"[26] refused to recognize it and promised Colonel Fulgenicio Batista—one of the officers who had put Grau in charge—that the next regime, if it was led by someone more acceptable, would reap great economic benefits.[27] That new regime, which Batista put in office in 1934 and controlled from behind the scenes, was indeed rewarded, and its policies greatly benefited US business interests in return. The conviction became widely accepted in US business and political circles that Batista, besides saving Cuba from Communism, was, as the Cuban strongman, indispensable.

FDR's administration, under criticism for having violated its recent acceptance of the principle that no nation "has the right to intervene in the internal or external affairs of another," deflected criticism by abrogating the Platt Amendment—which the administration had decided it no longer needed anyway, because "private political pressure and U.S. economic leverage seemed to be enough to make Cubans behave."[28] And this was true for 25 years, as the well-behaved Batista, who ruled Cuba (whether directly or indirectly) to the delight of US business interests and the continuing impoverishment of his own people, until he was overthrown in 1959 by another leader with the idea, still unacceptable to Washington, that Cuba should be for Cubans.

Support for Fascists in Europe and Asia

The fact that America's support for Mussolini's right-wing, fascist regime was no aberration was shown not only by the fact that it used him as a model for puppet leaders in the Western Hemisphere. It was also shown by the fact that FDR's administration did nothing to deter Franco's fascist overthrow of the Spanish Republic. This same administration also refused to break trade relations with Nazi Germany after learning about the concentration camps and then, after becoming aware of the "final solution," did very little to rescue Jews.[29] Neither did this administration demand that Japan's fascist regime quit slaughtering millions of Chinese. And for the sake of America's designs in China, it supported the completely corrupt, right-wing regime of Chiang-Kai Shek.[30]

The One and Only Empire

As shown by US policies in these and many other countries, the USA came out of the First World War with the determination to use its economic and military power to impose its will on much of the world for the sake of US business interests, even though this policy would not only violate America's professed belief in democracy, self-determination, and human rights, but also—as Wilson had acknowledged—would "outrage the sovereignty of unwilling nations." This growing ambition of the USA to be the one and only empire would increasingly bring it into conflict with the nationalism of many other countries, including those that had imperialistic ambitions of their own, thereby leading to its participation in a second world war.

2. Discussions about Modifying Global Anarchy

The central question created by the international order, given its anarchy, is whether it can be tamed, so as to prevent perpetual warfare, or whether this result can be attained only by modifying the international realm so as to overcome its anarchy. To call the international order *anarchical* is simply to say that there is no superior power over and above the states, which might regulate the behavior of the states toward each other. This section looks at thinkers in earlier centuries, primarily but not exclusively, who believed that the perpetual threat of war could be overcome only by overcoming global anarchy (see pages 170-71).

Dante Allighieri

The idea that the world needed an over-arching structure with which to prevent war was enunciated already in the Middle Ages.[31] The most famous of the early proposals, made early in the 14th century, was *De Monarchia*, by Dante Alighieri. Arguing that princes cannot be judged by other princes of the same rank because they are competitors, Dante advocated a world-state under an all-powerful emperor. Because there would be nothing to tempt the appetite of such an emperor, Dante said, "in him there may be judgment and justice more strongly than in any other." This emperor would impartially enforce a universal law.[32]

Although we, with our awareness of Lord Acton's dictum—"Power tends to corrupt, and absolute power corrupts absolutely"[33]—may be skeptical of Dante's solution to the problem of anarchy, he certainly recognized one of the conditions for fair arbitration of disputes between two rulers. The decision must be made by a *disinterested* party rather than by one of the parties to the dispute or even a third party that could benefit from the decision.

Eméric Crucé

In 1623, a monk named Eméric Crucé published a discourse on the "means to establish a general peace." Arguing that we needed a way of life befitting human beings, he appealed to the monarchs to create a world government, through which the world could be ruled by reason and justice, "and not violence, which is only suited to the beasts." Disputes between rulers would be settled by an assembly of ambassadors representing all the rulers.[34]

Thomas Hobbes

Much more influential, however, were two writers of the 17th century who made no effort to put an end to war. One of these was Thomas Hobbes, whose most famous work was entitled *Leviathan* (1651). Describing an anarchical realm in which there is no supreme ruler as a "state of nature," Hobbes used the international realm as his major illustration of a state of nature. Although he regarded this realm as a completely lawless realm of perpetual war—in the sense that any state *could* be attacked by any other state at any time—he made no proposal for overcoming this lawlessness. It had been necessary, he believed, for *individuals* to escape the state of nature by submitting themselves to a sovereign ruler (a "leviathan") within a territorial state. He argued, however, that the dangers created by the lawlessness of the international realm were not sufficiently intolerable to necessitate the creation of a *universal* sovereign to which the states would submit.[35]

Hugo Grotius

Another highly influential writer of the 17th century was Hugo Grotius, who published *The Rights of War and Peace* in 1625. In describing his motivation, Grotius said:

> I observed everywhere in Christendom a lawlessness in warfare of which even barbarous nations would be ashamed. Nations would rush to arms on the slightest pretext or even without cause at all. And arms once taken up, there would be an end to all respect for law, whether human or divine, as though a fury had been let loose with general license for all manner of crime.[36]

Grotius did not, however, try to prevent war. He tried only to humanize it. But his principles arguably did not even do that.

Jean Jacques Rousseau, later complaining that Grotius was widely "praised to the skies" while "Hobbes [was] covered with execration," said that in reality "their principles are exactly alike." Grotius, he said, could not have produced a philosophy "more favorable to tyrants."[37] One reason for this judgment was that Grotius, believing that most rulers could be trusted to enforce both the law of nations and the law of nature (the moral law) fairly, called on rulers to punish those who violated them.[38]

John Locke

Writing at the end of the seventeenth century, John Locke, like Dante before him, said that individuals in conflictual situations could *not* be trusted to apply the moral law impartially, because they would all interpret the law to their own advantage. Although Locke did not explicitly apply this principle to the international realm, he did refer to the relation between sovereigns as a state of nature.[39] Locke's insight therefore implied, as Cornelius Murphy said in his *Theories of World Governance*, the impossibility of "the unprejudiced enforcement of the fundamental law, which was an indispensable part of the whole Grotian system."[40]

William Penn

Probably the first truly practicable plan for overcoming war was *An Essay towards the Present and Future Peace of Europe*, published by William Penn in 1693. Arguing, like several before him, that Christendom's reputation could be recovered only if it learns to settle its disputes peaceably, Penn proposed that the European princes form a parliament, which would formulate rules of justice, then meet regularly to settle disputes. Voting would be by secret ballot (to avoid bribery—a principle the League of Nations and the United Nations should have embodied). Although Penn was a Quaker, he said that force would need to be used against any princes who refused to join, or to submit differences to the Parliament, or to abide by its rulings.

Although the Parliament would not destroy any country's sovereignty, Penn said, it would make it so that "the great Fish can no longer eat up the little ones." This plan, he pointed out, would also prevent the needless destruction of lives, cities, and countries. It would also, thanks to the disarmament it would allow, save enormous amounts of money.[41]

Jean Jacques Rousseau

In 1761, Rousseau published *A Project of Perpetual Peace*, his rewrite of "A Project for Settling an Everlasting Peace in Europe," which had been published in 1713 by Abbé de Saint-Pierre. Rousseau's own *Judgment on Saint-Pierre's Project for Perpetual Peace* was published posthumously in 1782. From this and his other writings, especially *The State of War*, Rousseau's position can be summarized by the following points:[42]

> 1. The misery created by war is so great that a plan to secure lasting peace must be found.
>
> 2. Recurrent war is evitable as long as states have absolute sovereignty.
>
> 3. Perpetual peace will be possible only on the basis of a federation with (a) laws to promote the common good, (b) a court and a parliament in which disputes can be settled, and (c) armed strength sufficient to enforce these rulings.
>
> 4. The advantages of this system will so outweigh its disadvantages, even from the perspective of the princes—they would, for example, be able to put an end to the ever-increasing cost of military preparations—that if they could distinguish their real from their apparent interest, they would adopt it.[43]

Rousseau knew, however, that princes might be unable to make this distinction and hence would reject his proposed federation because it would take away their "precious right of being unjust when they please." It would also take away "the apparatus of power and terror with which they love to frighten the world" and with which they can reap honors from "the glory of conquest."[44]

Immanuel Kant

If Rousseau was the first major philosopher to advocate a plan for overcoming war, Immanuel Kant—who greatly admired Rousseau—was the second. Although most Kant scholars have not focused on this dimension of his thought, it was actually the major concern of Kant's writings in his final years.[45] Most important for our purposes is the tension between Kant's best-known statements on this subject, contained in *Perpetual Peace* and *The Metaphysics of Morals*, which were published in 1796 and 1797, respectively,[46] and the position he had articulated a few years earlier.

In *Perpetual Peace*, he advocated the creation of a "pacific federation," which would extend gradually to encompass all states. "This federation [would not have] any power like that of a state," so the confederated states would *not* "need to submit to public laws and to a coercive power which enforces them."[47] In *The Metaphysics of Morals*, he made the point even clearer, saying that "this association must not embody a sovereign power as in a civil constitution, but only a partnership or *confederation*. It must therefore be an alliance that can be terminated at any time."[48]

In earlier writings, however, Kant had said the opposite. In 1784, three years after the appearance of *The Critique of Pure Reason*, he published *The Idea for a Universal History with a Cosmopolitan Purpose*, in which he said that people, through war, will be driven to abandon a lawless state of savagery and enter

> a federation of peoples in which every state . . . could expect to derive its security and rights not from its own power . . . but solely from . . . a united power and the law-governed decisions

> of a united will. However wild and fanciful this idea may appear—and it has been ridiculed as such when put forward by the Abbé St. Pierre and Rousseau . . .—it is nonetheless the inevitable outcome of the distress in which men involve one another. For this distress must force the states to make exactly the same decisions . . . as that which man was forced to make, equally unwillingly, in his savage state—the decision to renounce his brutish freedom and seek calm and security within a law-governed constitution.[49]

As this statement shows, Kant at that time was saying that warfare could be overcome through a federation with a constitution, a "united power," and a "united will." The step thought unnecessary by Hobbes—in which states, analogously to individuals, would leave the lawless state of nature by subordinating themselves to a higher authority, thereby giving up some freedom to gain security—was by Kant said to be necessary.

In a later essay, Kant, after saying that "a permanent universal peace by means of a so-called *European balance of power* is a pure illusion," argued that the distress produced by wars must finally lead the states, "even against their will, to enter into a *cosmopolitan* constitution."[50] But Kant cautioned against a universal monarch, adding:

> Or if such a state of universal peace is in turn even more dangerous to freedom, for it may lead to the most fearful despotism . . . , distress must force men to form a state which is not a cosmopolitan commonwealth under a single ruler, but a lawful *federation* under a commonly accepted *international right*.[51]

Whatever exactly Kant meant by this, he still intended that such a federation would be "based upon enforceable public laws to which each state must submit (by analogy with a state of civil or political right among individual men)." [52] Kant thereby still endorsed what has come to be called the "domestic analogy," a world government that is analogous to a domestic (national) government.[53]

With this background, we can now look more closely at Kant's still later statement in *Perpetual Peace*, according to which the federation would *not* have power to coerce the individual states. Although this vision has generally been taken as Kant's preferred position, he actually offered it as merely a "negative substitute" for his positive vision of a world republic, which would be the best option. In discussing this best option, he said:

> There is only one rational way in which states coexisting with other states can emerge from the lawless condition of pure warfare. Just like individual men, they must renounce their savage and lawless freedom, adapt themselves to public coercive laws, and thus form an *international state*. [54]

Kant clearly said that this approach, which involves the domestic analogy, is the *only* rational way to escape from the lawless state of nature. But Kant then made a fateful concession, saying:

> But since this is not the will of the nations . . . , the positive idea of a *world republic* cannot be realized. If all is not to be lost, this can at best find a negative substitute in the shape of an enduring and gradually expanding *federation* likely to prevent war. The latter may check the current of man's inclination to defy the law and antagonize his fellows, although there will always be a risk of it bursting forth anew.[55]

As this statement shows, Kant suggested his "negative substitute" only because a "world republic," which is what was really needed, was not "the will of the nations." By "nations" he did not mean the people—this was before the age of democracy—but the "great statesman" and the "heads of state," who, he had complained in his 1792 essay, always ridicule proposals of the type put forth by Abbé Saint-Pierre and Rousseau.[56]

Writers who are hostile to the idea of a global government often suggest that Kant himself said that such a government would degenerate into "soulless despotism." However, what Kant actually said, after speaking of the necessity for a "federal union to prevent hostilities breaking out," is that even the continuation of the present system would be preferable to "an amalgamation of the separate nations under a single power which has overruled the rest and created a universal monarchy."[57] It is *this* type of world government—one that had been achieved by conquest—that would be a "soulless despotism."

Kant knew, moreover, that this negative substitute, being devoid of coercive power, could not guarantee an end to war but was at best "likely" to prevent it. He probably even knew that the word "likely" was an exaggeration. He knew, in any case, that with such a federation "there will always be a risk of [war] bursting forth anew." Kant thereby settled for a compromise that could not guarantee perpetual peace. He would have many followers.

William Ladd

Although European politicians showed no inclination to adopt the schemes of Penn, Rousseau, or Kant (or even his water-downed version), thinkers who saw the need to overcome war kept making proposals. One of these was William Ladd, who in 1828 had founded the American Peace Society. In 1840, he published *An Essay on a Congress of Nations for the Adjustment of International Disputes without Resort to Arms*, which became very influential in both America and England.

Rejecting the Hobbesian dictum that "covenants without

swords are but words," Ladd believed that previous leagues for peace had failed because they did rely on the power of the sword. Accordingly, although his proposal called for congressional and judicial bodies, he said that the executive was to be public opinion, "the queen of the world." Once public opinion was enlightened, he suggested, its moral pressure would lead politicians to settle their disputes with reason instead of violence.[58]

James Lorimer

A more realistic proposal was put forward near the end of the century by James Lorimer, a Scottish legal philosopher, in *The Institutes of the Law of Nations*.[59] He was convinced that the relatively peaceful international relations that had characterized the 19th century would not continue without disarmament. He also argued that disarmament would not occur without the prior creation of an international government with the necessary military forces to provide security. The society of states would, however, not be undermined.[60] The international government would, in fact, be "the guardian of the freedom of all national governments."[61]

This international government would have its own legislature (consisting of a senate and a chamber of deputies), its own judiciary (with civil and criminal branches), and its own executive. It would also, in order to have the capacity to protect the freedom of the states, have its own power to tax and its own standing army.[62] Lorimer's proposal, accordingly, incorporated the domestic analogy in a strong sense.

However, said Cornelius Murphy, the proposals made by Lorimer and like-minded thinkers were not taken seriously: "the prevailing opinion in the late nineteenth century was that an international order could be achieved without the establishment of any permanent authority above the autonomous states."[63]

Nicolas Murray Butler and Lassa Oppenheim

An example of this optimism in the English-speaking world is provided in Nicolas Murray Butler's book *The International Mind*, in which he wrote:

> The civilized world is at peace and there is no ruler and no party bent on disturbing that peace. The more powerful nations are presided over by governments or monarchs whose faces are turned toward the light. . . . The German Emperor, against whom criticisms are sometimes leveled, is, I dare assert with confidence, a convinced believer in the policies of peace.[64]

The second edition of this book was originally published in 1913, one year before World War I broke out.

For an example of this optimism in the German-speaking world, we can turn to Lassa Oppenheim, a respected international lawyer who in 1911 published a book later translated as *The Future of International Law.*[65] According to Oppenheim, world government was unnecessary because the world was already a *society* of states, in which the independence of the members could be reconciled with the common interest of the whole human community. The law of nations would flourish when the principle of equality was more fully recognized, allowing the principle of "one state, one vote" to become operative. This was already happening, Oppenheim thought, so the traditional predominance of a minority of powerful states would soon be superseded.[66]

This happy development would occur, Oppenheim argued, because states are more moral than individuals and because unlimited progress is a law of the universe. Accordingly, the international interests of states would soon become stronger than their national interests. However, Murphy pointed out, while Oppenheim was drawing inspiration from the Hague Peace conferences, he was ignoring the political theory of the state that had been vigorously defended at those meetings.

> Diplomats emphasized the supremacy of the nation rather than the general interests in peace and disarmament . . . . Lip service was given

> to pacific ideas. But while states, through their representatives, were posing as moral entities, they were reinforcing their separate military power and increasing their capacity for unilateral action. . . . At the time of Oppenheim's optimistic prognosis neither disarmament, nor the pacific adjustment of differences, were of paramount importance to the leading European powers.[67]

The Concert of Europe

Just as these "leading European powers" ignored Lorimer's proposal at the end of the 19th century, they had ignored the proposals of Rousseau and Kant at the end of the prior century. Since 1815, after the defeat of Napoleon at Waterloo, issues related to war and peace had been largely determined by an informal alliance of Great Powers (at first Great Britain, Russia, Prussia, and Austria, with France and Italy added later).

At some point this alliance—which in reality "enjoyed no more than intermittent existence"—became known as the Concert of Europe.[68] It attempted to maintain peace by means of a balance of power[69]—an approach that Kant had warned would never bring lasting peace. The Concert had to rely entirely on power because it had "no provision for curbing the primacy of the national interest."[70]

As indicated above, the 19th century was, in comparison with previous centuries, relatively peaceful. There were, nevertheless, significant wars. One of these, the Franco-Prussian war of 1870-71, resulted in the emergence of the German Empire (which then took Prussia's place in the Concert). From then on, the Concert's basic problem—how to reconcile the competition between national interests with the desire for the avoidance of armed conflict—became increasingly difficult.[71] Meetings became less frequent. The last meeting was in 1913, meaning there was no meeting in 1914, the year World War I broke out.

3. The League of Nations

F. S. Northedge, in his history of the League of Nations, said: "The war which broke out in Europe in August 1914 was a bolt from the blue."[72] British political theoretician David Mitrany wrote that later generations "can hardly realize what a shock [the First World War] was," coming as it did after "a long period of stability and of liberal optimism."[73] This shock produced new thinking in many minds.

New Thinking Produced by World War I

In 1923, British law professor George Keeton, in a book entitled *National Sovereignty and International Order*, wrote:

> Whereas only a few years before many publicists thought that the Hague Peace Conferences had ushered in a new era in international relationships . . ., and while they were unanimous that the respect for international law was firmly based upon a public opinion whose censure would be sufficient to deter the potential lawbreaker, the war had made it necessary to abandon these doctrines.[74]

Even a chastened Lassa Oppenheim wrote in 1920, in his book's third edition, that the world needed an "international Parliament with power to legislate by a majority," a Permanent Court of International Justice with mandatory jurisdiction, and "an international Army and Navy to serve as a police force."[75]

Some prominent Americans agreed. In 1916, President Woodrow Wilson, speaking at the first convention of the League to Enforce Peace, declared:

> [T]he world is even now upon the eve of a great consummation, when . . . coercion shall be summoned not to the service of political ambition

> or selfish hostility, but to the service of a common order, a common justice, and a common peace.

He later said: "There must be, not a balance of power, but a community of power, not organized rivalries, but an organized common peace." Now that we have reached the limit of voluntary arbitration of disputes, said Senator Henry Cabot Lodge, "the next step is . . . to put force behind international peace." Former president Theodore Roosevelt devoted much of his 1915 book, *America and the World War*, to a proposal for a league for peace, saying: "If it is a Utopia, it is a Utopia of a very practical kind."[76]

The Launching of the League

New thinking of this type prepared the way for the creation of the League of Nations in 1920, as stipulated by the Treaty of Versailles in 1919. The League, as Northedge put it,

> was launched on the tide of revulsion, not only against the war just ended, but against all war, which swept the world when the fighting stopped in November 1918.[77]

The question would be whether this revulsion would be sufficient to persuade the Great Powers to give up what Rousseau had mockingly called their "precious right of being unjust when they please."[78] This question was largely answered in advance by developments in the two strongest countries, Great Britain and the United States, who together were most responsible for the failure of the League.

The League's Failure: Great Britain's Contribution

The greatest influence on official British thinking was *International Government*, a book written in 1915 by Leonard Woolf (Virginia's husband) as the proposal of the Fabian Society. In the Introduction, George Bernard Shaw, another Fabian, said that putting an end to international anarchy, with its war, would depend upon a "supernational sheriff" to "adjust the disputes of nations." What is needed, Shaw argued, is "a Supernational Legislature, a Supernational Tribunal, and a Supernational Board of Conciliation."[79]

In the book itself, however, Woolf made clear from the outset that he was not proposing any fundamental change of the international structure: "If we are to [conceive of] a definite international organization which will commend itself to the disillusioned judgment of statesmen and other 'practical' men," Woolf declared,

> we must build not a Utopia upon the air or clouds of our own imaginations, but a duller and heavier structure placed logically upon the foundations of the existing system.

We cannot change this system, he argued, because of "the theoretical sacredness of the independence and the sovereignty of independent and sovereign States." His scheme, he said, "falls far short of a cosmopolitan system or a world state," because "every state must remain absolute master of its own destiny." [80]

Arguing that the world was not forced to choose between Utopia and Chaos, Woolf presented his proposed International Authority as a "half-way house between a federation into a world-State and the existing splendid isolation of independent States."[81] For this International Authority to work, he pointed out, the nations composing it must agree

> to enforce, and actually enforce, by every means in their power the obligation of each independent State to refer a dispute or difference to the [Authority] before resorting to force of arms.[82]

To the criticism that this system would provide no guarantee against war, Woolf replied that "it is impossible to make war impossible," so we must settle for a plan that would "go far towards . . . making war extremely improbable." But he admitted that each State would remain "quite free to go to war, in the last resort." This admission made most unrealistic Woolf's statement about disarmament, namely, that

> national disarmament . . . is left to come about of itself, just as the individual carrying of arms falls silently into desuetude as and when fears of aggression die down before the rule of the law."[83]

This was unrealistic because the "international government" being proposed by Woolf was not at all analogous to a national government such as England's, which did make its citizens feel safe.

In any event, the main features of Woolf's proposal, which virtually admitted defeat in advance—being in essence the same as Kant's "negative substitute"—became incorporated into a memorandum drafted by the British Foreign Office, which then became the basis for the British position in the final Anglo-American negotiations prior to Versailles.[84] The British Empire, after losing almost a million of its citizens in World War I, would not even *propose* the creation of an organization with the power to prevent future wars from breaking out.

The League's Failure: America's Contribution

America contributed to the failure of the League of Nations in two ways. First, whereas the French, holding that "covenants without swords" are futile, wanted the League to have an international military force at its disposal, the Americans, like the British, would not endorse this idea. President Wilson argued that peace-loving world public opinion, backed up with the threat of economic sanctions, would be sufficient to prevent war.[85]

Accordingly, when the League's Council was created, it was "an essentially deliberative body" rather than a peace-keeping or peace-restoring body. The decisions of the League "were recommendations only and carried no binding force."

Accordingly, the later condemnation of the League as "the Geneva talking shop" was made virtually inevitable by its charter.[86] Also, in order to avoid a veto by the US Senate, Wilson insisted—even while recognizing the absurdity of the demand—that the Covenant stipulate that it would not affect "the validity of . . . regional understandings like the Monroe Doctrine."[87] This stipulation entailed that the United States could do as it pleased in Latin America with no censure from the League.

America's other major contribution to the failure of the League was the fact that, although Wilson had gotten the various demands of the US Senate built into the League's Covenant, the Senate then refused to ratify it.[88] The US Senate's refusal to ratify was based in part on politics. Republican Henry Cabot Lodge, the head of the Senate Foreign Relations Committee, wanted to undermine the pet project of Democrat Wilson, whom he loathed.[89] But the Senate's refusal to ratify the Covenant was also based on the desire of many of its more imperialistic members, such as Albert Beveridge and Lodge himself, not to allow any restrictions whatsoever on US freedom of action.

The strength of it is shown by the fact that Democratic Senator John Sharp Williams spoke against that sentiment, denouncing those Senators who say: "I want my nation left free and untrammeled to do whatever it please." Williams then asked:

> What would become of a municipal society composed of individuals founded upon that sort of basis? Suppose the Senator from Utah . . . went out and said: "I decline to be trammeled; I decline to enter into an agreement to abide by the pistol-toting law, or by the homicide law, or by the thievery law. . . . I will do right myself. I am my own sovereign, responsible to nobody but God." . . . Could you get civilization in a State out of citizens of that persuasion? Suppose each State in the Union said that to the other States of the Union? Could you get civilization in the

> American Union out of that? Why is it that thus far you have never gotten any civilization in the international world? Just simply because one nation after another, in blind chauvinism, has uttered that infernal, stupid selfishness.[90]

Although Williams' argument was unanswerable, the motion to ratify was defeated. As a result, the League of Nations had to try to maintain world peace without the nation that had become the world's greatest economic and military power.

The Senate had failed to ratify in spite of the prediction by Senator Joseph Randsdall that "if the League of Nations be not adopted . . . within a few years—ten or twenty years at most—another war far greater than [the recent war] will take place."[91] That was 1919, exactly 20 years prior to the beginning of World War II.

The Resulting Failure of the League

Not having the United States as a member surely contributed to the League's inability to achieve its major goals of keeping the peace and bringing about a general disarmament, as many commentators have said. But even if America had been in it, the League probably would not have been able to prevent war, due to weaknesses built into the Covenant.

One of these weaknesses was Article 5, which stipulated that "decisions at any meeting of the Assembly or of the Council shall require the agreement of all the Members of the League represented at the meeting." This article meant that every state—not just the Great Powers—had a veto. As a result, resolutions were generally watered down until they were innocuous.[92]

Even more important, because the League had no supranational legislature, executive, or army, "The League was not going to impose order from above—there was no-one in the world to do that; order would have to come from below."[93] In particular, it was up to the individual members of the League to decide if another member was violating the Covenant. If the answer was Yes, it was then up to the individual nations to provide the money and armed forces to stop the action. So although there were more rules than there were during the period of the Concert of Europe, "it rested with states whether they would make much or little of the new arrangements."[94] And they made little of them.

One consequence of the League's weakness was that "multilateral disarmament, which it was fervently believed the League would bring about," did not even begin, because disarmament would presuppose "foolproof collective security." This obvious truth, emphasized by James Lorimer decades earlier, was finally recognized in a resolution, passed in 1922, declaring:

> [I]n the present state of the world, many Governments would be unable to accept the responsibility for a serious reduction of armaments unless they received in exchange a satisfactory guarantee of the safety of their country.[95]

This the League could not supply, so although there was no issue on which the League spent more time and energy than disarmament, its efforts came to nought.[96]

The ultimate failure of these efforts occurred in a world conference on disarmament that, after much dawdling, finally began in 1932. The world's interest in the conference was intense:

> The tables were loaded with millions of petitions from people yearning for peace all over the world. The churches rang with prayers for the long-awaited talks.[97]

But this conference, in which each country focused on maximizing its own advantages, disbanded in failure in 1934. This failure "opened the way to the surge of rearmament among the European Powers which signaled the approach of the Second World War."[98]

This disarmament fiasco occurred at the same time as another major failure. In 1931, Japan began taking over Manchuria in an aggression that eventually resulted in the deaths of many millions of Chinese. When the League's Council, after much delay, finally issued its report, it endorsed the Chinese position. But that was as far as it went.

> There was no suggestion of economic or military measures to expel the Japanese, [because] none of the great Powers . . . was prepared for drastic action of that kind, despite the challenge to the whole international order implicit in Japan's strategy in Manchuria.[99]

This failure to stop Japan's aggression was "almost a fatal blow" to the League. The *truly* fatal blow occurred in 1935, after Mussolini's Italy invaded Ethiopia—then called Abyssinia—which was a member of the League. Besides the fact that the League refused to use force or even significant economic sanctions to force Italy to withdraw, its two most powerful members—Britain and France—came up with the notorious Hoare-Laval plan, according to which more than half of Abyssinia would be awarded to Italy. After a public outcry forced the plan's withdrawal, Mussolini simply took the entire nation.

> Abyssinia passed into the Duce's empire and the League's first and final experiment in the enforcement of international law was brought to a close.[100]

After these disasters, the League was simply ignored in 1938-1939, when Hitler began his aggression against Czechoslovakia, Austria, and Poland, thereby provoking World War II.[101]

Conclusion

In spite of portraying itself to the world, and even its own people, as the chief promoter of freedom and democracy, the United States, from almost the beginning, acted in imperialist ways, intervening in countries whose policies it found inconvenient. While attacking Russia and other Communist governments early on, the United States also used the "Communist threat" as an excuse to overthrow various governments that, although not Communist, were insufficiently supportive of America's goals. When World War I made peoples around the world, including the United States, see the need to prevent future wars, they created a League of Nations for this purpose. Although there were many reasons why this effort failed, one of the chief reasons was the refusal of the US Senate to allow this country to join the League, thereby guaranteeing its failure from the beginning.

Endnotes

1 Peter Evans, "World War I Centenary: Bolshevism & Communism," *Wall Street Journal,* 2017; "History of communism," Wikipedia. Accessed 17 December 2017.

2 Walter LaFeber, *The American Age: U.S. Foreign Policy Since 1750*, 2nd ed. (New York: Norton, 1993), 290.

3 David F. Schmitz, *Thank God They're On Our Side: The United States and Right-wing Dictatorships, 1921-1965* (Chapel Hill: University of North Carolina, 1999), 14.

4 "Dictatorships - The Great War and the Bolshevik Revolution," Encyclopedia of the New American Nation.

5 LaFeber, *The American Age*, 291.

6 On this intervention, see David S. Foglesong, *America's Secret War against Bolshevism: U. S. Intervention in the Russian Civil War, 1917-1920* (Chapel Hill: University of North Carolina Press, 1995).

7 Schmitz, *Thank God*, 14.

8 See Frank Costigliola, *Awkward Dominion: American Political, Economic, and Cultural Relations with Europe, 1919-1933* (Ithaca: Cornell University Press, 1984), 52-53; Schmitz, *Thank God,* 19; LaFeber, *The American Age*, 301.

9 LaFeber, *The American Age*, 310.

10 Schmitz, *Thank God*, 15.

11 Ibid., 11.

12 Ibid., 17-20.

13 This charge was made in 1926 by Frank Kellogg, who became secretary of state in 1925 under Harding's successor, Calvin Coolidge; see Schmitz, *Thank God,* 43.

14 Ibid., 43.

15 Ibid., 37, 41, 54.

16 This summary statement is based on Schmitz, *Thank God,* especially the Introduction and Ch. 1.

17 Ibid., 50-51.

18 See Frederick Gareau, *State Terrorism and the United States* (Atlanta: Clarity Press, 2004), 165. Also see Kevin A. Katovich,"Human Rights and Policy Wrongs," Illinois Wesleyan University, 1993, at https://digitalcommons.iwu.edu/cgi/viewcontent.cgi?referer=&httpsredir=1&article=1024&context=history_honproj

19 Ibid., 54-55; Walter LaFeber, *Inevitable Revolutions: The United States in Central America* (New York: Norton, 1984), 64-69.

20 LaFeber, *Inevitable Revolutions,* 69.

21 Ibid.; LaFeber, *The American Age,* 344.

22 Schmitz, *Thank God*, 4.

23 LaFeber, *Inevitable Revolutions,* 69.

24 LaFeber, *The American Age*, 267.

25 Noam Chomsky, *On Power and Ideology: The Managua Lectures* (Boston: South End, 1987), 67.

26 Schmitz, *Thank God*, 78, 80.

27 LaFeber, *The American Age*, 358; Schmitz, *Thank God*, 78; Bryce Wood, *The Making of the Good Neighbor Policy* (New York: Columbia University Press, 1962), 109; David Green, *The Containment of Latin America* (Quadrangle, 1971), 13-18.

28 LaFeber, *The American Age*, 359.

29 Ibid., 367; Henry L. Feingold, *The Politics of Rescue: The Roosevelt Administration and the Holocaust* (Rutgers University Press, 1970).

30 Gabriel Kolko, *The Politics of War: The World and United States Foreign Policy 1943-1945* (1968; New York: Pantheon, 1990), 209-41.

31 This survey of ideas and developments is limited to the West, the tradition in which the League of Nations and then the United Nations were created.

32 Quoted in Cornelius F. Murphy, Jr., *Theories of World Governance: A Study in the History of Ideas* (Washington, D.C. Catholic University of

America Press, 1999), 203.

33 Lord Acton, *Essays*, ed. Rufus F. Fears (Liberty Classics, 1985), Vol. II: 383.

34 Sylvester John Hemleben, *Plans for World Peace through Six Centuries* (Chicago: University of Chicago Press, 1943), 25-30.

35 Thomas Hobbes, *Leviathan* (New York: Liberal Arts Press, 1958), 108, 169.

36 Hugo Grotius, *De Jure Belli ac Pacis* ("The Rights of War and Peace"), in *Peace Projects of the Seventeenth Century* (New York: Garland, 1972), 35.

37 J. J. Rousseau, *Emile*, trans. by Barbara Foxley (New York: Everyman's Library, 1974), 458; *The Social Contract*, 47. A more recent critic, B.V.A. Röling, has said: "The enormous popularity of Grotius' doctrine becomes comprehensible when we recognize that in theory it could gratify the high-minded . . . while in practice it did not restrict in any way the endeavour to subjugate the non-European peoples to European authority" ("Are Grotius' Ideas Obsolete in an Expanded World," in *Hugo Grotius and International Relations,* ed. Hedley Bull, Benedict Kingsbury, and Adam Roberts [Oxford: Clarendon, 1992], 281-99, at 295, 297).

38 Murphy, *Theories of World Governance*, 15, 30.

39 John Locke, *Two Treatises of Government* (Cambridge and New York: Cambridge University Press, 1963).

40 Murphy, *Theories of World Governance*, 31.

41 In William Penn, *Essay Towards the Present and Future Peace of Europe* (1693), quoted in Wolfgang Mieder, *Proverbs: A Handbook* (Greenwood, 2004), 40.

42 For the sources of these points, see Hemleben, *Plans for World Peace*, 75-77.

43 Rousseau apparently believed that some such plan might eventually be adopted. Grace Roosevelt argued that previous interpreters of Rousseau, including Stanley Hoffman and F. H. Hinsley, had wrongly concluded, due to pages of *The State of War* being out of order, that he was pessimistic about the possibility of ending war; Grace Roosevelt, *Reading Rousseau in the Nuclear Age* (Templeton University Press, 1990), 10, 66.

44 Ibid., 104.

45 In one of his last books, in fact, Kant said that the "task of establishing a universal and lasting peace is not just a part of the theory of right within the limits of pure reason, but its entire ultimate purpose." See "The Metaphysics of Morals" as printed in Hans Reiss, ed., *Kant: Political Writings*, 2nd edition (Cambridge: Cambridge University

Press, 1991), 131-75, at 174.

46 Kant, "Perpetual Peace: A Philosophical Sketch," as published in 1796, is an enlarged edition of a version released in 1795.

47 Kant, "Perpetual Peace," in Reiss, ed., *Kant: Political Writings*, 93-130, at 104.

48 Kant, "The Metaphysics of Morals," 165.

49 Kant, "The Idea for a Universal History with a Cosmopolitan Purpose," as printed in Reiss, ed., *Kant: Political Writings*, 41-53, at 48-49.

50 Kant, "On the Common Saying: 'This May Be True in Theory, but It Does not Apply in Practice," as printed in Reiss, ed., *Kant's Political Writings*, 61-92, at 90.

51 Ibid., 90.

52 Ibid., 91-92.

53 See Hidemi Suganami, *The Domestic Analogy and World Order Proposals* (Cambridge: Cambridge University Press, 1989).

54 Kant, "Perpetual Peace," in Reiss, *Kant: Political Writings*, 105.

55 Ibid., 105.

56 Kant, "On the Common Saying," 92.

57 Kant, "The Metaphysics of Morals," 113.

58 Hemleben, *Plans for World Peace*, 106-08.

59 James Lorimer, *The Institutes of the Law of Nations*, 2 vols. (Edinburgh: E. Blackwood, 1883-84).

60 Murphy, *Theories*, 71-72, 139.

61 Lorimer, *Institutes*, II: 273.

62 Ibid., II: 273, 279.

63 Murphy, *Theories*, 73, 76.

64 *Nicholas Murray Butler's The International Mind: An Argument for the Judicial Settlement of International Disputes* (Charles Scribner's Sons, 1913).

65 Lassa Oppenheim, *The Future of International Law* (London: Clarendon Press, 1921).

66 I have here followed Murphy's summary in *Theories*, 78.

67 Murphy, *Theories*, 79.

68 Carsten Holbraad, *The Concert of Europe: A Study in German and British International Theory 1815-1914* (London: Longman, 1970), 2, 3.

69 Hemleben, *Plans for World Peace,* 186.

70 René Albrecht-Carrié, ed., *The Concert of Europe* (New York: Walker and Co., 1968), 11.

71 Ibid., 22, 241; Holbraad, *The Concert of Europe*, 2.

72 F. S. Northedge, *The League of Nations: Its Life and Times 1920-1946* (New York: Holmes and Meier, 1986), 3.

73 David Mitrany, *The Functional Theory of Politics* (1975), 4-5, quoted

in Hidemi Suganami, *The Domestic Analogy and World Order Proposals* (Cambridge: Cambridge University Press, 1989), 79.

74 George Keeton, *National Sovereignty and International Order* (London: Peace Book Company, 1939), 68.

75 Lassa Oppenheim, *International Law*, 3rd ed., ed. R. F. Roxburgh (London: Longmans, Green, 1920), II: 291-94.

76 These statements by Wilson, Lodge, and Roosevelt are all quoted in Alan Cranston, *The Killing of the Peace* (New York: Viking, 1945), 1-3, 9, 15.

77 Northedge, *The League of Nations*, 1.

78 Ibid., 1.

79 Bernard Shaw "Introduction," Leonard S. Woolf, *International Government: Two Reports* (New York: Brentano's, 1916), xvi, xvii.

80 Woolf, *International Government*, 4-5, 111, 125.

81 Ibid., 105.

82 Ibid., 118.

83 Ibid., 372.

84 Stephen J. Stearns, "Introduction," Leonard S. Woolf, *International Government* (New York: Garland Publishing, 1971 [reprint]), 19.

85 Northedge, *The League*, 30, 44.

86 Ibid., 49, 53, 44.

87 Ibid., 53.

88 Cranston, *The Killing of the Peace*, 43, 47, 91, 94-95.

89 Ibid., 22, 43, 47.

90 Ibid., 145.

91 Ibid., 149.

92 Northedge, *The League*, 53, 59-60.

93 Ibid., 69.

94 Ibid., 57, 69.

95 Ibid., 54, 118.

96 Ibid., 113.

97 Ibid., 122.

98 Ibid., 114.

99 Ibid., 160.

100 Ibid., 221-24, 243-45.

101 Ibid., 221. 267.

| Chapter 4 |

WORLD WAR II

Americans have liked to call World War II "the good war." The idea that it was good was based not only on the fact that America won the war (in its own estimation) but also on the idea that America participated in this war for the sake of liberating other peoples from tyranny. However, an examination of the actual history reveals that American policy continued to be guided by, in Bacevich's phrase, "unflagging self-interest and large ambitions."[1] This characterization of American policy was nowhere more apt than in the early days of World War II.

1. Preparing Postwar Plans

Within weeks after the war had begun in Europe in 1939, the Council on Foreign Relations, in collaboration with the US Department of State, formed a committee to make plans for the war and the ensuing peace. This "imperial brain trust," reported Laurence Shoup and William Minter, "worked out an imperialistic conception of the national interest and war aims of the United States" that "involved a conscious attempt to organize and control a global empire."[2]

The basic idea was that the United States, even with the rest of the Western Hemisphere as a source of markets and raw materials, was not self-sufficient and therefore, to prevent another economic depression, needed a "Grand Area" consisting of much of the world.

This committee declared that US policy makers, while privately formulating these war aims, needed to formulate different war aims for public consumption. The "formulation of a statement of war aims for propaganda purposes," said the brain trust, "is very different from formulation of one defining the true national interest."[3] In particular, the brain trust said:

> If war aims are stated which seem to be concerned solely with Anglo-American imperialism, they will offer little to people in the rest of the world, and will be vulnerable to Nazi counter-promises. . . . The interests of other peoples should be stressed, not only those of Europe, but also of Asia, Africa, and Latin America. This would have a better propaganda effect.[4]

The resulting propaganda statement was called the Atlantic Charter, drawn up by FDR and Churchill, which said that the war was being fought for "the right of all peoples to choose the form of government under which they will live"—which FDR certainly had no intention of allowing in Latin America nor Churchill in the British colonies—and "the enjoyment of all States, great or small," to "access, on equal terms, to the trade and to the raw materials of the world"—which America, as we have seen, was working hard to *prevent*.[5]

One sensitive soul who knew this, poet Archibald MacLeish—who was then an assistant secretary of state—said:

> [T]he peace we will make . . . will be a peace of oil, a peace of gold, a peace of shipping, a peace, in brief . . . without moral purpose.[6]

It was to be, as the imperial brain trust knew, a peace "concerned solely with Anglo-American imperialism."

The brain trust was, in fact, concerned with strictly *American* imperialism, as one of its goals was for America's empire to replace Great Britain's in the course of coming to exert world control.[7] (Control of the Grand Area was only a temporary measure.) "The preferred ideal," in the words of Shoup and Minter, "was even more grandiose—one world economy dominated by the United States," with "international political and economic institutions" that would "integrate all of the earth's nations under the leadership of the United States."[8]

The institutions planned were those that became the World Bank, the International Monetary Fund (IMF), and the General Agreement on Tariffs and Trade (GATT), the third of which later became the World Trade Organization (WTO). The idea of a fully global empire is not an idea that came to US policy makers only recently. This is the "stupendous project" that, Bacevich discovered, had guided US foreign policy for a long time.

America, in any case, got into the war by choking off Japan's supply of oil until the Japanese government felt forced to attack America, which it did at Pearl Harbor (see Chapter 5). Although the main concern of the United States was to get into the war in Europe, it did oppose Japan's drive to create a "Greater East Asia Co-Prosperity Sphere," which was Japan's euphemism for an Asian empire.

The American objection to Japan's plan, as Ambassador Joseph Grew explained, was that it would involve "a system of closed economy" that would "depriv[e] Americans of their long-established rights in China."[9] As this statement showed, America raised no objections to the imperialistic behavior of the Japanese as long as they were merely killing millions of Chinese. This behavior became objectionable only insofar as it threatened the "rights" of American business and banking interests.

In any case, the Japanese, in the final negotiations prior to Pearl Harbor, agreed to the US insistence on the open door principle in China—but only on the condition that this principle would be "adopted throughout the world." That would have meant, for example, that the Japanese would not face economic discrimination in Latin America. From the American point of view, of course, that was a non-starter, since the Monroe Doctrine had long been considered sacred. US Secretary of State Cordell Hull, accordingly, dismissed this demand out of hand, deploring the fact that the Japanese were too simple-minded "to see why the United States, on the one hand, should assert leadership in the Western Hemisphere with the Monroe Doctrine and, on the other, want to interfere with Japan's assuming leadership in Asia."[10] Whether or not Hull was here speaking with tongue in cheek, American leaders were quite conscious that they were simply using their superior power to enforce their double standard. No principle was involved other than "might makes right."

2. Playing Politics During Wartime

Once into the war, as Gabriel Kolko showed in his *Politics of War*, American leaders had already begun focusing on postwar political aims by 1943, as soon as victory seemed assured.[11] America's overall economic aim, as we have seen, was that governments in all parts of the world would have economic policies compatible with American interests. While this aim obviously entailed the subsidiary aim of preventing the rise of any governments likely to join with the Soviet Union in a Communist economic bloc, it equally entailed preventing the emergence of leftist or socialist governments of *any* type. America's overall aim also implied the need to replace the British empire with its own neo-colonial empire.

This combination of aims meant that while American leaders were cooperating with British and Soviet leaders in defeating the Axis Powers, they were simultaneously seeking to establish postwar dominance over Great Britain and the Soviet Union. This attempt repeatedly involved American insistence on double standards. The rest of this section looks at some examples of US attempts to implement these aims, complete with double standards, in both Asia and Europe.

The Philippines

Following the previously described takeover of the Philippines, which resulted in the establishment of a formal colony, America kept in charge the same plutocracy that had served the Spanish.[12] While claiming to bring democracy, the American governors of this colony allowed the vote only to a tiny, wealthy minority, which was concerned exclusively with maintaining its own privileges.[13] Although US leaders often *talked* about the need to overcome this "undemocratic oligarchy" by enlarging the political base, they never insisted upon it, with the result that the vast majority of the people lived in utter poverty.[14] Although this situation produced periodic revolts by the peasants, Washington never overruled the refusal of the wealthy class to mitigate the poverty of the peasants.[15]

Washington's indifference to the welfare of the Filipinos was further shown by the fact that, while being aware that it could not defend the islands in the case of an attack by Japan, Washington refused either to spend the money to fortify the islands or to grant independence to the Filipinos so that they could declare neutrality, hence avoiding attack.[16] As a result, the Filipinos suffered enormously, not only from the Japanese conquest and occupation[17] but even more from the American reconquest in 1944-1945, when General Douglas MacArthur fulfilled his "I shall return" pledge.[18]

The Japanese occupation had evoked the rise of guerrilla movements, especially the *Hukbong Bayan Laban sa Hapon* (the People's Anti-Japanese Army), abbreviated Hukbalahap or simply "the Huks." The leader of the Huks, Luis Taruc—who loved Washington, Jefferson, Lincoln, and the Gettysburg Address—wished to cooperate with the US army to defeat the Japanese. However, although the vast majority of the Huks were simple peasants and tenants with no ideological concerns, the organization had originally been formed by the Communist Party of the Philippines, so the American leaders considered the Huks to be enemies.

Accordingly, besides ignoring Taruc's offer of assistance, MacArthur ordered US-supported guerrilla groups to oppose them. The Huks, nevertheless, assisted US forces as well as carrying on their own offensive again the Japanese, taking over many towns and setting up local governing councils. When the American troops came into these areas, however, they quickly removed these Huk-appointed leaders from office, replacing them with Filipinos who had collaborated with the Japanese. American troops also disarmed Huks, after which they arrested them or allowed them to be massacred.[19]

Although MacArthur, in setting up a new government, had originally promised to "run to earth every disloyal Filipino," he soon decided, with backing from Washington, that it was more important to have a government that would keep the Philippines economically dependent on America, support the continued existence of its military bases, and press the battle against the Huks. MacArthur, therefore, exonerated his friend Manual Roxas, who had been one of the most prominent collaborators.[20] Roxas, seen "by the rest of the oligarchy as the wedge for their own political rehabilitation," was elected president, after which he granted amnesty to all (about 5000) collaborators, allowing the old plutocracy to return to full control.[21]

China

Much of US policy since the nineteenth century, as we have seen, was made with an eye to the "China market," with its seemingly infinite potential. US aid for Chiang Kai-shek's Nationalist forces was given primarily for the sake of Washington's postwar aims, geopolitical as well as economic. Geopolitically, Washington wanted a China that, being heavily dependent on US aid, would provide the base for America to become the dominant economic and military power in the Far East—a goal that led US leaders to prevent Great Britain from recovering its influence in China and Southeast Asia.[22]

Washington also wanted a China that, as a member of the UN Security Council,[23] would support Washington on all international issues.[24] Such a China, besides being "a united, but weak and dependent China,"[25] would also, of course, be anti-Communist. It was primarily this last stipulation that drove US policy in China prior to and during the war.

Without that stipulation, there would have been no reason to support Chiang Kai-shek in his civil war with the Communists under Mao Tse-tung and Chou En-lai. Chiang's government, besides refusing to fight the Japanese in spite of the hundreds of millions of dollars Washington gave it for this purpose, was perhaps the most corrupt government of the century (which is saying something), simply pocketing most of the money, then demanding more.[26] Washington, furthermore, was fully aware of Chiang's incompetence and venality, being told by its own people that Chiang was "the main obstacle to the unification of China and her cooperation in a real effort against Japan" and that he and his cohorts were simply "a bunch of crooks."[27]

All the reports about the leaders of the Communist insurgency, by contrast, were highly favorable. Besides being impressed with the honesty and efficiency of Mao and Chou, Americans reported on their nationalism, pragmatism, and moderation, regarding them as patriots more than Communist ideologues and even calling them "the only real democrats in China." Mao and Chou, furthermore, had also clearly indicated their readiness to cooperate with America and even to welcome US investments and private industry.[28]

All of this information, however, counted for naught, because US leaders, determined not "to permit an economic ideology alien to basic American war aims to predominate in China," simply would not entertain the idea of a Communist China.[29] The US therefore supported Chiang to the bitter end, thereby producing a China that, besides being Communist, was strongly anti-American.[30]

Although this "loss of China" resulted from the fact that Washington tried too hard to forestall a Communist victory, US political leaders would conclude that it resulted from not trying hard enough. This "lesson"—combined with another one derived from US action in the Philippines—would becoming a driving factor in US policy.

Italy

In Europe, the issue of double standards first emerged in Italy, the scene of the first Allied operation. The Atlantic Charter, as mentioned earlier, promised equal access to all. "After invading that country," however, "the Americans and British refused to allow the Soviets to have any influence in reconstructing the Italian government," in spite of the fact that the Soviet Union was fighting on their side and had lost far more troops than had the United States and Great Britain combined. The main reason for this refusal was the fear that Stalin's influence would result in political victory for Italy's large Communist party, which might remove Italy from the US-dominated economic system.[31]

This violation by FDR and Churchill of their own Atlantic Charter, with its promise of equal access to all, would repeatedly be used by Stalin to justify Soviet control of the countries of Eastern Europe. Stalin would have been content with different spheres of influence, being satisfied with "socialism in one zone."[32] However, the question was whether the Americans would accept this splitting of Europe into political spheres or try to have it both ways: exclude the Soviets from Italy but insist that the United States have a voice in Eastern Europe.[33]

The answer would be that the Americans would again insist on having it both ways. Given the Americans' belief that they needed to have "markets for their inevitable postwar surpluses in one world undivided and indivisible," they believed that, although the Eastern European market was not of great importance to them,

> Soviet control would present a great danger as a precedent. If Stalin succeeded there, he might use it as a lever to gain influence in the remainder of Europe. If he did forge a private sphere, moreover, his success might encourage the British to repudiate the Atlantic Charter and reestablish their own spheres. Instead of one world, there would again be, as in the 1930s, a world divided economically and politically.[34]

This was the US perspective, which it considered non-negotiable.

From Stalin's perspective, however, the USSR needed Eastern Europe for its economic security, just as the USA had Latin America. Stalin also maintained that the USSR needed Eastern Europe for its *political* security. Having been invaded repeatedly through Eastern Europe, losing twelve million citizens this last time, the Soviets felt the need for a buffer zone. But the Americans expressed no sympathy for this point of view.

Another wound to US-Soviet relations resulted from the fact that, although the "Russians had suffered frightful destruction at Italian hands," Washington "would not for a moment consider Italian reparations to the U.S.S.R." Washington feared that such reparations, besides helping the Soviet Union rebuild, would impoverish Italy, thereby increasing the attraction of Communism.[35] America's economic plan also led it to restore the old political order. Italy's ruling elite had, with King Victor Emmanuel, collaborated with Mussolini's fascist government and the Nazis. But once this group realized that Mussolini had chosen the losing side, they arrested him, then asked the allies to put the king back in power.

This plutocratic elite was opposed by the Partisans—the resistance movement that had fought against the fascist-Nazi alliance. However, although no single ideology dominated this movement, Communists formed the largest group.[36] Therefore, the British and American leaders, regarding the Partisans as "rampant Bolsheviks," supported the king and "the patriots who have rallied round him." FDR rationalized this support by agreeing with Eisenhower's judgment that the monarchists were not *really* fascists. In any case, this decision led the Allies not only to disarm, intimidate, and imprison the Partisans, but also to give the Nazis a free hand to massacre them.[37]

While doing all this in collaboration with the British, America also gradually eased the British out of Italy. By excluding the British and the Soviet Union, reinstating a right-wing government, and eliminating its domestic opposition, "the United States reintegrated the first defeated Axis power into its plans for a new world economy."[38] American court historians would, of course, later describe how America defeated Mussolini's fascism, helping Italians return to democracy.

France

In France, American leaders strove for similar results. American and British leaders agreed that, after the removal of the Vichy government, which had collaborated with Nazi Germany, the main task was to prevent the Communist Party, which was quite strong in France, from coming to power.[39]

But whereas Britain wanted the man in charge to be Charles de Gaulle, the United States, seeing de Gaulle as a British tool, chose Henri Giraud, an anti-Semitic, neofascist, anti-republican royalist, whose regime victimized members of the French Resistance. Although this appointment horrified the members of the Resistance in France and other European countries, it pleased France's elite class, terrified as it was by the Communist Party, which had provided the largest element of the Resistance.[40] In supporting this elite class, Washington, which had allowed American businesses to trade with the Vichy government in spite of its collaboration with Nazi Germany, was simply guaranteeing that US-French economic relationships would continue uninterrupted.[41]

In any event, deciding that de Gaulle was the only viable alternative to the Left, America finally let him come to power.[42] Through him they kept France generally supportive of American political and economic aims. This support for the old regime in France, which still had its own imperial ambitions, would eventually lead America into Vietnam.

3. American Exceptionalism?

The history of American expansionism and imperialism from the beginning of the Republic through the Second World War provides no basis for American Exceptionalism in the self-congratulatory sense. As discussed in the Introduction, American Exceptionalism holds that America, unlike other nations, is devoted not to furthering its own interests at the expense of others but to helping them achieve freedom, democracy, and affluence. Fortunately for Americans' self-image, most Americans have known little of the actual history of their country's behavior. But those Americans who will read the actual history can learn the same things that William Blum, Noam Chomsky, Gabriel Kolko, Walter LaFeber, David Schmitz, Stanley Karnow, and Howard Zinn—whose works I employed in this chapter—had learned. They can learn the same things that Andrew Bacevich and Chalmers Johnson have learned more recently. They can learn, in other words, the following:

- that there is a consistent US policy running back well over a century;
- that this policy is aimed at creating a worldwide American Empire;
- that economically this policy has meant forcing open the economies of other countries to American economic and financial interests;
- that because this policy entails exploiting the resources of these countries for US elite interests rather than the people of these countries, military force is often needed to keep rulers in power who will sacrifice the welfare of their own people in order to serve American interests; and
- that to prevent uprisings, America relies not only on force—both military and economic—but also on propaganda, through which it portrays its goals and policies as noble in a way that is convincing to a majority of its own citizens, who keep funding its military and economic warfare.

The image of America the Good, which can also be called the Myth of the Democracy-Promoting America, has been based to a great extent on the standard account of America's role in World War II, according to which America defended the free world first from fascist tyranny. According to this account, America selflessly devoted itself to defending the freedom of many peoples around the world from the threat of living under brutal, fascist regimes.

This, however, is not an accurate picture of American policies during the Second World War. Many peoples were, to be sure, liberated from terrible tyrannies by the Allied victories. But the fact that these peoples benefited was an incidental outcome, not a motive, of American policies. These policies, as Bacevich discovered, were based on "unflagging self-interest."[43]

Be that as it may, America's entrance into the war, according to the official account, was without fault. The following chapter discusses the event through which America got into World War II.

Endnotes

1 Andrew J. Bacevich, *American Empire: The Realities and Consequences of U.S. Diplomacy* (Cambridge: Harvard University Press, 2002), 4.

2 Laurence H. Shoup and William Minter, *Imperial Brain Trust: The Council on Foreign Relations and United States Foreign Policy* (New York: Monthly Review Press, 1977), 135.

3 Ibid., 145.

4 Ibid., 146.

5 Walter LaFeber et al., *The American Century: A History of the United States Since 1941*, 5th edition (Boston: McGraw-Hill, 1998), 289.

6 Howard Zinn, *A People's History of the United States* (1980; New York: HarperPerennial, 1990), 405.

7 Shoup and Minter, *Imperial Brain Trust*, 146.

8 Ibid., 140, 142.

9 Noam Chomsky, *Year 501: The Conquest Continues* (Boston: South End, 1993), 329

10 Cordell Hull, *Memoirs of Cordell Hull*, Vol. 2: 1032; quoted in Noam Chomsky, *American Power and the New Mandarins: Historical and Political Essays* (New York: Vintage, 1969), 205.

11 Gabriel Kolko, *The Politics of War: The World and United States*

Foreign Policy 1943-1945 (1968; New York: Pantheon, 1990),14.

12 Stanley Karnow, *In Our Image: America's Empire in the Philippines* (New York: Ballantine, 1989), 238.

13 Ibid., 231-32.

14 Ibid., 243, 250-51, 272.

15 Ibid., 274.

16 Ibid., 244, 247, 263-64, 272, 275-77, 296.

17 The Japanese were able to take over the islands quite easily, thanks to the fact that General Douglas MacArthur left his airplanes - America's largest array of planes - on the ground for nine hours after knowing of the attack on Pearl Harbor, thereby allowing the Japanese to destroy the majority of them. He said later that he had been ordered by Washington to allow Japan to strike first (ibid., 280-90).

18 Kolko, *The Politics of War*, 605-06.

19 Kolko, *Century of War*, 361-63; Karnow, *In Our Image*, 311, 340; William Blum, *Killing Hope: U.S. Military and C.I.A. Interventions Since World War II* (Common Courage, 2008), 39; Daniel B. Schirmeer and Stephen Rosskamm Shalom, *The Philippines Reader: A History of Colonialism, Neocolonialism, Dictatorship, and Resistance* (Boston: South End, 1987), 76-77.

20 D. Michael Shafer, *Deadly Paradigms: The Failure of U.S. Counterinsurgency Policy* (Princeton University Press, 1989), 212.

21 Schirmeer and Shalom, *The Philippines Reader*, 78-83; Karnow, *In Our Image*, 325-28.

22 Kolko, *The Politics of War*, 246.

23 The US insistence on this membership, which involved defining China as one of the "Great Powers," which it certainly was not in 1945, evoked Britain's insistence that France also be thus defined, with the hope that France would vote with it; Kolko, *The Politics of War,* 73, 218-19, 268.

24 Ibid., 218-20, 267-68.

25 Ibid., 226.

26 Ibid.,, 203, 212, 229.

27 Ibid., 214, 209.

28 Ibid., 215-17, 222-24, 234, 239, 525-26.

29 Ibid., 226.

30 Kolko, *Century of War*, 228-31, 526.

31 LaFeber et al., *The American Century*, 293.

32 Ibid., 303.

33 Ibid., 293.

34 Ibid., 290.

35 Kolko, *The Politics of War*, 582.

36 Ibid., 45, 47-49, 53.
37 Ibid., 45, 46-47, 61, 62.
38 Ibid., 60.
39 Ibid., 439-41.
40 Ibid., 67, 79.
41 Ibid., 64.
42 Ibid., 75, 82-84, 87, 92.
43 Bacevich, *American Empire*, 4.

| Chapter 5 |

PEARL HARBOR

Central to the view that World War II was the "good war" was the idea that America entered the war as a response to Japan's unprovoked surprise attack on Pearl Harbor (which killed over 2,000 servicemen, sank or heavily damaged 18 naval vessels, and destroyed 188 planes). "According to this view," said historian Stephen Sniegoski, "the cause of the war stemmed from the malign effort by Japan, run by aggressive militarists, to conquer the Far East and the Western Pacific."[1]

The day after the attack, President Roosevelt began his address to Congress by calling December 7, 1941, "a date which will live in infamy." The date should be so regarded, he said, because the attack on Pearl Harbor was "a surprise offensive" that had been "unprovoked," and occurred when the "United States was at peace with that nation."[2]

By means of these statements, the president told the American people that its government had been entirely blameless. It had not provoked the attack, and because the attack had come as a surprise, there would have been no way for the government to have prevented it. Insofar as America was at fault, the fault was that of the US military commanders in Hawaii, who were charged with dereliction of duty for being unprepared. Accordingly, although World War II turned America into the planet's supreme empire, there was nothing about its entrance into the war that contradicted the idea of American Exceptionalism.

However, there has long been a revisionist view of the Pearl Harbor attacks,[3] according to which all three major claims made by the standard view were false or at least misleading. (1) The claim that the Japanese government was malign and militarist is misleading. (2) The claim that the attack had been unprovoked was simply false. (3) The claim that the attack had been a surprise was equally false—a fact that means that the military commanders in Hawaii were not to blame. This chapter is organized in terms of these three claims, followed by a discussion of (4) various ways in which the truth was covered up.

1. Was Japan Malign and Militaristic?

The standard American view was that Japan was bent on conquest, which would threaten vital US interests (such as Hawaii and the Philippines). However, rather than being bent on conquering the Far East and Western pacific, said Sniegoski, "Japanese moves were fundamentally defensive efforts to protect vital Japanese interests."[4]

The fact was that Japan had very few natural resources, so it depended on foreign markets more than most countries. Japan was getting most of its natural resources from China, Manchuria in particular. Given the fact that the United States, with far less need, has acted aggressively to commandeer natural resources from various countries, it could hardly characterize Japan as uniquely evil in August 1941 because of its resource war with China. And this war was no sign that it meant to take over all of Asia and the Western Pacific. According to Sniegoski, prior to the American actions to cut Japan off from resources (as discussed below),

> Japan had been essentially satisfied with the status quo in China. . . . The revisionists portray the Japanese interests in China as similar to American interests in Latin America. . . . Japanese interests in China did not portend further aggression into Southeast Asia or threaten vital American interests.[5]

Similarly, Bruce Russett, in a book entitled *No Clear and Present Danger: A Skeptical View of the U.S. Entry into World War II*, wrote:

> [T]he Japanese attack on Pearl Harbor, and for that matter on Southeast Asia, is not evidence of any unlimited expansionist policy or capability by the Japanese government. It was the consequence only of a much less ambitious goal, centering on an unwillingness to surrender the position that the Japanese had fought for years to establish in China.

War resulted, said Russett, only when that unwillingness "met an equal American determination that Japan should give up many of her gains in China."[6]

To be sure, added Russett, "there were Japanese political and military leaders with wider ambitions, but they were not predominant in policy-making."[7] The militarists came to power only when the moderate government headed by Prince Konoye, the Prime Minister, fell because it was unable to work out a peace agreement with America. In one of the first and best of the revisionist books, journalist George Morgenstern wrote:

> The American diplomatic representatives in Tokyo noted that, almost until the very end, Konoye and the moderate elements were willing to go to almost any lengths to bring off the meeting [with Roosevelt] and avert war.[8]

Roosevelt refused to meet. As a result, Japan's government was taken over by a militant group headed by General Hideki Tojo.[9]

2. Was the Attack on Pearl Harbor Unprovoked?

The war in Europe had begun in 1939. Most Americans, at least 80 percent of them,[10] did not want their country to get involved in another European war. As a result, Roosevelt in his 1940 reelection campaign seemed to pledge to keep American out of the war, saying: "I have said this before, but I shall say it again and again and again: Your boys are not going to be sent into any foreign wars." He later rationalized his seeming violation of his pledge by saying, "If we're attacked it's no longer a foreign war."[11]

Roosevelt had usually qualified his pledge by saying, "unless we are attacked." Accordingly, he tried to bait Germany into attacking America: Although America was supposed to be neutral, FDR had US ships escort British ships in war zones; he had German submarines tracked and then reported to the British; and he provided armaments to Great Britain.[12] Although these actions constituted warfare, FDR feared that the Congress would not give him a declaration of war unless US forces were attacked, so he kept this "undeclared war" from it as well as the American public.[13] In any case, not wanting to fight the United States again, the Germans would never take the bait.

So FDR decided he would be able to get into the war only by going in by the "back door"—inducing Japan to attack America. Secretary of War Henry Stimson wrote in his diary: "We face the delicate question of the diplomatic fencing to be done so as to be sure Japan is put into the wrong and makes the first bad move—overt move."[14]

Lieutenant Commander Arthur McCollum, the head of the Far East desk of the Office of Naval Intelligence, regularly provided FDR with reports about Japan. In his 2001 book, *Day of Deceit: The Truth About FDR and Pearl Harbor*,[15] Robert B. Stinnett reported that in October of 1940, McCollum provided FDR with a plan for inducing Japan to make the first move. McCollum gave FDR an eight-action memorandum making the following argument:

- It is essential for the USA to get into the war—mainly because if the Axis Powers were to defeat Great Britain, thereby taking control of the British naval fleet, they could virtually rule the world.

- American public opinion would not presently allow the US government to declare war against Japan "without more ado."

- The recent signing of the Tripartite Pact, in which Germany, Italy, and Japan agreed to treat an attack by a new belligerent on any of them as an attack on all, provided an opportunity for more ado, because if Japan could be provoked into a war on the USA, then Germany would join in, providing the USA with a "back door" into the war in Europe.

Of the eight actions proposed, one was to keep most of the US Fleet in Hawaii as bait (rather than, at the conclusion of the spring training exercises, returning much of it to its normal location in San Diego).

Another important action in McCollum's list was to give more aid to the Chinese government of Chiang Kai-shek in support of its war with Japan. Sniegoski summarized:

> By 1940, the U.S. was providing substantial support for China, which had been at war with Japan since 1937. During that year, the U. S. loaned China $125 million. In 1941, the U.S. extended Lend-Lease to China, which enabled China to receive American war materials without involving payment.[16]

In addition, Sniegoski said:

> The U.S. government covertly sponsored an American-manned air force for China—General Claire Chennault's American Volunteer Group or the "Flying Tigers." Although officially "volunteers," they were actually closely connected to the American military.[17]

This aid to China was crucial, because it stiffened China's resistance, making it see no reason to agree to a peaceful settlement with Japan. "It was Japan's inability to terminate the war with China successfully," said Sniegoski, "that motivated its military expansion elsewhere."[18]

The third major part of McCollum's memo was to pinch Japan economically. The United States closed the Panama Canal to Japanese shipping, thereby reducing Japanese imports drastically, causing a downard spiral in the economy and food shortages. Most damaging, Roosevelt froze all Japanese assets in the US and—in cooperation with the Dutch and the British—placed a total embargo on all trade with Japan, including oil. This would mean that Japan would not be able to continue its war with China, "because neither Japan nor Japanese-controlled territory in China produced oil." *The New York Times* referred to this action as "the most drastic blow short of war."[19]

By such actions, McCollum said, Japan might "be led to commit an overt act of war."[20] In fact, said Stinnett, all the suggested actions were carried out before Japan's final decision to attack Pearl Harbor.[21] These actions left little choice. According to Robert Smith Thompson, "Japan had to strike—and strike first. . . . Japan's only salvation lay in taking out the U.S. Pacific fleet."[22]

The day after Roosevelt received McCollum's memo, he explained his plan to Admiral James Richardson, the fleet's commander. When Richardson refused to accept the idea of retaining the fleet in Hawaii, Admiral Husband Kimmel, who was *not* told of the plan, was put in charge of the Pacific Fleet.[23] General Walter C. Short, who was given responsibility for the defense of Hawaii, also was not told.[24]

3. Was the Pearl Harbor Attack a Surprise?

The Japanese attack was absolutely not a surprise to the nation's leaders in Washington. There were several means by which the Japanese plan was known.

Code "Purple"

One of the ways by which Washington knew the attack was coming involved Japan's secret diplomatic code, known as Purple.

> The code was so complex that it was enciphered and deciphered by machine. A talented group of American cryptoanalysts broke the code in 1940 and devised a facsimile of the Japanese machine. . . . The deciphered texts were nicknamed Magic.[25]

Although the texts did not reveal that Pearl Harbor was the target, they did let Washington know what the Japanese leaders were thinking.

Copies of Magic were promptly delivered to FDR, the secretaries of State, War, and Navy, the Army Chief of Staff (General George Marshall), and the Chief of Naval Operations (Admiral Harold Stark). Although Kimmel and Short asked for a code-breaking machine, this request was refused.[26]

"Winds" Signals

The Japanese had set up a "Winds System," by means of which consulates not having the code or a code-breaking machine could learn from weather reports about Tokyo's intentions. If diplomatic relations were broken, so that war was near, the message was to be repeated three times during a weather report. The message was "East wind, rain," with "East wind" indicating the United States and "rain" signifying the cut off of diplomatic relations. This message was broadcast, and picked up by Washington intelligence, on December 4.[27]

The Naval Code

Just as important as Stinnett's discovery of the McCollum memorandum was his discovery that US intelligence did *not*, as almost universally believed, lose track of the Japanese strike force while it was making its approach to Hawaii. That account—which has been part of the official story, according to which Washington could not have warned Hawaii of the impending attack because it had no precise advance knowledge of it—had been widely accepted. For example, historian Stephen E. Ambrose, repeating the story that "intelligence 'lost' the Japanese aircraft carrier fleet," charged in 1995 that US intelligence was "terrible."[28]

One of the two crucial elements in this story was that, although US cryptographers had deciphered the diplomatic code (Purple), the cryptographers were unable to read any of the intercepts of military (naval) messages until *after* Pearl Harbor. For example, in his 1997 book, *The Clash,* Walter LaFeber said that "the intercepts—codenamed MAGIC—allowed U.S. officials to listen in on the many secret Japanese diplomatic and, after the Pearl Harbor attack, the military messages."[29] However, Stinnett discovered that the naval code had been partly deciphered by the fall of 1940, and all four of the codes employed for the expedition to Hawaii had been solved by the fall of 1941.[30]

Radio Contact

The other crucial element in the official account was that the Japanese maintained radio silence during the strike force's approach to Hawaii. For example, Lafeber said that "U.S. intelligence had no idea where the fleet was located" because it sailed "without radio contact."[31] However, far from being silent, wrote Stinnett, the Japanese were "blasting away on the lower marine frequencies," averaging over 6 messages a day.[32] Thanks to the intercepts for these messages, US intelligence was able to track the movement of the strike force to the Kurile Islands, then eastward, and then southward to Hawaii.[33] Beginning on November 20, several intercepts, which FDR himself received,[34] indicated that "Hawaii" or "Pearl Harbor" was the target, with intercepts on December 2 and 3 revealing that the "Hawaii attack" would occur on December 7.[35]

Spy Messages

All this information was reinforced, furthermore, by intercepted messages from Japan's spy in Honolulu, who in response to requests from Tokyo sent grid coordinates for Pearl Harbor, from which Tokyo could prepare bombing maps.[36] On December 6, his intercepted message informed Tokyo that "a considerable opportunity is left for a surprise attack."[37]

The "Pilot" Message

Early in the morning of December 6, US intelligence intercepted the so-called "pilot" message, which contained Japan's response to America's demands. This message came in 14 parts, the first 13 of which were received and decoded on that day. FDR saw that the message "means war." Then the 14th part was received and decoded on the morning of December 7. It indicated that the Japanese ambassador to the United States was to deliver the message breaking diplomatic relations to Secretary of State Cordell Hull at 1:00 PM (Eastern time), which meant that this was about when the attack was to begin.[38] Accordingly, the Pearl Harbor attack was not a surprise for Washington, which knew where and when the attack would come, almost down to the minute.[39] But it was a surprise for Hawaii.

A Surprise for Kimmel and Short

The wife of William Friedman, the cryptographer credited with solving the Purple code, said that, after the attack, he paced about muttering: "But they knew, they knew, they knew."[40] Although *they*—FDR, General Marshall, and a few other people—knew, Marshall and FDR had taken pains to ensure that Admiral Kimmel and General Short would *not* know. In addition to the fact that none of the intercept information summarized above was given to them, they were also explicitly lied to by their intelligence officers, being told the day before the attack, for example, that the Japanese "carriers are lost."[41]

They were also not told after Kimmel, who had sent part of his fleet to the sea north of Hawaii for surveillance purposes, was ordered to bring the ships back to Oahu. This order reflected a more general "Vacant Sea" policy, which was evidently implemented to ensure that the Japanese strike force would not encounter any US ships.[42]

On November 27, Kimmel and Short did receive a war warning, but it was explained so as to prevent them from making preparations: They were told that the attack would probably be "against either the Philippines or KRA Peninsula or possibly Borneo"; that if hostilities could not be avoided "the United States desires that Japan commit the first overt act"; and that any defensive measures should be carried out so as "not to alarm civil population or disclose intent"—which meant that they could do virtually nothing.[43]

When Short wrote back to say that he interpreted the message to mean that he should be alert "to prevent sabotage," no one corrected him.[44] Finally, after Washington on December 7 received the information about the exact minute of the attack several hours in advance, General Marshall sent this information to Hawaii in such a way that it would arrive only after the attack had begun.[45]

4. The Cover-Up

The authorities went to great lengths to prevent the public from knowing the truth about the Pearl Harbor attack. This cover-up, which still to a great extent continues, was achieved by various means.

The first investigation, which occurred in 1942, concluded that the lack of preparedness for the attack was the fault of Kimmel and Short. This should have been no surprise, because the investigation was headed by Supreme Court Justice Owen Roberts, who had been handpicked by FDR, and the Roberts Commission was comprised of, with only one exception, "personal cronies of Roosevelt and Marshall."[46] The one member of the Commission who was not a crony was Admiral William Standley. Having arrived late to the hearing in Washington, Standley

> was startled by the inquiry's chummy atmosphere. Admiral Harold Stark and General Marshall were asked no difficult or embarrassing

> questions. Furthermore, all testimony was taken unsworn and unrecorded—an irregularity that, at Standley's urging, was corrected.[47]

The commission then moved to Hawaii.

> When Admiral Husband Kimmel was summoned, he brought a fellow officer to act as counsel. Justice Roberts disallowed this on grounds that the investigation was not a trial, and the admiral not a defendant. Because Kimmel and General Walter Short were not formally "on trial," they were also denied all traditional rights of defendants: to ask questions and cross-examine witnesses. Kimmel was also shocked that the proceeding's stenographers—one a teenager, the other with almost no court experience—omitted much of his testimony and left other parts badly garbled. Permission to correct the errors . . . was refused.[48]

Standley said that Roberts' handling of the investigation was "as crooked as a snake," but he did not submit a minority report, because he was told that it "might jeopardize the war effort by lowering the nation's confidence in its leaders." Admiral Richardson, whom Kimmel had replaced, called the report "the most unfair, unjust, and deceptively dishonest document ever printed by the Government Printing Office."[49]

Kimmel and Short were inundated with hate mail and called traitors who should be shot. There were cries for courts-martial, but although Kimmel and Short wanted them, as the only way in which they could save their reputations, the administration did not want courts-martial, because sharp defense attorneys might uncover the secrets. So it was announced that the courts-martial would not occur until safety would permit.[50]

By 1944, the Allies were clearly winning, so national security could no longer be an excuse, and the courts-martial were scheduled. In preparation for the Naval Court of Inquiry, one of the defense attorneys obtained 43 of the Magic intercepts.

> The admirals on the Court listened to them being read with looks of horror and disbelief. . . . The verdict of the Roberts Commission was overturned. Admiral Kimmel was exonerated on all charges.

The intercepts were also leaked to the Army Pearl Harbor Board, saying that the guilt was not that of General Short but that of General Marshall. (The proceedings were not allowed to criticize the President.)[51]

It was announced, however, that the courts-martial verdicts would not be released until the war was over, and this gave the Roosevelt administration time to reverse the verdicts. It announced that there would be some additional inquiries, and these were not run with the rigor of the courts-martial but "in an informal manner and without regard to legal or formal requirements." As a result, most of the witnesses who had testified against the Roosevelt administration reversed their earlier testimony, fearing that telling the truth would end their chances for promotion. One naval officer was intent on repeating his testimony, but he "was thrown into a psychiatric ward at Bethesda Naval Hospital" and told that "his testimony had better change or he'd be in the ward for the rest of his life."[52]

Having gotten all the problematic testimonies reversed, the administration publicized the revamped versions of the courts-martial findings, and the public never knew what the findings of the courts-martial had been.[53]

Although Short and Kimmel died in 1949 and 1968, respectively, their families kept trying to clear their names. In 1999, the Senate, in light of new information, approved a resolution saying that the two officers had performed their duties "competently and professionally," so the losses at Pearl Harbor were "not the result of dereliction of duty."[54]

Conclusion

Although the Senate repaired the reputations of Kimmel and Short (long after they died), it did not go on to explain who, if not these two men, *had* been responsible for the losses. In the mind of the general public, accordingly, the standard story is still the truth about the Pearl Harbor attacks. For those who know the facts, however, it is obvious that the official story was a lie.

This episode provides further evidence against the self-congratulatory version of American Exceptionalism, because it shows that the American government lies as do other governments. Moreover, although Japan was accused of perfidy, this attribute was exemplified more by the behavior of the American government in this episode than by that of the Japanese government. However, although the Roosevelt administration was guilty of perfidy, and most Americans upon learning the truth about the Pearl Harbor attacks will immediately feel outrage, there is still the question: Was FDR's deceit justified? Statements in Stinnett's book showed that he was of two minds. On the one hand, he wrote: "As a veteran of the Pacific War, I felt a sense of outrage as I uncovered secrets that had been hidden from Americans for more than fifty years." Stinnett's sense of outrage, moreover, is reflected throughout his book.

On the other hand, speaking of "the agonizing dilemma faced by President Roosevelt," Stinnett said that "he was forced to find circuitous means to persuade an isolationist America to join in a fight for freedom," a fight that led to the "victory of allied forces over the Axis nations that threatened the liberties we all cherish." Stinnett also expressed this side of his mind in a chapter titled "A Pretty Cheap Price," in which he quoted one of the military men who was in on the conspiracy, who concluded: "It was a pretty cheap price to pay for unifying the country."[55]

Endnotes

1 Stephen J. Sniegoski, "The Case for Pearl Harbor Revisionism,"

Occidental Quarterly, Winter 2001.

2 "'A Date Which Will Live in Infamy': FDR Asks for a Declaration of War," History Matters.

3 Frank Paul Mintz, in *Revisionism and the Origins of Pearl Harbor* (University Press of America, 1985), laid out the views of various Pearl Harbor revisionists.

4 Sniegoski, "The Case for Pearl Harbor Revisionism."

5 Ibid.

6 Bruce Russett, *No Clear and Present Danger: A Skeptical View of the U.S. Entry into World War II* (New York: Harper & Row, 1972), 57.

7 Ibid.

8 George Morgenstern, *Pearl Harbor: The Story of the Secret War* (New York: Devin-Adair Company, 1947), 140.

9 Ibid., 150-52.

10 Sniegoski, "The Case for Pearl Harbor Revisionism." In 1939, a Gallup Poll showed that 88 percent of the population wanted America to stay out of the War (James Perloff, "Pearl Harbor: Hawaii Was Surprised; FDR Was Not," New American, 7 December 2016). Later polls put the opposition at 80 percent of the population ("America and the Second World War," America in the World Briefings).

11 David Greenberg, *Republic of Spin: An Inside History of the American Presidency* (New York: W.W. Norton, 2016), 233.

12 Jacob G. Hornberger, "FDR's Pearl Harbor Bait," Hornberger's Blog, The Future of Freedom Foundation, 7 December 2016.

13 Walter LaFeber, *The American Age: U.S. Foreign Policy Since 1750*, 2nd ed. (New York: Norton, 1993), 376-77, 382; see also William L. Langer and S. Everett Gleason, *The Undeclared War, 1940-1941: The World Crisis and American Foreign Policy* (New York: Harper & Brothers, 1953), and F. R. Fehrenbach, *FDR's Undeclared War, 1939-1941* (New York: D. McKay, 1967).

14 James Perloff, "Pearl Harbor: Hawaii Was Surprised; FDR Was Not," *New American*, 7 December 2017.

15 Robert B. Stinnett, *Day of Deceit: The Truth About FDR and Pearl Harbor* (New York: Touchstone, 2001). Although the book was originally published in 2000, the Afterword to the Touchstone (paperback) edition has additional information.

16 Sniegoski, "The Case for Pearl Harbor Revisionism," citing Wayne S. Cole, *An Interpretive History of American Foreign Relations,* revised ed. (Homewood, Il.: Dorsey Press, 1974), 377.

17 Ibid., citing Robert Smith Thompson, *A Time for War: Franklin D. Roosevelt and the Path to Pearl Harbor* (New York: Prentice Hall Press, 1991), 322-23.

18 Ibid.

19 Ibid.

20 Stinnett, *Day of Deceit*, 275.

21 Ibid., 321-22.

22 Thompson, *A Time for War,* 352, 379.

23 The occasion for Richardson's removal was the creation of a two-ocean navy, with Kimmel put in charge of the Pacific Fleet (ibid., 11).

24 Perloff, "Pearl Harbor: Hawaii Was Surprised; FDR Was Not."

25 Perloff, "Pearl Harbor: Hawaii Was Surprised; FDR Was Not."

26 Ibid.; Sniegoski, "The Case for Pearl Harbor Revisionism."

27 Perloff, "Pearl Harbor: Hawaii Was Surprised; FDR Was Not."

28 Stephen E. Ambrose, *Pearl Harbor Revisited* (New York: St. Martin's, 1995), 99-100. Ambrose repeated this charge in an opinion piece in the *Wall Street Journal*, 27 May 1999 (both cited in Stinnett, *Day of Deceit,* 208, 374).

29 Walter Lafeber, *The Clash: U.S.-Japanese Relations Throughout History* (Norton 1997), 197.

30 Stinnett, *Day of Deceit*, 23, 71.

31 LaFeber, *The Clash,* 211.

32 Stinnett, *Day of Deceit*, 196.

33 Ibid., 47, 72, 154, 164, 269.

34 In November, FDR had asked to be given the raw intercepts, not simply the summaries that had previously been supplied (ibid., 47, 169).

35 Ibid., 45, 72, 210, 219, 269.

36 Ibid., 98-104.

37 Ibid., 85.

38 Sniegoski, "The Case for Pearl Harbor Revisionism."

39 Consistent with these facts were reports about FDR's state of mind on the day of the attack - that upon receiving the report, he did not seem alarmed, and that his overriding concern about the attack seemed to be the public's reaction to it: whether it would unite Americans behind a declaration of war (Stinnett, *Day of Deceit*, 3, 233). Reflecting a similar attitude, FDR's secretary of war, Henry Stimson, wrote in his diary that his "first feeling" upon hearing the news "was relief that the indecision was over and that a crisis had come in a way which would unite all our people" (*The Diary of Henry Stimson* [available in the Sterling Library, Yale University], 7 December 1941; quoted by LaFeber, *The Clash*, 212).

40 John Toland, *Infamy*: *Pearl Harbor and Its Aftermath* (Doubleday, 1982), 15, citing Ronald Clark, *The Man Who Broke Purple* (Boston: Little, Brown, 1977), 170.

41 Stinnett, *Day of Deceit*, 207.

42 Ibid., 144-45, 150-51.

43 Ibid., 171-72. On November 25, 1940, reported Henry Stimson in his diary, FDR and his "war cabinet" discussed the question "how we should maneuver them [the Japanese] into the position of firing the first shot without allowing too much danger to ourselves" (quoted by LaFeber, *The Clash,* 209).

44 Ibid., 174-76.

45 Ibid., 234-35.

46 Perloff, "Pearl Harbor: Hawaii Was Surprised; FDR Was Not."

47 James Perloff, "Pearl Harbor: Scapegoating Kimmel and Short," New American, 4 June 2001.

48 Ibid.

49 Ibid.

50 Ibid.

51 Ibid.

52 Ibid.

53 Ibid.

54 Ibid.

55 Stinnett, *Day of Deceit*, xiii, xiv, 203.

| Chapter 6 |

HIROSHIMA AND NAGASAKI

After having tricked Japan into striking Pearl Harbor, the US government then attacked it mercilessly with conventional bombs and two atomic bombs. Although most of the discussion has been about the dropping of atom bombs on Hiroshima and Nagasaki—justifiably, because nuclear weapons were a new type of warfare, and each atomic bomb is enormously more destructive than any conventional weapon—the conventional bombing of Japan was truly horrific. Mark Selden, a historian in Cornell University's East Asia Program, wrote:

> In the final six months of the war, the US threw the full weight of its air power into campaigns to burn whole Japanese cities to the ground and terrorize, incapacitate and kill their largely defenseless residents in an effort to force surrender. . . .
>
> The full fury of firebombing and napalm was unleashed on the night of March 9-10, 1945 when [Major General Curtis] LeMay (the head of the Twenty-First Bomber Command) sent 334 B-29s low over Tokyo. . . . Their mission was to reduce the city to rubble, kill its citizens, and instill terror

> in the survivors, with jellied gasoline and napalm that would create a sea of flames. . . . [A police cameraman] described the streets of Tokyo as
>
> > rivers of fire . . . flaming pieces of furniture exploding in the heat, while the people themselves blazed like 'matchsticks' as their wood and paper homes exploded in flames. Under the wind and the gigantic breath of the fire, immense incandescent vortices rose in a number of places, swirling, flattening, sucking whole blocks of houses into their maelstrom of fire. . . . No previous or subsequent conventional bombing raid ever came close to generating the toll in death and destruction of the great Tokyo raid of March 9-10. . . .
>
> Following the Tokyo raid . . . the firebombing was extended nationwide. . . . Between January and July 1945, the US firebombed and destroyed all but five Japanese cities, deliberately sparing Kyoto, the ancient imperial capital, and four others [saved to be targets for atomic bombs].[1]

The atomic bombings in Hiroshima and Nagasaki killed about 130,000 people immediately and another 130,000 by the end of 1945. By 2016, about twice that many had died because of the bombings.[2]

It has commonly been thought that the US government, having seen how terrible were the effects of the bombings of Hiroshima and Nagasaki, decided never to use them again. Actually, however, the next month after the bombings, the Pentagon said that it wanted 204 atomic bombs in order to destroy 66 Soviet cities of "strategic importance."[3] In 1948, the Joint Chiefs of Staff made plans for preemptive atomic strikes, such as "Plan Trojan," which would incinerate 30 Soviet cities.[4] After the outbreak of the Korean War in 1950, General Douglas MacArthur wanted to use 30-50 atomic bombs against the Chinese in Manchuria.[5] During the Vietnam war, American leaders came close to dropping nuclear weapons on that country.[6] Overall, US presidents have threatened to use nuclear weapons at least 25 times.[7]

1. The Manhattan Project

Having learned that Nazi Germany was trying to create an atomic bomb, President Franklin Roosevelt created the Manhattan Project in order to make a bomb before the Germans could.[8] Fearing that Hitler would use the bomb to enslave the world, "U.S. and British scientists believed they were in a desperate winner-take-all race with German scientists. That was especially true of the émigré scientists who came to the Manhattan Project," as they had experienced Nazism first-hand, "and their fear and loathing of Hitler was intense."[9]

However, during 1943 and 1944, the US government became increasingly convinced that the German scientists had given up the attempt to create an atomic bomb.[10] Indeed, by May 1943, the government had already decided that the bomb would be used on Japan instead.[11] But General Leslie Groves, who was in charge of the Manhattan Project, did not tell his scientists about the change of target. Instead, he used the "fear of a German bomb to drive his team onward" and also, evidently, to prevent them from resigning.[12]

One might ask, of course, why the US government, after realizing that it would not need an atomic bomb to defeat Germany, did not simply cancel the Manhattan Project. Was it because the government thought it would need the bomb to defeat Japan? No, the political and military leaders knew that they would be able to defeat Japan without any nuclear weapons.

Of course, one could say that the government could not know this long in advance, so they justifiably completed the Manhattan Project, in case the Japan military proved to be stronger than expected. But even if we assume this to have been the case, we still have the difficult question of why, after realizing that atomic bombs were not necessary to defeat Japan's military, the United States dropped them on Japanese civilians?

2. The Hiroshima Myth

To be sure, Americans have been told that the atomic bombs *were* necessary. The most effective claim to this effect was a 1947 article by the Secretary of War, Henry Stimson, entitled "The Decision to Use the Atomic Bomb." In this article, Stimson claimed that, without the bombs, the war would have continued "until the latter part of 1946" and "cost over a million casualties, to American forces alone."[13] However, Stimson's claims conflict with what several top military figures had said. For example:

- Dwight D. Eisenhower, the supreme commander of the Allied Forces, said at the Potsdam Conference (before the bombings) that "there was no question but that Japan was already thoroughly beaten." In addition, Eisenhower later said that "the Japanese were ready to surrender and it wasn't necessary to hit them with that awful thing."[14]

- Admiral William "Bull" Halsey Jr., Commander of the US Third Fleet, stated publicly that "the first atomic bomb was an unnecessary experiment. . . . It was a mistake to ever drop it."[15]

In fact, Stimson had been asked to write his essay to drown out the voices of military men and others who said that atomic bombs were not necessary to defeat Japan. The idea for this article came from James B. Conant, a prominent scientist (who had worked on poison gas during World War I), and who eventually served as the president of Harvard University. During World War II, Conant was chairman of the National Defense

Research Committee and one of the central figures overseeing the Manhattan Project.[16]

According to an article by John Denson entitled "The Hiroshima Myth," Conant had become "concerned about his future academic career, as well as his positions in private industry, because various people began to speak out concerning why the bombs were dropped."[17] These people included not only military men, such as Eisenhower and Halsey, but also Einstein, who said that the dropping of the bomb was a political-diplomatic decision, not a military or scientific decision, and Norman Cousins, the editor of *The Saturday Review of Literature,* who spoke of the "crime of Hiroshima and Nagasaki" and who also, referring to Halsey's statement, asked: "[W]hat happens to the argument that numberless thousands of American lives were saved?"[18] Given this situation,

> Conant came to the conclusion that some important person in the administration must go public to show that the dropping of the bombs was a military necessity, thereby saving the lives of hundreds of thousands of American soldiers.[19]

Conant approached Harvey Bundy and his son, McGeorge Bundy, and the three of them agreed that Stimson was the one to write it, with McGeorge Bundy revising it.

With regard to the origin of the claim that the bomb prevented over a million American casualties: Truman, who later repeated this estimate, claimed that he had gotten it from General George Marshall. However, Marshall had estimated that an invasion of Japan would result in 31,000 casualties.[20] As to the real source of the claim, Kai Bird and Martin Sherwin reported that "McGeorge Bundy, the man who first popularized the 'over 5 million casualties' figure, later confessed that he had pulled it out of thin air in order to justify the bombings."[21]

In addition to this fabrication, there were three other problems with Stimson's article: It ignored the fact (a) that the

US military had long rejected the idea of an invasion of Japan,[22] (b) that Stimson himself had believed that, if Truman had clarified the meaning of "unconditional surrender," the Japanese would have surrendered without any bombs,[23] and (c) that he himself had believed that the Soviet entrance into the war would cause such a shock that Japan would surrender.[24] In other words, Stimson's entire article was a lie. Aside from its lies, this article was contradicted by many more people than Eisenhower and Halsey. For example:

- Henry "Hap" Arnold, the commanding general of the US Army Air Forces, said after the bombings that "the Japanese position was hopeless even before the first atomic bomb fell."[25]

- Major General Curtis LeMay, the hawkish head of the Twenty-First Bomber Command, told the press that "the atomic bomb had nothing to do with the end of the war at all."[26]

- Admiral Chester Nimitz, Commander in Chief of the Pacific Fleet, said: "The atomic bomb played no decisive part, from a purely military standpoint, in the defeat of Japan."[27]

- Admiral William D. Leahy, President Truman's Chief of Staff, said that "the use of this barbarous weapon at Hiroshima and Nagasaki was of no material assistance in our war against Japan. The Japanese were already defeated and ready to surrender."[28]

Even Robert Oppenheimer, who headed the scientific project at Los Alamos (which led to the creation of the atomic bombs), later said that the bombs were dropped on "an essentially defeated enemy."[29]

3. Why Were Atomic Bombs Dropped on Japan?

Given this situation, why did the US government drop atomic bombs on Japan? According to Arjun Makhijani (who was quoted extensively above), "the all-out US effort had created its own momentum." A large part of this momentum was based on the fact that "a host of war-related projects were in fierce competition for industrial and intellectual resources," so "officials connected with [the Manhattan Project] were compelled to demonstrate that it would have a decisive effect on the outcome of the war."[30]

Roosevelt's director of the Office of War Mobilization, James F. ("Jimmy") Byrnes, was "acutely aware of the potential for intense political problems if atom bombs were not produced and used in the war." Byrnes told Roosevelt that, if the bombs are not produced and used, the Manhattan Project would be "subjected to relentless investigation and criticism."[31] After Roosevelt died on April 12, 1945, and Byrnes became President Harry Truman's secretary of state, Byrnes said that he wanted the atomic bomb used "as quickly as possible in order to 'show results.'"[32]

This answer by itself would suggest that the United States chose to drop atomic bombs on Japan for political and bureaucratic, not military, reasons. However, the US government did bomb Japan for a military reason, just not for the sake of defeating Japan. In 1944, General Groves revealed that the real military purpose for making the bomb was to *subdue the Soviets.*[33]

This fact became evident in relation to the question as to why Japan had refused to surrender, even after it was clear that it had been defeated. Besides refusing to surrender before Hiroshima was bombed, Japan would not even surrender afterwards. It was even ready to refuse to surrender after Nagasaki was bombed.

Unconditional Surrender and the Emperor

The Japanese refused because the Truman administration had insisted that Japan surrender *unconditionally.* This stipulation was understood by Japanese leaders to mean that Japan's emperor, Hirohito, would be removed and be subject to prosecution for war crimes. To the Japanese, that was completely unacceptable, partly because they believed their Emperor to be a god, a direct descendant of the sun goddess, Amaterasu.[34]

In his classic work, *Japan's Decision to Surrender,* Robert Butow wrote: "The one thing [the Japanese] could not do was sign a death warrant for the imperial house," and if it appeared that the Allies would take steps against the Emperor, "then even the most ardent advocates of peace would fall into step behind the [pro-war] fanatics."[35] In "The Hiroshima Myth," John Denson wrote:

> The stark fact is that the Japanese leaders, both military and civilian, including the Emperor, were willing to surrender in May of 1945 if the Emperor could remain in place and not be subjected to a war crimes trial after the war. This fact became known to President Truman as early as May of 1945.[36]

Truman was repeatedly advised that he should clarify the meaning of the "unconditional surrender" he demanded—that it did not mean the loss of the throne. He received this advice from Democrats, Republicans, newspapers, radio shows, and religious leaders (such as Reinhold Niebuhr).[37]

In addition, in preparation for the Potsdam conference (July 17-August 2)—the last of the conferences of Truman, Churchill, and Stalin to achieve agreement about various matters after the war—Stimson and his assistant secretary of war, John McCloy, had prepared a draft for Truman's proclamation, which included explicit assurances about the Emperor's status.[38]

Nevertheless, when the Potsdam Proclamation—which was written by Truman and Byrnes—was made public, it demanded "the unconditional surrender of all the Japanese armed forces"—without saying anything about the retention of the Emperor's position. Moreover, the Proclamation contained assertions that seemed threatening to the Emperor.[39]

Given the fact that Byrnes and Truman, immediately

after the bombings, made clear that they wanted the Emperor to remain in office, commentators have asked why they did not say this earlier, thereby finishing the war without using the bombs.[40] But these commentators did not understand the goal of Byrnes and Truman. This goal was explained by the authors of two major books about this issue.

In *The Decision to Use the Atomic Bomb,* University of Maryland political economist Gar Alperovitz explained:

> [I]n making the decision to excise the recommended language concerning the Emperor, American officials understood that the warning to Japan [the Potsdam Proclamation] almost certainly could not be accepted—and that therefore the atomic bomb would be used.[41]

University of California at Santa Barbara historian Tsuyoshi Hasegawa, in a book entitled *Racing the Enemy*, stated the point even more bluntly:

> Truman knew that the unconditional surrender demand without any promise to preserve a constitutional monarchy would be rejected by the Japanese. He needed Japan's refusal to justify the use of the atomic bomb.[42]

Why Did Truman and Byrnes Want an Excuse?

But why were Truman and Byrnes intent on having an excuse to use the bombs? They refused to modify the unconditional demand, said Denson, "so that the bombs could actually be dropped thereby demonstrating to the Russians that America had a new forceful leader in place."[43] In fact, Byrnes told Truman, the atomic bomb might put the United States in position to "dictate" terms to the Soviets at the end of the war.[44]

This idea—that the bombs were dropped with the Soviets in mind—is now widely held. For example, Kai Bird and Martin J.

Sherwin, the authors of *American Prometheus: The Triumph and Tragedy of J. Robert Oppenheimer,*[45] said: "Truman and his closest advisor, Secretary of State James Byrnes, quite plainly used it primarily to prevent the Soviets from sharing in the occupation of Japan."[46]

4. Why Did Japan Finally Surrender?

However, having dropped the bombs, the Americans still had the problem of how to get the Japanese to surrender. This should not have been a problem, because the Japanese were desperate to surrender to the Americans. Why? Americans had from the beginning been told that the second atomic bomb—the one that hit Nagasaki—caused Japan to surrender. This view is still repeated in newspapers, magazine stories, and in essays on the Internet.[47] But the opinions of scholars have changed.

One of the first statements of this new view was written by journalistic legend Murray Sayle. In a 1995 *New Yorker* essay asking "Did the Bomb End the War?", Sayle wrote:

> Once, like everyone else, I thought that the atomic bombs had caused the surrender. Now I know that they did not. . . . [T]he Soviet invasion of Manchuria was what eventually led to the sudden unexpected surrender offer to the US in the days following Hiroshima and Nagasaki.[48]

This is now the dominant view among scholars. For example:

- Tsuyoshi Hasegawa wrote: "Without the Soviet entry, it is not likely that the Nagasaki bomb would have changed the situation."[49] Hasegawa's argument was so convincing that it persuaded Richard Rhodes, the author of the Pulitzer Prize-winning book *The Making of the Atomic Bomb*. Rhodes said: "Hasegawa has changed my mind: The Japanese decision to surrender was not driven by the two bombings."[50]

- "It was only with the entry of the Soviet Union's Red Army into the war," said Gar Alperovitz, "that the Japanese moved to finally surrender."[51]

This Soviet entrance into the war was what made the Japanese anxious to surrender to the Americans. Australian writer Paul Ham, in his book *Hiroshima Nagasaki*, wrote:

> A greater threat than nuclear weapons—in Tokyo's eyes—drove Japan finally to accept the surrender: the regime's suffocating fear of Russia. The Soviet invasion on 8 August crushed the Kwantung Army's frontline units within days. . . . The invasion invoked the specter of a communist Japan.[52]

The Soviet invasion was also frightening because of its sheer size. As Tristin Hopper explained:

> On Aug. 9, just three days after the bombing of Hiroshima, as many as 1.6 million Soviet troops launched a surprise attack on Japanese positions in Manchuria. . . . When Imperial Japan came to the United States to talk surrender, they weren't just facing nuclear bombs, they were staring down an unstoppable communist juggernaut.[53]

However, there was also a second reason why the Japanese finally surrendered. Although they were anxious to surrender to the Americans, the demand for unconditional surrender stood in the way. When Japan submitted its surrender proposal, it insisted on one condition. It was "ready to accept the terms" of the Potsdam Declaration, the proposal said, on the understanding that it "does not comprise any demand which prejudices the prerogatives of His Majesty as a Sovereign Ruler."[54]

However, the Truman administration would not accept a

surrender labeled "conditional," even if it had only one condition. How could the Americans overcome this impasse? The solution they reached was to suggest (in Ham's words) a "conditional unconditional surrender." Byrnes' task was to write "a compromise that read as an ultimatum." While presupposing the continuation of the Emperor, the statement fashioned by Byrnes declared that "the authority of the Emperor shall be subject to the Supreme Commander of the Allied Powers." Implicitly, therefore, the Americans had accepted Japan's condition, while still calling the surrender unconditional.[55]

As this episode showed, "Truman did not hesitate [observed Alperovitz] to modify the 'unconditional surrender' policy after the atomic bomb was used."[56] In other words, the insistence on unconditional surrender had simply been a ploy to give Truman and Byrnes a pretext to use the bombs. In fact, reported the History Channel, "the leaders [of the Potsdam conference] issued a declaration demanding 'unconditional surrender' from Japan, concealing the fact that they had privately agreed to let Japan retain its emperor."[57]

5. American Morality

The Truman administration had reasons for creating and using its nuclear weapons. But these reasons were not even close to justifying the American decisions. Besides resulting in the suffering and needless deaths of a great number of Japanese civilians, these decisions resulted in a loss of reputation for America and a subjection of the world to enormous risks. Regarding *America's reputation*:

- Admiral Healy said: "The lethal possibilities of atomic warfare in the future are frightening. My own feeling was that in being the first to use it, we had adopted an ethical standard common to the barbarians of the Dark Ages."[58]

- According to an article in the *Christian Century* entitled

"America's Atomic Atrocity," the bombings put the United States in "an indefensible moral position."[59]

- Raymond Swing, a popular broadcaster on ABC, said that "in using the bomb we became the most ruthless nation in warfare on earth."[60]

Regarding *the risks*:

- Leo Szilard, who was instrumental in the decision to create the Manhattan Project, said: "By demonstrating the bomb and using it in the war against Japan, we might start an atomic arms race between America and Russia which might end with the destruction of both countries.[61]

- George Kennan, one of the six "wise men" of that era,[62] wrote: "[T]he readiness to use nuclear weapons against other human beings... and, in doing so, to place in jeopardy the natural structure upon which all civilization rests, . . . this is nothing less than a presumption, a blasphemy, an indignity—an indignity of monstrous dimensions."[63]

In addition, there was a final monstrous action: General Henry "Hap" Arnold, the head of the Army Air Force, wanted to stage a big finale. So he asked for, and received, permission to launch a massive bombing raid. This raid occurred after the Japanese had "broadcast their offer of surrender through every country in the world," but "before the message had reached Washington through official channels." Arnold had 1,014 aircraft drop 6,000 tons of conventional explosives on Honshu—Japan's largest island, which, of course contains Tokyo.[64]

Conclusion

This episode in the American trajectory provides further evidence against the belief that this country is divine or even morally exceptional in any positive sense. Indeed, it demonstrated rather the reverse: that America was exceptionally immoral. Could Americans claim that their country is especially guided by God, if they realize that the United States, knowing that the atomic bombs were not necessary to end the war, nonetheless *chose* to subject a half-million Japanese civilians to an agonizing death? Could Americans claim that their country is exceptionally moral, if they realize that their government, knowing that the Japanese had announced their surrender, allowed the Army Air Force to drop thousands more bombs on them?

Endnotes

1 Mark Selden, "A Forgotten Holocaust: US Bombing Strategy, the Destruction of Japanese Cities and the American Way of War from World War II to Iraq," *Asia-Pacific Journal*, 2 May 2007.

2 Dan Listwa, "Hiroshima and Nagasaki: The Long Term Health Effects," Columbia Center for Nuclear Studies, 9 August 2012; Serina Sandhu, "Hiroshima: The Legacy of the Atomic Bombing in Numbers," inews, 27 May 2016.

3 Paul Ham, *Hiroshima Nagasaki: The Real Stories of the Atomic Bombings and their Aftermath* (St. Martin's Press, 2011), 488-89.

4 Ibid., 498-500.

5 Ibid., 503-04.

6 Marjorie Cohn, "Daniel Ellsberg: United States Nearly Used Nukes During Vietnam War," Truthout, 9 June 2014.

7 Fred Kaplan, "Dr. Strangelove Was a Documentary," Slate, December 2017.

8 William J. Broad, "Why They Called It the Manhattan Project," *New York Times*, 30 October 2007.

9 Arjun Makhijani, "'Always' the Target?: While U.S. Bomb Scientists Were Racing against Germany, Military Planners Were Looking toward the Pacific," *Bulletin of the Atomic Scientists* 51/3 (May/June 1995): 23-27.

10 Alex Wellerstein, "When Did the Allies Know There Wasn't a German Bomb?" The Nuclear Secrecy Blog, 13 November 2015.

11 Makhijani, "'Always' the Target?"

12 Ibid.

13 Henry L. Stimson, "The Decision to Use the Atomic Bomb," *Harper's*

Magazine, February 1947.

14 John LaForge, "No One Saves Lives by Dropping Bombs on Cities," Deluth Reader, 5 August 2015; "Ike on Ike," *Newsweek*, 11 November 1963.

15 Hew Strachan and Sibylle Scheipers, *The Changing Character of War* (Oxford University Press, 2011), 99.

16 See James G. Hershberg, *James B. Conant: Harvard to Hiroshima and the Making of the Nuclear Age* (Stanford University Press, 1995).

17 John V. Denson, "The Hiroshima Myth," MISES Institute, 2 August 2006.

18 Norman Cousins, "The Literacy of Survival," *Saturday Review of Literature* (14 September 1946), 14.

19 Denson, "The Hiroshima Myth."

20 Ham, *Hiroshima Nagasaki*, 477.

21 Kai Bird and Martin J. Sherwin, "The Myths of Hiroshima," *Los Angeles Times*, 2 August 2005.

22 Ham, *Hiroshima Nagasaki*, 472, 476.

23 Gar Alperovitz, *The Decision to Use the Atomic Bomb* (Vintage Books, 1995), 235.

24 Ibid., 465; Ham, *Hiroshima Nagasaki,* 476.

25 Gar Alperovitz, "The War Was Won Before Hiroshima—and the Generals Who Dropped the Bomb Knew It," *The Nation,* 6 August 2015.

26 Major General Curtis E. LeMay, *New York Herald Tribune,* 20 September 1945.

27 Daniel Russ, "Chester Nimitz Also Thought the Atom Bomb Was Not Why Japan Surrendered," Civilian Military Intelligence Group, 28 February 2017.

28 William D. Leahy, *I Was There* (Ayer Co. Publisher, 1979).

29 J. Robert Oppenheimer, "Address to the American Philosophical Society," 16 November 1945.

30 Makhijani, "'Always' the Target?"

31 Ibid.

32 Ibid.

33 Joseph Rotblat, "Leaving the Bomb Project," *Bulletin of Atomic Scientists*, August 1985: 16-19.

34 Ibid.

35 Robert J.C. Butow, *Japan's Decision to Surrender* (Stanford University Press, 1954), 141.

36 John V. Denson, "The Hiroshima Myth," MISES Institute, 2 August 2006.

37 Alperovitz, *The Decision to Use the Atomic Bomb,* 228-32, 235, 243, 300-01.

38 Ibid., 235.

39 Pacific War Research Society (with John Toland), *The Day Man Lost: Hiroshima,* 6 August 1945 (Kodansha America, 1981), 212-14; The Potsdam Proclamation said: "There must be eliminated for all time the authority and influence of those who have deceived and misled the people of Japan into embarking on world conquest," and "stern justice shall be meted out to all war criminals."

40 James Reston, *Deadline: A Memoir* (Random House, 1991); Hanson W. Baldwin, *Great Mistakes of the War* (Harper and Brothers, 1950); Henry L. Stimson and McGeorge Bundy, *On Active Services in Peace and War* (Harper & Brothers, 1947), 629.

41 Alperovitz, *The Decision to Use the Atomic Bomb*, 302.

42 Tsuyoshi Hasegawa, *Racing the Enemy: Stalin, Truman, and the Surrender of Japan* (Harvard University Press, 2005), 292.

43 Denson, "The Hiroshima Myth."

44 Alperovitz, *The Decision to Use the Atomic Bomb*, 213.

45 Kai Bird and Martin J. Sherwin, *American Prometheus: The Triumph and Tragedy of J. Robert Oppenheimer* (Alfred A. Knopf, 2005).

46 Kai Bird and Martin J. Sherwin, "The Myths of Hiroshima," *Los Angeles Times*, 5 August 2005.

47 See for example: G. V. Glines, "The Bomb that Ended the War," History Net, 12 June 2006 ("for all practical purposes, the Nagasaki mission had ended the war"); David Kaiser, "Why the United States Dropped Atomic Bombs in 1945," Time.com, 25 May 2016 ("The United States, then, dropped the bombs to end the war"); "Timeline: The Road to Hiroshima," *NPR,* 5 August 2005 ("Three days later, U.S. forces detonated a second atomic bomb over Nagasaki, Japan, forcing an end to World War II"); "The Manhattan Project and the Atomic Bomb," Khan Academy ("In 1945, the United States dropped two atomic bombs on Japan, ending World War II").

48 Murray Sayle, "Did the Bomb End the War?" *New Yorker,* 31 July 1995.

49 Hasegawa, *Racing the Enemy,* 296-97.

50 Quoted in Gareth Cook, "Why Did Japan Surrender?" Boston.com, 7 August 2011.

51 Gar Alperovitz, "The War Was Won Before Hiroshima—and the Generals Who Dropped the Bomb Knew It," *The Nation,* 6 August 2015.

52 Paul Ham, *Hiroshima Nagasaki: The Real Stories of the Atomic Bombings and their Aftermath* (St. Martin's Press, 2011), 474.

53 Tristin Hopper, "Did the Atomic Bombings of Hiroshima and Nagasaki Really End the War?" *The National Post,* 4 August 2017.

54 Oliver Stone and Peter Kuznick, *The Untold History of the United States* (Gallery Books, 2012), 173.

55 Ham, *Hiroshima Nagasaki*, 386, 480.

56 Alperovitz, *The Decision to Use the Atomic Bomb*, 39.

57 History Channel, "Potsdam Conference" (www.history.com).

58 Leahy, *I Was There,* 441.

59 Ham, *Hiroshima Nagasaki,* 461.

60 Ibid., 473.

61 Ibid., 186.

62 See Walter Isaacson and Evan Thomas, *The Wise Men: Six Friends and the World They Made* (Simon & Schuster, 1986).

63 Alperovitz, *The Decision to Use the Atomic Bomb,* 627.

64 Alperovitz, *The Decision to Use the Atomic Bomb,* 419; citing Barton J. Bernstein, "The Perils and Politics of Surrender: Ending the War with Japan and Avoiding the Third Atomic Bomb," Pacific Historical Review (February 1977), 13-17, and W. F. Craven and J. L. Cate, *The Army Air Forces in World War II: Volume Five: The Pacific: Matterhorn to Nagasaki June 1944 to August 1945* (Chicago, 1953), 732-33.

Chapter 7

THE UNITED NATIONS

According to F.S. Northedge, although human weakness certainly played a role in the League of Nations' failure, the main problem was "a fatal drawback in the League system" itself—"an inconsistency between the theory of collective security and the necessities of action in the anarchical international system."[1]

1. More Proposals to Overcome Global Anarchy

This realization led many thinkers to propose the creation of an organization that would truly overcome this system.

G. Lowes Dickinson

Perhaps the best-known book of this type was G. Lowes Dickinson's 1926 book, *The International Anarchy, 1904-14,* which made the phrase "international anarchy" famous.[2] Rather than focusing on the particular causes of particular wars, Dickinson said, we need to focus on the underlying cause of all wars, which is international anarchy. It is a mistake to believe that war is inevitable, but "whenever and wherever the anarchy of armed States exists, war does become inevitable."[3]

The continuation of this conditional inevitability was no longer acceptable, Dickinson argued, because the technology of warfare had become so destructive. Although civilization had thus far survived war, "survival cannot be counted upon in the future." This was written, it should be noted, two decades prior to the invention of atomic weapons.[4] Given this analysis of the problem of war and its seriousness, Dickinson said:

> [T]he way to salvation is the development of the League of Nations into a true international organ to control, in the interests of peace, the policies of all States. . . . The legal openings left for war must be closed. . . . There must be, by consequence, a complete apparatus for the peaceable settlement of all disputes. . . . [T]here must be arrangements for an equitable distribution of important raw materials. . . . And, above all, there must be general, all-round disarmament.[5]

One major problem, of course, was that neither the emerging American empire nor the British empire, to which Dickinson belonged, wanted an "equitable distribution of important raw materials." The main purpose of imperialism is to garner the lion's share of these materials. Nevertheless, some scholars of international relations have thought that a Dickenson-type arrangement might be possible.

Frederick Schuman and Georg Schwarzenberger

In *International Politics* (1933), a very successful international relations textbook, Frederick Schuman, like Dickinson, argued that war could not be eliminated by attempts at disarmament, arbitration, adjudication, conciliation, or collective security. Schuman was a member of the school of thought known as "political realism," which emphasizes international anarchy as the underlying cause of war. Although most realists have followed Hobbes in rejecting a call for global government to overcome war, Schuman argued for overcoming "the Western state system" through the political unification of the world by means of a world federation.[6]

Another major political realist who argued this case was Georg Schwarzenberger. In a 1941 book, *Power Politics*, he said that because "[p]ower politics, international anarchy and war are inseparable," the "antidote [to war] is international government."[7] By an international government he meant a "world State," preferably of the federal type.[8]

A Widespread Consensus

Many additional illustrations could be given. But more important than the views of individual thinkers was the growth of a widespread consensus, after the outbreak of a second world war, that an organization much more powerful than the League needed to be created. In fact, said Robert Hilderbrand in his great book *Dumbarton Oaks* on the origins of the United Nations, the League was "perceived to have failed [so fully] . . . that its main role . . . was to serve as an example of what the new organization ought not to do."[9] In particular, said Northedge, "there was a general agreement that the League had failed because it lacked 'teeth' . . . . [T]he new world organisation would need to be created on vastly different lines."[10]

Creating such a vastly different organization was, moreover, widely taken to mean one that would, finally, overcome the international anarchy. In F.S. Northedge's words:

> The League was decidedly not a super-state, and it was for this reason that, in 1944, when the United Nations forces allied in defeating the Axis powers met . . . to plan a successor to the League, the idea which inspired them was that the League had failed *because* it was not a super-state, and that something like a super-state would have to be created if aggressor states as strong as Nazi Germany were going to be halted in their tracks in future.[11]

This intention to create such an organization really did exist. "As originally developed in each of the Big Four nations," wrote Hilderbrand, "the dream that led to the creation of [the United Nations] was a vision of lasting peace."[12]

While World War II was still going on, the US State Department was—as discussed in Chapter 4—involved in intense planning for the post-war world. A central part of this planning involved an idea for an organization that eventually came to be known as the United Nations Organization (now usually known simply as the United Nations, or UN). As originally conceived, it was to be an organization whose purpose was to maintain peace. This organization, since its founding in 1945, obviously has not done this.

The UN has not even had any substantive effect on US foreign policy. The United States continued to intervene in foreign countries, except that it did so more covertly (at least until recently), usually through the Central Intelligence Agency, which was also created at that time. Or else, for its large-scale interventions, the US used the UN as a cover.[13] When the United States, more recently, has been unable get UN authorization, it has simply gone ahead and done what it wanted without it.

Criticism of the UN as an ineffective organization has been common in the United States, especially so in recent years. Most of this criticism implies that the problem is rooted in the UN's personnel—that they are failing to apply the resources at their disposal effectively. The UN's ineffectiveness in maintaining peace and curtailing imperialism is rooted, however, primarily in the UN charter. It is ineffective primarily because it was intended to be so by its architects, the primary architect having been the United States itself.

To understand why the United Nations has been a failure with regard to its primary stated purpose—"to save succeeding generations from the scourge of war"[14]—and hence why structuring of the UN was a missed opportunity of tragic proportions, it is necessary to understand the main issues in the history of the discussion that led up to this event.

2. Why the United Nations Failed

The United Nations did not, of course, bring lasting peace. Indeed, wrote Northedge in 1986, "the United Nations is almost as much a lost cause [with regard to the maintenance of peace] as the League was in the late 1930s."[15] Why?

The Great Powers' Postwar Ambitions

As Hilderbrand noted, "the final plans for the [United Nations] made a stronger U.N. impossible by vitiating the strongest features of the Great Powers' original ideas."[16] And why did this change occur?

> [T]he United States, Great Britain, and the Soviet Union decided that their own, individual interests were too important to entrust to a world body, that the wartime dream of an international peacekeeping agency might interfere with their own nationalistic dreams of hegemony. . . . As the postwar period drew nearer, other concerns, especially the protection of their own sovereignty and freedom of action, seemed more important to them than permanent peace.[17]

Emphasizing the central point, Hilderbrand wrote: "At the heart of the new organization's political difficulties lay the expansive postwar ambitions of the Great powers themselves."[18] For example, the United States wanted to be able to "take over strategic islands and bases in the Pacific" while "Stalin viewed a Soviet-led Communist hegemony in Eastern Europe as his most important postwar objective."[19] In short,

> the Big Three saw the defense of their own security, the protection of their own interests, and the enjoyment of the fruits of their victory in the world war as more important than the creation of an international organization to maintain future world peace.[20]

The importance of Hilderbrand's answer cannot be exaggerated. Hilderbrand's answer means that the world since 1945 has suffered the wars in Korea, Vietnam, Nicaragua, El Salvador, the Balkans, Iraq, Syria, the ongoing deadly struggles in Israel-Palestine and beyond, and the coups and massacres in Iran, Nicaragua, Chile, Greece, and elsewhere, not because the leaders of the Great Powers discovered that maintaining peace would be impossible. It was because they, just like the princes at the time of Penn, Rousseau, and Kant, did not *want* peace badly enough to give up their "freedom of action" and their "dreams of hegemony."

One implication of Hilderbrand's answer is that most criticisms of the United Nations for its irrelevance to issues of war and peace reflect a misunderstanding about what was intended.

> [T]he U.N.'s shortcomings did not develop out of a failure of application; they were an intentional part of the plans for the world body as negotiated by the Great Powers in the summer of 1944.[21]

The UN has not been able to maintain peace because it was deliberately denied the power to do this. Hilderbrand wrote his book about the Dumbarton Oaks Conference to explain "how the wartime dream of world peace led to plans for a postwar organization lacking the authority to achieve it."[22] What happened in the summer of 1944 was the Dumbarton Oaks Conference, in which (prior to the official end of the war) the Great Powers worked out the basic ideas for the UN (which were to be taken to the 1945 meeting in San Francisco at which organization would be founded).

The Change from Dream to Reality

The writings of Penn, Rousseau, Kant, Lorimer, Oppenheim, Dickinson, Schuman, and Schwarzenberg, especially when taken together, laid out the elements needed by an organization capable of maintaining peace. It would need executive, legislative, and (mandatory) judicial power; it would need the power to tax and to maintain its own military or police force, so that the nations could disarm. In short, it would need to be a superstate. (For the superstate to have a monopoly on military power would not be an unacceptable threat, if the legislature would consist of members from all countries, if the executive power would be exercised by a prime minister, not a president, if the executive power would be rotating; see the final statement in the Epilogue). This was the original dream. However:

> [A]s the war moved toward its conclusion, the Great Powers began to wonder if they really wanted to create an organization with so much force. Might it not be employed against them?

So they moved to the idea of "creating a revitalized League of Nations that would be less threatening to the[m]."[23]

In reading Hilderbrand's book, one can see that, on issue after issue, the Great Powers deliberately did everything possible to prevent the United Nations from being anything like a superstate. With regard to the name of the organization, for example, Andrei Gromyko, negotiating for the Soviet Union, "suggested the name 'World Union,'" but this was "far too suggestive of a superstate to suit American tastes."[24]

Rejecting "a worldwide peacekeeping organization based on the equality of all states—a 'Federation of the World'—that could threaten their interests as well as their dominance," the Great Powers opted for "an organization that they could control, at least where their own vital interests were concerned."[25] An "organization that they could control" would be one without the features listed above. In particular:

1. The UN has no power to tax the citizens of the world. Rather, it relies on payments from the member states. Accordingly, if the United States, for example, does not like some UN policy, it can withhold payment until the policy is modified. This practice is, to be sure, prohibited by the UN Charter, which says that any nation seriously in arrears will lose its vote in the Assembly.

But although the United States has been seriously in arrears, it has never been thus disciplined. Without its own money, the UN has no independence from the most powerful states, especially the United States: Having by far the largest economy, the US supplied one-fourth of the UN's budget. The resulting ability of the United States to discipline the UN, rather than be disciplined by it, was articulated by Charles William Maynes, who had been the assistant secretary of state in charge of supervising US policy toward the UN during the Carter administration. The United States, said Maynes, should be a "sympathetic but tough parent . . . towards the United Nations. You don't give this dependent child everything it wants."[26]

2. The UN was not given its own police or military force. The Soviets and many analysts in Great Britain and the United States believed that the "absence of an international police force was a major reason for downfall of the league." But FDR said: "We are not thinking of a superstate with its own police forces and other paraphernalia of coercive power."[27] The UN was not even given the power to order states to provide their fair share of troops for a particular operation. Rather, no state could be forced to provide troops without its consent. The UN, accordingly, can exert only as much military force as member states are willing to provide.

A compromise idea, proposed by the Soviet Union, was for "an international air force to punish aggressor states." Such a force had attractive features: "it could respond quickly, bringing awesome force to bear against a guilty nation," and it would require relatively few personnel, thereby being less costly and allowing each state to keep most of its troops at home. But America vetoed this idea, too, partly because the Pentagon feared that even this would "pose a threat to American sovereignty and freedom of action."[28] As a result of the first two points:

3. The UN could not provide security for the various states, hence no basis for them to disarm. Unlike the League, in fact, the UN Charter did not even advocate disarmament as a goal for the future. There was also no mention of regulating either the size of armed forces or the manufacture and sale of arms.[29]

4. The UN had no power to prevent war. The main weakness that had afflicted the League—its lack of "teeth"—was addressed by the creation of the Security Council, with the power to take military action. Two fateful decisions, however, meant that the Security Council's ability to maintain peace was severely restricted. The first decision was that the Security Council would not have the authority to impose pacific settlements prior to the outbreak of hostilities. The British and the Americans both feared that giving the Council this police function "would turn the organization into something too close to an international superstate."[30]

5. The Great Powers gave themselves veto power. The second fateful decision about the Security Council involved the most contentious issue of the negotiations: the power of the veto. The paralysis of the League had been caused in large part, as we saw, by the fact that every nation had veto power. The four Great Powers involved in the founding of the UN did not repeat *this* mistake. But they also did not agree to have all Security Council decisions decided by a majority or even two-thirds of its members. Rather, *the four Great Powers made themselves (along with France)*[31] *permanent members of the Security Council, then gave the veto to all permanent members of the Security Council*—which they could use even when they were one of the parties to a dispute. Those who were against this decision pointed out that it would make the UN impotent in relation to the Great Powers, so that its enforcement could be applied only to lesser powers.[32] But the decision was made anyway—making the UN a useful instrument for Great Power imperialism.

6. There is no legislature empowered to pass laws. Proposals for a world based on law, rather than force, have always included a global legislature, which could pass laws that all nations would have to obey. However, only the Security Council, which currently has fifteen members, was given coercive power. The General

Assembly, which has representatives from all countries, cannot pass laws, only "resolutions." And these resolutions are enforced only if the Security Council decides to enforce them.

7. **The World Court was given no power.** The other major basis for a world of laws has been the idea of a world court with mandatory jurisdiction and enforced edicts. There was a strong push by many of the conferees at the 1945 meeting in San Francisco, where the final charter was worked out, to make the Security Council the executor of the court's decisions. However:

> The conferees [thereby] threatened to replace the political hegemony of the Great Powers with the legal authority of a panel of more or less independent jurists. . . . [S]uch a provision would render the veto meaningless following a court decision. . . . In addition, mandatory enforcement of court decisions would give the new organization too much of a supranational aspect, which [Great Britain, the USSR, and the USA] wished to avoid.[33]

Whatever these Great Powers wanted to avoid was avoided. The world court, accordingly, is largely impotent. Its decisions are enforced only when all of the permanent members of the Security Council want them enforced, rendering enforcement highly arbitrary.

Conclusion

Through these decisions, the United Nations was given "teeth," but *not* "the kind of teeth required to maintain permanent peace." More generally, the United Nations Organization created at San Francisco was far different from the idea originally espoused. But not because that idea was found to be impractical. Rather, to repeat Hilderbrand's conclusion:

> [T]he United States, Great Britain, and the Soviet Union decided that their own, individual interests were too important to entrust to a world body, that the wartime dream of an international peacekeeping agency might interfere with their own nationalistic dreams of hegemony... [which] seemed more important to them than permanent peace.[34]

As Hildebrand pointed out, the inscription on the mansion at Dumbarton Oaks, where the Big Three worked out the basic ideas for the UN, is *Quod severis metes*: One reaps what one sows.

Because the three Great Powers decided to retain the anarchical order, so as to be able to continue to use their power to advance their individual interests, the world reaped: (1) The Cold War; (2) a nuclear arms race that could easily have resulted in nuclear extinction, and still may; (3) dozens of hot wars, bringing unspeakable suffering in many countries, including Korea, Vietnam, Central America, Serbia, Afghanistan, Iraq, and Syria; (4) the US drive to replace global anarchy with the tyranny of a global American empire; (5) a global ecological crisis, especially global climate change, which if it continues will bring civilization to an end.

Endnotes

1 F. S. Northedge, *The League of Nations: Its Life and Times 1920-1946* (New York: Holmes and Meier, 1986), 73.

2 This according to Hedley Bull, *The Anarchical Society: A Study of Order in World Politics* (London: Macmillan, 1977), 46.

3 G. Lowes Dickinson, *The International Anarchy, 1904-14* (London: Allen and Unwin, 1926, 1937), 2, ix.

4 Ibid., 9.

5 Ibid., 493.

6 Frederick L. Schuman, *International Politics: An Introduction to the Western State System* (New York: McGraw-Hill, 1933), 642, 661-63, 828-30. Schuman continued to affirm this idea in the subsequent

editions, the 7th of which appeared in 1969, and in other books.

7 Georg Schwarzenberger, *Power Politics: An Introduction to the Study of International Relations and Post-War Planning* (London: J Cape, 1941), 430, 399.

8 Ibid., 401-04.

9 Robert C. Hilderbrand, *Dumbarton Oaks: The Origins of the United Nations and the Search for Postwar Security* (Chapel Hill: University of North Carolina Press, 1990), 1.

10 Northedge, *The League of Nations*, 279, 278.

11 Ibid., 51.

12 Hilderbrand, *Dumbarton Oaks*, ix.

13 Thomas M Campbell, in *Masquerade Peace: America's UN Policy, 1944-1945* (Tallahassee: Florida State University Press, 1973), argued that the US government's aim already in 1944 and 1945 was "to make the UN policy cover allied power politics with a Wilsonian coating palatable to the American people" and that shortly thereafter the Truman administration used "the United Nations as a mask for building an anticommunist Western entente".

14 It is important to emphasize that the focus here is on the UN's primary purpose, to prevent war, with brief attention to its secondary purpose, to protect human rights. In these areas it has largely been a failure. Some of the agencies of the United Nations, however, have done very good work.

15 Northedge, *The League of Nations*, 1.

16 Hilderbrand, *Dumbarton Oaks*, ix.

17 Ibid., x, 3.

18 Ibid., 246.

19 Ibid., 170, 215.

20 Ibid., 246.

21 Ibid., x.

22 Ibid., x.

23 Ibid., 3.

24 Ibid., 105.

25 Ibid., 3.

26 Maynes' statement, made during an interview, is quoted in Linda M. Fasulo, *Representing America* (New York: Praeger, 1984), 285; quoted in Rosemary Righter, *Utopia Lost: The United Nations and World Order* (New York: Twentieth Century Fund, 1995).

27 Hilderbrand, *Dumbarton Oaks,* 140, 65.

28 Ibid., 142-43.

29 Ibid., 161-63.

30 Ibid., 130-31.

31 Neither China nor France was really a Great Power at that time. But the United States insisted on including China among the permanent members of the Security Council. Then Britain, thinking (probably correctly) that the US motive was to give itself an automatic second vote (at that time, it was still assumed that the US-supported Nationalists would defeat the Communists), insisted on including France, believing that it (Britain) would be able to count on France to vote with it.

32 Hilderbrand, *Dumbarton Oaks*, 183-84.

33 Ibid., 119.

34 Ibid., x, 3.

| Chapter 8 |

CREATING THE COLD WAR

The United States would emerge from World War II with enormous economic and military power relative to all the other nations of the world. It would claim, and to some extent even believe, that it was wielding this power to achieve moral ends. In preparing to examine some of the record, we should recall that a point of view is moral to the degree that it approximates the perfect knowledge, benevolence, and compassion of the ideal observer.

Human beings seeking to approximate this point of view as closely as humanly possible would seek to acquire a disinterested understanding of the various relevant facts, including the perspectives of the various affected parties, and then to ask which policies would truly promote the good, and minimize the suffering, of all affected parties. Human beings could best do this by gathering information from people from all parts of the world, then basing policies on decisions made democratically by a body composed of representatives of these various peoples. In this way, the ignorance, self-centeredness, and indifference to the well-being of most other people that typically characterize the perspectives of human beings could be partially overcome.

The United Nations, with all its imperfections, provided a means by which a move in this direction could have been made. US leaders could have regularly consulted the UN General Assembly about how best to exercise its enormous postwar power. US leaders, however, assumed that they already knew, or could figure out on their own, what policies would be best for the peoples of the world—policies that also, coincidentally, would serve the interests of the American people, at least the portion that counted. US politicians, therefore, proceeded to use their vast power to reshape the world on the basis of equally vast ignorance, self-centeredness, and indifference. The destructiveness of this combination was increased by the rise of what would be called the Cold War.

The Cold War is sometimes said to have begun in 1950, sometimes 1947, and sometimes as early as 1945. One reason the date is difficult to pin down is that America's fight against socialism, Communism, and Russia actually began in 1917, after the Bolshevik Revolution, as discussed in Chapter 3. As explained in that chapter, President Woodrow Wilson said that priority must be given to "keeping Bolshevism out of the rest of Europe."[1] In 1918, in violation of the sixth of his famous "fourteen points"—that the United States would promote the "unhampered and unembarrassed opportunity for the independent determination of her [Russia's] own political development"[2]—Wilson as mentioned in Chapter 3 sent thousands of troops into northern and eastern Russia, leaving them there until 1920.[3] In 1919, Wilson's food administrator, Herbert Hoover, used a food blockade to bring down a Communist government in Hungary.[4] And at home, Wilson helped foment the Red Scare of 1919-1920 by charging that "apostles of Lenin in our own midst" were spreading "the poison of disorder, the poison of revolt."[5]

As Chapter 3 further explained, the importance of this Red Scare was incalculable because, as David Schmitz pointed out, it helped to usher in the twelve-year Harding-Coolidge-Hoover period, through which "the fear of revolution and radical thought became a fixture in American thought"—a fixture that long allowed American leaders to justify support for right-wing dictators as the lesser of evils.[6]

Opposition to Communism also provided justification for the support of Mussolini and then for putting collaborators with fascists back in power in countries such as Italy, France, and the Philippines. Moreover, even though the Soviet Union was officially an ally in the war against the Axis Powers, the United States treated it more like an enemy, excluding it from any role in Italy and Japan and denying it the anticipated war reparations.

In light of all these facts, there is no right date for the beginning of "the Cold War," if by that term one means actual political hostility. However, if by that term one means the mutual public acknowledgment of this hostility, along with the use of this mutual hostility to justify policies, we can say that the Cold War began sometime between 1945 and 1947, then became fully rationalized, at least on the American side, in 1950. This chapter looks at this period.

1. Early Steps

As we saw in Chapter 2, Washington took several actions during the first world war that can in retrospect be considered first steps toward the Cold War, especially the actions involving the employment of double standards with regard to spheres of interest. After the war, Washington took several more such steps.

It is crucial to realize that in each case, Washington initiated the hostility. The American self-image, suggested Gore Vidal, rests primarily on myths, one of which is that "the Soviets began the Cold War."[7] The record shows, however, that the Cold War was basically an American creation. One can, to be sure, still read histories of the Cold War produced by American "court historians," which continue to lay the blame at the feet of Stalin and/or Communist ideology.[8] But these accounts are contradicted by the facts.

US Atomic Policy

The Truman Administration's change of policy regarding atomic energy, which Stalin and Secretary of State James F. Byrnes had previously agreed should be put under international control, was another step in creating the Cold War. In 1946, before Dean Acheson became secretary of state, he had worked out such a plan to be proposed to the United Nations. Truman gave the task of making the presentation to Bernard Baruch, a 75-year-old multimillionaire who—considering himself far too important to be a mere "messenger boy"—demanded the right to revise the plan.

Acheson correctly predicted that these revisions, which put atomic-energy policy entirely under US control, would "almost certainly wreck any possibility of Russian acceptance." The Truman administration, however, refused to undo the damage, in spite of warnings that it had inaugurated an atomic arms race.[9] It would, in fact, use the Soviet refusal to accept the "Baruch Plan" as evidence of Communist treachery.

Turkey and the Dardenelles

Still another step in creating the Cold War was the Truman Administration's refusal to honor pledges that FDR had made to Stalin. One instance was the promise that Russia would have access to the Dardenelles, which would give Russian ships a passageway from the Black Sea to the Mediterranean. But in 1946, when Stalin put pressure on Turkey for joint control of the Dardenelles, the Truman administration encouraged Turkey to refuse and sent a giant aircraft carrier to enforce that position.[10]

2. Soviet Reparations and the Division of Germany

Another issue involved war reparations. The German invasion had destroyed Soviet industrial machinery, with the result that Stalin needed large reparations from Germany to rebuild the devastated Soviet economy. But despite the approval of reparations for Allied governments at Potsdam, and their subsequent approval for additional countries such as Greece, Israel, the Netherlands and Poland, this request was denied.

Stalin's only other solution was to get loans from America, but US officials "refused to discuss postwar aid to Russia unless the Soviets essentially opened Eastern Europe as the Atlantic Charter asked." This refusal left Stalin, as he saw it, with only one option:

> Impose such absolute control over Eastern Europe (including East Germany) that Eastern Europe would serve as a Russian-dominated buffer zone between Germany and the Soviet Union and also be forced to surrender its industry for Russia's benefit.[11]

Furthermore, although this control over East Germany, along with the Berlin Wall, have been portrayed in the West as symbols of Soviet perfidy, Carolyn Woods Eisenberg showed that "the division of Germany was fundamentally an American decision." She continued:

> The Soviet Union was strongly opposed to this development because the effect was to exclude it from the most populous, powerful, and wealthy part of the nation. . . . President Roosevelt himself had tilted U.S. directives toward a program of deindustrialization and draconian reform. This seemed to meet Stalin's economic and security requirements.[12]

But with FDR's death, America's German policy was taken over by conservatives who were "determined to rebuild postwar Germany so that it could be integrated with the capitalist economies of Europe."

The final decision was made in 1947, when an emerging economic crisis in Europe led Americans to conclude that Europe could be kept within America's economic empire only through a dramatic increase in German production, which would require massive American aid (the Marshall Plan [see below]) and freedom from Soviet constraints, both of which in turn required partition.[13] Insofar as we take the division of Germany as the beginning of the Cold War, this war was started by America in 1947.

3. Reversing Course in Japan: 1945-1950

Washington's priorities, exemplified by its behavior in Europe, were also revealed in its behavior during its post-war occupation of Japan, especially by the famous "reverse course" that occurred in 1947. Prior to this reversal, during what LaFeber called the "first occupation," American policies aimed at punishment and reform. Punishment included reparations to devastated countries and purges of individuals deemed guilty of war crimes. Reform, aimed at preventing any future outbreak of Japanese militarism, included democratizing the political system, breaking up the huge financial houses (*zaibatsu*), which had benefited from the country's militarism, and virtually disbanding the military. The watchword for this period was "democratization."

From Punishment to Economy Recovery

In 1947, Washington's plans for Japan began changing. The primary cause was the growing realization that China, long expected to provide the primary base in Asia for America's global economic plan, was not going to play this role. (Truman admitted that America, in having supported Chiang Kai-shek, had backed "the wrong horse.")[14] This role would have to be played by Japan. But Japan's economy was bankrupt. The primary concern henceforth would be to bring about Japan's economic recovery.

Washington's growing Cold War mentality, reflected in the concurrent announcement of the Truman Doctrine (see below) and the anticipation of the "loss of China," helped shape this change of course. In this context, economic recovery in Japan was seen as essential to stimulate economic recovery in East Asia as a whole, thereby immunizing it from Communism. Ironically, accordingly, America's postwar aims were to be achieved primarily through its two major wartime enemies, Germany and Japan, because the recovery of Europe and Asia, said Dean Acheson, could come about only through "those two great workshops."[15]

This change of emphasis to economic recovery was manifested in several ways. Reparations were no longer sought (as they would further weaken Japan while strengthening some of America's enemies, especially the USSR). Also, punitive measures were curtailed: there were no more purges of military men (who often were, US officials pointed out, the best businessmen); and no continued detention of war criminals.[16] There were still purges, but given the change of emphasis from democratization to economic strength, the purges were now directed against the Left, not the Right. Communist organizations were outlawed and attacked. Unions were forbidden, with about 5,500 being destroyed. Trust-busting of remaining *zaibatsu* was replaced by rebuilding those that had been dismantled.[17]

Central to the US plan to make Japan the hub of its Asian activities was the need to ensure its security from both external attack and internal subversion, and to provide the US military with bases. Washington, therefore, made its peace treaty, and hence Japan's independence, contingent upon its acceptance of an expanded police force and of numerous US naval bases, complete with "extraterritoriality" (meaning that US military personnel committing crimes, such as rape, against Japanese would not be subject to Japanese law).

Keeping Japan Open to American Interests

Although this change of course involved almost a complete change of policies, the underlying US attitude toward Japan remained the same. In LaFeber's words:

> One U.S. policy objective remained consistent: keeping Asia open to American interests while integrating the region within an open, global, capitalist framework. If that objective required opposing Japan, so be it. If the objective required rebuilding Japan and reintegrating it with Asia, so be it. Japanese culture was . . . viewed as malleable. It could be put into the service of the American worldview. Japan was less an end in itself than the means, in Washington's eyes, for

> achieving the larger regional and global purposes of U.S. foreign policy.[18]

Japan was not unique, of course, in being viewed by Washington in this purely instrumentalist way. Japan was, however, assigned unique roles in Washington's grand design. It was to provide the primary base for US military power in East Asia, along with the Philippines, and to serve as "a model and a showcase of what Asians might expect if they threw in their lot with the Americans instead of the Communists."[19]

Because of Japan's virtual absence of natural resources combined with America's desire that it no longer turn to China to make up for this lack, this second role required that the resources of the other East Asia countries remain available. America, therefore, set out to create for Japan just the kind of "co-prosperity sphere" that America had gone to war to prevent.[20] The difference was that this time Japanese economic exploitation would be exercised in line with, rather than in opposition to, US economic interests.

This US service to the economic needs of Japan—which was even more central to America's plan for Asia than Germany was to its plan for Europe[21]—would be crucial for American policy in Asia in the coming decades. A book by Michael Schaller, *The American Occupation of Japan,* was subtitled *The Origins of the Cold War in Asia.*[22]

4. Greece, the Truman Doctrine, and the Guinea Pig Experiment

Illustrating the fact that US postwar policies in Europe and Asia were closely intertwined, the reason for reversing course in Japan is closely related to America's 1947 intervention in Greece. This intervention constituted a crucial chapter in the history of American imperialism for many reasons. It provided the occasion for the Truman Doctrine, which is sometimes considered the beginning of the Cold War; it was the first clear demonstration of

American willingness to take over and continue the policies of a European imperialist power; and, by virtue of being considered a successful example of the deployment of US power to defeat a leftist movement, it achieved paradigmatic status.

A look at the character of this intervention will, therefore, be especially helpful for understanding the nature of America's postwar foreign policy, which in turn requires an understanding of the postwar British policy in Greece. This British policy involved taking sides in a longstanding battle of Greece's wealthy ruling class, which supported the king, against citizens who supported republican government and some relief for the poor.

British Policy

The tension between these sides had been intensified by the war, partly because the devastation of the war in Greece, already Europe's poorest country, put millions below the level of subsistence,[23] and partly because the monarchists, with their pro-Nazi sympathies, had collaborated with the German occupation, contributing little to the resistance.

The Greek resistance had been led by the ELAS (the People's Liberation Army) and its political wing, EAM. ELAS wrested much of the country from the Germans, and by the time British troops arrived in 1944, the Germans had departed and "EAM was running Greece with efficiency and order and the support of the majority of the population."[24] Finding this situation intolerable, Churchill claimed that EAM planned to "Bolshevize Greece," setting up "a tyrannical Communistic Government."[25] After Churchill tricked EAM's forces into disarming, the coalition of British and right-wing Greeks, including Nazi collaborators, began a reign of terror against EAM's supporters.[26]

However, although Britain had been heavily financed by America, it was unable to defeat ELAS/EAM, to which about a fourth of the population belonged. So early in 1947, Britain told the Truman administration that it was leaving Greece, asking the United States to take over the battle against ELAS/EAM.

Replacing the British Empire

The Truman administration, which had already been giving over $250 million a year in support of this imperialist effort, was more than ready to do so, because it wanted to replace the British Empire.[27] Secretary of State George Marshall famously said that the British request was tantamount to "British abdication from the Middle East with obvious implications as to their successor."[28]

In that situation, the Truman administration saw an opportunity. Although ELAS/EAM partisans were receiving support from Yugoslavia's independent Communist leader, Marshal Tito, they were not at all supported by Stalin, who was honoring his promise not to interfere in Greece. The Truman Administration decided, nevertheless, to portray the issue as a battle of "Communism vs. Democracy" in order to get money from Congress to support US economic policies in Greece and also in Turkey, where Stalin's pressure regarding the Dardenelles was the basis for claiming that he was trying to take the country over.

Communism vs. Democracy

One of Truman's assistants said: "The only way we can sell the public on our new policy is by emphasizing the necessity of holding the line: communism vs. democracy should be the major theme."[29]

Dean Acheson, then Under Secretary of State, had already developed early versions of what would come to be called—in relation to the Vietnam war (see the following chapter)—the "domino theory" and the "credibility argument." According to this version of the domino theory, if Greece fell to Communists, it would take with it "the whole Near and Middle East and northern Africa."[30] As for this version of the credibility argument, the problem was not so much "saving the Greek people" (said a State Department official) as it was "preventing Greece from becoming a Soviet base and permitting the impression . . . that the United States is lacking in resolution when faced with aggression."[31]

One might have responded, of course, that the war in Greece was a civil war, that insofar as there was external aggression it was that of the British, that the EAM forces were internal freedom fighters (most of whom were not Communists), and that, in any case, there was certainly no aggression against the United States.

It must be recalled, however, that Washington had by then defined its interests as global. So the US regarded any movement that was likely to refuse to play its assigned role in the US grand design as an aggressor, and was developing the notion that any group that refused this role was Communistic and that all Communist forces were directed by the Kremlin. Accordingly, even seemingly indigenous leftist movements could be considered external aggression. Working up a justification for this intervention involved formulating the so-called Truman Doctrine

The Truman Doctrine and the Marshall Plan

Greece has the distinction of being the country in which the United States first used the "Communist menace" to win congressional support for its global economic plan. The administration was getting nowhere with members of Congress until Acheson pulled out the domino theory. In a statement that, he later admitted, made the matter "clearer than truth,"[32] Acheson told congressional leaders that if the Communist "infection" were successful in Greece and Turkey it could spread to the Mid-East, Africa, Asia, and Europe.[33]

A convinced Senator Vandenberg told Truman that to get financial support for this program he would need "to scare hell out of the American people."[34] The president did this in a speech before Congress in which he expressed the policy that came to be called the Truman Doctrine—that the United States must "support free peoples who are resisting attempted subjugation by armed minorities or by outside pressures." Dividing the world's governments between "free" and "totalitarian," he said that Turkey and Greece, now in the first group, would fall into the second group unless Congress appropriated $400 million to aid them.[35]

The money for Greece and Turkey was merely the first phase of a more ambitious plan, which was to obtain $13 billion for European aid. The twofold purpose of this "Marshall Plan"—named for Secretary of State George Marshall—was to prevent any European countries from going Communist and to provide them with money to buy enough US goods to prevent another depression in America.

When Stalin learned of this plan, which included the thing he feared most—the reconstruction of Germany—he retreated behind what Churchill dubbed the "iron curtain" (where Stalin set up his "Molotov Plan"), cracked down in Hungary and Poland, and overthrew the Czech government. Thanks to this coup, plus a telegram from Gen. Lucius Clay (the military governor of Germany) falsely claiming that the Soviets had suddenly become warlike, Congress approved the Marshall Plan.[36]

Creating the CIA to Promote Freedom

Henry Wallace, who had been fired as Secretary of Commerce for saying that US atomic policy would lead to an atomic arms race, now pointed out that the government in Greece was not, as Truman said, merely an "imperfect democracy," but completely fascist. By supporting such governments, Wallace prophesied, the America of the Truman Doctrine would "become the most hated nation in the world."[37] As if seeking to fulfill this prophesy, the Truman Administration passed the National Security Act of 1947, which created, among other things, the Central Intelligence Agency (CIA).[38]

After the communist coup in Czechoslovakia, the CIA was authorized to conduct covert operations to carry out the Truman Doctrine's intent to promote free governments—with "free" defined, of course, by the US government. Thanks to the CIA, plus the enormous amount of money at its disposal through the Marshall Plan (about $200 billion in current dollars), US officials were able to control political events throughout western Europe, primarily by having the CIA engage in clandestine operations with the help of right-wing organizations in order to frighten people away from voting for left-wing politicians.

For example, as World War II in Europe was nearing its

end, the Nazi leaders, being anxious—in the words of Hitler's appointed successor, "to save German territory and the German race from Bolshevism"—had sought an anti-Bolshevik alliance with America and Great Britain.[39] Although no formal alliance was formed, the Allied forces did cooperate with Nazi commanders by enabling as many Germans as possible to surrender to them, rather than to the Russians.[40]

Its role in this collusion foreshadowed US government occupation policies, during which, while removing Nazi leaders (at least from all visible roles), it would also keep the Left out of power, oppose the payment of large reparations to Russia, and restore the old order, with its alliance between big business and right-wing politics.[41] In these operations, the CIA recruited Nazi war criminals, such as Klaus Barbie, because of their expertise and strong anti-Communist attitudes. This use of former Nazis was only the most shocking form of America's systematic support for fascist rather than anti-fascist forces, which demonstrated that its interventions against "Communist" governments had nothing to do with their alleged suppression of political freedom and everything to do with their economic policies.[42] Such operations in Italy, France, Turkey, and Belgium are discussed in Chapter 11.

The Guinea Pig Experiment

After the administration obtained congressional funding, it used part of it to provide Greece's military establishment with weapons, including napalm bombs, and 250 US officers, who would henceforth direct much of the war. In the ensuing three-year war, many tens of thousands of EAM's troops—once called "those gallant guerrillas" by Churchill—were killed, and with them the hope that Greece would have a democratic government devoted to the welfare of its people.[43]

The decision to intervene meant that the US Government would be supporting one of the most corrupt regimes in the world. US officials would have liked to find a strong leader who, by eliminating corruption and instituting at least minimal land and tax reforms, would win popular support. The problem, reported the

US ambassador, was that "the best men . . . are the heads of the Communist movement," so unless America was willing to "lose the country" it had to keep "trying to make bricks without straw."[44]

As would be the case in virtually every other country in which Washington took on similar tasks, it did at first genuinely try to get the Greek leaders to institute reforms, suggesting that its money was conditional on such reforms. But the Greek leaders, knowing that they were indispensable to Washington's plans, refused to make the reforms. Rather than overcoming the regressive tax, for example, the Greek upper classes "reduced their contribution to tax revenues by half," thereby increasing their "assault on the poor majority's standard of living." The United States, nevertheless, "dropped the reform effort and threw its support behind the Greek government and its wealthy supporters."[45]

This support included backing for brutal methods. As a result, although Truman assured Congress that its money would help Greece "perfect its democratic processes,"

> the Right applied the new resources to old-fashioned Greek winner-take-all politics of the most violent kind. . . . [A]nybody suspected of republican or leftist leanings was jailed or exiled. . . . [R]ightist mobs lynched suspected leftists, and home guard units murdered others to collect the official bounty for the killing of "bandits." . . . [The military] began a three year campaign of mass arrests. Thousands were banned to desolate islands and more fled to neighboring countries. . . . In short, the right took American support to eliminate or intimidate all other contenders, not to form a more perfect union.[46]

The US-backed programs also included the execution of thousands for political crimes, even labor strikes, and the forced evacuation of hundreds of thousands from the countryside.[47] By the end, rather than trying to instill moderation, US officials were encouraging their Greek mercenaries to be even more violent, with the US ambassador arguing that, because stopping the executions would "play directly into Soviet hands," the US task is "to see that nothing prevents Greeks from finishing [a] job well started."[48]

The difference between this brutal policy and proclaimed US ideals led US officials to engage in dubious justifications and outright lies. The main strategy was simple denial, with the US ambassador telling Congress that reports that people were being arrested, executed, and sent into exile were "half-truths, distortions of the truth, and down-right lies originating in the propaganda mill of the Kremlin."[49] Insofar as "excesses" were admitted, they were said to result from "a reaction against Communist terrorism rather than any real tendency toward fascism."[50]

The fact that the Greek rulers were anti-Communistic was, indeed, taken to override every other consideration. "The only question we should ask," said Acheson, "is whether they are determined to protect their independence against Communist aggression, and if they are we should recognize our basic unity with them."[51] In this "basic unity, of course, Acheson was completely right, as both governments shared a commitment to protecting plutocratic privileges over against people fighting for a decent standard of living.

This plutocratic alliance was eventually successful, with the guerrilla forces giving up at the end of 1949, with the decisive factor being the split between Stalin and Tito, which finally led Tito to withdraw support and close his borders, no longer allowing guerrillas to find sanctuary in Yugoslavia.[52] But US leaders, not considering the unique factors involved, simply celebrated their victory in what one of them called "the guinea pig experiment of Greece," taking it as evidence that the same strategy would work elsewhere.[53]

5. NSC-68: The Founding Document of the Cold War

Although the Cold War, as we have seen, began several years

before 1950, National Security Council paper 68 (known as NSC-68), which appeared that year, has been "widely recognized as the founding document of the Cold War."[54] NSC-68 was itself evoked by era-creating events: the 1949 victory of Communism in China (which seemed to put an end to the long-time US dream of an almost limitless "China market"); the explosion that same year of an atomic bomb by the USSR (which "changed everything," Acheson later remarked); and the formation early in 1950 of an alliance between China and the USSR.[55] The year 1950 also marked the beginning of US involvement in the civil war in Korea, the USA's first full-scale war billed as a war against a Communist dictatorship.

NSC-68 was primarily the work of Paul Nitze, who had replaced George Kennan as head of the State Department's policy staff. Kennan had inspired the government's policy of "containing" the Soviet Union, but now Kennan, who had never defined the Soviet threat or its containment in military terms, was seen by Acheson as insufficiently confrontational. Nitze, by contrast, defined Communism as "a new fanatic faith" that, seeking to use military force "to impose its absolute authority over the rest of the world," had to be checked by US military power.

This solution would require a massive military buildup, including the development of a "thermonuclear" bomb, which together would require the quadrupling of US military spending—from $13 to $50 billion. Nitze, a Wall Street lawyer, pointed out that this massive, heretofore unthinkable, peacetime spending would, incidentally, stimulate the slowing economy. He thereby inaugurated "military Keynesianism," upon which the US economy has relied ever since, requiring an endless supply of enemies to justify the maintenance of a huge military machine and the acquisition of ever-new weapons.

To drum up support for this massive increase in spending and hence taxes, Acheson traveled widely, giving speeches saying that America is in a "cold war" with the Soviet Union, which "has one purpose and that is world domination"—speeches that indeed "scared hell out of" at least some listeners.[56]

6. Korea

Although most references to American involvement in Korea suggest that it began in 1950, after North Korea invaded South Korea, the truth is quite different. The USA—which was responsible for the line at the 38th parallel separating "North" from "South" Korea and even for the very distinction between them—had been in control of the southern part since 1945.[57]

The background to the nature of the US involvement was the fact that Korea, which had been a Japanese colony since 1910, was divided between the vast majority of the people, who were impoverished, and a tiny minority of rich landowners. After the defeat of the Japanese, the Korean People's Republic (KPR) was organized in Seoul by leaders who favored land reform and grassroots democracy, based on "people's committees" throughout the country.[58] The key leader was a Christian, a Wilsonian democrat, and a socialist—but *not* a Communist.[59]

The Deadly Restoration of Plutocracy

The US leaders, however, regarded the KPR as a Communist, Soviet-backed government and promptly sought an alternative. General Hodge, who was in charge of the US occupation, realized that Korea was a "powder keg," because the majority of the Koreans hated the tiny, rich minority, which had collaborated with the Japanese. And he knew that the majority wanted independence immediately. However, fearing that immediate independence would lead to "the establishment of Communism," General Hodge decided to support the rich minority—which would protect foreign interests—and to continue the American occupation until, as a Truman advisor put it, "a democratic (capitalistic) form of government is assured." (Because this was a private report, the fact that the word "democratic" meant "capitalistic" could be freely stated.)[60]

Having such a government was crucial for America's economic plans for Asia, which required that the economy of Korea be structured to serve the rebuilding of Japan's industrial economy, which together with Europe was to provide markets for

America. Hodge's plan to create an anti-Communist government in South Korea involved the following steps:

- Creating an army of South Koreans to defend the 38th parallel - a task later described by a US officer as "train[ing] 100,000 guys to do the shooting for you" so as to be a "watchdog over the [American] investments placed in this country."

- Building up the Korean National Police to "pacify" the South.

- Bringing Syngman Rhee back from America to be the head of what would in 1948 become the Republic of Korea. Although Rhee had been living in the USA for almost four decades and had an Austrian wife, he had the virtues of sharing "the American point of view" and being rabidly anticommunist.[61]

The immediate result of this US decision to create an anti-Communist government out of a tiny, despised portion of the population was a civil war that, between 1945 and 1950, led to some 100,000 South Korean deaths—all this before the start of "the Korean War."[62] Furthermore, this American action between 1945 and 1950, by creating a permanent division between the northern and the southern parts—with a government in the south totally at odds with that in the north—provided the precondition for the war to come.

At this time, Acheson was working hard to provide support for the kind of massive military spending recommended by NSC-68, which would be required to fulfill the plans of the imperial brain trust. Acheson even had help from Senator Joseph McCarthy, who was creating anti-Communist hysteria in the country. Even this atmosphere, however, had not yet provided Acheson with the huge military buildup he desired.

The Korean War

But then came a godsend: Acheson received word that Communist North Korean troops had entered South Korea, initiating a war that, Acheson later said, "confirmed in our minds the correctness of the analysis of NSC 68," because it showed that "the USSR was willing to use forces in battle to achieve objectives."[63]

However, the claim about the Soviet Union was misleading. Although Kim Il Sung evidently received permission for a war to try to reunify Korea, Stalin, who had withdrawn his forces from Korea in 1948, gave the permission only reluctantly and told Kim—as he told the US government as soon as the fighting started—that Soviet troops would stay out, a pledge that he kept.[64]

But the facts were irrelevant. Although Washington had not wanted a war prior to 1950, by June of that year it did. Acheson, under severe criticism from Republicans for "losing China" by not applying the Truman Doctrine to Asia, announced that Korea would be added to those countries saved from Communism by the Democratic administration.[65]

In line with NSC-68's policy to "rollback" Communism, American forces attacked North Korea mercilessly. The really wild men—who wanted to drop dozens of atomic bombs, even on China—were restrained. (Douglas MacArthur later said: "I could have won the war in Korea in a maximum of 10 days," because "I would have dropped between 30 and 50 atomic bombs on North Korea.")[66]

But some two million people, mainly civilians, were killed by America's conventional and napalm bombs—more bombs than were dropped during the war against Japan during World War II.[67] General Curtis LeMay said: "Over a period of three years or so we killed off—what—twenty percent of the population."[68] Dean Rusk, later to become secretary of state, said that the United States bombed "every brick that was standing on top of another, everything that moved."[69] Supreme Court Justice William O. Douglas wrote: "I had seen the war-battered cities of Europe, but I had not seen devastation until I had seen Korea."[70]

Although the war finally ended in 1953 with a stalemate

at the 38th parallel, all those American and Korean deaths were not in vain, from the point of view of the US government, because what really led to the rebuilding of the Japanese economy was the demand for Japanese products that the war created. The Korean War, in fact, has been called "Japan's Marshall Plan."[71]

7. George Kennan's 1948 Statement

As indicated earlier, George Kennan was a major figure in the US government, highly respected for his wisdom. In fact, he was one of six men included in a 1986 book entitled *The Wise Men,* which was a study of the evolution of US foreign policy vis-à-vis the Soviet Union.[72] Kennan was central to shaping America's Cold War policies, as indicated by another book, *George F. Kennan and the Making of American Foreign Policy, 1947-1950.*[73] Although Kennan often wrote about dealing with foreign relations from a Christian point of view, as in his 1959 article "Foreign Policy and Christian Conscience,"[74] in 1948 he had said:

> [W]e have about 50% of the world's wealth but only 6.3% of its population. . . . In this situation, we cannot fail to be the object of envy and resentment. Our real task in the coming period is to devise a pattern of relationships which will permit us to maintain this position of disparity without positive detriment to our national security. To do so, we will have to dispense with all sentimentality and day-dreaming; and our attention will have to be concentrated everywhere on our immediate national objectives. We need not deceive ourselves that we can afford today the luxury of altruism and world-benefaction. . . . The day is not far off when we are going to have to deal in straight power concepts. The less we are then hampered by idealistic slogans, the better.[75]

It is unclear how this statement showed the influence of a Christian conscience. Perhaps this statement was satire. In any case, Kennan's statement reflected the policy that was actually followed by America during the Cold War and beyond.

Endnotes

1 David F. Schmitz, *Thank God They're On Our Side: The United States and Right-wing Dictatorships, 1921-1965* (Chapel Hill: University of North Carolina, 1999), 14.

2 Walter LaFeber, *The American Age: U.S. Foreign Policy Since 1750*, 2nd ed. (New York: Norton, 1993), 291.

3 On this intervention, see David S. Foglesong, *America's Secret War against Bolshevism: U. S. Intervention in the Russian Civil War, 1917-1920* (Chapel Hill: University of North Carolina Press, 1995).

4 LaFeber, *The American Age*, 301; Schmitz, *Thank God*, 19; see also Frank Costigliola, *Awkward Dominion: American Political, Economic, and Cultural Relations with Europe, 1919-1933* (Ithaca: Cornell University Press, 1984), 52-53.

5 LaFeber, *The American Age*, 310.

6 Schmitz, *Thank God*, 15.

7 Gore Vidal, *Dreaming War: Blood for Oil and the Cheney-Bush Junta* (New York: Thunder's Mouth/Nation Books, 2002), 75.

8 A well-known example of this genre is John Lewis Gaddis, *We Now Know: Rethinking Cold War History* (Oxford: Oxford University Press, 1997). A devastating critique of his book was provided by Melvyn P. Leffler in a review essay entitled "The Cold War: What Do 'We Now Know'?" (*American Historical Review* 104 [April 1999]: 501-24). An implicit critique of Gaddis's viewpoint was provided by Walter LaFeber in his *America, Russia, and the Cold War 1945-2006* (McGraw-Hill Education, 10th edition, 2006). One of the interesting differences between the Gaddis and LaFeber books is that the latter cites evidence.

9 Walter Isaacson and Evan Thomas, *The Wise Men: Six Friends and the World They Made: Acheson, Bohlen, Harriman, Kennan, Lovett, McCloy* (New York: Simon & Schuster, 1986), 360-61; LaFeber, *The American Age*, 447. In a speech early in 1946, Stalin, saying that socialism was better than capitalism, announced that the Soviet Union would not be opened up to world markets by cooperating with the World Bank and the IMF, which had been recommended by the

imperial brain trust and established at the famous Bretton Woods conference "to ensure an open, capitalist world." Leading US thinkers responded hysterically, calling his speech "the declaration of World War III" (LaFeber, *The American Age*, 410; Richard J. Barnet, *The Rockets' Red Glare: When America Goes to War* [New York: Simon and Schuster, 1990], 257, 260). Shortly thereafter Churchill gave his famous "iron curtain" speech, in which he said that God had willed Anglo-Saxon countries to get the atom bomb first. Stalin rejected the racist view that English-speaking people were to "decide the destinies of the entire world" (LaFeber, *The American Age*, 447).

10 LaFeber, *The American Age*, 445-46; LaFeber et al., *The American Century*, 315.

11 LaFeber et al., *The American Century*, 298.

12 See Carolyn Woods Eisenberg, *Drawing the Line: The American Decision to Divide Germany, 1944-1949* (Cambridge: Cambridge University Press, 1996), 9.

13 Ibid., 9-10.

14 LaFeber, *The Clash*, 270.

15 Ibid., 272.

16 Ibid., 272-73, 276-77.

17 Ibid., 275, 277, 279.

18 Ibid., 271.

19 Chalmers Johnson, *Blowback: The Costs and Consequences of American Empire* (New York: Henry Holt, 2000), 177.

20 Bruce Cumings, *Korea's Place in the Sun: A Modern History* (New York: Norton, 1997), 210.

21 Ibid., 210.

22 Michael Schaller, *The American Occupation of Japan: The Origins of the Cold War in Asia* (New York: Oxford University Press, 1985).

23 Gabriel Kolko, *Century of War: Politics, Conflict, and Society Since 1914* (New York: New Press, 1994), 376.

24 Kolko, *The Politics of War*, 183.

25 Ibid., 182.

26 Ibid.

27 LaFeber, *The American Age,* 452.

28 Walter LaFeber, *America, Russia, and the Cold War 1945-2006* (McGraw-Hill Education, 10th edition, 2006), 52.

29 Richard J. Barnet, *The Rockets' Red Glare: When America Goes to War* (New York: Simon and Schuster, 1990), 269.

30 Shafer, *Deadly Paradigms,* 177.

31 Ibid., 177-78.

32 Barnet, *The Rockets' Red Glare*, 261.

33 The idea that Marxist communism, with its atheism, would have appeal in the Muslim countries of North Africa and the Mid-East was, of course, unlikely, as many critics of Acheson's scenario pointed out. But "communism" was used broadly to include "radical nationalism," which was an "infection" that really might spread to those countries, leading to "the possible loss of the petroleum resources of the Middle East," in the words of a CIA study (Chomsky, *Deterring Democracy*, 55).

34 Richard M. Freeland, *The Truman Doctrine and the Origins of McCarthyism* (1972; New York: New York University Press, 1985), 89.

35 Barnet, *The Rockets' Red Glare,* 267.

36 Alex Bosworth, "Did Harry Truman Use Scare Tactics to Get the Marshall Plan Approved?" History News Network, 18 November 2004.

37 Robert A. Divine, *Foreign Policy and U. S. Presidential Elections* (New York: New Viewpoints, 1974), Vol. I: 170.

38 A more complete account would need to deal with still more institutions created at that time, including NATO, which was created (in Melvyn Leffler's words) "to integrate Western Europe and England into an orbit amenable to American leadership" (*A Preponderance of Power* [Stanford: Stanford University Press, 1992], 17).

39 Kolko, *The Politics of War*, 370, 384.

40 Ibid., 382-88.

41 Kolko, *The Politics of War*, 509, 517-20.

42 Schmitz, *Thank God,* 133, 140, 174, and Chap. 9.

43 Blum, *Killing Hope, 35;* Walter LaFeber et al., *The American Century: A History of the United States Since 1941*, 5th edition (Boston: McGraw-Hill, 1998), 318.

44 LaFeber, *America, Russia, and the Cold War*, 56.

45 Shafer, *Deadly Paradigms*, 193.

46 Ibid., 193.

47 Kolko, *Century of War,* 379-80.

48 Shafer, *Deadly Paradigms,* 194.

49 Ibid., 194.

50 Ibid., 185.

51 Ibid., 195.

52 Ibid., 199-203; Kolko, *Century of War,* 380-85.

53 This phrase was used later by Ambassador MacVeagh, after he had become disillusioned with what he considered many mistakes in this experiment (Shafer, *Deadly Paradigms,* 204). The dominant attitude, however, was that the experiment had been a great success.

54 Noam Chomsky, *Rogue States: The Rule of Force in World Affairs*

(Cambridge: South End Press, 2000), 175.

55 LaFeber, *The American Age*, 477-79.

56 Ibid., 485-86.

57 Cumings, *Korea's Place*, 186.

58 Ibid., 185, 191.

59 Ibid., 191.

60 Ibid., 190, 193, 198, 199.

61 Ibid., 194-95, 200, 255.

62 By contrast, the North Korean leader, Kim Il Sung, had been fighting the Japanese since 1932, was chosen to be the leader by fellow North Korean guerrillas (not the Soviet Union), and was not under either Soviet or Chinese control nearly to the degree that Rhee was under US control. Furthermore, although his government instituted a rigorous program of indoctrination, it did not engage in a massive slaughter of its own people (ibid., 195-96, 225, 231-32).

63 Ibid., 486.

64 Cumings, *Korea's Place*, 263-64.

65 Barnet, *The Rockets' Red Glare*, 310-12.

66 "Texts of Accounts by Lucas and Considine on Interviews with MacArthur in 1954," *New York Times,* 9 April 1964.

67 Charles K. Armstrong, "The Destruction and Reconstruction of North Korea, 1950-1960," *The Asia-Pacific Journal*, 16 March 2009.

68 Richard Rhodes, "The General and World War III," *New Yorker*, 19 June 1995.

69 Blaine Harden, "The U.S. War Crime North Korea Won't Forget," *Washington Post,* 24 March 2015.

70 Sven Lindquist, *A History of Bombing* (New Press, 2003), 128.

71 Ibid., 322.

72 Walter Isaacson and Evan Thomas, *The Wise Men: Six Friends and the World They Made* (Simon & Schuster, 1986).

73 Wilson D. Miscambel, *George F. Kennan and the Making of American Foreign Policy, 1947-1950* (Princeton University Press, 1992).

74 See "Foreign Policy and Christian Conscience," *The Atlantic Monthly*, May 1959.

75 George F. Kennan, Policy Planning Study 23 (PPS23), *Foreign Relations of the United States*, 1948. (For a helpful discussion of the so-called "Kennan Quotation," see Gilles d'Aymery, "Context and Accuracy: George F. Kennan's Famous 'Quotation'" [Swans Commentary, 28 March 2005].)

| Chapter 9 |

AMERICAN IMPERIALISM DURING THE COLD WAR

1. The Philippine Neo-Colony: Finding the First Magsaysay

By the end of 1945, after the war with Japan was over, the US Army was training and equipping a Filipino force of 50,000, which an Army spokesman candidly said was "essential for the maintenance of internal order, not for external difficulties at all." It was, in other words, directed at the Huks (discussed in Chapter 4). Although, as an Army report later admitted, the Huks' movement resulted from "peasant grievances, not Leninist designs," it was seen as a threat to, in William Blum's words, "the neo-colonial condition of the Philippines."[1]

Because there was no intention on the part of Washington and its client state to accommodate the concerns of the Huks politically, the solution to the threat they posed had to be military force.

The Huks themselves tried at first to challenge the US-backed plutocracy in the Philippines by means of the political process. Having disarmed after the war, the Huks took part in the national elections in 1946 as part of a "Democratic Alliance" of peasant political groups, and ten Alliance candidates, including the Huks' leader, Luis Taruc, won seats in the House and the Senate.

Their election, however, meant almost certain defeat of the Philippine-US Trade Act, passage of which the US government had made a last-minute condition of the long-promised $620 million to rehabilitate the islands from war-related destruction.[2] The United States was at last granting formal independence to the Philippines, and the purpose of the Trade Act was, as one US Senator put it critically, "to keep the Philippines economically even though we lose them politically."[3] The "parity" provision of the Trade Act would give American citizens the same economic rights as Filipinos, so that US-owned companies had full access to all natural resources.

Knowing that Taruc and the other Alliance senators and representatives would vote against the Trade Act, President Roxas, in violation of the nation's constitution, denied them their seats.[4] As a result, the Trade Act passed. This passage meant that when formal independence was received two days later, "the Philippines went from colony to neo-colony," with American domination of the country becoming, in fact, even greater.[5]

Besides excluding the former Huks from the political process, Roxas then began a reign of terror against them, leading Taruc and others again to take up arms, now under the name of the People's Liberation Army. In the ensuing conflict, the government forces had no lack of troops, training, or weaponry; all these were guaranteed by American taxpayers in connection with the Military Bases Agreement of 1947. But the Huks grew ever stronger, thanks to their positive program for peasants combined with the brutality and indifference of the government—which had, among other things, made the tax system even more regressive.[6]

By 1950, official Washington documents were declaring the need "to remove the Huk threat without delay."[7] Lying behind Washington's heightened concern was the intensified Cold War mentality following the "loss of China" and the outbreak of the war in Korea.[8] There was plenty of evidence, if anyone had been interested, that the Huks, besides not being supported by either Moscow or Peking, were also not dominated by Communist ideology or even anti-imperialism. They merely wanted participation in the political process, some agrarian reform, economic relief for peasants, and an end to the violence against them.[9] Even an analysis by the US National Security Council recognized that the problem resulted from "the wealthy propertied class [which has] failed to appreciate the need for reform [to help] the less prosperous and more numerous groups."[10]

Washington officials decided, nevertheless, that "the situation in the Philippines cannot be viewed as a local problem," because a Huk victory would mean "Soviet domination of these islands." This would in turn, these officials argued, lead to Communist domination of many other countries, so America must help the "wealthy propertied class" defeat the peasant-based Huk movement.[11]

The primary impediment to this defeat, Washington believed, was the new president, Elpido Quirino. Besides being hopelessly corrupt, he was also unwilling to carry out even minimal reforms, so he would never win the peasants over.[12] The main "lesson to be learned from the China debacle," suggested US Secretary of State Acheson, "is that if we are confronted with an inadequate vehicle, it should be discarded or immobilized in favor of a more propitious one."[13]

Coincidentally, such a vehicle, Ramón Magsaysay, had recently offered himself to Colonel Edward Lansdale, then working on covert operations for the Office of Policy Coordination, soon to be absorbed into the CIA. It was agreed that, if Magsaysay would act as America's surrogate, Washington would provide covert support for his political career. Quirino was then induced, by the offer of a huge increase in military assistance, to make Magsaysay Secretary of National Defense, which put him in charge of battling the Huks. The CIA sent Lansdale to be Magsaysay's coach.[14]

They were a formidable team. Lansdale, a former advertising man who was already familiar with the Filipino people, undertook a massive campaign of propaganda and psychological warfare. Through millions of flyers, thousands of meetings, and various dirty tricks, he portrayed the Huks as dangerous terrorists and Magsaysay as an honest, courageous reformer.

Magsaysay, for his part, was an easy product to sell. Besides being honest and unsullied by collaboration, he was a charismatic speaker with a man-of-the-people style. Through these characteristics and a few modest reforms—such as some "land for the landless" and a halt to the abuse against peasants—he was able to win the trust of the people.[15] Also, besides doubling the size of the army, he improved both efficiency and morale by purging incompetence and rewarding achievement.[16] Through these various means, combined with several weaknesses in the Huks' situation and leadership, they lost their mass base and were heavily demoralized by 1952.[17]

On the basis of this success, Magsaysay ran for president in 1953. With lots of help from the US press, which considered Magsaysay "America's boy," and plenty of illegal contributions from US business interests,[18] Lansdale engineered for Magsaysay an overwhelming victory, earning him the name "Colonel Landslide."[19]

By 1954, Taruc surrendered and the Huk rebellion was officially over. In 1957, in a most ironic development, the Huks were outlawed on the grounds that they aimed at placing the government "under the control and domination of an alien power."[20] From Washington's point of view, of course, America itself was not an alien power but the rightful ruler of the Philippines.

In any case, one US official, describing Magsaysay's tactics before becoming president, concluded: "He wasn't able to accomplish the social reforms, but [the peasants] believed that he would. And that defeated the Hukbalahaps."[21] After becoming president, Magsaysay still did not accomplish any significant reforms, partly because he could not have done so even if he had tried, given the plutocratic oligarchy, and partly because, with the Huks defeated, his US sponsors were no longer concerned.[22] By 1954, Washington was preoccupied with threats to its empire in other places, including Vietnam, where Lansdale had been sent with instructions to find "a Vietnamese Magsaysay."[23] Magsaysay himself died in a plane crash in 1957. A year later, a new CIA agent assigned to Manila was told: "Find another Magsaysay."[24]

By 1965, however, the country's plutocratic structure produced the presidency of Ferdinand Marcos.[25] Although he suspended the constitution, ruled by martial law, and headed one of the most corrupt governments in world history, Marcos was given complete support by a series of American administrations. These administrations were anxious to maintain US military bases in the Philippines, which were heavily used for the operations in Vietnam, Laos, and Cambodia (this being another illustration of the centrality of military bases in the American empire). These administrations saw Marcos as the best barrier to a Communist takeover, which would surely have meant that the Americans would have been asked to leave.[26]

In 1968, Marcos' chief opponent, Senator Benigno "Ninoy" Aquino - who would later be assassinated by Marcos - described the Philippines as a land where freedom is "a reality for the minority and an illusion for the many," a land "consecrated to democracy but run by an entrenched plutocracy."[27] In 1983, shortly before he was assassinated, Aquino admitted that even if he succeeded in wresting the presidency from Marcos, he would not be able to bring about any real change. The presidency of his widow, Corazon (Cory) Aquino, who displaced Marcos in 1986, bore out this prediction.

Until 2016, after a full century of US colonialism and neo-colonialism, things remained essentially the same in what the *New York Times* once called "democracy's showcase in Asia."[28] This description inadvertently expressed the truth about the plutocratic type of democracy America had been imposing on countries around the world—when, that is, it supported democracy of *any* kind.[29]

In 2016, something new happened. The new president, Rodrigo Duterte, expressed anti-American views, saying in particular that he wanted to have a foreign policy independent from Washington. He made clear that he has deep resentments, feeling that the Philippines has been insulted by America.[30]

2 Iran: Creating Lasting Hatred

BP is one of the world's largest oil-and-gas companies. In 2010, it became notorious for being responsible for the *Deepwater Horizon* oil spill, the largest-ever accidental release of oil in marine waters. This release resulted in severe environmental and economic consequences, for which BP was heavily fined. But BP, was earlier responsible for an event with even more disastrous consequences.

In the 1940s, BP was known as the Anglo-Iranian Oil Company, but it was entirely owned by Great Britain. It was exploiting Iran terribly and keeping it in poverty, giving Iran only 16 percent of the profits, even though the going rate was 50 percent.[31] After Britain refused to negotiate, the Iranians in 1951 nationalized the company. This move was led in the parliament by Mohammad Mossadegh, who was elected prime minister. Defending Iran's decision to the UN Security Council, Mossadegh said:

> My countryman lack the bare necessities of existence. Their standard of living is probably one of the lowest in the world. Our greatest natural asset is oil. This should be the source of work and food for the population of Iran. . . . [T]he revenue from it should go to improve our conditions of life. As now organized, however, the petroleum industry has contributed practically nothing to the well-being of the people. . . . The oil resources of Iran, like its rivers, its rivers and mountains, are the property of the people of Iran. They alone have the authority to decide what shall be done with it, by whom and how.[32]

Mossadegh's statement was made in response to the British spokesman, who had said that the oil beneath Iran's soil was "clearly the property of the Anglo-Imperial Company."[33] This attitude was expressed by the British Chancellor of the Exchequer, who said that Mossadegh failed to recognize the fact that "our own economic viability was at stake, which was much more important than Persia's."[34]

The UN Security Council rejected the British claim. In response, although the British government was given a generous settlement, it organized, with American support, an economic blockade, which plunged the already impoverished country into destitution. Although Mossadegh offered Britain generous compensation, British leaders in late 1952 approached the CIA about organizing a coup. They knew that President Truman would not support such a plan, but they believed that the incoming Eisenhower administration would be amenable. They were right.

The Eisenhower administration had many reasons to desire regime change. Iran's nationalization of a foreign oil company, if allowed to stand, might inspire similar seizures elsewhere.[35] Also, if there were a friendly government in Tehran, Iran could be used for surveillance of the Soviet Union and otherwise protecting US interests in the Gulf region.[36] Furthermore, Eisenhower's secretary of state, John Foster Dulles, and his brother, Allen Dulles, the new director of the CIA, had both previously worked for the law firm representing Standard Oil of New Jersey, which would certainly get a big share resulting from a coup to take over the oil company.[37]

Finally, although Mossadegh was not a Communist, the claim had been made that he was, and the Eisenhower administration had swept into office by charging the Democrats with having lost both China and Korea to the Communists. In addition, the Dulles brothers were strongly anti-Communist.[38]

This issue was crucial. A British intelligence agent sold the Dulles brothers on the coup by telling them that Mossadegh was a Communist, who would lead Iran to Communism. This claim was totally false: Mossadegh was a convinced democrat, who did not allow Communists in his government.[39] Nevertheless, the Dulles brothers argued that America needed to overthrow Mossadegh to prevent Iran from embracing Communism.

To organize the coup, the Dulles brothers chose Kermit

Roosevelt, a grandson of President Theodore Roosevelt. The idea that the CIA would orchestrate such a coup was opposed by several members of the CIA, especially Roger Goiran, who was the chief of the CIA station in Tehran. He said that if such a coup was carried out, Iranians would forever view the United States as a supporter of "Anglo-French imperialism." Allen Dulles fired Goiran and ordered the coup to go ahead.[40]

Roosevelt planned the coup along with former Nazi collaborator General Zahedi and the young shah of Iran. Roosevelt convinced the shah to join the coup by telling him that, if Mossadegh were left in power, he would lead Iran to Communism.[41] Roosevelt's coup plan, dubbed Operation Ajax, had many lines of attack.

- First, a campaign in the streets, the mosques, and the press would undermine Mossadegh's popularity, as he would be portrayed as corrupt, pro-Communist, and anti-Islam.

- Second, thugs would be paid to launch staged attacks on religious leaders, making them appear to be ordered by Mossadegh.

- Third, General Zahedi would bribe military officers to be ready to help with the coup.

- Fourth, money was also used to bribe members of the parliament.

- Fifth, on "coup day," thousands of paid demonstrators were paid to stage a massive anti-government rally, and the bribed members of parliament would arrange a vote to demand Mossadegh's resignation.

- Sixth, army units under Zahedi's control would arrest Mossadegh and take charge of command posts, police and radio stations, and the national bank.

- Seventh, General Zahedi would accept the shah's nomination to be the prime minister.[42]

Although the US-backed ouster of Mossadegh was bitterly denounced by the people of Iran, the young shah gave thanks to Allah and the CIA[43]—as presumably did Standard Oil, which started receiving 40 percent of Iran's oil profits. In spite of having earlier pointed out that Mossadegh had "acquired a reputation as an honest patriot,"[44] the *New York Times* declared that his ouster would be a good learning experience:

> Underdeveloped countries with rich resources now have an object lesson in the heavy cost that must be paid by one of their number which goes berserk with fanatical nationalism.[45]

"Fanatical nationalism" was, of course, the idea that a country's resources should benefit its own people, rather than the corporations of America and its allies. This object lesson exemplifies the way in which the US government has, like Rome and other empires, used terror to intimidate.

The after-effects of this object lesson were even more deadly. Although Allen Dulles declared that Iran had been saved from a "Communist-dominated regime,"[46] democratic freedom was not to be the result. The coup gave Mohammad Reza Shah the opportunity to become a dictator, as the CIA gave him over $1 billion a year, with which he bought weaponry and crushed dissent by whatever means necessary. The shah's regime instituted, in the words of Amnesty International, "a history of torture which is beyond belief."[47] This torture was the work of the shah's secret police, SAVAK, which was trained by Norman Schwartzkopf (the father of the man who was to lead US forces in the first Bush administration's attack on Iraq, discussed later).[48]

For saddling the Iranian people with this regime and stealing their one source of wealth, America earned their long-term hatred, which was manifested when the shah was replaced in 1979 by the rabidly anti-American government headed by Ayatollah Khomeini, which allowed students to take over the American embassy in Tehran and hold its diplomats hostage. One of the militant students explained later that the hostage-taking was a delayed reaction to Operation Ajax.[49]

Prior to Operation Ajax, Iranians admired America, liking it much better than both Britain and the Soviet Union.[50] But America's Operation Ajax began a series of events that led to a state of permanent hatred between these two countries.

Interestingly, Eisenhower had asked why it was not possible "to get some of the people in these down-trodden countries to like us instead of hating us."[51] He answered his own question when he OK'd the plan of the Dulles brothers to overthrow Iran's beloved leader, Mohammad Mossadegh. This episode, Kinzer pointed out, had another effect:

> Operation Ajax taught tyrants and aspiring tyrants there that the world's most powerful governments were willing to tolerate limitless oppression as long as oppressive regimes were friendly to the West and Western oil companies.[52]

A final observation: Kermit Roosevelt warned the CIA that its success in Iran should not be taken as evidence that it could overthrow governments at will. "The Dulles Brothers, however, took it to mean exactly that," observed Kinzer. "They were already plotting to strike against the left-leaning regime in Guatemala."[53]

3. Guatemala: Deterring the Threat of a Good Example

Insofar as America has acknowledged that it is imperialistic, it has portrayed its imperialism as benign because, although it pursues its own self-interests, it does so by promoting the growth of democratic governments around the world. Given the standard definition, which speaks of governments that are freely elected (without outside influence), reflect the interests of the majority, and protect human rights, American influence has generally been used for—to use the title of one of Noam Chomsky's books—"deterring democracy."[54]

This fact has nowhere been more clearly illustrated than in Guatemala, where the Eisenhower administration in 1954 overthrew what author Piero Gleijeses called "the first truly democratic government in Guatemala's history" and "the best government it has ever had." The United States thereby returned Guatemala, for the remainder of the century and beyond, to the condition that has led it to be called "the land of eternal tyranny."[55]

In doing so, the Eisenhower administration also destroyed the man most responsible for the ten years of democracy that Guatemala enjoyed from 1945 to 1954, Jacobo Arbenz. Strangely, the Guatemalan side of this story revolves around four men whose names began with "Ar": Arévalo, Arana, Armas, and Arbenz himself. The decisive factor, however, would be a fifth "Ar": the Army.

Once the center of Mayan civilization, Guatemala, having none of the resources that interested Spain, had become a neglected, impoverished country during the three centuries of Spanish rule. At the end of the 19th century, however, the rising demand for coffee provided a source of riches. The indigenous Mayan peoples were, accordingly, further dispossessed of land and forced to provide inexpensive labor for the large landholders.[56] When the market for coffee collapsed during the global financial crisis of 1929, it caused further unrest among the native population. In response, Guatemala's wealthy class, wanting a "strong leader" to thwart any challenge to its interests, selected Jorge Ubico, who modeled himself on Napoleon, Franco, and Mussolini. Living up to his "reputation for efficiency and cruelty" during his 13-year dictatorship, he legalized the murder of Mayans by landowners, crushed labor unions, and had spies and secret police everywhere, creating a society of fear.[57]

Although hated by the masses, Ubico was appreciated by the Guatemalan upper class—and also by the US government and corporations, to which he was deferential. He was especially generous to the biggest US enterprise, the United Fruit Company (UFCO), to which he gave free land and a free hand.[58] Although Washington's support had been unstinting, FDR's administration finally, in response to a student-led uprising, encouraged Ubico to resign, confident that he would be replaced by another deferential leader.[59] And this is what would have happened, had it not been for a young army captain, Jacobo Arbenz.

Having no money to attend the university, Arbenz had won a scholarship to the military academy, where he had excelled, first as a student and then as an officer. But he was an unusual officer, one "whose concern for the future of his country was intense," one who told his future wife, "I would like to be a reformer."[60] The occasion for embarking on this course was provided by General Federico Ponce, who, after Ubico's resignation, brought his troops to the Guatemalan Congress, thereby "persuading" it to make him president.

Furious, Arbenz resigned from the army in protest and then led a victorious battle against Ponce's forces. Although the other soldier most responsible for the victory, Francisco Arana, wanted to set up a military government, Arbenz insisted that they prepare for free elections and thereby civilian rule. The elections, Arbenz told his wife, "will be completely free. Therefore, Arévalo will win [and] we will have written a brilliant and patriotic page in our history."[61]

He was referring to Juan José Arévalo, who became president after "the revolution of 1944," which had begun with the student-led revolt against Ubico. Given Arévalo's Ph.D. in education and his emphasis on spiritual matters—he called himself, in opposition to the materialist concerns of the Marxists, a "spiritual socialist"—he seemed safe enough to the upper classes and US businesses.

And he *was*, being firmly committed to capitalism. He did, to be sure, introduce some significant reforms, allowing workers the right to unionize and permitting the passage of a Labor Code. Believing in political freedom, he even tolerated Communists, although he did not legalize their party. But he did not touch the biggest issue, the fact that 2 percent of the landowners owned 72 percent of the land, while most of the rest were crowded onto parcels too small to feed a family.[62] He also did not change the country's extremely regressive tax code, which, among other things, allowed US corporations to pay little.[63]

In spite of the moderate nature of Arévalo's reforms, however, the upper classes and American corporations--which were outraged by any deviation from the conditions they had enjoyed under Ubico--protested, with UFCO (the United Fruit Company) complaining to Washington that it was being "persecuted" and that Arévalo was a Communist.[64] Although the Truman administration spent much time debating whether Arévalo was, in fact, a Communist, it decided that there was no basis to take action.[65]

But Arana, now the chief of the armed forces, precipitated a crisis. Having been encouraged by the landed elite to stage a coup, he gave Arévalo an ultimatum: either be deposed or else replace his ministers with those chosen by Arana. Instead of accepting the ultimatum, Arévalo simply had Arana dismissed, then ordered Arbenz, who was the minister of defense, to have him arrested. When Arana resisted arrest, he was killed by Arbenz's men in a shootout.[66] Upon hearing of Arana's death, his supporters revolted but were defeated by the loyalist forces, skillfully led by Arbenz.[67]

Arbenz, with his prestige reinforced—he had saved democracy again—won a landslide victory in the next presidential elections, in spite of being opposed by the landed elite.[68] The only other challenge was an inept coup attempted by one of Arana's former officers, Castillo Armas, who was captured but later escaped from prison, thereby becoming available as an American tool.[69] In any case, Arbenz, taking office in March of 1951, quickly articulated the moral vision behind the reforms he envisaged:

> I grant great importance to economic policy, but only as a means to achieve our social goals. All the riches of Guatemala are not as important as the life, the freedom, the dignity, the health and the happiness of the most humble of its people.

> How wrong we would be if—mistaking the means for the end—we were to set financial stability and economic growth as the supreme goals of our policy, sacrificing to them the well being of our masses. . . . Our task is to work together in order to produce more wealth. . . . But we must distribute these riches so that those who have less—and they are the immense majority—benefit more, while those who have more—and they are so few—also benefit, but to a lesser extent. How could it be otherwise, given the poverty, the poor health, and the lack of education of our people.[70]

Although this statement was unsettling to the landed elite and US companies, it was generally dismissed as mere rhetoric, especially because nothing changed during the next year. Arbenz, however, was working quietly but intensely with his advisers on an integrated plan to carry out his redistributive vision, at the center of which was agrarian reform.[71]

Presented to a stunned Congress in April of 1952, Decree 900 was approved in June, with implementation beginning in January of 1953—the month the Eisenhower administration came to power.[72] Although it was a moderate program, expropriating only uncultivated land from larger estates, it was extremely successful, being implemented with little violence, resulting in an immediate increase in production (rather than a temporary decrease, as in most such programs), and helping a large percent of Guatemala's people.[73] Arbenz, Piero Gleijeses pointed out, had "accomplished a unique feat: the first true agrarian reform of Central America. . . . For the first time since the Spanish conquest, the government returned land to the Indians."[74] The landed elite, UFCO, and the US government, however, had different perspectives.

Although UFCO was duly paid for expropriated land, it claimed that the amount was far too little. The problem resulted from the fact that Decree 900 stipulated that the amount paid for expropriated land would reflect the value that had been declared by the owners for tax purposes. UFCO had been declaring that the land was worth only $1 million, but it now claimed that the expropriated land was really worth $19 million. Although UFCO thereby admitted that it had been grossly undervaluing its land to keep its taxes down, the US State Department endorsed its claim of unjust treatment.[75]

The Eisenhower administration, having had the CIA overthrow the government of Iran in 1953, decided to have a repeat performance in Guatemala. Contrary to most previous accounts, however, the fact that the Eisenhower administration was closely connected with UFCO was probably not a primary reason in this decision. Far more important was the very fact that the agrarian reform *was* successful. It was a classic case of "the threat of a good example." As a letter to the assistant secretary of state for inter-American affairs put it:

> Guatemala has become an increasing threat to the stability of Honduras and El Salvador. Its agrarian reform is a powerful propaganda weapon; its broad social program of aiding the workers and peasants in a victorious struggle against the upper classes and large foreign enterprises has a strong appeal to the populations of Central American neighbors where similar conditions prevail.

American leaders did not, of course, use this reason in their public discussions. The *expressed* concern was that Arbenz's government constituted a "Soviet beachhead" in Central America.[76] This, however, was not true.

It *is* true, contrary to some accounts, that Arbenz had become a Communist and had Communist friends, who served as his "kitchen cabinet," helping him formulate the plan for agrarian reform. But Arbenz had become a convinced Communist through reading Marx, finding that the Marxian analysis illuminated the situation of Guatemala, and also through the fact that the Communist intellectuals in Guatemala were hard working, dedicated, incorruptible people who were, like Arbenz, genuinely concerned to help their country, especially the poor.[77] There was no connection to the Soviet Union whatsoever; the two countries did not even have diplomatic relations.[78]

Even if there had been, this would have provided no justification for the United States to overthrow a duly elected government.[79] After all, the US government was busy establishing "beachheads" all around the Soviet Union. The claim that it had a right to do this while the Soviets had no right to assist governments in the Western Hemisphere was just one more example of American double standards. But this parallel need not even be raised in this case, because there was no Soviet connection in Guatemala.

Given Washington's mindset, however the mere fact that Arbenz was a Marxist, combined with the fact that he was in the process of carrying out successful and popular land reform-thereby establishing a precedent that people in neighboring countries might want to duplicate—was sufficient for Washington to set in motion a plan to get rid of Arbenz.[80]

Although much has been made in some accounts of razzle-dazzle orchestrated by the CIA, the coup was successful simply because the United States bribed, persuaded, and intimidated the Guatemalan army. Hence, when Castillo Armas led a little band of soldiers across the border from Honduras, he was victorious not because of CIA tricks, as some accounts have claimed, but only because the Guatemalan army had decided not to fight. They had been told that Armas' army was simply a proxy for the Americans, so that if it was defeated, the US military would invade the country in full force.[81] This intimidation worked. Arbenz was forced from office due to this threat from the United States. Secretary of State John Foster Dulles, of course, gave the American people a different interpretation, saying that the "people of Guatemala have now been heard from."[82]

As a result of the puppet subsequently installed by US officials, land reform was scuttled, labor unions were outlawed, labor organizers were killed, and political parties and opposition newspapers were banned.[83] Longer term, the US overthrow of Guatemala's fledgling democracy resulted in decades of state terror, much of it carried out by death squads. It also resulted in widespread poverty, with some 20,000 people, mainly children, dying of hunger each year, and many other children avoiding this fate only through prostitution.[84]

This condition continued. According to a 2014 report: "Guatemala suffers from a level of inequality and widespread poverty that is extreme even within Latin America. According to the World Bank's Guatemala Poverty Assessment, many developing countries are poor, multi-ethnic, and overwhelmingly rural. Yet Guatemala stands out for the magnitude of these characteristics."[85]

Beginning in 1944, the "land of eternal tyranny" had experienced ten years of hope. But American foreign policy was committed, as suggested by the title of a book by William Blum, to *Killing Hope*. Accordingly, the hope of the Guatemalans became, as the title of the book by Piero Gleijeses put it, *Shattered Hope*. In Eisenhower's memoirs, nevertheless, the overthrow of Arbenz was listed as one of his proudest accomplishments.[86]

In removing Arbenz, Eisenhower was acting in harmony with the recommendation of his treasury secretary, George Humphrey, who advised fellow members of the National Security Council that they should "stop talking so much about democracy" and instead "support dictatorships of the right if their policies are pro-American." Speaking in agreement, Eisenhower said: "They're OK if they are *our* s.o.b.'s." Alfred McCoy commented: "The president had just articulated, with crystalline clarity, the system of global dominion that Washington would implement for the next fifty years."[87]

4. Cuba: Creating a Communist Neighbor

Known as the July 26 Movement because its first major attack occurred on July 26, 1953, Fidel Castro's campaign to overthrow the US-supported regime of Fulgencio Batista had gained substantial backing by 1958. By January 1, 1959, the July 26 Movement took control. Had Eisenhower and Dulles considered this movement even remotely Communist, they would have eliminated it long before this. And their assessment was correct. Castro was a middle-class lawyer; he was not strongly anti-American; he desired foreign investment and US aid; and his Movement had no relations, except one of mutual hostility, with Cuba's Communist Party. Shortly after coming to power, he even suggested at an OAS meeting that the USA provide a $30 billion, ten-year package to Latin America to overcome social conditions that could bring Communists to power.[88]

Castro did, however, speak critically of the 60 years of American control, of the resulting impoverishment of the Cuban masses, and of the military presence at Guantánamo, and he declared that Cuba would henceforth be neutral in the Cold War.[89] It was this neutralist nationalism that was crucial, because if it were emulated by other countries, the status of the United States as the de facto ruler of the non-Communist world would be threatened. "A defection by any significant number of Latin American countries to the ranks of neutralism," a NSC paper had declared in February, "would seriously impair the ability of the United States to exercise effective leadership of the Free World."[90] Compared with a Communist government, in fact, a neutralist nationalistic government was far more dangerous, because it would probably be more influential. It would also be more difficult to overthrow without severe criticism.[91]

Washington's ire was increased when Castro introduced a land reform law. Although it was rather mild, it did affect US business interests. Washington took retaliatory action in October of 1959, not only blocking a sale of jet fighters from Britain but also beginning a series of bombing and strafing attacks on Cuba.[92] This twofold action, from which Castro concluded that Washington would soon try to overthrow his government, led him to turn to Moscow to purchase arms.[93]

Castro was right about US intentions. Allen Dulles, director of the CIA, had begun planning for an invasion, and by March of 1960 Eisenhower had approved Dulles' covert plan to "bring about the replacement of the Castro regime with one more devoted to the true interests of the Cuban people and more acceptable to the U.S."—but, of course, "in such a manner as to avoid any appearance of U.S. intervention."[94] The CIA began training Cuban exiles, composed largely of former supporters of Batista, and even hired a mobster to assassinate Castro.[95]

Washington's hostility increased when Castro nationalized the sugar industry and then the American oil companies—after they had refused to refine Soviet oil.[96] Washington's imposition of an embargo drove Cuba into even greater dependence on the Soviets.. Given that America had during the previous 60 years structured Cuba's economy to be almost totally dependent on its own, this embargo was devastating.

When John Fitzgerald Kennedy (JFK) became president in 1961, he inherited the CIA's invasion plan. Holding a similar view of the problem posed by Castro, he approved the invasion in April, which later became known as the Bay of Pigs debacle. Although the Kennedy men hoped to repeat the 1954 overthrow of Arbenz in Guatemala, Castro's military, unlike Arbenz's, remained loyal to him.[97] The invasion was a complete failure except in one respect: It forced Castro to become even more dependent on the Soviet Union. That same month, furthermore, Castro for the first time proclaimed the Cuban revolution to be socialist. A few months later, an alliance between Castroism and the Communist Party was formed, and that December Castro announced his acceptance of Marxism-Leninism.[98]

This allowed the US war against Castro—which involved not only a continuation of the economic embargo but also a continuing series of attacks aimed at further destroying the Cuban economy—to be justified as an attempt to rid the hemisphere of a Communist dictatorship. Most Americans, nevertheless, had little knowledge of this war, which was called the "dirtiest, most secret war in American history."[99] And to this day few Americans know that Castro was deliberately pushed into association with the Soviet Union and the Communist Party by the United States itself.

In any case, Cuba's dependence upon the Soviet Union and its fear of another American invasion, combined with Washington's hostility to Cuba, communism, and the Soviet Union, would lead to the missile crisis of 1962. From the Cuban point of view, the missiles provided by the USSR were necessary to deter another US invasion. From the point of view of the Soviet leaders, the missiles in Cuba were parallel to the American missiles in Turkey and Western Europe pointed at the USSR. In the words of Premier Nikita Khrushchev,

> the United States had no moral or legal quarrel with us. We hadn't given the Cubans anything more than the Americans were giving to their allies. We had the same rights. . . . Our conduct in the international arena was governed by the same rules and limits.

Khrushchev failed to realize, however, that America's moral superiority gave it special rights. As *Time* magazine explained, anyone who accepted Khrushchev's argument was suffering from "intellectual and moral confusion":

> The purpose of the U.S. bases [in Turkey] was not to blackmail Russia but to strengthen the defense system of NATO, which had been created as a safeguard against Russian aggression. . . . [Also] there is an enormous moral difference between U.S. and Russian objectives. . . . The U.S. bases, such as those in Turkey, have helped keep the peace since World War II, while the Russian bases in Cuba threatened to upset the peace. The Russian bases were intended to further conquest and domination, while U.S. bases were erected to preserve freedom. The difference should have been obvious to all.[100]

As with many statements justifying America's double standards, it is hard to tell whether this one was written with tongue in cheek.

In any case, the propaganda advantage provided by Castro's open embrace of Marxist-Leninism was great, given the true significance of the "Cuban threat." This threat, JFK was told by a team he had appointed to evaluate Latin America, is "the spread of the Castro idea of taking matters into one's own hands." This idea has great appeal, they reported, because "the distribution of land and other forms of national wealth greatly favors the propertied classes." That by itself was not a problem, of course, but only the fact that "the poor and underprivileged, stimulated by the example of the Cuban revolution, are now demanding opportunities for a decent living."[101]

Given Washington's concept of "national security," according to which it is threatened unless the whole world, and especially the whole Western Hemisphere, follows US leadership, Cuba was a threat to US national security. As a US diplomat to Mexico pointed out, however, "If we publicly declare that Cuba is a threat to our security, forty million Mexicans will die laughing."[102]

But now American leaders did not have to make this ludicrous claim. Having forced Castro into embracing Marxism and the USSR, US leaders could portray themselves as nobly standing up for human rights, while conveniently ignoring the fact that in terms of social and economic rights—such as the rights to food, health care and education—Cuba, in spite of the embargo, far excelled all the Latin American countries in the American camp.[103] This fact was, of course, precisely what made the Cuban threat—another threat of a good example—so dangerous.[104] As the CIA told the White House in 1964:

> Cuba's experiment with almost total state socialism is being watched closely by other nations in the hemisphere, and any appearance of success there could have an extensive impact on the statist trend elsewhere in the area.[105]

Given the American government's task of helping US business, successive administrations would make every attempt, from tightening the embargo to sporadic military strikes on economic targets, to make sure the Cuban economy would not thrive.

5. Brazil: The Alliance for Progress Centerpiece

JFK's Alliance for Progress, which was created in response to Castro's victory in Cuba, declared that it would discontinue support for "dictatorships or regimes based on plutocracies," because that policy had "lent plausibility to the Communist charge that America's only interest was to enlarge her investment opportunities and markets, and to the Marxian charge that American capitalism equated to imperialism."[106] Intending "peaceful revolutions," JFK's basic idea was that economic aid could be used to create a growing middle class and a democratic alternative to both right-wing dictatorships and left-wing revolutions.[107]

Brazil was to be the centerpiece of the Alliance.[108] Brazil's economy had long been dominated by America's. Gerald Haines, the senior historian of the CIA, frankly said that Washington had guided "Brazilian industrial development for the benefit of private U.S. corporations," developing "a neocolonial relationship, with Brazil furnishing the raw materials for American industry and the United States supplying Brazil with manufactured goods." Any industrial development in Brazil had to be "complementary to U.S. industry. . . . Brazilian development was all right as long as it did not interfere with American profits and dominance."[109] As a result, Brazil had become one of the most economically divided societies in the world, with an enormous gap between the rich and the poor.

In 1961, João Goulart, the vice-president, was elevated to the presidency when the former president was forced out of office by the Kennedy Administration, which was angered by his refusal to support the US embargo against Cuba.[110] Goulart, a Roman Catholic, a millionaire landowner, and a critic of Castro, was not even close to being a Communist. But he, like his predecessor, did favor moderate economic nationalism and social reform, which led him to raise the minimum wage, to initiate some mild agrarian changes, and to restrict the profits of US businesses. Also, favoring democracy and neutralism, he opposed sanctions against Cuba and extended democratic rights to Communists, even appointing some of them to government posts. Being suspicious of US machinations, furthermore, he promoted nationalist over pro-American officers in the military.[111]

In the minds of these US-trained officers as well as Brazilian plutocrats and Washington officials, these actions raised the possibility that Goulart was planning to establish a Communist dictatorship—which, even as a mere possibility, had to be eliminated.[112]

The Kennedy Administration, besides starting to discuss a coup with Brazilian officers, began increasing the percentage of Alliance funds going for military aid. The CIA spent millions of dollars supporting anti-Goulart candidates and an anti-Goulart propaganda campaign, spreading stories about outrages he was allegedly planning.[113]

A few months after Kennedy's assassination, the administration of Lyndon Baines Johnson (LBJ) gave the military planners the green light for the coup, which became known as the March 31 Revolution. Although Secretary of State Dean Rusk would later swear to Congress that the United States had nothing to do with it, Washington sent oil, money, and arms.[114] After the coup's success, the American ambassador called it "the single most important victory for freedom in the hemisphere in recent years," the meaning of which was clarified by the CIA's statement that the change "will create a greatly improved climate for private investment."[115]

Freedom in the layperson's sense, however, was not facilitated. The March 31 Revolution, which was said to be necessary to prevent a *possible* left-wing dictatorship, ushered in an *actual* right-wing military dictatorship that, besides lasting for two decades, was especially brutal. The people were subjected to "disappearances," death squads, extreme torture, and gang rapes of women in front of their husbands and children—all underwritten by Uncle Sam. The income of this already extremely inegalitarian country was redistributed upward.

By the 1980s, in spite of having the world's eighth largest economy, fueled by billions of dollars in US aid and investment, Brazil ranked among the worst countries of the world in terms of health, education, and general welfare. Over two-thirds of the population were malnourished, hundreds of thousands of children were dying of starvation each year, and millions of children were surviving only by becoming slaves or prostitutes—at least until murdered for the price their organs would bring.

Washington never withdrew support for this regime, which survived until Brazil's economy, having followed the IMF's neoliberal, wealth-producing policies, collapsed.[116] The fact that America supported this regime while persecuting Cuba's, with its successful promotion of health care and education in spite of a crippling embargo, by itself showed that America was not fit to run the world.

6. The Dominican Republic: The Johnson Doctrine and the Credibility Gap

Although the brutal dictatorship of Rafael Trujillo in the Dominican Republic had received unwavering US support for almost three decades, Batista's fall to Castro's forces in Cuba in 1959 gave US policymakers several reasons to begin plans for Trujillo's removal: the realization that right-wing dictators might be fostering revolution rather than checking it; the criticism by Latin American governments that America, while always opposing leftist governments no matter how good, supports right-wing governments no matter how bad; and Eisenhower's realization that, because these countries believed "that the Trujillo situation is more serious than the Castro situation," they will not "reach a proper level of indignation in dealing with Castro" until Trujillo is eliminated.[117]

Although Eisenhower hesitated, for fear that the elimination of Trujillo would open the door for a left-leaning government, the new Kennedy administration, ready to show that it would oppose right-wing dictatorships, apparently gave the green light, and in May of 1961 Trujillo was assassinated by a conservative group.[118] Then, after almost two years of new right-wing governments backed by the USA, Juan Bosch was elected president with a large majority in the first free election in the country's history.

This was what JFK's administration said it supported, and Bosch was the kind of moderate reformer it hoped to promote in the hemisphere. But in September of 1963—only seven months after his election—Bosch was removed in a US-sanctioned coup. The reforms themselves—land reform, higher wages, and some modest nationalization of businesses—upset the upper class, the military, and US companies.[119] What most bothered Washington, however, was that Bosch, a believer in democracy, maintained that Communists should not be persecuted unless they broke the law. Observing all this, the CIA said that, because of insufficient evidence, "the possibility that he was secretly pro-Communist or a party member could not be ruled out."[120]

Given the US principle that, with regard to Communism, one is guilty until proven innocent, the Dominican Republic's seven months of democracy was terminated by a military coup. "Democracy," explained *Newsweek*, "was being saved from Communism by getting rid of democracy."[121] In April of 1965, however, a group of "constitutionalists" instigated a rebellion to return Bosch to power. LBJ had just intensified US involvement in Vietnam to prevent its "going Communist" on his watch and evidently saw the Dominican Republic in the same light. "If the Castro-types take over the Dominican Republic," a close advisor told him, "it will be the worst domestic political disaster any Administration could suffer."[122] Within days, 23,000 marines were in the country, preventing the military government from being overthrown by the citizens trying to restore constitutional rule.

This intervention violated not only the Charter of the United Nations but also the Charter of the Organization of American States (OAS), which prohibits intervention "directly or indirectly, for any reason whatever, in the internal or external affairs of any other state." That, however, was an irrelevancy to LBJ, who, expressing himself with his usual delicacy, said that the OAS "couldn't pour piss out of a boot if the instructions were written on the heel."[123]

Attempting, nonetheless, to justify the intervention, LBJ offered three of the standard excuses: American lives at risk, rebel atrocities, and Communist domination of the rebel movement—telling a national audience that "the establishment of another Communist government in the Western Hemisphere" could not be permitted.[124] The administration then launched a massive propaganda campaign to convince the world of the truth of its claims. American reporters in the Dominican Republic, however, refuted all of them. The claim of Communist domination, which was most emphasized, was undermined by the twofold fact that no Communists could be found and that the Communist Party in the Dominican Republic, the CIA reported, had been "unaware of the coup attempt."[125]

After hearings conducted later that year, Senator William Fulbright, chairman of the Senate Foreign Relations Committee, concluded that the administration had used the communist threat and danger to American lives only as a pretext to prevent Bosch's government from returning to power. Another Senate critic, Frank Church, said that US leaders "downgrade freedom by equating it with the absence of Communism" and "upgrade a host of dictatorial regimes by dignifying them with membership in what we like to call the 'Free World.'"[126] The *New York Times* asked why American soldiers should be sent to kill Dominicans who were "fighting and dying for social justice and constitutionalism."[127]

One legacy of this intervention, due to the number of the government lies that were exposed, was the entry of the expression "credibility gap" into American popular language.[128] While that legacy reflected the perspective of much of the public, Washington, reflecting another perspective, launched an attack on the concept of non-intervention, calling it obsolete.

LBJ said that "with enemies of freedom talking about 'Wars of national liberation,' the old distinction between 'Civil War' and 'International War' has already lost much of its meaning." LBJ's statement revealed perhaps more than he intended: From the perspective of a government that sees itself as the rightful government of the whole world, there *is* no distinction between civil and international wars.

In any case, the House of Representatives, evidently sharing this perspective, passed a resolution (315 to 52) justifying the unilateral use of force on foreign territory by any nation that considers itself threatened by "international communism, directly or indirectly." Although the House Resolution referred to "any nation," it meant, of course, only America and its junior partners. The essence of this "Johnson Doctrine," commented Richard Barnet, is "a virtually unlimited claim of legitimacy for armed intervention in civil strife."[129]

For the people of the Dominican Republic, the legacy was predictable. In the election of 1966, the people, having been massively propagandized and told in effect that the military occupation would not end unless they voted for the US-backed candidate instead of Bosch, did so. As a result, in William Blum's summary statement:

> The rich became richer and the poor had . . . hungry babies; democracy remained an alien concept; the police and military regularly kidnapped, tortured and murdered opponents of the government and terrorized union organizers. . . . The pot was sweetened for foreign investors. . . . And the men who ran the United States . . . were satisfied.[130]

The United States did not limit its regime-change interventions only to the Western Hemisphere, of course. We will turn next to an illustration in Europe, then one in Asia.

7. Greece: Whacking a Flea, Screwing a Constitution

The US devotion to fostering democracy in the land of its birth, which was illustrated in the 1940s (as discussed in Chapter 8), was manifested again in the 1960s, by which time Greece had become a central base of American power, with dozens of US military installations and a vast intelligence network closely intertwined with the CIA. In 1964, George Papandreou became prime minister. Having been the British-installed prime minister who led the oligarchy's war against the left in the 1940s, he should have been fully acceptable to US officials.

But he had moved toward neutralism and was also resisting Washington's solution to Greece's dispute with Cyprus, having his ambassador explain to LBJ that it would be unacceptable to Greece's parliament and in violation of its constitution. "Then listen to me, Mr. Ambassador," LBJ reportedly replied,

> fuck your Parliament and your Constitution. America is an elephant. Cyprus is a flea. If these two fleas continue itching the elephant, they may just get whacked by the elephant's trunk. . . . We pay a lot of good American dollars to the Greeks. . . . If your Prime Minister gives me talk about Democracy, Parliament and Constitutions, he, his Parliament and his Constitution may not last very long.

They did not. In 1965, the CIA helped King Constantine bribe enough members of Papandreou's party to topple his government.[131]

Part of Washington's reason for wanting Papandreou removed involved his son, Andreas Papandreou, who was a member of his father's cabinet. In this role, he had learned that the KYP—the Greek equivalent of the CIA—had become a shadow government, with powers beyond the control of the formal government, and that the KYP was closely linked to the CIA, so that the United States could virtually control Greek policy.[132] Although young Papandreou was unsuccessful in most of his attempts to reform and regulate the KYP, he was able to transfer the KYP agent who served as the liaison with the CIA, George Papadopoulos.

In any case, after having been removed in 1965, George and Andreas Papandreou were about to be returned to power by the voters in 1967. Two days before the election, however, a military junta, led by Papadopoulos, staged a coup. Claiming that the action was necessary to prevent a Communist takeover, Papadopoulos made himself prime minister. The Johnson administration, knowing months before that such a coup was being planned, let it occur. The CIA was, in fact, surely involved in the planning. Papadopoulos, who had been on the CIA payroll for 15 years, was widely considered "the first CIA agent to become Premier of a European country."[133]

In any case, by removing both the elder and the younger Papandreou, the American elephant had eliminated two irritating fleas with one whack.

As its reward for being the locus of this historic event, Greece experienced a seven-year nightmare, with thousands subjected to extreme forms of torture, some for merely criticizing the government. American leaders, however, defended Greece's military junta, which one U.S. general called "the best damn Government since Pericles." The Papadopoulos regime appreciated this support, with one notorious torturer regularly telling his victims: "You can't fight us, we are Americans."[134]

8. Indonesia

Indonesia, the world's largest Islamic country, had long been a colony of the Netherlands. At the end of World War II, during which Indonesia had fallen under Japanese control, America initially supported the attempt by the Netherlands to regain control of Indonesia, just as it had supported France's effort to regain control of Vietnam. Eventually, however, America pressured the Netherlands to withdraw, partly because it had refused to obey a Security Council order to do so. (The French effort in Vietnam was able to continue, by contrast, because France had veto power, so there were no Security Council resolutions against it.) The battle for Indonesia's independence was led by Sukarno, who was then elected president.

However, America found him insufficiently obedient to its wishes. Sukarno was not a Communist, he did not allow any members of the Communist Party (the PKI) into his cabinet, and he even ruthlessly suppressed Soviet-oriented Communists. But he did not persecute *nationalistic* Communists, who had sided with him against the Soviet-oriented Communists.[135]

The Eisenhower administration became obsessed with the possibility that, because of Sukarno's tolerance of the PKI, this organization might become strong enough "to take power through legal . . . means" (even though it was the smallest of Indonesia's four major parties). Washington hence decided on a covert policy, in the words of Secretary of State Dulles, "to bring about a new government on Java" (which is Indonesia's dominant island, where most of the people live).[136] The plan was to exploit the dissatisfaction of the outer islands with the central government in Java (in Jakarta), thereby turning their movement for a federal system into a full-blown civil war.

This war, which occurred in 1957, was supported by massive military assistance and generous funding, courtesy of American taxpayers, who were not informed that their money was being used to foment war against a democratically elected government. The idea was to establish a pro-American government on the island of Sumatra, which has Indonesia's oil, then use it as a base for taking over the whole country.[137] However, in spite of the massive American support given to the rebels, Java's forces held them off, partly because they foiled an American plan for a false flag operation. (The plan was to burn the US-owned oil fields on Sumatra, then blame it on the Javanese, to provide, in the words of a US soldier, "a pretext to send in marines.")[138]

One result of this imperialist adventure, which fulfilled Sukarno's prediction that American support for the rebels would be the "way to hell," was the loss of some 40,000 Indonesian lives.[139] But that was merely a foretaste of the hell to come.

Fearing that Indonesia's parliamentary system would allow the PKI to win the 1959 elections, Washington bribed the army to postpone the elections and then to eliminate the parliamentary system altogether.[140] Later, in 1965, the US Ambassador to Indonesia, in view of the fact that the PKI had become stronger, told President Johnson that "an unsuccessful coup attempt by the PKI might be the most effective development to start a reversal of political trends."[141] Within months there was such an attempt, fabricated by the CIA and the Pentagon in collusion with army strongman General Suharto, who blamed it on the PKI. Suharto then used this "failed coup attempt" as a pretext to begin a general slaughter, for which the Johnson administration provided arms and "shooting lists."[142]

The resulting holocaust resulted in the deaths of one to three million people; the CIA itself compared it to the Nazi and Soviet mass murders.[143] Many of the victims were simply peasants, school teachers, and union organizers accused of being Communist sympathizers. In addition, hundreds of thousands of people were put in jail or concentration camps, many for the rest of their lives.[144]

The long-term consequences were also devastating. Indonesia would not enjoy free elections or representative government for the rest of the century.[145] Landlessness increased, wages fell, and Indonesia became the poorest nation in Southeast Asia, with much of the population living in stark poverty with insufficient food. America's 1965 intervention in Indonesia did, however, serve a few interests. Suharto, being careful not to upset the United States, ruled the country dictatorially until 1999 and became "a fabulously wealthy man." And Indonesia, having been saved, like Iran, from the nationalists, became a "paradise for investors."[146]

The CIA was extremely proud of the 1965 intervention, regarding it as a model for future operations.[147]

9. The Iran-Iraq War (1980-1988)

After forces of the Ayatollah Khomeini overthrew the shah in 1979 and took 53 American hostages, the Carter administration was desperate, knowing that it would not be re-elected unless it could obtain the release of these hostages. Accordingly, after a rescue attempt failed, Washington encouraged Iraq, now headed by Saddam Hussein, to attack Iran, partly by exaggerating Iran's weakness, partly by hinting of US assistance.[148] The idea, articulated by Carter's national security advisor Zbigniew Brzezinski, was that Iran—which, thanks to military assistance given to the shah's regime, was using American military equipment—would soon run out of parts and need to turn to America to get replacements. It was a parts-for-hostages plan.

This plan was thwarted, however, because of a previous imperial adventure: Iran was able to turn to Vietnam, which had plenty of spare parts from the equipment left there when American troops made a hasty retreat in 1973. The Carter-Brzezinski plan was also thwarted because candidate Ronald Reagan had made a secret deal with Khomeini (the "October Surprise"),[149] promising that if he did not release the hostages until after the US election, Reagan's administration would lift the US embargo on parts.[150]

This agreement, however, did not mean that Reagan would support Iran or even stay neutral. Indeed, Washington soon put Iran on its list of countries who supported terrorism—while taking Iraq *off* the list, so that Washington could supply it with arms, which it did.[151] Then in 1986, fearing that Iran was about to defeat Iraq, Washington, which had long been providing arms to Iraq, actively intervened on its side. This support occurred in spite of the fact that the Reagan Administration was fully aware that Saddam's troops had repeatedly used chemical weapons.[152] Indeed, after the war this administration even actively prevented Iraq from being punished for its violations of the Geneva Protocol on Chemical Weapons.[153] In any case, this war, which was encouraged by America and then prolonged by its intervention, lasted for eight years, claiming over a million casualties in these two Islamic countries.[154]

Another result of the war was that Iraq had to borrow about $90 billion, which was a major factor in its decision in 1981 to invade Kuwait (see Chapter 13).

Conclusion

As this chapter and the following one show, virtually all of America's imperialistic interventions were justified on the basis of claims about Communism.

As these chapters also show, the Dulles brothers - as Stephen Kinzer documented in his 2013 book, *The Brothers* - were responsible for much of the havoc wreaked by the United States during the Cold War (with continuing effects to this day). After quoting John Quincy Adams' 1821 statement that the United States "goes not abroad in search of monsters," Kinzer wrote: "The Dulles brothers, however, did. Six impassioned visionaries in Asia, Africa, and Latin America became the monsters they went abroad to destroy." These six visionaries included five men discussed in the present book: Mohammad Mossadegh, Jacobo Arbenz, Sukarno, Fidel Castro, and Ho Chi Minh.[155]

Endnotes

1 William Blum, *Killing Hope: U.S. Military and C.I.A. Interventions Since World War II* (Common Courage, 2008), 40.

2 Daniel B. Schirmeer and Stephen Rosskamm Shalom, ed., *The Philippines Reader: A History of Colonialism, Neocolonialism, Dictatorship, and Resistance* (Boston: South End, 1987), 90, 94; Alfred W. McCoy, Catherine B. Reach, and Leonard D. Adams, *Politics of Heroin in Southeast Asia* (New York: Harper & Row, 1972), 58.

3 Schirmeer and Shalom, *The Philippines Reader*, 94.

4 Gabriel Kolko, *Century of War: Politics, Conflict, and Society Since 1914* (New York: New Press, 1994), 393.

5 Schirmeer and Shalom, *The Philippines Reader*, 87, 92-93, 125.

6 Ibid., 111.

7 D. Michael Shafer, *Deadly Paradigms: The Failure of U.S. Counterinsurgency Policy* (Princeton University Press, 1989), 213-14.

8 Stanley Karnow, *In Our Image: America's Empire in the Philippines* (New York: Ballantine, 1989), 324, 334; Kolko, *Century of War*, 393.

9 Schirmeer and Shalom, *The Philippines Reader*, 113; Shafer, *Deadly Paradigms*, 211, 213, 232-33; Blum, *Killing Hope*, 40; Kolko, *Century of War*, 233, 388.

10 Schirmeer and Shalom, *The Philippines Reader*, 108.

11 Shafer, *Deadly Paradigms*, 213.

12 Ibid., 221-24.

13 Ibid., 229.

14 Karnow, *In Our Image*, 346, 350; Schirmeer and Shalom, *The Philippines Reader*, 113.

15 Kolko, *Century of War*, 393; Karnow, *In Our Image*, 353.

16 Shafer, *Deadly Paradigms*, 234; Karnow, *In Our Image*, 350.

17 Karnow, *In Our Image*, 352; Kolko, *Century of War*, 393.

18 In the Philippines, it was illegal for foreigners to contribute to election campaigns (Schirmeer and Shalom, *The Philippines Reader*, 122).

19 Karnow, *In Our Image*, 353.

20 Blum, *Killing Hope*, 44.

21 Schirmeer and Shalom, *The Philippines Reader*, 117.

22 Both of these problems were illustrated by the fact that when an American land expert in Manila in 1952 recommended real land reform, he was brought home after being called a Communist by Filipino politicians (Karnow, *In Our Image*, 351; Schirmeer and Shalom, *The Philippines Reader*, 119-20).

23 Marilyn B. Young, *The Vietnam Wars: 1945-1990* (New York: HarperPerennial, 1991), 44; George McT. Kahin, *Intervention: How America Became Involved in Vietnam* (New York: Anchor, 1987), 70.

24 Karnow, *In Our Image*, 355, 362.

25 "The state-based accumulation of capital and economic power that culminated in the Marcos regime from 1966 to 1985," said Kolko, "was merely the logic of a political structure with which the United States endowed the Philippines during the colonial period and which persists to this day" (Kolko, *Century of War*, 386).

26 Karnow, *In Our Image*, 378-88; Schirmeer and Shalom, *The Philippines Reader*, 143-69.

27 Karnow, *In Our Image*, 25.

28 Blum, *Killing Hope*, 43.

29 Bill Fletcher Jr., "The Philippines: Invisible Neo-Colony," Telesur, 8 August 2015; "US Military Basing Deal in the Philippines: A Step towards Neocolonial Rule," World Socialist Web Site," 17 May 2014.

30 Prashanth Parameswaran, "Why the Philippines' Rodrigo Duterte Hates America," *The Diplomat*, 1 November 2016.

31 Stephen Kinzer, *All the Shah's Men: An American Coup and the Roots of Middle East Terror* (John Wiley, 2003), 50, 89; Stephen Kinzer, *Overthrow: America's Century of Regime Change from Hawaii to Iraq* (Henry Holt, 2006), 117.

32 Stephen Kinzer, *All the Shah's Men: An American Coup and the Roots of Middle East Terror* (John Wiley, 2003), 123-24.

33 Ibid., 121.

34 Ibid., 129.

35 Walter LaFeber et al., *The American Century: A History of the United States Since 1941*, 5th ed. (Boston: McGraw-Hill, 1998), 385.

36 Blum, *Killing Hope*, 70.

37 Ibid., 71.

38 Audrey R. Kahin and George McT. Kahin, *Subversion as Foreign Policy: The Secret Eisenhower and Dulles Debacle in Indonesia* (Seattle: University of Washington Press, 1995), 4; Stephen Kinzer, *Overthrow: America's Century of Regime Change from Hawaii to Iraq* (Henry Holt, 2006), 4, 114, 117.

39 Kinzer, *Overthrow,* 121.

40 Kinzer, *All the Shah's Men*, 164.

41 Ibid., 10.

42 Ibid., 10, 163.

43 Walter LaFeber, *The American Age: U.S. Foreign Policy Since 1750*, 2nd ed. (New York: Norton, 1993), 518.

44 Blum, *Killing Hope*, 70.

45 Noam Chomsky, *Deterring Democracy*, 2nd ed. (New York: Hill and Wang, 1992), 50 (quoting the *New York Times*, 6 August 1954).

46 LaFeber, *The American Age*, 518.

47 Blum, *Killing Hope*, 72.

48 William Rivers Pitt, *War On Iraq* (New York: Context Books, 2002), 17.

49 Pitt, *War On Iraq*, 17; Kinzer, *Overthrow,* 202.

50 Kinzer, *All the Shah's Men*, 85-86.

51 Ibid., 158.

52 Ibid., 204.

53 Ibid., 202.

54 This section is based primarily upon Piero Gleijeses, *Shattered Hope: The Guatemalan Revolution and the United States, 1944-1954* (Princeton: Princeton University Press, 1991), and Nick Cullather, *Secret History: The CIA's Classified Account of Its Operations in Guatemala 1952-1954* (Stanford: Stanford University Press, 1999), which draws on both Gleijeses's book and CIA files, which were originally intended only for internal CIA use. Their accounts differ significantly from older accounts, especially with regard to the Communism of Jacobo Arbenz,

the importance of the United Fruit Company, and the cause for the success of the US operation. There is a newer book: Mario Overall and Dan Hagedorn, *PBSuccess: The CIA's Covert Operation to Overthrow Guatemalan President Jacobo Arbenz June-July 1954* (Helion and Company 2016). But its new material deals only with the use of air power by the CIA and the Guatemalan Air Force.

55 Gleijeses, *Shattered Hope*, 3.

56 Ibid., 10; Nick Cullather, *Secret History*, 9.

57 Gleijeses, *Shattered Hope*, 9-19.

58 Ibid., 19-21; Cullather, *Secret History*, 10.

59 Gleijeses, *Shattered Hope*, 22-23.

60 Ibid., 135-35.

61 Ibid., 53, 140; Cullather, *Secret History*, 11.

62 Gleijeses, *Shattered Hope*, 36-37.

63 Ibid. 41-47, 91, 117, 377.

64 Ibid., 94, 96, 99-100, 103, 105.

65 Ibid., 119-21.

66 Although there were rumors that Arbenz simply had Arana murdered, this was, Gleijeses showed, most improbable. The rumors persisted partly because Arévalo, rather than telling the truth about Arana's betrayal, claimed that he was killed by right-wing reactionaries. Although Arbenz had advised Arévalo simply to tell the truth, he remained silent (ibid., 67-71).

67 Ibid., 54-56, 59, 62-71.

68 Ibid., 73, 83; Cullather, *Secret History*, 11.

69 Gleijeses, *Shattered Hope*, 81-83.

70 Ibid., 150.

71 Ibid., 144-45.

72 Ibid., 145, 150-51, 231.

73 Ibid., 152, 155-60, 163.

74 Ibid., 135, 160.

75 Ibid., 151, 164.

76 Gleijeses, *Shattered Hope*, 257, 262, 298.

77 Gleijeses, *Shattered Hope*, 78-79, 140-41, 143-46, 182, 190, 192, 216, 233-34; Cullather, *Secret History*, 142.

78 Cullather, *Secret History*, 107-08.

79 When David Atlee Phillips, then a recent CIA recruit, was tapped for the assignment, he reportedly said: "But Arbenz became President in a free election. What right do we have to help someone topple his government and throw him out of office?" This story was told by Phillips himself in *The Night Watch: Twenty-five Years of Peculiar Service* (New York: Athenaeum, 1977), 34-35.

80 This was actually the Eisenhower administration's second attempt to overthrow Arbenz. After the first attempt, Arbenz discovered and published evidence of American involvement. The US State Department called the accusations "ridiculous and untrue," adding: "It is the policy of the United States not to interfere in the internal affairs of other nations" (Blum, *Killing Hope*, 78). What it meant, of course, is that it is the policy of the United States to lie whenever it gets caught.

81 Gleijeses, *Shattered Hope*, 246-47, 254, 256, 305, 313, 335, 338-39, 341, 365, 375, 380; Cullather, *Secret History*, 60, 64, 68, 82, 84-85, 89.

82 Schmitz, *Thank God*, 196.

83 Blum, *Killing Hope*, 82.

84 Chomsky, *Year 501*, 174-76.

85 "Telling Common Hope's Story 2014."

86 Gleijeses, *Shattered Hope*, 235, citing Dwight D. Eisenhower, *Mandate for Change, 1953-1956* (Garden City: Doubleday, 1963), 421-27, 573-75.

87 Alfred W. McCoy, *In the Shadows of the American Century* (Haymarket Books, 2017), 62-63.

88 Gabriel Kolko, *Confronting the Third World: United States Foreign Policy 1945-1980* (New York: Pantheon, 1988), 141.

89 Blum, *Killing Hope*, 192.

90 Schmitz, *Thank God*, 227.

91 Kolko, *Confronting the Third World*, 142.

92 Ibid., 141; Schmitz, *Thank God*, 219; Blum, *Killing Hope*, 186.

93 Kolko, *Confronting the Third World*, 141-42.

94 Schmitz, *Thank God*, 220, citing "A Program of Covert Action against the Castro Regime," 17 March 1960.

95 Blum, *Killing Hope*, 192; Warren Hinckle and William Turner, *Deadly Secrets: The CIA-Mafia War Against Castro and the Assassination of J.F.K.* (New York: Thunder's Mouth, 1992), xv-xvi, 24-25.

96 Kolko, *Confronting the Third World*, 142-43.

97 Walter LaFeber, *Inevitable Revolutions: The United States in Central America* (New York: Norton, 1984), 149.

98 Kolko, *Confronting the Third World*, 144.

99 Hinckle and Turner, *Deadly Secrets*, xi.

100 Blum, *Killing Hope*, 185, quoting *Time*, 2 November 1962.

101 Chomsky, *Rogue States*, 2, citing "American Republics," vol. XII of *Foreign Relations of the United States* (US Dept. of State, 1961-63), 13-14, 33.

102 Chomsky, *Year 501*, 146, quoting Ruth Leacock, *Requiem for Revolution* (Kent State University Press, 1990), 33.

103 In 1980, the World Health Organization reported that "Cuba has the best health statistics in Latin America." In 1992, a report in Australia

said that "despite the economic difficulties, the average Cuban is still better fed, housed, educated, and provided for medically than other Latin Americans." Both reports are quoted in Chomsky, *Year 501*, 151-52.

104 Washington's concern for the human rights of the Cuban people has been so great that in 1997 it continued its embargo on medicine to Cuba because supplying it would be "detrimental to US foreign policy interests" (Chomsky, *Rogue States*, 148).

105 LaFeber, *Inevitable Revolutions*, 157.

106 Schmitz, *Thank God*, 238-39.

107 LaFeber, *Inevitable Revolutions*, 149.

108 Schmitz, *Thank God*, 269.

109 Chomsky, *Year 501*: 159, quoting *Gerald Haines, The Americanization of Brazil*.

110 Schmitz, *Thank God*, 269; Blum, *Killing Hope*, 156.

111 Blum, *Killing Hope*, 164-66; Chomsky, *Year 501*, 162; Schmitz, *Thank God*, 269.

112 The language used by US officials reflects the fact that there was no evidence that Goulart was a Communist. The charges were that "we *may be* witnessing the early stages of an attempted slow-motion coup"; there is a "*danger* that he will become a captive of the left"; there is "a *good chance* that the course of Brazilian politics will continue moving toward leftist solutions"; there are "*fears* of Goulart's intentions to maneuver a Left-wing takeover"; Goulart "*may be able* to neutralize [the] military . . . bulwark against a Leftist takeover"; "a communist takeover is *conceivable*"; and, most frightening, present tendencies "*could* lead ultimately to . . . an extreme leftist regime with a strongly anti-US character" (Schmitz, *Thank God*, 270-73; emphases added).

113 Blum, *Killing Hope*, 166; Schmitz, *Thank God*, 271-72.

114 Blum, *Killing Hope*, 167-69.

115 Schmitz, *Thank God*, 276, 275.

116 Blum, *Killing Hope*, 170-71; Chomsky, *Deterring Democracy*, 227-28; *Year 501*, 165-69, 177.

117 Blum, *Killing Hope*, 175; Schmitz, *Thank God*, 231.

118 Blum, *Killing Hope*, 176.

119 Ibid., 179; Schmitz, *Thank God*, 260.

120 Schmitz, *Thank God*, 258.

121 Blum, *Killing Hope*, 180.

122 Schmitz, *Thank God*, 284.

123 LaFeber, *Inevitable Revolutions*, 158, quoting Philip Geyelin, *Lyndon B. Johnson and the World* (Frederick A Praeger, 1966), 254.

124 Ibid., 157.

125 Schmitz, *Thank God*, 284-85; Blum, *Killing Hope*, 182-83.

126 Schmitz, *Thank God*, 284-85; Blum, *Killing Hope*, 182-83.

127 Young, *The Vietnam Wars*, 152.

128 Blum, *Killing Hope*, 183, citing David Wise, *The Politics of Lying: Government Deception, Secrecy, and Power* (Random, 1973), 32.

129 Blum, *Killing Hope*, 183, citing Richard Barnet, *Intervention and Revolution: The United States in the Third World* (World Pub. Co.,1972), 178-79.

130 Ibid., 184.

131 Ibid., 216.

132 Ibid., 217.

133 Ibid., 218.

134 Ibid., 215, 220.

135 Kahin and Kahin, *Subversion as Foreign Policy,* 32, 40, 42-43, 50-51; Chomsky, *Powers and Prospects: Reflections on Human Nature and the Social Order* (Boston: South End, 1996), 190. It was only with the publication of the book by the Kahins in 1995 that the information about America's 1965 intervention was made public. It had been kept secret for 30 years and is evidently still unknown to most Americans.

136 Kahin and Kahin, *Subversion as Foreign Policy*, 91, 92, 93, 126, 161.

137 Ibid., 10, 15, 74, 84, 87-88.

138 Ibid., 149-51; cf. 124.

139 Ibid., 86, 99, 102, 119-20, 128, 132, 134, 136, 138, 140, 150-51, 158, 161, 186, 216.

140 Ibid., 193-94, 208.

141 Ibid., 225.

142 On arms, see Noam Chomsky, *Year 501*, 126, and Gabriel Kolko, *Confronting the Third World: United States Foreign Policy 1945-1980* (New York: Pantheon, 1988), 181. On shooting lists, see Kathy Kadane, *San Francisco Examiner*, 20 May 1990. For additional evidence of U.S. responsibility, see Kahin and Kahin, *Subversion as Foreign Policy*, 123, 225, and Blum, *Killing Hope*, 195-97.

143 Kahin and Kahin, *Subversion as Foreign Policy*, 227-28; Noam Chomsky and Edward S. Herman, *The Washington Connection and Third World Fascism* (Montreal: Black Rose, 1979), 207.

144 Kahin and Kahin, *Subversion as Foreign Policy*, 227-28; Noam Chomsky, *Rogue States: The Rule of Force in World Affairs* (Cambridge: South End Press, 2000), 6, 144; Chomsky and Herman, *The Washington Connection*, 208-09, 228; John Stockwell, *The Praetorian Guard: The U.S. Role in the New World Order* (Boston: South End, 1991), 72.

145 Kahin and Kahin, *Subversion as Foreign Policy*, 194; 217; Chomsky and Herman, *The Washington Connection*, 209-10; Robert Gellately

and Ben Kiernan, ed., *The Specter of Genocide: Mass Murder in Historical Perspective* (Cambridge University Press, 2003); Syarina Hasibuan, "Indonesia's Killing Fields," Al Jazeera, 21 December 2002.

146 Kolko, *Confronting the Third World*, 185; Chomsky and Herman, *The Washington Connection*, 209-10.

147 Ralph W. McGehee, *Deadly Deceits: My 25 Years in the CIA* (New York: Sheridan Square Publications, 1983), 57-58; Stockwell, *The Praetorian Guard*, 72-73.

148 John Tirman, *Spoils of War: The Human Cost of America's Arm Trade* (New York: Free Press, 1997), 102-03; Dilip Hiro, *The Longest War: The Iran-Iraq Military Conflict* (New York: Routledge, 1991), 71-72.

149 Barbara Honegger, *October Surprise* (Tudor, 1989); Gary Sick, *October Surprise* (Crown, 1991); Robert Parry, *Trick or Treason: The October Surprise Mystery* (Sheridan Press, 1993).

150 Tirman, *Spoils of War*, 102; Hiro, *The Longest War*, 71-72.

151 Tirman, *Spoils of War*, 105.

152 Hiro, *Iraq: In the Eye of the Storm* (New York: Thunder's Mouth/ Nation Books, 2002), 30-31.

153 Ibid., 238-39.

154 Hiro, *The Longest War*, xxii; Tirman, *Spoils of War*, 103.

155 Stephen Kinzer, *The Brothers: John Foster Dulles, Allen Dulles, and Their Secret World War* (Times Books, 2013), 117.

| Chapter 10 |

THE VIETNAM WAR

The wars to seize Spanish colonies provided, as we saw in Chapter 1, a revelation of the early manifestations of US imperialism and its nonbenign nature. However, although this revelation led to the formation of the Anti-Imperialist League, its effects were not comparable to those of later revelations.

The revelatory impact of the 20-year before American war in Vietnam was so great that US political and military leaders were obsessed for decades thereafter with overcoming the "Vietnam Syndrome." This term, suggesting a pathological condition, referred to the reluctance of the American people to commit their troops to fight abroad, partly because of widespread skepticism about Washington's motives. The revelatory impact of the Vietnam War was so much greater than that of the wars of 1898-1902 partly because of the power of television, which brought the reality and the horrors of the war in Vietnam into American homes, and partly because this war lasted so much longer, dragging on for another decade after 1965—the year by which a significant percentage of the American public started to realize what was going on.

During the ensuing debates, the term "American imperialism" came back into currency in public discourse, after having virtually disappeared for 60 years, and the picture of "America the Good" was widely replaced by radically different portraits. The government came to be widely seen as one that breaks international law with impunity, regularly lies to its own people, kills hundreds of thousands of people with indifference, and, while claiming to promote freedom, democracy, and self-determination, does exactly the opposite.

I was one of those for whom the war in Vietnam served as a revelation, although the revelation was only partial. I recall nodding in assent when a friend in the summer of 1965 denounced America's participation in the war, declaring that we were supporting the wrong side in a civil war. Only later would I realize that, insofar as what was going on could be called a "civil war," it would not have even existed without American intervention—that we *were* "the wrong side."

The awakening brought about by the Vietnam War was so widely perceived partly because of the publication in 1971 of *The Pentagon Papers*, the Pentagon's own top-secret history of US decision-making about Vietnam. Whereas prior to that time criticisms of American policy could be dismissed as distortions by leftist radicals, this document showed that US officials were fully aware that they were breaking promises, violating international law, and systematically lying to the American people. The significance of this document was illustrated by the reaction of then Secretary of Defense Robert McNamara, who had commissioned the study in 1967. After reading it, McNamara reportedly remarked to a colleague, "They could hang people for what's in there."[1]

For some observers, the Vietnam War's revelation of the immorality and illegality of US foreign policy was slow to be absorbed. An example is provided by Neil Sheehan, the journalist through whom *The New York Times*—which, along with *The Washington Post*, began publishing selections from *The Pentagon Papers* in 1971—came into possession of these papers. Many years later, Sheehan, who had reported from Vietnam, said of himself and fellow correspondents during the early 1960s: "Our ignorance and our American ideology kept us from discerning the larger truths of Vietnam beneath the surface reality we could see."[2] By 1971, however, Sheehan was suggesting, in a review of 31 books on the war in Vietnam, that "if you apply the law of war to American conduct there, then the leaders of the United States for the past six years at least, including the incumbent President, Richard Milhous Nixon, may well be guilty of war crimes."[3]

The Vietnam War was not, to be sure, perceived to have such moral and legal significance by everyone. Henry Kissinger, the national security advisor during Richard Nixon's first term and secretary of state during his second, said about the growing number of young men who were refusing to fight in Vietnam on moral grounds: "Conscientious objection must be reserved only for the greatest moral issues, and Vietnam is not of this magnitude."[4]

The revelatory significance of the Vietnam War was not grasped even by some professional ethicists. Jean Bethke Elshtain, for example, said: "When Americans look back with sadness and even shame at the Vietnam War, it is horrors like the My Lai *massacre* they have in mind."[5] She italicized the word *massacre* because her point was that this event, which involved "the slaughter of more than four hundred unarmed men, women, and children," cannot be called a *battle* because of the US soldiers' failure to distinguish between combatants and noncombatants. She was certainly right about this. But her statement implied that My Lai was an aberration, not typical of the US military's regular practice in Vietnam.

In 1971, however, the Vietnam Veterans Against the War—an organization of men who had just returned from Vietnam—held an event to demonstrate that "My Lai was not an isolated incident" but "only a minor step beyond official United States policy in Indochina."[6] Elshtain's statement also seemed to imply that, except for some occasional "horrors," there was no reason for Americans to look back on Vietnam in shame. Our intentions were, as always, noble. But it was precisely the fact that the Vietnam War showed the falsity of this deeply held assumption that it constituted such a powerful, life-transforming revelation for many people.

The Vietnam War was perceived as a "revelation" insofar as its law-breaking, lying, and indifference to massive death and devastation were perceived to be only an especially clear example of, rather than an exception to, the US government's more general policies. The account in this chapter, taken in the context of the other chapters in this book, is intended to show the accuracy of this perception. I have given more attention to this example of US intervention than to any other partly because of its overwhelming importance, partly because of the length of its duration (almost 30 years), partly because it continued to be regarded as a watershed event (as the term "Vietnam syndrome" showed), and partly because it seemed important that this book have one example in which US behavior is analyzed in considerable detail.

1. Getting Involved

The most general lie told about the war in Vietnam by American leaders was that they were—as an official statement in 1966 put it—seeking "only to insure that the South Vietnamese have the right and opportunity to control their own destiny."[7] The record shows that, from beginning to end, American policies were aimed at exactly the opposite effect. The vast majority of the people of Vietnam, in the South as well as the North, wanted their country unified and to be free from foreign domination. The United States spent thirty years seeking to frustrate this desire.

American involvement with Vietnam began at the end of World War II. For over 80 years prior to the war, Vietnam had been under the control of France, which called the whole area, including Laos and Cambodia, "Indochina." During the war, Vietnam fell under Japanese control. After the war, the French wanted Vietnam back, at least the southern part of it (Cochin), which included Saigon. French leaders argued that, unless the United States assisted them in this effort, the Communist Party might come to power in France.

American leaders, anxious to keep the Communists out of power and, more generally, to gain French cooperation with America's postwar economic plans for Europe, decided to help France recover some of its "grandeur."[8] Accordingly, two months after the end of World War II, which most Americans assumed was fought to defeat "the unjust imperialist ambitions of two oppressive nations: Germany and Japan," American ships transported some 13,000 French troops to Saigon so that France could recover part of its empire.

Betraying a Friend and Admirer

Vietnamese leaders had reason to expect better from America. During the war against the Japanese, the most effective nationalist party fighting for independence, the Vietminh—short for Vietnam Doc Lap Dong Minh (League for the Independence of Vietnam)—had a friendly working relationship with American forces. The leader of this party, Ho Chi Minh, had long been a great admirer of America. At the peace conference at Versailles in 1919, Ho had appealed to Woodrow Wilson to fulfill one of America's stated war aims: self-determination for all peoples. Although Ho's plea went unfulfilled, he retained his faith in America and its ideals.

Proclaiming Vietnam's independence on September 2, 1945, Ho used words from the American Declaration of Independence, saying: "All men are created equal. The Creator has given us certain inviolable Rights: the right to Life, the right to be Free." Then, rehearsing the fact that the French had robbed them of their natural resources, deprived them of their democratic liberties, and slain their patriots, Ho added, with an allusion to the founding of the United Nations, that he was certain that the Allied nations, which "have acknowledged the principle of self-determination and equality of nations, will not refuse to acknowledge the independence of Vietnam."[9]

Ho wrote at least eight letters to President Truman and the US State Department, asking America to help the Vietnamese to win independence from France and to bring the case before the United Nations.[10] In his final letter to Truman, Ho reminded him that it was the Viet Minh who had fought against the Japanese, while the French had collaborated with them; that all wartime conferences had promised independence to subject peoples; that there had been peace and order in Vietnam during the five months his party had been in office; and that France's "aggression on a peace-loving people is a direct menace to world security."[11]

However, Truman and other US officials did not even acknowledge Ho's letters, having "no thought," in the words of Acting Secretary of State Acheson, "of opposing the reestablishment of French control in Indochina."[12]

Financing France

This US stance was maintained, furthermore, despite the fact that the French were setting out to reestablish their control by double-crossing the Vietnamese. After Ho had realized that he would get no help from the United States, he had signed an agreement allowing French troops into the northern part of Vietnam on three conditions: that Ho's Democratic Republic of Vietnam in the north would be recognized as a free state, that all French troops would be withdrawn by 1952, and that there would be a referendum on reunification with the southern part (in which Viet Minh resistance to the French would continue). France, however, had no intention of honoring these commitments. Once their troops were there, they refused to allow the vote on reunification and began working to gain complete control.[13]

Far from seeking to thwart this effort, the United States armed and financed it. With US knowledge, France's share of Marshall Plan money, which was supposed to be for rebuilding the French economy, was used to fund its effort in Vietnam. The same was true of much of the modern weaponry ostensibly intended for the defense of France. As one member of the US Marshall Plan mission to France later wrote, America supplied France with the means "for a colonial reestablishment."[14] Indeed, as John Prados put it, "by 1950 President Truman had . . . com[e] full circle from the anticolonial policy of World War II to one supporting a French neocolonial state."[15]

American military and financial support would continue to grow. "When Dwight D. Eisenhower became president in January 1953, the United States was already paying 40 percent of the cost of the French war."[16]

2. The Eisenhower Administration: Shaping and Sabotaging the Geneva Accords

By the end of 1954, the Eisenhower administration would be paying 78 percent of France's war to recolonize Vietnam.[17] By then, in fact, the United States was more committed to the war than were the French. With the French people wanting to withdraw their troops from what had come to be called the "dirty war" in Vietnam, the Eisenhower administration warned France's leaders that "French acquiescence in a Communist take-over of Indochina" would mean that "U.S. aid to France would automatically cease."[18]

As that statement illustrated, US leaders saw the French-American effort as a battle against "Communists." This was at best a misleading perception. Although Ho Chi Minh did indeed turn to Communist theory after his plea at Versailles was ignored, he was first of all a nationalist. What this meant concretely was that the nationalist task of gaining independence was to be given priority over the social revolution, with Vietnamese of all classes encouraged to work together for this goal. Because of Ho's stance, he had long been denounced by Vietnam's Communist Party as a nationalist, a reformist, and even a collaborationist. And when the Viet Minh was formed in the 1940s, it adopted Ho's stance rather than that of the Communist Party.[19]

This fact about Ho and the Viet Minh was conveyed to Washington by virtually all American officials who spent time in Vietnam. These officials also pointed out that Ho was by far the most capable and popular leader, so that if the power of self-determination were granted to the Vietnamese people, they would overwhelmingly vote for Ho as their leader. Most of this message was received in Washington, with State Department officials acknowledging in 1948 that they were "all too well aware of the unpleasant fact that Communist Ho Chi Minh is the strongest and perhaps the ablest figure in Indochina and that any suggested solution which excludes him is an expedient of uncertain outcome."[20]

As this statement showed, the one point Washington

could not acknowledge was that Ho was not primarily motivated by Communist ideology. Washington declared that Communists could not be true nationalists. And although US intelligence could find no evidence of Soviet influence in Vietnam, Washington declared that all Communists in colonial countries were Stalinists, who sought to put their countries under the Kremlin's control. The State Department in 1949, therefore, could say that the real conflict in Vietnam was not that between Asian nationalism and Western imperialists, as "Vietnamese propaganda" claimed, but the "conflict between nationalism and Stalinism." In helping the French and their puppet government, therefore, America purported to support the genuine nationalists![21]

It has often been said, incidentally, that leading US officials were so blinded by their anti-Communism that they could not see that Ho and his Viet Minh party were nationalists rather than agents of Soviet and/or Chinese Communism, with the result that US policy was based on a "tragic error." However, wrote Noam Chomsky and Edward Herman:

> This claim is thoroughly refuted by the documentary record, which reveals that from the beginning U.S. analysts understood perfectly well that "the source of Viet Minh strength lay in its credentials as the leading force in Vietnamese nationalism," so that the United States intervened on the basis of "quite rational imperial motives that are carefully outlined in planning documents."[22]

Concealing these motives, however, required portraying Ho and the Viet Minh as agents of "international Communism."

Threatening Intervention to Prevent "Losing Vietnam"

The American conviction that the Viet Minh must not prevail had been increased by the victory of the Communists in China in 1949. Eisenhower's Republican Party had achieved victory partly by blaming the Democrats for "losing China" to Communism.

Now, having portrayed the Viet Minh as part of this international Communist threat, they could not afford to have Vietnam "lost to Communism" on *their* watch. Also, the "domino theory," which would become infamous, was articulated early in 1950 in a National Security Council document, which said that, if Indochina fell to Communism, then Thailand, Burma, the Philippines, Indonesia, and Malaya would be in grave danger of falling also.

After these developments of 1949, 1950, and 1952, American leaders became willing to go to even greater lengths to prevent a victory by the Viet Minh. In addition to paying for an ever greater part of France's war, the United States even threatened to intervene militarily on its behalf.

This occurred in relation to the long battle of Dien Bien Phu in 1954. When French defeat appeared imminent, Secretary of State John Foster Dulles declared that the possible "imposition on Southeast Asia of the political system of Communist Russia and its Chinese Communist ally . . . would be a grave threat to the whole free community." Accordingly, Dulles said, "that possibility . . . should be met by united action," by which he meant military action by US, British, and French forces.[23] Some members of the administration, including Vice-President Richard Nixon, recommended the introduction of US ground forces; some advocated air strikes; and some, including Nixon and Admiral Arthur Radford, Chairman of the Joint Chiefs of Staff, even advocated the use of nuclear weapons.[24]

President Eisenhower, however, rejected these proposals. On the use of ground troops, he said that if America put a single combat soldier in Vietnam, its "entire prestige would be at stake, not only in that area but throughout the world."[25] He also had no intention of using nuclear weapons or even of authorizing any air strikes whatsoever, whether alone or as part of some "united action."

Although it had long been thought that Eisenhower and Dulles really did want to intervene militarily and did not do so only because the British government refused to go along, the fuller documentary evidence that became available showed that

Eisenhower and Dulles merely wanted to pose a united *threat* for the purpose of persuading the Soviets and the Chinese, at the soon-to-start phase of the 1954 Geneva conference devoted to Indochina, not to support the Viet Minh's goals. This phase began, in fact, the day after May 7, when the French, having lost the battle of Dien Bien Phu, accepted defeat.

Although London refused to participate in any such united threat, Washington continued to issue threats of military intervention to cause Moscow, Beijing, and Hanoi to worry that, if the US did not find acceptable the agreements reached at Geneva, it would take over the effort to prevent the Viet Minh from taking control of the southern part of Vietnam. The United States had not been one of the belligerents, so it should have had no say in the matter. But its strategy worked.

The US Shapes the Geneva Accords

Besides failing in its effort to keep France fighting, the United States had earlier failed to prevent it from putting Indochina on the agenda of the 1954 Geneva conference, which had originally been scheduled to deal only with Berlin and Korea. America's fallback strategy was to shape the resulting agreements in such a way that it would be able to sabotage them.

For the Viet Minh, the brilliant victory at Dien Bien Phu was the climax of their nine-year battle to win independence from France. Being in control of virtually the whole country, both politically and militarily, they naturally expected their position to be reflected in the resulting agreements. US officials, however, took steps to make sure this would not happen. Their first step was to threaten military intervention, which they continued to do during the first five weeks of the conference.[26]

This threat was effective due to the fact—of which both US and the Communist leaders in Moscow and Beijing were aware—that US military power, especially in strategic nuclear weapons, outweighed that of China and the Soviet Union. This imbalance resulted from a massive build-up in US strategic forces that began after the Soviets tested an atomic bomb in 1949. Being designed to give the United States greater freedom of action and to create a situation in which the Communist world, in the words of the National Security Council, "would find it expedient to accommodate itself," the resulting strategic superiority, which was mutually evident by 1953, had two effects.

- The United States developed "more aggressive and interventionist policies."[27]

- The Communist bloc adopted a new international line based on the twin principles of "peaceful co-existence" and the peaceful resolution of all disputes. As one manifestation of this new stance, "the Communist powers," in the words of Gareth Porter, "pursued a conscious policy of appeasement of the United States in Vietnam."[28]

This second point meant that, at the Geneva conference, both Moscow and Beijing, far from supporting Ho Chi Minh's demands, made "stunning diplomatic concessions," which Ho was then forced to accept.[29] Getting these concessions was the Eisenhower administration's second step in preventing the Vietnamese from obtaining the type of agreement to which their victory over the French should have entitled them. The concessions were three.

- Although Ho wanted an immediate settlement, he was forced to settle for an immediate *armistice*, during which there would be a "regroupment" of military forces into two temporary zones (with the Viet Minh in the northern zone and the French in the southern), which would endure only until a free, all-country election took place.

- In light of the territory the Viet Minh controlled, the line dividing the northern and southern zones, Ho said, should be the 13th parallel, which is just above Saigon. Ho was forced, however, to agree to the 17th parallel, which is several hundred miles north. This meant that the southern zone, rather than constituting only about one eighth of Vietnam, constituted about half of it and included the important cities of Hue and Danang.

- Ho said that the election, through which the country would become unified, should occur within six months, but Moscow and Beijing forced him to accept a two-year delay.[30]

Ho made these concessions, Ho told his party leaders back in Hanoi, in return for the pledge by the French that elections would be held by July 20, 1956.[31]

In spite of being very unhappy with the terms that had been forced upon him, Ho still had five reasons to believe that Vietnam would soon be united:

1. The Geneva Accords explicitly stated that the line of demarcation at the 17th parallel was to be "provisional and should not in any way be interpreted as constituting a political or territorial boundary."

2. The Accords stipulated that "general elections will be held in July 1956, under the supervision of an international commission." Ho knew that he could easily win a free election against his rival, Bo Dai, who had been France's puppet ruler.

3. The Accords also stipulated that, in the intervening two years, the struggle for control would be strictly political, with all military activity prohibited. The Accords expressly prohibited the introduction of any troops or weapons from outside; they also prohibited the formation of any military alliances with other countries.

4. It was understood that the French would stay to enforce these provisions until the election occurred.[32]

> 5. Although the United States dissociated itself from the agreements, it did promise, through its Undersecretary of State Walter Bedell Smith, that it would "refrain from the threat or the use of force to disturb them." It also reaffirmed its support for its general policy of having free elections to reunify divided nations.[33]

To understand discussions about the Geneva Accords, it is necessary to understand that they consisted of two parts. The first part was a bilateral cease-fire agreement between the two belligerents: Ho's Democratic Republic of Vietnam (DRV) which was headquartered in the north, and France, which was recognized as acting on behalf of all the 'Vietnamese in the southern zone, which it still controlled.

The second part was a multinational 13-point Final Declaration, which was orally endorsed by the DRV, France, Britain, China, and the Soviet Union. (The World Court had established in 1933 that oral agreements between authorized representatives of countries are legally binding.[34]) Although the United States did not join in this oral endorsement, it did, through Walter Bedell Smith, make the promises cited above.

Given these guarantees by the international community and the promises of the United States in particular, Ho was willing to compromise in the short run, being certain that, after two years, Vietnam would be united under the leadership of the Viet Minh and hence finally be free of foreign occupation.

The US Begins to Sabotage the Geneva Accords

The Eisenhower administration, however, had no intention of keeping its word. A few days before the discussion of Indochina began at Geneva, Secretary of State Dulles was asked whether the US government would allow "a victory of Ho Chi-Minh or a coalition in a free election." Dulles replied: "[T]he United States should not stand passively by and see the extension of communism by any means into Southeast Asia. We are not standing passively by."[35] The phrase "by any means" included, of course, free elections. Further indication of the Eisenhower administration's intentions from the outset was provided by Dulles' statement, in an executive session of the Foreign Relations Committee, that "the military regrouping will be apt to gradually become a live *de facto* political division."[36]

So, although Geneva did not, in Kahin's words, "leave two separate states but, rather, two contesting parties within a single national state,"[37] Eisenhower and Dulles were determined, contrary to the Geneva Accords, to turn the provisional line between the northern and southern *zones* into a *permanent* line between two separate *states*.[38]

So the United States, while publicly pledging to honor the Geneva Agreements, had from the outset planned to subvert its three major ideas: (1) that the division was temporary, (2) that free elections would be held in 1956 to determine under which party the country would be unified, and (3) that in the meantime there would be no military activity.

In preparation for this subversion, the United States sabotaged the fourth of the above five points, which was that France would remain in order to supervise the provisions until the elections: By starting to pay all salaries for the government and military in the south directly and otherwise withdrawing financial support for the French, American leaders assured speedy French withdrawal. This departure left Washington as the policy-determining power in Vietnam's southern zone This was essentially the time when America took over the war.[39]

One of its first moves was to find a suitable person to head the government in this zone, which the United States treated as a separate country.

Ngo Dinh Diem: The Vietnamese Magsaysay

American officials were confident that they could succeed in Vietnam because of their previous successes in subverting democratic results of which they disapproved in Greece, Iran, Guatemala, and the Philippines. Of these, the CIA's success in getting Ramón Magsaysay elected president of the Philippines in 1953 was the most important.[40]

In fact, John Foster Dulles—whose brother Allen Dulles was the CIA director—brought CIA operative Edward Lansdale, who had engineered Magsaysay's election in the Philippines, to Vietnam, telling him: "Do what you did in the Philippines."[41]

Lansdale's assignment involved Ngo Dinh Diem, a Roman Catholic who had been living in the USA until the United States got Bo Dai, still the head of the government in the South, to make him his prime minister. Lansdale was told to turn Diem into the "Vietnamese Magsaysay."[42] Diem, however, was very different from Magsaysay, who was honest, charismatic, and had a man-of-the-people style. By contrast, Diem was cold, aloof, and elitist. The idea that he would become a popular leader was made still more unlikely by three other facts: besides being a member of a minority religion and having long lived abroad, he had collaborated with the French.

Diem, however, had two attributes deemed essential by the Eisenhower administration: He was a fierce anti-Communist, who would surely never accept a neutralist coalition government (meaning one that would be aligned neither with the American-led West nor with the Communist world), and he was opposed to fulfilling the Geneva agreement for an all-Vietnam election in 1956.[43]

There was, however, one election he was keen to have. As prime minister, he in 1955 set up a referendum for the voters to choose between him and Bo Dai to be the head of state. Lansdale, knowing that the votes would be counted by Diem's own men, urged him to be content with "a fairly large majority," but Diem insisted on receiving 98 percent of the vote.

His victory in the Saigon area was especially impressive: "[O]ut of a total of 450,000 registered voters, an astonishing 605,025 voted for Diem."[44] This episode revealed much about the wisdom as well as the character of the man around whom the American plan was to be built.

In any case, with Diem in place, the US could proceed to carry out its plan to subvert the crucial provisions of the Geneva Accords.

Further Violations of the Geneva Accords by the Eisenhower Administrations

The Provision against Threatened Violence: To shore up support for Diem in the South, Lansdale resorted to "scaring the hell out of Vietnamese in the North."[45] He spread rumors, for example, that the Communists were planning reprisals against Catholics in the North and that America planned to attack those Communists with atomic weapons.[46] Also, American taxpayers paid $375 million to help the Catholics, almost a million, who decided to move to the South in response to this scare campaign as well as in response to promises of land and work, combined with assurances from Catholic priests that Christ had moved to the South.[47] A large percentage of the people who went to the South, moreover, had no choice, because they had supported the French.[48] The Eisenhower administration claimed, nevertheless, that all of these people were "voting with their feet."

The Provision Against Importing Weapons: Having with its threat of atomic warfare flagrantly violated one provision of the Geneva Accords, the Eisenhower administration violated a second by smuggling weapons into the country to arm troops supporting Diem's regime.[49]

The Provision Against Military Alliances: American leaders also violated the prohibition against alliances with foreign countries by forming SEATO, the Southeast Asia Treaty Organization, two months after the end of the Geneva conference. Seeing that the Geneva Accords would thereby be violated, France blocked the US effort to make the southern zone, called "the State of Vietnam," a member of SEATO. But American officials got around this technicality with a protocol extending SEATO's mantle of protection over "the free territory under the jurisdiction of the State of Vietnam." As a "protocol state" of SEATO, "South Vietnam" was now effectively a member of a foreign alliance.[50]

Besides violating the spirit of Geneva, the White House's creation of SEATO was at the heart of its ability to trick the

American people, and even the US Congress, into believing that the United States had, with international backing, made a formal commitment to intervene militarily to prevent Communist domination of a country called "South Vietnam."

In Senate hearings, Secretary Dulles reaffirmed, as the language of the treaty itself put it, that US forces would respond unilaterally only in the event of "armed *aggression*" from a foreign country—meaning *a country other than Vietnam, understood as one country*. (China in particular was in view.) Dulles explicitly said that the United States would *not* respond unilaterally to mere (political) *subversion*, even from Communists.[51]

But Dulles did not tell the senators that, shortly before the conference to form SEATO, an undisclosed National Security Council directive had said that, if any government required assistance "to defeat local Communist subversion or rebellion not constituting armed attack," the president should request "Congressional authority to take appropriate action, which might . . . include the use of U.S. military forces"—even though to do so would be in express violation of the charter of the United Nations. This secret document, in other words, said that the administration should use the SEATO treaty to do exactly what Dulles was assuring the senators it would *not* be used to do.[52]

As Kahin suggested, once the US Senate had accepted the treaty, a president would later, thanks to "an apathetic and poorly informed Congress," be able "to define insurgency as outside aggression."[53]

The Temporary Nature of the Line of Demarcation: In the meantime, the task was to turn the temporary line between the northern and southern zones into a *political* line dividing two *countries*: the Democratic Republic of Vietnam (DRV) in the north and the Republic of Vietnam (RVN) in the south.

The Provision for Free Elections: The first step in changing the nature of the line of demarcation was to tell Diem that he need not participate in the electoral consultations. Dulles had originally meant to put the onus for cancelling the all-Vietnam elections on the North by specifying such stringent conditions for free elections that Hanoi would refuse.

However, Kenneth Young, an Asian expert in the US State Department, convinced Dulles that Ho Chi Minh's government was so much more popular than Diem's that it would win "any type of election which could be held in Viet-Nam in 1956."[54] (In his 1963 memoirs, Eisenhower himself acknowledged this fact, saying that if elections had been held, "possibly 80 percent of the population would have voted for the Communist Ho Chi Minh as their leader."[55]) Young also argued that, if Diem refused to hold elections, the Viet Minh in the South would be able to overthrow his government only with military support from the North, but that Moscow and Beijing, fearing a conflict with the United States, would pressure Hanoi not to provide this support.[56]

On this twofold basis, Dulles told Diem in 1955 that he would not need to hold elections the following year (even though the British warned that this breach of the Geneva accords would inevitably lead to a breach of the peace).[57]

The seriousness of this violation of the Geneva Accords cannot be exaggerated. As Kahin said, "without the firm and explicit assurance of national elections aimed at reunifying the country, the Vietminh would never have agreed to an armistice."[58] They would, instead, have simply gone ahead and completed their military reunification of the whole of Vietnam. Having earlier been double-crossed by the French, the Viet Minh were now double-crossed by the Americans.

Telling Another Lie, Risking Another War

The Eisenhower administration did not, of course, tell the American people that they were opposing the elections because it knew that its side would lose. The Eisenhower administration instead told another lie, claiming that the Geneva Accords had stipulated that elections were not to be held until there were "fundamental freedoms and democratic institutions" in both the northern and the southern zones. Elections had to be postponed, it claimed, because those conditions did not presently exist in the North. However, although the Accords did indeed speak of "fundamental freedoms and democratic institutions," they spoke of them only as the anticipated *consequences* of the election, not as prerequisites.[59]

The Eisenhower administration understood fully what it was doing. As a State Department intelligence report said: "If Diem is emboldened to reject or continue postponement of the elections stipulated in the Geneva Agreements, the DRV can be expected to seek its goal of unification (and control) through other means." US officials understood, in other words, that if their side violated an agreement they found distasteful, they could not expect the other side to continue honoring the other agreements, such as "respect for [the] demarcation line and ceasefire."[60]

US officials were, on behalf of the American people, willing to accept this risk, saying that if cancellation of the elections resulted in a renewal of hostilities, the United States must be willing to oppose the Viet Minh "with U.S. armed forces if necessary."[61] The Eisenhower administration hence knowingly took a crucial step towards another Asian war, after having only recently (in 1953) ended America's four-year war in Korea.

Was the US Motivated by the "Domino Theory"?

Why was the Eisenhower administration willing to take this risk? It has long been assumed that it did so because of its commitment to the "domino theory," according to which the loss of Vietnam would lead to a "chain reaction" in which most of the Southeast Asia countries, most importantly Thailand and Indonesia, would become Communist or at least neutral. In support of this assumption is the fact that in April 1954, when Eisenhower was trying to get the British to join in a "united action" to save French Indochina, he said: "you have a row of dominos, you knock over the first one, and what will happen to the last one is the certainty that it will go over very quickly."[62]

However, Gareth Porter argued convincingly that, although the CIA and the State Department did indeed hold this view from early 1950 (when NSC 64 spoke of "Communist plans to seize all of Southeast Asia") through the first part of 1953, the perception shifted in the latter part of that year, partly because of the US strategic superiority but also partly because of a more realistic appraisal of the Communist world's intentions and limitations. In November 1953, a CIA estimate said that, although the loss of southern Vietnam would be a "major blow to U.S. power and prestige in Asia," it would not necessarily lead to losses beyond Indochina. In early 1954, Undersecretary of State Walter Bedell Smith, who had previously told the Senate Foreign Relations Committee that the loss of Indochina would lead to the collapse of Southeast Asia as a whole, said: "I do not believe that now. . . . [P]art of Indochina might be lost without losing the rest of Southeast Asia." In saying this, he reflected the changed outlook of Eisenhower and Dulles themselves, who made similar statements.[63]

The domino theory would continue to be invoked by officials of the Eisenhower administration (as well as officials in subsequent administrations), but only as an argument that was found to be "useful," in Porter's words, "for various political and diplomatic purposes." As such, it was directed both at the Communist bloc, to convince it that the United States considered southern Vietnam so vital that it would intervene militarily to prevent it from going Communist, and to the US Congress and the American people, to retain their support. This was one more way, therefore, in which the Eisenhower administration (as well as subsequent administrations) did not tell the American people the truth about its Vietnam policy.[64]

The Eisenhower Administration's Plan

If Eisenhower and Dulles did not consider southern Vietnam sufficiently vital to US interests to commit military forces to save it, why did they think it important enough to cancel the elections, thereby risking the possibility that Hanoi, perhaps supported by China and/or the USSR, would resume its effort to unify the country through military means? The reason was evidently the fear that the charge that they had "lost Vietnam" would be used against them in coming elections, combined with the belief that Hanoi probably would not send troops down to the south, so that the risk was small.

But if so, what was the Eisenhower administration's plan for shoring up the Saigon regime, so that it could withstand possible attacks from members of the Viet Minh party who had remained in the South? Its plan was to duplicate what it had done in Iran in 1953 after engineering a coup to replace the government of Mohammad Mossaddeq with that of the shah, namely, to use covert operations to help the shah's government destroy Iran's Communist Party.

This approach was codified in a 1955 document on national security policy that, after calling for "destroying the effectiveness of the Communist apparatus in the free world," added: "[D]irect action against the Communist apparatus must rest largely with the local governments concerned, although the United States should be able to help significantly, chiefly through covert means."[65]

Having carried out this approach effectively in Iran without provoking intervention from the Soviet Union, even though Iran was on its periphery, the Eisenhower administration was confident that it could get away with it in Vietnam. This approach resulted in a terrorist state.

Diem's Terrorist State

Shortly after becoming head of state in 1954, Diem, in violation of the Geneva Agreements' prohibition against political reprisal, began eliminating all possible opposition, having tens of thousands of Viet Minh sympathizers—real and merely suspected—executed or thrown into prisons and concentration camps. "Arrests through 1957 averaged 5,000 a month, with about 150 executed each month."[66] By 1957, according to a writer for *Foreign Affairs*, South Vietnam was "a quasi-police state characterized by arbitrary arrests and imprisonment."[67]

By 1959, it was a full-fledged terrorist state, in which anyone accused of being a threat to the security of the state could be arrested, tried by military tribunal, and executed within three days, with no right of appeal.[68] Although this terror campaign "was in theory aimed at the Communists," wrote Philippe Devillers, it in fact "affected all those . . . who were bold enough to express their disagreement with the line of policy adopted by the ruling oligarchy."[69]

This campaign was carried out with the knowledge and financial support of the Eisenhower administration, which was providing the Diem government hundreds of millions of US tax dollars a year and had people working with "Diem's propaganda apparatus, his economic ministries, and, of course, the South Vietnamese military."[70]

The US-Diem policy of destroying the Viet Minh as a political force in South Vietnam almost succeeded. The party's membership in the Mekong Delta, for example, was reduced from 60,000 to 5,000 by 1959.[71] The Viet Minh party in the South came so close to being liquidated because it was not allowed to fight back, even though an estimated 5,000 to 10,000 of its guerrilla fighters had remained in the South (while about 80,000 had gone North in the post-Geneva regroupment). The party leaders in the North, having adopted the general Communist bloc line of peaceful co-existence and peaceful resolution of disputes, ordered that the struggle in the South must be purely political, not also military. Party members were not, therefore, able to defend themselves.[72]

In 1958, however, some former guerrillas, contrary to orders, took up arms and started a resistance movement.[73] In response to this movement and the danger that the party in the South would be completely destroyed, Hanoi in 1959 finally authorized its use of force and agreed to send it supplies. It declared, however, that the military struggle must remain subordinate to the political, making no effort to overthrow the Diem regime. Only in 1961, after seeing the successes of the insurgency, did Hanoi allow the military and political struggles to be put on an equal footing. (It would not be until 1964, moreover, that North Vietnam would send regular army troops to the South.)[74]

Diem's murderous reign of terror cannot be excused,

therefore, on the grounds that he was simply defending himself from a Hanoi-backed Communist insurgency. The Viet Minh insurgency, which eventually won Hanoi's backing, arose because the Eisenhower administration unilaterally canceled the Geneva-ordained election. The Viet Minh then supported Ho's National Liberation Front (NLF).[75]

3. The Kennedy Administration

When the Kennedy administration took over, the unspeakable truth was that the United States was backing an extremely unpopular government, which had evoked an uprising within the South which had been officially created in 1955 as the Republic of Vietnam. As a result of Diem's personality and his policies, he had little support except from the few Vietnamese who were prospering financially under his regime. American intelligence reported that only 5 percent of the people in the southern zone supported Diem, while 75 percent supported the NLF (with 20 percent being neutral).[76]

Realizing that its puppet government was so unpopular, the Kennedy administration decided that it could be propped up only by the use of US military force. Throughout the Eisenhower administration, America's violation of international law was limited, for the most part, to its support for Diem's state terror. By the end of Eisenhower's presidency, accordingly, there were only 800 US military personnel in Vietnam, serving primarily as advisors for the Army of the Republic of South Vietnam (ARVN).

But the Kennedy administration changed the policy from merely supporting Diem's regime to fully Americanizing the war.[77] By the end of Kennedy's first year, there were 3,000 US military personnel in Vietnam. By the end of 1962, there were 11,000. Kennedy obviously agreed with his advisor who, having pointed out that sending US forces to Vietnam would "require circumvention of the Geneva Accords," added that "we should not let this stop us."[78]

This intensified commitment to Vietnam reflected not

merely the Kennedy administration's realization that ARVN would never attain victory on its own, even with US advice and equipment. It also reflected the belief of some members of this administration that US "credibility" was at stake in this contest.

This justification for US involvement did not replace the older justification—the domino theory. Rather, as Gabriel Kolko put it: "The domino and credibility theories began to merge into a unified conception, credibility growing weightier over time."[79] Both theories were part of imperial logic, but they were different. The domino theory could be understood in strictly economic and geopolitical terms, in which America's concern was to have the countries of Southeast Asia politically aligned with it and open to its economic exploitation.

The credibility theory, by contrast, involved the world's perception of US military power: America's willingness and ability to use its military power to achieve its goals. The idea was that, if other nations saw that American power could be defeated in Vietnam, then enemies around the world would be emboldened to challenge US hegemony, while repressive allied governments would lose faith that American commitments to them would be kept. This theory was classically expressed in 1964 by General Maxwell Taylor (who was the Chairman of the Joint Chiefs of Staff from 1962 to 1964, then US ambassador to Saigon in 1964 and 1965). Taylor said: "If we leave Vietnam with our tail between our legs, the consequences of this defeat in the rest of Asia, Africa, and Latin America would be disastrous."[80]

At the outset of the Kennedy administration, said Kolko, "the issue of U.S. potency possessed Washington." One reason was the success of Castro's revolution in Cuba combined with the Bay of Pigs debacle, which was "a humiliating reverse for the counterinsurgency and local-war concepts just then coming into great vogue." So Kennedy established a special task force on Vietnam, making Vietnam a test case for the ability of counterinsurgency to defeat "subversion" everywhere. Having imbued Vietnam with global symbolic significance, "the administration would begin a long series of escalations, each raising the ante to establish credibility."[81]

Under Kennedy, the Vietnam War became more of an American enterprise, with the US-trained ARVN playing an increasingly subordinate role and the American taxpayer assuming an ever larger responsibility. To finance his counterinsurgency warfare, in fact, Kennedy brought about the largest peacetime increase in military spending in US history to date. Some of the money was for US troops and their fighting machines, which included armored personnel carriers, bombers, and helicopters equipped with napalm and massive machine guns.

This increase also financed the beginning of Operation RANCH HAND, through which 100 million pounds of herbicides would be dropped on South Vietnam between 1962 and 1970 to poison food crops that could be used by NLF troops and to strip foliage that could hide them. Although this program had a dark-humor motto—"Only We Can Prevent Forests"—there was nothing funny about its consequences for the health of the Vietnamese people for generations to come.[82] In any case, at the very center of the Kennedy administration's plan was the "strategic hamlet program," in which millions of South Vietnamese—reportedly about 2/3 of the rural population—were forced into concentration camps to prevent contact between them and NLF forces.[83]

All this death, destruction, and relocation brought about by American military might did nothing, however, to increase the viability of Diem's regime. In 1960, Diem had been warned by the Eisenhower administration that if his government did not reform, American leaders would consider "alternative courses of action and leaders in order to achieve our objective."[84] He, in other words, could be replaced by another puppet. By 1963, Diem had not reformed, and Kennedy was advised: "The war could not be won with the present regime."[85] Kennedy decided on a radical change of course, albeit one he would not live to implement.

The Kennedy administration had learned that Diem's brother and principal advisor, Ngo Dinh Nhu, wanted to negotiate a "neutralist" government. That, of course, was not acceptable to US leaders: South Vietnam had to be *anti*-Communist, not simply *non*-Communist. Shortly thereafter, some generals were given the green light for a coup, the CIA supplied the funds, and on November 2 Diem and Nhu were deposed and executed. Three weeks later, Kennedy himself was assassinated—a fateful event, given the convincing evidence in several books that Kennedy planned to leave Vietnam after the next election.[86]

4. The Johnson Administration: First Steps

The next president, Lyndon Johnson, cancelled the plan to leave Vietnam and escalated the war, but otherwise, having inherited the Kennedy administration advisors,[87] continued its policies, a fact that gave the "credibility" rationale a double meaning. As Kahin analyzed the problem:

> [I]t had become starkly evident to Johnson's advisers that the policies they had been shaping ever since John F. Kennedy assumed the presidency had failed. However, since their own reputations were so closely bound up with these policies, it was difficult for them to call for a shift from a military to a political track. Even if more attuned to American interests, such a move would have exposed their own previous counsel. . . . On the other hand, moving to a policy of heavier and geographically expanded military intervention would be perceived by the American Congress and public as having consistency and continuity and would not [at least immediately] disclose the erroneous nature of the assumptions and perceptions upon which interventionism rested. . . . It was usually not difficult for these men to equate the U.S. national interest with their own reputations.[88]

"Using the phrase, 'protecting our commitment,' to explain American presence in Viet-Nam," Robert Gallucci observed, "may be as pertinent in its application to individual actors as it is to the nation as a whole."[89]

In any case, the assumption behind the coup on the part of these Kennedy-Johnson advisors was that American leaders would be able "to achieve our objective" through the military junta composed of the generals who carried out the coup, led by Duong Van ("Big") Minh. "Our requirements," said William Bundy, "were really very simple—we wanted any government which would continue to fight." Big Minh, however, objected to some of the US military's views, especially the idea that it should start bombing North Vietnam. Also his junta, being non-Communist rather than anti-Communist, favored a neutral government that, while leaning towards the West, would be a government of reconciliation, working for peaceful coexistence with Hanoi.

Johnson was advised by Kennedy's former aides to reject this possibility. McGeorge Bundy, the national security advisor, said it would cause a loss of US prestige. Walt Rostow, another influential advisor, argued that the neutralization of South Vietnam would be "the greatest setback to US interests on the world scene."[90] In March of 1964, the National Security Council defined the war as "a test case of U.S. capacity to help a nation to meet the Communist 'war of liberation.'"[91] As these assessments illustrated, the United States, far from fighting for the right of the people of the southern part of Vietnam to determine their own form of government, constantly acted to *prevent* this in the name of America's own "prestige" and "credibility."

Accordingly, less than two months after Big Minh's military junta assumed power, it was removed in another coup, led by General Nguyen Khanh. What US officials found in Khanh, said Marilyn Young, "was a Vietnamese government that would follow orders." And this, they assumed, was the key. Secretary of Defense Robert McNamara, when asked by a reporter why he thought the American cause was now finally going to succeed, said: "Because we now have a leader in South Vietnam, General Khanh, who himself is ready to put that nation on a war footing." But it would be less than a year before Khanh would be replaced by still another leader through whom the US government would seek to achieve its objective in Vietnam.[92]

The only way to achieve this objective, the Johnson admin istration decided, was by more fully exerting America's military might.

The Gulf of Tonkin "Incident"

As it became clear that things were proceeding no better under General Khanh, Johnson's advisors decided that Khanh and his troops needed a boost in morale, which could be provided by air strikes against North Vietnam.

These advisors agreed that this escalation of the war would require a congressional resolution, but also that without some "drastic change in the situation to point to" and "a substantial increase in national attention and international tension," it would be hard to get the public and the US Congress to support this escalation.[93] Secretary of State Dean Rusk added that, according to his (incorrect) reading, SEATO would provide the basis for a congressional resolution to attack North Vietnam if Hanoi did something that could be regarded as an "armed attack."

Shortly after these discussions, which took place during a conference in Honolulu in June 1964,[94] the desired "drastic change in the situation" came about.

On August 4, shortly after Washington had told General Khanh (in late July) that it was considering attacks on North Vietnam, Johnson told congressional leaders that the North Vietnamese had made unprovoked attacks against American ships in international waters.[95] Was this a fabricated incident? The evidence suggests that it was.

OPLAN 34-A and "the Scenario": One part of this evidence is the fact that, on the basis of discussions that began at the Honolulu conference in November 1963, the CIA and the US military worked up a clandestine military campaign called Operations Plan 34 Alpha (OPLAN 34-A), which would involve secret forays into the North.

In June 1964, moreover, a committee chaired by Assistant Secretary of State William Bundy worked up a scenario—called, in fact, "the scenario"—that would lead to a congressional resolution for the use of force. Bundy's committee even prepared a draft of a resolution, so that it would be ready when the opportunity arose, and contingency plans for airstrikes against the North, which would be ready if the desired resolution were to be forthcoming.[96]

OPLAN 34-A Provocations: Then in mid-July, the US destroyer *Maddox* was ordered to head to the Gulf of Tonkin to carry out electronic espionage. On July 30, South Vietnamese gunboats, with American advisers, made commando raids against two DRV islands in the Gulf, these raids being part of OPLAN 34-A.

On July 31, the *Maddox*, having reached the Gulf, exchanged greetings with South Vietnamese gunboats that were leaving after the day's raids (contrary to later claims that the *Maddox* had no awareness of these gunboats). That same day, the North Vietnamese sent a note to the International Control Commission, saying that the raids, which they called acts of the American and South Vietnamese administrations, were violations of the DRV.[97]

Then on August 2, the *Maddox* cruised near DRV islands that were under attack by the South Vietnamese gunboats. Three DRV patrol boats charged repeatedly at the *Maddox*, veering off at the last moment. The *Maddox* then opened fire on them, and they fired torpedoes in return, but missed.

On August 3, Rusk sent a cable to Maxwell Taylor, the US ambassador in Saigon, saying: "We believe that present Op Plan 34 A activities are beginning to rattle Hanoi, and Maddox incident is directly related to their efforts to resist these activities."[98]

A similar point was made by the commodore of the *Maddox*, who sent a message to the commander of the 7th Fleet saying that he had intelligence indicating that the North Vietnamese considered the patrol by the *Maddox* to be directly involved with the attacks by the South Vietnamese gunboats. Clearly the North Vietnamese attack, if it can even be called that, was not unprovoked, and the Americans knew that the North Vietnamese certainly did not consider it unprovoked.

The incident that provided the basis for the Gulf of Tonkin Resolution, however, was not the one that occurred on August 2, but the one that did *not* occur on August 4.

The August 4 "Incident": On the night of August 4, the *Maddox*, along with the *Turner Joy* (another destroyer sent into the Gulf on August 3), fired their huge guns for several hours, having evidently been told by their sonarmen that torpedoes were headed at them. But no torpedoes hit them. James Stockdale, a naval commander flying low directly over the destroyers, saw nothing: "No boats, no wakes, no ricochets off boats, no boat impacts, no torpedo wakes—nothing but black sea and American firepower." Also, Captain John Herrick of the *Maddox*, who had not been informed about OPLAN 34-A,[99] decided that his ship might have been firing at nothing. He sent a radio message saying:

> Review of action makes many reported contacts and torpedoes fired appear very doubtful. . . . No actual sighting by *Maddox*. Suggest complete evaluation before any further action.

Stockdale, receiving this message, was relieved that "there's a commodore up there in the Gulf who has the guts to blow the whistle on a screw-up." Nevertheless, the next morning (August 5), Stockdale was given orders to retaliate against North Vietnamese targets, which he did, even while thinking that the president was "going off half-cocked" and asking: "Retaliate for what?" At the same time, Johnson was telling congressional leaders about the "unprovoked attack."[100]

Johnson administration members knew, however, that even if there had been an attack, it would *not* have been "unprovoked." In addition to having set OPLAN 34-A into motion, they acknowledged among themselves that the North Vietnamese actions, such as they were, were in response to this plan's provocations.

On August 3, National Security Advisor McGeorge Bundy,

talking about the behavior of the North's patrol boats on August 2, had told Undersecretary of State George Ball that "he was persuaded . . . it's a reaction to the 34 enterprise the day before." LBJ himself, talking to a former Eisenhower administration official, said: "There have been some covert operations up in that area that we have been carrying on, so I imagine they wanted to put a stop to it." Robert McNamara, discussing with Johnson a briefing to be set up for congressional leaders, said: "I think that . . . we should . . . , Mr. President, explain this OPLAN 34-A, these covert operations. There's no question but what that had [a] bearing on [the events]."[101]

On August 5, nevertheless, Johnson would assure Congress that the attacks had been "unprovoked."

First, however, Johnson gave orders to dust off "the scenario" that had been worked out by William Bundy—both the plans to attack North Vietnam and the draft resolution, saying with regard to the latter: "[N]ow's the time to get it through the Congress."[102]

The Gulf of Tonkin Resolution

On August 5, shortly after Johnson had assured Congress that that there had been "unprovoked attacks" on a US ship exercising the right of innocent passage through international waters, the US Congress did pass the resolution, which came to be called the Gulf of Tonkin Resolution. The Johnson administration got this resolution by lying.

Lying to Congress: When asked if the United States had done anything to provoke an attack, McNamara said that the attacks were "deliberate and unprovoked" against a ship on "routine patrol in international waters." Besides failing to mention that this ship had been carrying out electronic espionage, McNamara also did not, of course, volunteer the information that there were real doubts whether there had even been an attack on August 4.

When Wayne Morse of Oregon, one of two senators who voted against the resolution, asked—on the basis of a tip from a source in the Pentagon—whether there was a connection between the *Maddox* and the South Vietnamese commando raids, McNamara continued to lie, saying:

> Our Navy was not associated with, was not aware of, any South Vietnamese actions, if there were any. The *Maddox* was operating in international waters, was carrying out a routine patrol. . . . It was not informed of, was not aware of, had no knowledge of . . . any possible South Vietnamese actions in connection with the two islands, as Senator Morse referred to.[103]

When Morse tried to interest other senators in the information he had to the contrary, one of them told him: "Hell, Wayne, you can't fight with a President at a time when the flags are waving." Besides, this fellow senator added: "[Johnson's] the kind of president who follows the rules and won't get the country into war without coming back to Congress."[104]

Senator William Fulbright, chairman of the Senate Foreign Relations Committee, felt the same way, adding that he had been assured by his "good friend Lyndon" that the resolution was "just backing the President on his Tonkin response, not giving him a blank check for war." Years later, Fulbright, having learned better, said: "I don't normally assume a President lies to you."[105]

The US Congress unanimously, except for Morse and Senator Ernest Gruening of Alaska, quickly passed the Gulf of Tonkin Resolution, which authorized the president "to take all necessary measures to repeal any armed attack against the forces of the United States and to prevent further aggression."[106]

Lying to the American People and the World: The rationale for the Gulf of Tonkin resolution was filled with falsehoods, including the following:

> Whereas naval units of the Communist regime in Vietnam, in violation of the principles of the Charter of the United Nations and international law, have deliberately and repeatedly attacked United States naval vessels lawfully present in international waters [untrue]. . . and Whereas these attacks are part of a deliberate and systematic campaign of aggression that the Communist regime in North Vietnam has been waging against its neighbors and the nations joined with them in the collective defense of their freedom [untrue]; and
>
> Whereas the United States is assisting the peoples of southeast Asia to protect their freedom [untrue] and has no territorial, military or political ambitions in that area [untrue], but desires only that these people should be left in peace to work out their own destinies in their own way [untrue]....[107]

Lying about SEATO: The resolution also, besides ignoring the fact that it was the United States that was violating the Charter of the United Nations, falsely implied that this Charter, in conjunction with SEATO, provided authorization for the United States "to take all necessary steps, including the use of armed force, to assist any member or protocol state of the Southeast Asia Collective Defense Treaty requesting assistance in defense of its freedom."

Accordingly, although the US Congress had explicitly been assured in 1954 that SEATO could not be used to authorize unilateral military intervention by the United States on behalf of South Vietnam, the Congress in 1964 allowed the Johnson administration to use it for just that.

As soon as Johnson had won reelection—in a landslide victory based largely on the public's belief that he would be less likely to escalate the war than his opponent, Senator Barry Goldwater—he appointed a National Security Council Working Group to consider options in Vietnam, suggesting that they make "maximum use of a Gulf of Tonkin rationale."[108] Johnson planned to use the resolution in precisely the way he had assured his "good friend" Senator Fulbright that he would not. He would use it, in fact, to bring about three major escalations, all of which occurred in 1965, and all of which reflected indifference to the welfare of the people of Vietnam.

US Indifference to Vietnamese Welfare

An examination of the Working Group's first draft about US aims in South Vietnam is revealing. These aims were said to be:

> to protect US reputation as a counter-subversion guarantor; to avoid domino effect especially in Southeast Asia; to keep South Vietnamese territory from Red hands; to emerge from crisis without unacceptable taint from methods.[109]

The aims, in other words, were all about protecting America's reputation.

Noticeably absent from this internal document was anything about the welfare of the people of Vietnam. In a quantitative evaluation of US aims offered by John McNaughton, the assistant secretary of defense, this concern did find a place—but only barely. According to his memo, US aims were:

- 70% - To avoid a humiliating US defeat (to our reputation as guarantor).

- 20% - To keep SVN = South Vietnam (and then adjacent) territory from Chinese hands.[110]

- 10% - To permit the people of SVN to enjoy a better, freer way of life.

- ALSO – To emerge from crisis without unacceptable taint from methods used.[111]

Given that last point, introduced by the capitalized ALSO, even the 10 percent initially allotted to concern for the people of South Vietnam seemed to be negated.

In public statements, to be sure, the relative importance of the first three rationales was reversed, with Johnson saying that the American objective was that the Vietnamese "be allowed to guide their own country in their own way" and "free from outside interference."[112]

The internal memos, however, reflected the Johnson administration's indifference to the welfare of the Vietnamese people. This attitude had, in fact, already been reported in 1964 by a war correspondent who said: "Coldbloodedly, we really don't care what happens here providing the Communists don't get it and with it Southeast Asia."[113]

5. The Johnson Administration's Repeated Escalations

This coldblooded lack of concern for the people of Southeast Asia would be further illustrated by the escalations ordered by the Johnson administration.

The First Escalation: Bombing the South

The Johnson administration's first escalation was occasioned by its awareness that most of the South Vietnamese wanted peace, combined with the realization that the Buddhists, who had become active opponents of the war, were being increasingly effective. Johnson's advisors became alarmed at the possibility that, in Kahin's words,

> Buddhist leaders could channel the mounting tide of antiwar sentiment in South Vietnam into the creation of a government that would demand a cease-fire, a negotiated settlement with the NLF, and ultimately the departure of the Americans.[114]

Given this alarm, combined with the continued

deterioration of ARVN's military effectiveness—due to a growing unwillingness to fight and increasing desertion rates—the US military was in February of 1965 given authorization for a "systematic bombing of South Vietnam." This bombing of the South was, Chomsky and Herman have noted, "at three times the level of the more publicized—and more protested—bombing of the North," which was soon to follow.[115] "Largely unnoticed by the American news media," commented Kahin, "this major escalatory decision had immense physical consequences for the people and land of Vietnam."[116]

One of the consequences of unleashing the US military machine was an enormous number of civilian deaths. American leaders were aware of this consequence. For example, Ambassador Henry Cabot Lodge, Jr. (the son of the Henry Cabot Lodge discussed in Chapter 1), said:

> [T]he superiority of Allied forces . . . lies largely in almost unlimited quantities of sophisticated equipment of war. We have weapons of tremendous power. . . . [I]t is inevitable that they will produce civilian casualties, most of which we will never learn about.[117]

US leaders, however, were not deterred by this consequence. Lodge, for example, warned against letting restrictions on the use of these weapons "inhibit our military activities to [a] point where our superiority in weapons is completely negated."[118]

With regard to what to do about the bad press that could result from causing so many civilian deaths, Lodge gave the administration this advice:

> [C]ontinue to impress on [the] public and Congress that [the] reason for civilian casualties is [the] essentially cruel yet totally deliberate VC tactic of using civilians . . . and that casualties

> caused by VC, being deliberate, are much more cruel and morally reprehensible than those inadvertently caused by Allied forces.[119]

The Congress and most of the press let the administration get away with this propaganda.

In 1967, however, Bernard Fall tried to call attention to the significance of Johnson's first escalation, writing:

> [W]hat changed the character of the Vietnam war was *not* the decision to bomb North Vietnam; *not* the decision to use American ground troops in South Vietnam; but the decision to wage unlimited aerial warfare inside the country at the price of literally pounding the place to bits.[120]

This initiation of an all-out aerial attack on the people, land, and hamlets of South Vietnam, which would continue for another decade, certainly deserves at least equal mention, even if Fall's claim that it was more fundamental than the other two escalations was debatable.

The Second Escalation: Bombing the North

The Johnson administration next decided to use the Gulf of Tonkin Resolution, originally employed to justify only sporadic raids against the North, as authorization for a sustained bombing campaign in the North.

The Rationale for Bombing the North: Johnson's advisors favored this campaign for four reasons.

1. Assuming that the battle in the South was directed by the leaders in the North, who could call it off at will, Johnson's advisors said that the bombing would be an attack on the will of the Northern leaders, through which they would "be brought to their knees."

2. The bombing would also be a "shot in the arm" for the

Southern leaders, through which their morale would be increased, making them less inclined to desert and more willing to fight.[121]

3. The bombing would protect the administration's reputation, because even if it failed, William Bundy argued, "it will damp down the charge that we did not do all that we could have done."[122]

4. The bombing would increase American credibility,[123] with this same Bundy brother adding that, even if the bombing failed, it would "set a higher price for the future upon all adventures of guerrilla warfare."[124] North Vietnam was to be devastated, in other words, to discourage other peoples from being disobedient.

This planned bombing campaign, in any case, faced the following two obstacles.

Obtaining a "Request" to Bomb the North: One obstacle was the fact that the bombing of the North had to be presented as an American response to a request from the government of South Vietnam. This was an obstacle because, although the current president, General Khanh, had been brought to power on the assumption that he would carry out US wishes, he did not favor the bombing. Worse yet, he was, in alliance with Buddhist leaders, contacting the NLF about a negotiated settlement.

American officials overcame this obstacle by arranging yet another coup, through which Khanh was replaced by a military triumvirate of generals all named Nguyen: Nguyen Cao Ky, Nguyen Chanh Thi, and Nguyen Van Thieu.

This coup, which occurred on February 19, 1965, gave America a puppet government that finally removed the threat of a negotiated peace: General Ky—who would later express admiration for Hitler—announced that he would replace any prime minister who "threatened to betray the country" by proposing a negotiated settlement.[125]

Accordingly, General Ky and his military companions "asked" the United States to start a bombing campaign against the North.

Proving "Aggression" from the North: The second obstacle to the proposed systematic bombing of the North was the lack of public support in America and the rest of the world. The sporadic bombings of the North had already produced worldwide protests, and a poll showed that 75 percent of the American public favored settling the war through negotiations.

The US solution to this obstacle was to portray the war in general, and the bombings in particular, as responses to aggression from the North. This was the task of an administration White Paper, entitled *Aggression from the North: The Record of North Vietnam's Campaign to Conquer South Viet-Nam*. Its central thesis was that the United States was aiding South Vietnam, which was "fighting for its life against a brutal campaign of terror and armed attack inspired, directed, supplied, and controlled by the Communist regime in Hanoi," which was trying to conquer "a sovereign people in a neighboring state."[126]

This, however, was a difficult thesis to support. The administration had no evidence that many of the "Viet Cong," as the US government called the Viet Minh, were from the North. The *New York Times* had recently reported, moreover, that "the majority of Vietcong weapons are American-made ones captured in battle from South Vietnamese forces."[127]

Even evidence that men and weapons were coming from the North, moreover, would not have provided any legal or even moral justification for bombing the North, because the idea that "North Vietnam" was another state or country, distinct from "South Vietnam"—so that it could be guilty of "aggression" against the latter—was merely an American invention, not accepted by the Vietnamese and not sanctioned by the Geneva Accords. The Johnson administration, however, could safely assume that this fact, which had seldom if ever been recently mentioned in the American press, had long been forgotten, and that if they could convince the American people that men and weapons were coming from the North, they would consent to the bombing campaign.

The Johnson administration achieved this objective through additional subterfuge. Phillip Liechty, who was then a

CIA officer, later stated that the CIA filled a North Vietnamese boat with 100 tons of military supplies made in Communist countries, then sank it in shallow water off the South Vietnamese coast.[128] After a phony firefight on February 16, 1965, during which the boat was supposedly sunk by the South Vietnamese, foreign correspondents were invited to inspect the boat's contents.

When the White Paper was released on February 17, this "evidence" was included as "dramatic new proof . . . exposed just as this report was being completed . . . that North Viet-Nam is carrying out a carefully conceived plan of aggression against the South." In spite of the suspicious timing, a *New York Times* story cited this feature of the White Paper as "conclusive proof" of "an increased southward flow of more sophisticated weapons."[129]

Results of the Bombing Campaign: The day after the White Paper's release, Johnson announced the beginning of sustained bombing, and soon a hundred US airplanes were regularly attacking targets in the North.[130]

However, this bombing campaign, called Operation Rolling Thunder, brought none of the benefits in the South that had been predicted. Rather, "the political and military fabric of the southern regime continued to unravel even more rapidly than before."[131]

Also, far from breaking the will of the DRV, the bombing *produced* the invasion from the North that had been the bombing's purported justification. As Kahin explained:

> Hanoi had always held back from dispatching combat units, for fear of provoking further U.S. military intervention. Now that the bombing had in fact been launched, however, it had little to lose.

In spite of the administration's earlier claims about "aggression from the North," US intelligence had spotted no North Vietnamese combat units operating in the South before April 21, 1965.[132]

Johnson's Third Escalation: US Ground Troops

The bombing campaign against the North, combined with the continued disintegration of the army of South Vietnam, produced yet another problem. The airfields in the South, from which some of the bombing missions in the South and now in the North were launched, were becoming increasingly vulnerable to attacks from the NLF, which would soon be joined by forces from North Vietnam.

In response, the Johnson administration decided that American ground forces were needed to protect these airfields. Early in March of 1965, Marine battalions arrived to defend the giant airfield at Danang, and a few weeks later they were given authorization to fight up to 85 kilometers away. As *The Pentagon Papers* later noted, this was "a major decision made without much fanfare—and without much planning."[133] It was a major decision because it was the beginning of the Johnson administration's third major escalation: the introduction of US ground forces into South Vietnam.

Although the troops sent to protect US airfields inaugurated this new phase, it was not until July, after long discussions, that Johnson finally accepted the position of the majority of his advisors, namely, that large numbers of US ground forces should be sent to fight, as distinct from simply protecting airfields. The rationale was that, although the bombing of the North and the South and the use of forces to protect US airfields had neither increased ARVN's morale nor broken the will of the enemy, the large-scale introduction of American ground forces would have both of these benefits.[134]

Having been told by Congressional leaders that he would have no chance of replacing the Gulf of Tonkin Resolution with a more explicit grant of authority to wage war, Johnson simply employed that resolution as a "functional equivalent,"[135] demonstrating again that he was using it as the "blank check" he had promised it would not be.

At the end of July, Johnson ordered 50,000 troops to be sent, bringing the total up to 125,000. He did this on the basis of another "request" from General Ky, who had in the meantime been appointed prime minister by the triumvirate to which he belonged, after the former prime minister had refused to request more American troops.[136]

Further Escalations and the Complete Americanization of the War

In any case, this escalation, like the previous ones, made little difference, so more troops were sent time and time again. By the end of 1966, there were over 383,000 American troops in South Vietnam. By the end of 1967, there were over a half million.[137]

With the Johnson administration's escalations, the war had become totally Americanized, with ARVN serving a purely auxiliary role. Furthermore, this American war became, in Marilyn Young's words, "a war against Vietnam as such, North and South," and, in Gabriel Kolko's words, a "relentless, unconscionable attack on the bodies and minds of virtually the entire people of Vietnam."[138]

With the Saigon government in the hands of a military junta, moreover, "there was no longer any pretense that the United States was supporting a genuine political entity in South Vietnam."[139] The fact that this had been a pretense all along—that the Republic of South Vietnam had virtually no indigenous support but was "essentially an appendage of the United States"[140]—explained why all the escalations, while creating enormous death and destruction, could not turn the RSV into a viable government.

Seeing both that it was unable to win the war on its own and also that it needed to make the effort appear multi-national, the Johnson administration formulated a "Many Flags" Program, under which it tried to get help from allies. This program was largely a failure, as no European countries, and very few other countries, would send troops. And what little success the program had was mostly a charade. Of the five countries that did send troops, only Australia and New Zealand sent them as allies. The other countries—South Korea, Thailand, and the Philippines—demanded very high prices.[141]

For example, the concessions extracted by South Korea—such as the agreement that its soldiers would receive 20 times their normal remuneration—cost the United States almost $1 billion in the period between 1966 and 1970 alone. Ferdinand Marcos, the dictator of the Philippines, worked out a similarly sweet deal before sending Filipino troops.

The State Department worked hard to keep these arrangements secret, fearing, it said, that publication "might create the impression that [these] troops went to South Vietnam . . . as mercenary troops paid by the United States."[142] This "impression" would, of course, have been the truth. But by successfully keeping these arrangements secret, "the administration was able to refer to Korea, Thailand, and the Philippines as 'stanch allies' who were 'volunteering to fight for the Free World.'"[143]

In any case, even with its escalations, reinforced by tens of thousands of mercenary troops, the United States was no closer to its goal of creating a viable anti-Communist, pro-American government in the South.

6. The Domestic Rebellion Against the War

By the late 1960s, there was a growing rebellion in the United States against the war.

The Senate Foreign Relations Committee: This rebellion was aided by televised hearings on the war and the underlying principles of American foreign policy, which were conducted by the Senate Foreign Relations Committee. Senator William Fulbright, as the committee's chairman, led the attack on the administration's arguments, including its assumption that America had a moral or legal right to be in Vietnam. Addressing Secretary of State Dean Rusk, Fulbright said:

> Vietnam is their country. We do not even have the right the French did. We have no historical right. We are obviously intruders from their point of

> view. We represent the old Western imperialism in their eyes.[144]

Citizens against the War: Some of the rebellion was reflected in anti-war marches, speeches, and teach-ins. The teach-ins, which were led by intellectuals such as Noam Chomsky and George Kahin, began with small groups but increasingly attracted larger audiences, which led to anti-war marches.

The first big anti-war march, complete with draft-card burnings, occurred in April 1967, with 75,000 marching in San Francisco and perhaps 250,000 in New York City.[145] One of the marchers in New York was Martin Luther King, Jr., who shortly before, in a sermon at New York's Riverside Church, had compared the Vietnam War to a "demonic, destructive suction tube" and described the US government as "the greatest purveyor of violence in the world today." King also said that "we have no honorable intentions in Vietnam" and that "we have been wrong from the beginning of our adventure in Vietnam."[146]

A year after beginning to speak against the war, King would be silenced by an assassin's bullet. (Although James Earl Ray was accused and convicted of the crime, a civil trial in 1999 showed that he was merely a patsy for an assassination planned by FBI Director J. Edgar Hoover, the U.S. military, and others.[147]) But after King's death, the protest against the war, much of it religiously motivated, would continue. In 1968, two Catholic priests, Daniel and Philip Berrigan, used napalm to destroy draft board records. At the subsequent trial, Daniel offered an apology "for the fracture of good order, the burning of paper instead of children."[148]

Rebellion within the Army: At the same time, a rebellion against the war was going on within the army itself.

- In 1965, a young officer in Vietnam, saying that the war was "not worth a single American life," was court-martialed because he refused to follow orders.[149]

- In 1966, three privates, who would come to be known as the "Fort Hood Three," refused orders to leave for Vietnam.[150]

- Also in 1966, Donald W. Duncan, a highly decorated Green Beret, having refused to re-enlist, wrote an indictment of the war for *Ramparts* magazine called "The Whole Thing Was a Lie!"[151]

- In 1967, an Army doctor refused to train Special Forces soldiers, because to train "murderers of women and children" would be to violate his Hippocratic Oath.[152]

- That same year (1967) also brought the formation of Vietnam Veterans Against the War (VVAW). One of many soldiers who sent contributions to this organization wrote that, if anyone back home told him that "Viet Nam was worthwhile or it was our obligation—I'll hit him right in the face."[153]

Within the Johnson Administration: Changes of heart were even occurring within the administration. In 1967, reflecting on the widespread feeling in the country "that 'the Establishment' is out of its mind," Assistant Secretary of Defense John McNaughton wrote a memo to his boss suggesting that he persuade the president to repudiate the 1964 National Security Memorandum—drafted by McNaughton himself—which had justified the war as "a test case of U.S. capacity."[154]

Agreeing, McNamara wrote a memo to the president stating that the United States should clarify that its commitment was "only to see that the people of South Vietnam are permitted to determine their own future," which would mean that US commitment was *not:*

- to ensure that a particular person or group remains in power. . . .

- to guarantee that the self-chosen government is non-Communist . . . .
- to insist that the independent South Vietnam remain separate from North Vietnam.[155]

A few months later, McNamara would read the history of US policy toward Vietnam that he had commissioned, which led him to make his comment that "they could hang people for what's in there."[156] That same month, McNamara testified before the Senate Armed Services Committee that Operation Rolling Thunder had been a failure. Furious that his Secretary of Defense had gone "dovish" on him, Johnson decided that McNamara would make an excellent president of the World Bank.[157]

Within another year, Johnson would in effect fire himself.

The Tet Offensive

One of the major factors leading to Johnson's decision was the Tet Offensive early in 1968, which Kolko called "the most important . . . event of the Vietnam War."[158] It was so important because it revealed the enormous gap between what the White House and the Pentagon had been telling the Americans about Vietnam and the reality, showing that "the supposedly defeated adversary could strike anywhere, even in the heart of Saigon, in great force."[159]

The Tet Offensive, by exposing the wishful thinking behind the claim that there was "light at end of the tunnel," induced a massive change in public perception. Whereas 50 percent of the public thought America was making progress in Vietnam late in 1967, only 33 percent thought so after Tet, and "an astonishing 49 percent believed the United States should never have intervened in Vietnam to begin with."[160] Tet also, as one insider put it, "changed absolutely everything in Washington."[161] Johnson, finding that the country's "wise men" no longer thought it worthwhile to continue the war, announced on March 31 that he would not seek reelection.[162]

The Nixon Years: Déjà Vu All Over Again

Although Richard Nixon won the 1968 presidential election partly because his opponent, Vice-President Hubert Humphrey, had been discredited by association with Johnson's Vietnam policy, Nixon also won partly by claiming that he had a "secret plan" to end the war. Believing Nixon just as they had believed Johnson four years earlier, the American people—not to mention America's victims in Indochina—had to suffer through several more years of horrible, meaningless, criminal war.

During Johnson's final year in office, he had a two-part policy to salvage American credibility: (1) increase the use of American firepower in both the North and the South and (2) turn more of the effort to "pacify" the South over to Saigon.[163] Nixon, believing as much as his predecessors in the need to save American credibility, continued this two-part approach, dubbing the latter part "Vietnamization."[164]

A central part of the American effort to pacify South Vietnam was a CIA operation called the Phoenix program, which had been started during the Johnson administration. Its goal was to eliminate the "Viet Cong infrastructure (VCI)," meaning the network of people, including soldiers and political thinkers, providing leadership for the NLF.

Operating on a quota system, with a goal of 3,000 VCI to be "neutralized" per month, and using financial incentives, the program encouraged indiscriminate killing. Those who were arrested were usually tortured and, as the Saigon police liked to say: "If they are innocent beat them until they become guilty."[165]

One military intelligence officer testified that interrogation by Marine Counterintelligence often involved "the use of electronic gear [attached to] the women's vagina and the men's testicles." Some of the methods he reported, such as starvation and tapping dowels through ears into the brains of prisoners, resulted in death.[166]

This same officer, Barton Osborne, testified that the Phoenix bureaucracy encouraged killing captured suspects on the spot to save time, so that Phoenix "became a sterile depersonalized murder program." Contradicting the official line that there was "a triple reporting system for verification," he said: "There was no verification and there was no discrimination."[167] The indiscriminateness was such that one AID advisor refused to return to the interrogation center, because "war crimes are going on there." It would be claimed, to be sure, that the Americans were less guilty than their Saigon colleagues, because when the latter decided to kill 80 percent of their suspects outright, the Americans encouraged them to reduce this figure to merely 50 percent![168]

Between the Phoenix program and the increased bombing of South Vietnam, there were, according to one source, 165,000 civilian casualties for each of the five years of Nixon's presidency, for a total of over 800,000 Vietnamese deaths attributable to this last effort to save America's all-important credibility.

Expanding the War into Laos and Cambodia

Part of the increase in firepower involved an expansion of the war into Cambodia and an intensification of the bombing of Laos, which had been going on for many years—two grotesque dimensions of the overall US war against Indochina, involving multiple war crimes and crimes against humanity, not treated here.[169]

The Ignominious End

This massive bombing of the South reflected the fact that, although the Johnson administration had learned otherwise, Nixon's secretary of state, Henry Kissinger, believed that he could, in Kolko's words, "bludgeon the DRV into negotiating on American terms."[170] A central part of this effort involved massive bombing of the North, about which Kissinger had no compunction, because the North Vietnamese, he reportedly told Nixon, were "just a bunch of shits."[171]

In April of 1972, there were 700 B-52 raids, including a 48-hour attack on Hanoi and Haiphong. Contrary to later claims that America lost the war in Vietnam because it fought with "one hand tied behind its back," one of Kissinger's aides said: "we had a free hand to use all our force to end the war."[172] This fact was exemplified by the notorious "Christmas bombing" at the end of 1972. Starting on the 17th of December, 200 B-52s began 24-hour bombings of Hanoi and Haiphong.

This was finally too much. Besides the public protests, there were work stoppages in the Air Force. The Democratic caucuses of the House and the Senate voted to cut off all funding for the war. Nixon and Kissinger were forced to accept the agreement they had worked out with Hanoi months earlier, on which they had reneged.[173] By the end of March 1973, the last US troops had left Vietnam.

The American war in Vietnam would, however, continue for two more years, in the sense that the Saigon regime, with continued US funding and advice, would continue to fight to retain power. Finally, on April 30, 1975, the North Vietnamese army captured Saigon. After giving US officials and their Vietnamese collaborators time to evacuate—with helicopters flying from the US embassy and the roof of a CIA safe house—the victors took over the presidential palace, which had been home to a long succession of leaders who had been corrupt, ineffective, or both. "The American war in Vietnam ended that day."[174]

America's longest war of the century had ended, in Kolko's words, "ignominiously, without the hope of the slightest shred of dignity or honor."[175]

America tended to focus on the war's effects on herself, giving little attention to the number of Vietnamese killed. The American public was led to believe that only about 100,000 Vietnamese had been killed, Vietnamese had been killed, whereas the true figure was closer to 4,000,000. Perhaps the government kept the true figure a secret because it knew that many Americans, unlike Kissinger and others like him, did not think of the Vietnamese as "just a bunch of shits," whose lives were matters of indifference, but as fellow human beings.[176] In any case, that was a lot of human beings to kill in a war that was illegal and—being based on lies—immoral from the outset

In any case, approximately 700,000 Cambodians and

60,000 Laotians were also killed during the US incursions into those countries, and another approximately 2,000,000 Cambodians perished during Pol Pot regime, which surely would not have come to power apart from the US military attacks in that country. The total number of deaths in Indochina for which the United States was responsible, therefore, was almost 7,000,000. That was a lot of human beings to kill in a war that was also immoral and illegal.

Also not a matter of indifference were the lives of 58,000 Americans, one of whom was my beloved brother-in-law, who wanted nothing to do with this war—the kind of war, the United States pledged at the time, in which we would never be involved again. In 1967, Senator Morse said: "We're going to become guilty, in my judgment, of being the greatest threat to the peace of the world. It's an ugly reality, and we Americans don't like to face up to it."[177]

There was, however, one beautiful aspect of the Vietnam War: the anti-war movement that resulted from it. In a critique of Ken Burns' 2017 PBS Series, "The Vietnam War," Robert Levering, while praising it for its "depiction of the gore of war and the criminality of the warmakers," said that it missed the significance and effectiveness of the anti-war movement:

> [A]s many Americans took to the streets to protest the war on one day (October 15, 1969) as served in Vietnam during . . . the war (about 2 million for both). . . .The peace movement was . . . the largest domestic opposition to a warring government in the history of modern industrial society. . . . "The Vietnam War" fails to tell the story of the organized movement of draft resisters that grew to such proportions that the draft itself became virtually unworkable and that was a major factor why Nixon ended the draft. . . . [T]he radical anti-war movement [was] among the factors that led Johnson to refuse General Westmoreland's pending request for 206,000 more troops and why

> the president himself refused to run for another term just six months later. . . . Congress cut off funds to the war largely because of the intensive lobbying efforts by such groups as the American Friends Service Committee and Indochina Peace Campaign, or IPC, led by Tom Hayden and Jane Fonda. . . . [T]he success of the anti-Vietnam war movement provides hope and illustrates the power of resistance.[178]

Endnotes

1 David Halberstam, *The Best and the Brightest* (New York: Random House, 1972), 769.

2 Neil Sheehan, *A Bright Shining Lie: John Paul Vann and America in Vietnam* (New York: Random House, 1988), 315.

3 Quoted in Marilyn Young, *Vietnam Wars 1945-1990* (HarperCollins, 1991), 259-60. Sheehan received a copy of the Pentagon Papers after Daniel Ellsberg, who had worked on the papers while he was on the Pentagon staff, saw Sheehan's review.

4 Quoted in Young, *Vietnam Wars*, 240.

5 Jean Bethke Elshtain, *Just War Against Terror: The Burden of American Power in a Violent World* (New York: Basic Books, 2003), 18.

6 Young, *Vietnam Wars,* 257, quoting Al Hubbard, executive director of VVAW.

7 *Vietnam in Brief* (Department of State Publication 8173, Far Eastern Series 153, Bureau of Public Affairs, 1966); quoted as the final sentence in George McT. Kahin, *Intervention: How American Became Involved in Vietnam* (Garden City: Anchor Press/Doubleday, 1987), 432.

8 Young, *Vietnam Wars*, 22; Kahin, *Intervention*, 4, 5, 9.

9 Young, *Vietnam Wars*, 2, 10-11.

10 *The Pentagon Papers*, New York Times Edition (New York: Bantam, 1971), 4, 5, 8, 26; cited in William Blum, *Killing Hope: U.S. Military and C.I.A. Interventions Since World War II* (Common Courage, 2008), 123.

11 Young, *Vietnam Wars*, 14, quoting text in Robert M. Blum, "Ho Chi Minh and the United States: 1944-46," in *The United States and Vietnam, 1944-1947*, Staff Study No. 2: 10.

12 Gareth Porter, ed., *Vietnam: A History in Documents* (New York: New American Library, 1981), 38-39.

13 Kahin, *Intervention,* 22-26; Young, *Vietnam Wars*, 18-19.

14 This statement, made by Robert Blum, is contained in "Digest of the Discussion," Council on Foreign Relations Study Group on Indo-China, 6 February 1957; quoted in Kahin, *Intervention,* 8.

15 John Prados, *Vietnam: The History of an Unwinnable War, 1945-1975* (Lawrence: University of Kansas Press, 2009), 22-23.

16 Ibid., 23.

17 Kahin, *Intervention,* 42.

18 *The Pentagon Papers*, New York Times Edition, 36; quoted in Blum, *Killing Hope*, 124.

19 Young, *Vietnam Wars*, 4-5, 13.

20 Department of State Policy Statement on Indochina, 27 September 1948, in *Foreign Relations of the United States 1948* 6:48, quoted in Kahin, *Intervention,* 27.

21 Young, *Vietnam Wars*, 23-24. Although it is difficult to discern how fully this rationalization was believed at the highest levels, it enabled American officials to believe, or at least to pretend, that they were not violating American ideals in supporting the French attempt to recolonize Vietnam. As Marilyn Young said: "Here was a formula that at one blow met the needs of America's anti-colonial ideology and the reality of its postwar position as hegemon of world capitalism. By definition, Communists could not be genuine nationalists; by definition, America supported genuine nationalism. Therefore, those people the United States supported were nationalists, the rest were Communist stooges" (*Vietnam Wars,* 25).

22 Noam Chomsky and Edward S. Herman, *After the Cataclysm: Postwar Indochina and the Reconstruction of Imperial Ideology* (Montreal: Black Rose Books, 1979), 28.

23 Quoted in Porter, ed., *Vietnam,* 76.

24 Kahin, *Intervention,* 46-47; Prados, *Vietnam*, 28-29, 33.

25 Kahin, *Intervention,* 49.

26 Prados, *Vietnam*, 30, quoting George Herring, *America's Longest War: The United States and Vietnam, 1950-1975* (New York: McGraw-Hill, 1996), 40, and adding: "This can now be affirmed from a host of evidence."

27 Porter, ed., *Vietnam*, 1-2.

28 Ibid., 35, 32.

29 Ibid., 87.

30 Young, *Vietnam Wars*, 38-39.

31 Porter, ed., *Vietnam*, 108.

32 Kahin, *Intervention,* 61-62; Young, *Vietnam Wars*, 41.

33 Kahin, *Intervention,* 61; Young, *Vietnam Wars*, 41-42. The full text, along with the oral declarations, can be found in Robert F. Randle, *Geneva 1954: The Settlement of the Indochinese War* (Princeton: Princeton University Press, 1969), 572-607.

34 Kahin, *Intervention*, 452 n. 78.

35 Young, *Vietnam Wars*, 37.

36 Kahin, *Intervention*, 75.

37 Ibid., 63.

38 Ibid., 67-68.

39 Ibid., 71; Porter, ed., *Vietnam*, 94-95; Prados, *Vietnam*, 53. : The official beginning of American involvement in the war as recognized by the Vietnam Veterans Memorial was November 1, 1955, which was when President Eisenhower deployed the Military Assistance Advisory Group to train the Army of the Republic of Vietnam (Wikipedia), "Role of the United States in the Vietnam War."

40 Kahin, *Intervention*, 69-70. Stanley Karnow, *In Our Image: America's Empire in the Philippines* (New York: Ballantine, 1989), 346-53; Daniel B. Schirmeer and Stephen Rosskamm Shalom, ed., *The Philippines Reader: A History of Colonialism, Neocolonialism, Dictatorship, and Resistance* (Boston: South End, 1987), 113-22.

41 Young, *Vietnam Wars*, 44; Kahin, *Intervention,* 81.

42 Ibid., 44.

43 Kahin, *Intervention*, 81-82.

44 Young, *Vietnam Wars*, 53; see also Kahin, *Intervention*, 95.

45 Prados, *Vietnam*, 41.

46 Kahin, *Intervention*, 76-77.

47 Ibid., 75-77; Young, *Vietnam Wars*, 45.

48 Prados, *Vietnam*, 42.

49 Young, *Vietnam Wars*, 45.

50 Ibid., 46-47.

51 Kahin, *Intervention*, 73-74; Porter, ed., *Vietnam*, 84-85.

52 Kahin, *Intervention*, 74-75.

53 Ibid., 74.

54 Ibid., 89; Porter, ed., *Vietnam,* 97-97.

55 Dwight D. Eisenhower, *Mandate for Change, 1953-56* (Garden City: Doubleday & Company, 1963), 372.

56 Porter, ed., *Vietnam*, 101-02. *The Pentagon Papers* referred to this fact, saying: "Without the threat of U.S. intervention, South Vietnam could not have refused to even discuss the elections called for in 1956 under the Geneva settlement without being immediately overrun by the Vietminh armies." Quoted in James W. Douglass, *JFK and the*

Unspeakable: Why He Died and Why It Matters (Simon & Schuster, 2008), 105.

57 Porter, ed., *Vietnam*, 102.

58 Kahin, *Intervention,* 61.

59 Ibid., 90.

60 Ibid., 88-89.

61 Ibid., 90.

62 *Public Papers of the Presidents: Dwight D. Eisenhower, 1954* (Washington, DC: Government Printing Office, 1955), 382; quoted in Prados, *Vietnam*, 29.

63 CIA, "Probable Consequences in Non-Communist Asia of Certain Possible Developments in Indochina before Mid-1954," cited in Porter, ed., *Vietnam*, 232-33.

64 Porter, ed., *Vietnam*, 233;xii.

65 Ibid., 86, n. 58.

66 Prados, *Vietnam*, 57.

67 Kahin, *Intervention*, 97; Young, *Vietnam Wars*, 63.

68 Young, *Vietnam Wars*, 62.

69 Philippe Devillers, "The Struggle for the Unification of Vietnam," 302 *China Quarterly* 9 (January-March 1962), 12; quoted in Kahin, *Intervention*, 97.

70 Prados, *Vietnam*, 57-58.

71 Porter, ed., *Vietnam*, 91.

72 Ibid., 110-13; Prados, *Vietnam,* 65.

73 Prados, *Vietnam*, 66.

74 Porter, ed., *Vietnam*, 114-15.

75 Young, *Vietnam Wars*, 73.

76 Noam Chomsky, *Rethinking Camelot: JFK, the Vietnam War, and US Political Culture* (Boston: South End, 1993), 25.

77 Young, *Vietnam Wars*, 77.

78 Gabriel Kolko, *Anatomy of a War: Vietnam, the United States, and the Modern Historical Experience* (New York: Pantheon Books, 1985), 112.

79 Ibid., 113, quoting *The Pentagon Papers: The Defense Department History of United States Decisionmaking on Vietnam*, 4 vols., Senator Gravel Edition (Boston: Beacon Press, 1971), II: 336.

80 Ibid., 112-13.

81 Young, *Vietnam Wars*, 87, 82.

82 Although America was supposedly seeking to win "the hearts and minds" of the Vietnamese people, nothing could have been more alienating than American policies. "Everything that peasants held precious," said Kolko, "was now being threatened, including the very existence of the family system and the traditional culture" (*Anatomy of*

a War, 135).

83 Young, *Vietnam Wars*, 74.

84 Ibid., 101.

85 Ibid., 101-02.

86 See John M. Newman, JFK and Vietnam: Deception, Intrigue, and the Struggle for Power (Warner Books, 1992); David Kaiser, American Tragedy: Kennedy, Johnson, and the Origins of the Vietnam War (Harvard University Press, 2000); Howard Jones, Death of a Generation: How the Assassinations of Diem and JFK Prolonged the Vietnam War (Oxford University Press, 2003); and, more recently, James W. Douglass, JFK and the Unspeakable: Why He Died and Why It Matters (Simon & Schuster, 2008).

87 Kahin, *Intervention,* 387.

88 Ibid., 245.

89 Robert Gallucci, *Neither Peace nor Honor: The Politics of American Military Policy in Viet Nam* (Baltimore: Johns Hopkins Press, 1975), 44; quoted in Kahin, *Intervention*, 245.

90 Young, *Vietnam Wars*, 106-07.

91 Kolko, *Anatomy of a War*, 114, quoting *The Pentagon Papers*, Gravel Edition, III: 51. 303

92 Young, *Vietnam Wars*, 111-13.

93 Kolko, *Anatomy of a War*, 124.

94 Kahin, *Intervention*, 217-19.

95 Young, *Vietnam Wars*, 119.

96 Prados, *Vietnam*, 83, 96.

97 Young, *Vietnam Wars*, 116-17; Kahin, *Intervention,* 221.

98 Kahin, *Intervention*, 221.

99 Daniel Ellsberg, *Secrets: A Memoir of Vietnam and the Pentagon Papers* (New York: Viking, 2002), 9-10.

100 Young, *Vietnam Wars*, 118-19; Kahin, *Intervention,* 222-23.

101 Prados, *Vietnam*, 95-96.

102 Ibid., 96, 98.

103 Kahin, *Intervention*, 220.

104 Young, *Vietnam Wars*, 120.

105 Ibid., 120-21.

106 William Appleman Williams et al., *America in Vietnam: A Documentary History* (Garden City: Anchor Press/Doubleday, 1985), 237.

107 As quoted in Young, *Vietnam Wars,* 119 (although the bracketed inserts are mine).

108 This according to William Bundy, who was chairman of the Working Group (Young, *Vietnam Wars*, 130).

109 Ibid., 130.

110 Although it was often said, as here, that the motivation was to prevent Vietnam from falling into Chinese hands, the deeper concern was revealed by William Bundy's statement that a Communist Vietnam independent of China would be "just as humiliating" (quoted in Kahin, *Intervention,* 263).

111 Young, *Vietnam Wars*, 135, citing a memorandum to McNamara from John McNaughton, contained in the *Pentagon Papers*, Gravel Edition, III: 695.

112 Kahin, *Intervention*, 313-14.

113 Young, *Vietnam Wars*, 112.

114 Kahin, *Intervention*, 271.

115 Chomsky and Herman, *After the Cataclysm*, 3.

116 Kahin, *Intervention*, 271.

117 Ibid., 404.

118 Ibid., 404.

119 Ibid., 404.

120 Bernard Fall, *Last Reflections on a War* (New York: Doubleday, 1967); quoted in Chomsky, *Rethinking Camelot*, 56.

121 Young, *Vietnam Wars*, 122, 131; Kahin, *Intervention*, 236, 263-64, 272-275. 304 122 Kahin, *Intervention*, 283.

123 Young, *Vietnam Wars*, 110; Kahin, *Intervention*, 360; Kolko, *Anatomy of a War,* 164.

124 Kahin, *Intervention*, 283.

125 Ibid., 305, 345.

126 Young, *Vietnam Wars*, 141; Prados, *Vietnam*, 123.

127 Kahin, *Intervention*, 291.

128 Liechty's account, summarized by Kahin (*Intervention,* 290), was reported in a story by Michael Getler in the *Washington Post*, 20 March 1982.

129 Kahin, *Intervention*, 290-91, quoting Max Frankel, *New York Times*, 27 March 1965.

130 Kolko, *Anatomy of a War*, 609.

131 Kahin, *Intervention*, 306.

132 Ibid., 307.

133 Kolko, *Anatomy of a War*, 165.

134 Kahin, *Intervention*, 306, 319.

135 Prados, *Vietnam*, 182; Young, *Vietnam Wars*, 160.

136 Kahin, *Intervention*, 344.

137 Ibid., 399.

138 Young, *Vietnam Wars*, 177; Kolko, *Anatomy of a War*, 177.

139 Kahin, *Intervention*, 345.

140 Ibid., 323.

141 Ibid., 333.
142 Ibid., 334.
143 Ibid., 334.
144 Young, *Vietnam Wars*, 205.
145 Young, *Vietnam Wars*, 197. I reached the figure for the New York march by compromising between the highest estimate, 400,000, and the lowest, 125,000.
146 Young, *Vietnam Wars*, 199; David J. Garrow, "When Martin Luther King Came Out Against Vietnam," *New York Times,* 4 April 2017.
147 See William F. Pepper, *An Act of State: The Execution of Martin Luther King*, Updated with a New Afterword (London: Verso, 2008); a more recent and fuller account was provided by Pepper in *The Plot to Kill King: The Truth behind the Assassination of Martin Luther King, Jr.* (Skyhorse Publishing, 2016).
148 Young, *Vietnam Wars*, 202.
149 Ibid., 203.
150 Ibid., 204.
151 Ibid., 195.
152 Ibid., 204. 305
153 Ibid., 257.
154 Ibid., 206.
155 Ibid., 206-07.
156 Ibid., 211.
157 Ibid., 208.
158 Kolko, *Anatomy of a War*, 303.
159 Prados, *Vietnam*, 240.
160 Young, *Vietnam Wars*, 220-22, 226.
161 Ibid., 222.
162 Kolko, *Anatomy of a War*, 316-20; Young, *Vietnam Wars*, 229.
163 Kolko, *Anatomy of a War*, 324.
164 Ibid., 341-42, 352; Young, *Vietnam Wars*, 237, 324-25.
165 *The Washington Post*, 17 February 1970, quoted in Noam Chomsky and Edward S. Herman, *The Washington Connection and Third World Fascism* (Montreal: Black Rose Books, 1979), 325.
166 "Military Intelligence and the Phoenix Program," House of Representatives, July 15-August 2, 1971, cited in Young, *Vietnam Wars*, 213.
167 Quoted in Chomsky and Herman, *The Washington Connection*, 327.
168 Reported in a UPI story in *Le Monde*, 5 November 1971, cited in Chomsky and Herman, *The Washington Connection*, 327.
169 On American action in Laos, see Blum, *Killing Hope*, 140-45, and Young, *Vietnam Wars*, 46-47, 78-79, 131, 234-35; on American action

in Cambodia, see Blum, *Killing Hope,* 133-39, and Young, *Vietnam Wars*, 236-38, 245-53, 305-08, 312-13.

170 Kolko, *Anatomy of a War*, 352.

171 This statement is quoted from *RN: The Memoirs of Richard Nixon* (New York: Grosset & Dunlap, 1978) in Seymour M. Hersh, *The Price of Power: Kissinger in the Nixon White House* (New York: Summit Books [Simon & Schuster], 1983), 620.

172 Young, *Vietnam Wars*, 272.

173 Ibid., 278-79.

174 Prados, *Vietnam*, 530-31.

175 Kolko, *Anatomy of a War*, 538.

176 Chomsky, *Rethinking Camelot*, 62. Nick Turse estimated the most reasonable estimate to be 3.8 million (*Kill Anything That Moves: The Real American War in Vietnam* (Picador, 2013), 13).

177 Quoted in Norman Solomon, "A Lonely Voice Against the Gulf of Tonkin Resolution," *San Francisco Bay Guardian*, 19 September 2001.

178 Robert Levering, "Ken Burns' Powerful Anti-War Film on Vietnam Ignores the Power of the Anti-War Movement," Waging Nonviolence, 17 October 2017

| Chapter 11 |

FALSE FLAG OPERATIONS

The idea of "false flag attacks" has recently become much better known than previously. Originally, a false flag attack was one in which the attackers, perhaps in ships, literally showed the flag of an enemy country, so that it would be blamed. But the expression has come to be used for any attack made to appear to be the work of some country, party, or group other than that to which the attackers themselves belong.

While not being doubtful that other countries, especially enemies of the United States, employ false flag attacks, Americans have tended to be skeptical of the idea that its own government would ever arrange such attacks. Americans are especially skeptical of any claim that their government would have attacked citizens of friendly countries. And they would consider most dubious any suggestion the American government would attack its own citizens. Accordingly, it is important to look at the evidence that America has, in fact, employed all of these types of false flag attacks. Indeed, the trajectory of the American Empire has relied on these types of attacks so heavily that one could describe it as a *false flag empire.*

This chapter begins with some examples of false flag attacks carried out by other countries. It next looks at some examples of false accusations by the US government to enable it to start wars. It then examines more extensively some examples of US-sponsored false flag attacks on innocent citizens in friendly countries. The fourth section describes a Pentagon plan for the US government to attack its own citizens as a pretext for war.

1. False Flag Operations by Other Countries

From at least the time of the Roman Empire, imperialist and would-be imperialist powers have staged false flag attacks to justify various types of action, such as "retaliatory" attacks on countries they wanted to conquer, and operations to eliminate domestic opposition. Three of the best-known examples of such attacks in the 20th century were orchestrated by Japan and Germany.

The Mukden Incident

In the early decades of that century, Japan, hoping to establish economic self-sufficiency, was exploiting resource-rich Manchuria. The chief instrument of this exploitation was the South Manchuria Railway, controlled by Japan. In 1930, Chiang Kai-shek's increasingly successful effort to unify China was causing Japanese leaders to fear that their position in Manchuria would be threatened.

On September 18, 1931, Japanese army officers secretly blew up a portion of the railway's tracks near the Chinese military base in Mukden. Then, blaming the sabotage on Chinese solders, the Japanese army used this incident, in LaFeber's words, "as an excuse to conquer Manchuria."[1] This military operation is considered by many historians to be the beginning of World War II. Therefore, the Mukden incident—which the Chinese call 9/18—was one of the most important false flag incidents of the twentieth century.[2]

The Reichstag Fire

An equally fateful false flag operation was the burning of the Berlin Reichstag, which was the home of Germany's parliament.

The fire occurred on the night of February 27, 1933, less than a month after the Nazis took power. The fire is now known to be have been orchestrated by Hermann Göring, the president of the Reichstag, and Joseph Göbbels, Hitler's propaganda minister, who had the fire started by members of the SA (Storm Troops).

The Nazis then blamed the arson on the German Communist Party, claiming that the fire was intended to be the signal for a Communist uprising. The only evidence the Nazis presented for this claim was the "discovery" on the site of a feeble-minded left-wing radical from Holland named Marinus van der Lubbe, who had evidently been brought to the site by the SA troops.[3]

The Reichstag fire then became "the excuse for a hitherto unparalleled persecution of Communist and Social Democratic workers, intellectuals and party leaders."[4] Thousands of people allied with the workers movement were arrested, all left-wing newspapers were shut down, and two so-called fire decrees annulled civil rights provided by the constitution of the Weimar Republic. These decrees "formed the pseudo-legal basis for the entire Nazi dictatorship."[5]

Operation Himmler

Nazi Germany attacked Poland on the morning of September 1, 1939. In Hitler's speech to the Reichstag later that day, he referred to 21 "border incidents" of the previous night in which Polish troops had allegedly initiated hostilities. The attack on Poland was hence presented as a defensive necessity. But this attack had been planned long before. The Nazis only needed a pretext, so that the war would not be strongly opposed by the German people and, hopefully, other nations.

After Heinrich Himmler came up with the basic idea for the pretext, the task of planning and directing it was assigned to Reinhard Heydrich (who would later be centrally involved in the "final solution") and Heinrich Müller, the head of the Gestapo. The plan, dubbed "Operation Himmler," was to have members of the Gestapo and the Security Service, dressed as Poles, stage various raids near the Polish-German border on the night of August 31.

The plan in some cases was to take some German convicts, dress them as Poles, give them fatal injections, take them to the sites, shoot them, then leave them there as proof that they had been killed while attacking German troops.

The most famous of these raids was the Gleiwitz incident, which was headed by Alfred Naujocks (who later testified about all this at Nuremberg). Naujocks had one of the convicts, who had been injected and shot, delivered to the German radio station at Gleiwitz. Then he and his men seized the station, broadcast a message in Polish urging Poles to attack Germans, and left. The body of the dead convict, "discovered" shortly thereafter, was used as proof that an attack by Poles had occurred. The invasion of Poland on September 1 was the beginning of World War II, as France and the United Kingdom declared war on Germany two days later.[6]

These three false flag operations—the Reichstag Fire, the Mukden Incident, and Operation Himmler—were all crucial events on the road to World War II. The fact that this war caused millions of deaths and enormous suffering illustrates how important it is that false flag operations be exposed before the true perpetrators can use them as pretexts for carrying out their designs.

Many Americans may, to be sure, agree with this principle while assuming that US leaders would never engage in such deadly deceit. But this assumption is contradicted by the historical record.

2. US Wars Based on False Charges of Enemy Aggression

American leaders have in several cases knowingly used false charges of enemy aggression to start a war. The examples of Cuba and Vietnam have already been covered. The Mexican-American war and the war to take the Philippines provide two more examples.

The Mexican-American War

One factor in the background to the Mexican-American War of 1846-1848 was a border dispute between Mexico and the

Republic of Texas, after the latter had won its independence in 1836. According to Mexico, the border was marked by the Nueces river, whereas the Texans placed the border much farther south, at the Rio Grande. Another factor was American expansionism, especially that of President James Polk. Although he was mainly interested in acquiring California, Polk had committed himself to annexing Texas, promising to support its border claim.

In 1846, after being rebuffed in his attempt to purchase California, Polk ordered the US army to build a fort on the Rio Grande, about 150 miles south of what Mexico considered the border. Facing humiliation as the only alternative, Mexico reportedly initiated hostilities. When the good news reached Polk, he told Congress that Mexico had "shed American blood upon the American soil." A congressman named Abraham Lincoln called Polk's claim that Mexico had been the aggressor "the sheerest deception."[7] Frederick Douglas, speaking of "the present disgraceful, cruel, and iniquitous war with our sister republic," added that "Mexico seems a doomed victim to Anglo Saxon cupidity and love of dominion."[8]

In any case, Mexico, being out-gunned, signed a peace treaty in 1848, ceding what is now California, Arizona, Nevada, New Mexico, Utah, and part of Colorado. In compensation, the US government paid $15 million, which was a paltry sum even in those days (the USA would later offer Spain $100 million for Cuba). The United States, in other words, used the trumped-up war to steal about half of Mexico.[9]

One newspaper concluded, nevertheless, that "we take nothing by conquest. . . . Thank God."[10] This would not be the last time the US government would deliberately provoke a conflict in order to justify an imperial conquest, then rely on the mass media to interpret it as illustrating the fact that America is under divine guidance.

The War to Take the Philippines

Although the US war against the Philippines was discussed in Chapter 1, that discussion did not include the issue of how the war got started. In January of 1899, General Arthur MacArthur ordered all Filipino soldiers out of a village they had occupied for several months. Another US general set up a sentry at a position in this disputed area known as the "pipeline," ordering the men to fire on any intruders. On the evening of February 4, the sentries, approached by four Filipino soldiers—who were probably drunk and unarmed—opened fire on them. US troops, having been prepared for this "pipeline incident," then fired on Filipino positions for the next six hours. Few shots were fired in return by the Filipinos, but the war was on. The US secretary of war, giving the official version of what happened, said:

> On the night of February 4th. . . an army of Tagalogs. . . attacked, in vastly superior numbers, our little army . . . and after a desperate and bloody fight was repulsed in every direction.

This statement was part of a more general "propaganda offensive to prove that the Filipino army started the war."

Years later, MacArthur and three US officers who had been on the scene confessed that the whole battle was prearranged and that American troops had fired first.[11] By then, however, it did not matter much.

3. US False Flag Attacks in Europe

Some Americans, being confronted with the preceding evidence of the willingness of US leaders to provoke and lie about incidents to justify going to war, might reply: "I grant that American leaders have done such things to enemies, but they would not deliberately kill citizens of friendly countries for political reasons." That assumption, however, would be false.

In a 2005 book entitled *NATO's Secret Armies: Operation Gladio and Terrorism in Western Europe*,[12] Swiss historian Daniele Ganser extensively documented the fact that, during the Cold War, the United States sponsored false flag terrorist incidents in many countries of Western Europe in order to discredit Communists, and socialists more generally. In 2015, journalist Paul Williams published a book entitled *Operation Gladio: The Unholy Alliance between the Vatican, the CIA, and the Mafia.*[13] The discussion in this section draws from these two books. After some historical background, examples from four countries will be provided.

Historical Background

Allen Dulles, whose activities have already been mentioned in Chapter 8 (in relation to Iran, Guatemala, and Cuba) and Chapter 10 (on Vietnam), was in 1942 recruited by the Office of Strategic Services (OSS) - which would later become the CIA - to direct its operations in Switzerland. Having learned that the Nazis wanted to work out a separate peace with the United States (from which the Soviet Union would be excluded), and having connections with the German High Command, Dulles told William ("Wild Bill") Donovan, the head of the OSS, that he would like to pursue this possibility.[14]

Having received permission, Dulles contacted the head of German military intelligence, General Reinhard Gehlen, who had conceived the idea of developing clandestine guerrilla squads, the members of which would be known as "werewolves" (ordinary citizens by day, Communist killers at night). These squads would be "stay-behind units," which would remain behind lines in the case of a Soviet postwar invasion of Western Europe, thereby being in position to mobilize a resistance movement.[15]

These secret armies never played this role, of course, since no such invasion ever occurred. They only engaged in terrorism and other forms of subversion, which, insofar as they have been officially admitted, have been portrayed as secondary operations. It is not clear, however, that the United States ever believed that there would be a Soviet invasion. All of the so-called stay-behind armies may have from the first, as some critics have charged, been created entirely to do battle against domestic Communist parties, with the stay-behind function serving simply as a cover story.[16] In any case, Dulles decided that the OSS should provide the stay-behind armies with material, tactical, and strategic assistance.[17]

Gehlen would work out this plan, Dulles informed Donovan, in collaboration with SS General Karl Wolff, whose main task had been arranging the transportation of Jews to concentration camps. After the Yalta meeting between Roosevelt, Stalin, and Churchill, Dulles took Gehlen to Virginia, "where they were wined and dined by Donovan and other US officials." It was agreed that "Gehlen would return to Germany under US protection to establish the Gehlen Organization, which would receive full funding." The name of the soldiers would be changed from "werewolves" to "gladiators," as the operation would be called Gladio, referring to the short swords used by Roman gladiators to kill their opponents.[18]

Also directing the stay-behind armies would be James Jesus Angleton, who was the commander of the OSS's Secret Counterintelligence (SCI) unit. Through Angleton's pro-Hitler father, who had been the president of the American Chamber of Commerce in Italy, he met Price Junio Valerio Borghese, who was the leader of a commando unit called X MAS. This unit had been set up by the Nazis to attack Italy's partisan bands, which were sponsored by the Italian Communist Party. Borghese accepted the idea of Dulles, Wolff, and Angleton that they would continue their war against the Soviets by deploying X MAS under the covert direction of the OSS. "Angleton needed Borghese and the 10,267 fascists who fought under his command to help establish the stay-behind units."[19]

Thanks to a mandate by the US State Department, the operational resources of "the Italian police, the Italian military intelligence, and the Italian secret service were placed at the disposal of Angleton and the SCI." Due to the efforts of Gehlen and Wolff, there were soon new gladiators in Austria, France, and Germany, and by 1946 "hundreds of Gladio units were in place throughout Western Europe." These units "were equipped by the CIA and the MI6 with machine guns, explosives, munitions, and high-tech communication equipment hidden in arms caches in forests, meadows, and underground bunkers across Europe."[20] By the 1950s, there were 622 stay-behind units it Italy alone.[21]

Such a huge operation would, of course, require a lot of money. The idea of how to get it was provided by Paul E. Helliwell, who was the OSS's Chief of Special Intelligence. Seeing how Chaing Kai-shek had raised money for his Chinese National Army by selling opium to Chinese addicts, Helliwell decided that money for Gladio could be raised by selling heroin to black communities in America's ghettos. This way, the OSS could "purchase the services of foreign agents, foreign politicians, and foreign assassins without the approval of any elected official."[22]

In 1947, the Truman administration successfully sponsored the National Security Act, which created the Central Intelligence Agency (CIA) and its superior, the National Security Council (NSC). The CIA was to carry out covert operations "against hostile foreign states or groups . . . but which are so planned and conducted that any US government responsibility for them is not evident to unauthorized persons."[23] The CIA did not have to account for the money it spent except to the President. Accordingly, unless the President said otherwise, the CIA "could hire as many people as it wanted. . . . It could hire armies; it could buy banks."[24]

With the creation in 1949 of the North Atlantic Treaty Organization (NATO), these operations came to be coordinated by a secret unit within NATO called the Clandestine Planning Committee (CPC), which was guided primarily by the CIA and the Pentagon. (US control of NATO was guaranteed by the fact that its Supreme Commander would always be an American general. When NATO was expelled from France in 1966 by French President Charles de Gaulle, it moved to Brussels, Belgium. But the real headquarters—of NATO in general and the CPC in particular—remained in the Pentagon.[25])

Although the right-wing armies engaged in many kinds of operations, including coups, the focus here is on false flag operations, giving examples from four countries.

Italy

Existing primarily to prevent the victory of Communist parties in European elections, the NSC and its CIA first targeted Italy, spending $30-50 million annually for covert operations in that country.[26] Directive NSC 4-A ordered the CIA to undertake covert activities to prevent a victory by the Communists in the 1948 elections. After these operations succeeded, directive NSC 10/2 created the Office of Policy Coordination, which was authorized to carry out covert operations in *all* countries in the world. Such operations were to include:

> propaganda; economic warfare; preventive direct action, including sabotage [and] demolition. . . ; subversion against hostile states, including assistance to underground resistance movements, guerrillas . . . and anti-Communist elements.[27]

Although Gladio continued waging war for the next two decades, it became much more violent during the presidency of Richard Nixon (1969 - 1974). Nixon's National Security Advisor, Henry Kissinger, gave orders for the implementation of terrorist attacks and coups.[28]

- On December 12, 1969, four bombs exploded in Rome and in Milan's Piazza Fontana, killing 16 people and injuring another 80. This attack, known as the Piazza Fontana massacre, was blamed on the left by the military secret service, which destroyed evidence (a bomb that had failed to go off), then planted bomb parts in a leftist editor's villa.[29]

- In 1972, some members of Italy's paramilitary police were set up to be killed by a car bomb near Peteano. An anonymous caller implicated a Communist group called the Red Brigades, after which some 200 Communists were arrested.[30]

- In 1978, after the Communist Party had won an unprecedented number of seats in parliament, President

Aldo Moro decided—against the strongly stated wishes of Washington—that he had to include them in his government. But before he could do so, he was kidnapped and murdered. (Henry Kissinger had told Moro: "You must abandon your policy of bringing all the political forces in your country into direct collaboration, or you will pay dearly for it."[31])

- The deadliest attack in Italy occurred in 1980, when a massive explosion at the Bologna railway station killed 85 people and wounded another 200. Blame was initially placed on the Red Brigade, but the terrorists had made a mistake: The bomb was a complicated device that "had been developed for use by the US military."[32]

For over a decade, the Italian public believed that Communists had committed these atrocities.[33] However, Italian authorities, beginning in 1984 with an investigation of the Peteano incident, discovered that these crimes were actually orchestrated by right-wing forces. Judge Felice Casson, who spearheaded the investigation, later said: "the Peteano attack is part of what has been called 'the strategy of tension' . . . to create tension within the country to promote conservative, reactionary social and political tendencies."[34] This interpretation was later confirmed by a member of the extreme right-wing organization Ordine Nuovo, who confessed to having planted the Peteano bomb, adding:

> You had to attack civilians, the people, women, children, innocent people. . . . The reason was . . . to force these people, the Italian public, to turn to the State to ask for greater security. This is the political logic that lies behind all the massacres and the bombings.[35]

In 1990, Judge Casson discovered documents revealing the existence of Gladio and its connection to NATO and the United

States. The truth of these discoveries was then confirmed by Prime Minister Giulio Andreotti, who emphasized the responsibility of the White House.[36]

In 2000, an Italian parliamentary committee to study Operation Gladio concluded that "those massacres . . . had been organized or . . . supported by men . . . linked to the structures of United States intelligence." This conclusion was confirmed in 2001 by General Giandelio Maletti, former head of Italian counter-intelligence, who said of the Piazza Fontana massacre: "The CIA, following the directives of its government, wanted to create an Italian nationalism capable of halting what it saw as a slide to the left." It seemed to him, he added, that to achieve this goal, "the Americans would do anything."[37]

One of the things the Pentagon evidently did was to have its own secret service, the Defense Intelligence Agency (DIA), prepare an instruction book, called Field Manual 30-31, for Gladio and NATO's other secret armies.[38] This manual came with two "supplements," entitled simply A and B. Supplement B, dated March 18, 1970, came to be known as the "Westmoreland Manual," because it contained the signature of General William Westmoreland, who, after commanding US military operations in Vietnam, served as US Army Chief of Staff from 1968 to 1972.

The Westmoreland Manual instructed these armies to carry out acts of violence, then blame them on Communists, and also to infiltrate left-wing organizations, then encourage them to use violence. Through these means, Supplement B said, "US army intelligence [will] have the means of launching special operations which will convince Host Country Governments and public opinion of the reality of the insurgent danger." However, the manual continued: "These special operations must remain strictly secret. . . . [T]he involvement of the US Army in the internal affairs of an allied country . . . shall not become known under any circumstances."[39]

The existence of FM 30-31 first became publicly known in 1973, when a Turkish newspaper announced that one of its journalists had come into possession of it. This journalist soon disappeared, never to be heard from again. But the manual was translated into Turkish in 1975, after which it became known in Spain and Italy.

In 2006, after Ganser's book appeared, the US Department of State claimed that Supplement B was a Soviet forgery. Its evidence for this claim, however, was extremely weak, consisting merely of this claim: "Field Manual 30-31B . . . was exposed as a 'total fabrication' in February 1980 hearings before the U.S. House of Representatives Permanent Select Committee on Intelligence."[40] The State Department did not reveal whether this was a conclusion reached by the committee as a whole or simply a statement of someone testifying at the hearings. It also did not mention the discovery of the document in Turkey and the disappearance of the journalist who discovered it.

The State Department did not mention that Ganser, far from being oblivious to the claim that Supplement B was a forgery, had pointed out that this claim was made by Michael Ledeen (who had worked at the Pentagon, the National Security Council, and the Department of State, was involved in the Iran-Contra Affair, and was earlier reportedly involved in Operation Gladio). The State Department also did not mention that Ganser presented two strong pieces of evidence against that claim.

1. When Ray Cline, former CIA Deputy Director of Intelligence, was asked about FM 30-31B in a BBC-aired film about Gladio produced by investigative journalist Allan Francovich, Cline said: "I suspect it is an authentic document. I don't doubt it. I never saw it but it's the kind of special forces military operations that are described."

2. When Licio Gelli, the leader of one of Italy's anti-Communist organizations, was asked in the same film how he came into possession of the document, he replied: "The CIA gave it to me."[41]

The State Department, in spite of providing such a weak

defense of the claim that FM 30-31B was a Soviet forgery, then used this defense to claim to support its more sweeping conclusion: that the idea "that West European 'stay-behind' networks engaged in terrorism . . . at U.S. instigation" is "not true." That conclusion would not follow, however, even if the State Department had made a good case for its allegation that FM 30-31B was a forgery, because Ganser's conclusion rested on far more than this document, as we have already seen and will further see below.

France

After World War II, the French Communist Party (PCF) was very popular, due to the leading role it had played in the resistance against the fascist Vichy regime, which had collaborated with the Nazis. These Vichy collaborators in military and business circles were frightened by the prospect that the PCF might come to power. The United States shared this fear.[42]

US. fears increased in 1946, when national elections showed the PCF to be the strongest party. As a result, Ganser said, "Washington and the US secret service were convinced that the PCF had to be attacked and defeated in a secret war."[43] The resulting strategy, known as "Plan Bleu," was "to escalate the already tense political climate in France by committing acts of terror, blame them on the left, and thus create suitable conditions for [a] coup d'état." There was reportedly even a plan to assassinate former Prime Minister Charles de Gaulle to increase public resentment.[44]

This secret plan was exposed in 1947 by the French Socialist party, then in power, before it could be carried out. But this exposure did not end the secret war. It was carried on by a new anti-Communist secret army, code-named "Rose des Vents," a reference to NATO's star-shaped symbol.[45] Although France experienced some false flag violence, it evidently did not suffer as many such attacks as occurred in other countries from the late 1960s through the 1980s, perhaps because in 1966 de Gaulle expelled NATO and its covert agents from France. France did, nevertheless, suffer some such attacks.[46]

An especially important person in this respect was Yves

Guerain Serac, who was recruited by the CIA. In 1962, Serac went to Portugal, where he created the Aginter Press, a front for a secret CIA-sponsored army. Aginter Press set up training camps to teach bomb terrorism and other kinds of clandestine operations. Between 1967 and 1968, for example, some of its agents went to Rome to teach the use of explosives to members of Avanguardia Nazionale, one of the right-wing organizations behind the 1969 Piazza Fontana massacre.

Serac also became influential through his writings. Describing how to target a democratic state that is insufficiently anti-Communist, Serac wrote:

> The destruction of the state must be carried out as much as possible under the cover of "Communist activities". . . . [W]e must . . . demonstrate the weakness of the present legal apparatus. . . . Popular opinion must be polarized in such a way, that we are being presented as the only instrument capable of saving the nation.[47]

Serac explicitly advocated, as this statement showed, false flag operations to turn the public to the right.

The Pentagon's involvement in the French and Italian secret armies was revealed in a 1952 top-secret memorandum of the US Joint Chiefs of Staff entitled "Operation Demagnetize." It laid out ways in which "political, paramilitary and psychological operations" are to be used "to reduce . . . the danger that Communism could gain strength in Italy and France and endanger the interests of the United States in the two countries." (Note that in this memo, intended to remain secret, there was nothing about protecting democracy or the freedom of the French and Italian peoples; the only concern was "the interests of the United States.") This memo added that "the limitation of the strength of the Communists in Italy and France is a top priority objective," which is "to be reached by the employment of all means," a standard phrase to refer to the use of violence.

Turkey

In Turkey, the CIA and the Pentagon used a secret army that had been set up by Colonel Alparsan Türks, a Nazi collaborator. This army, known as Counter-Guerrilla, was composed largely of fascists.[48]

One of the most active periods for Counter-Guerrilla was "the terror of the 1970s," during which some 5,000 people were killed, most of whom were identified with the political left. The attacks suddenly came to an end in 1980 after a CIA-planned military coup, which gave the presidency to General Kenan Evren, the head of Counter-Guerrilla. The terror of the 1970s, a right-wing extremist on trial later said, had been a strategy to bring Evren and the military right to power.[49]

In the 1990s, the Turkish people learned that this secret army was funded by the CIA and run by NATO—which means, of course, by the Pentagon.[50] A book written by a former paramilitary commander who had battled the PKK (the organization fighting for an independent Kurdish state) revealed that Counter-Guerrilla had run false-flag operations. In order to turn Kurds against the PKK, he reported, Counter-Guerilla troops would dress up as PKK fighters and attack Kurdish villages, then engage in rapes and random executions.[51]

Belgium

In the 1980s, Belgium suffered a terrifying series of terrorist attacks known as the Brabant massacres. (Brabant is the geographic area around Brussels, where NATO has been headquartered since 1966.) The attacks usually occurred at shopping centers, especially supermarkets. In November of 1985, for example, three hooded men got out of their car and started firing at shoppers with a pump-action shotgun. Eight people were killed.

> A husband and wife and their 14-year-old daughter were finished off in cold blood. . . . Another father and his nine-year-old daughter were killed in their car trying to flee.

Between 1982 and 1985, there were 16 such attacks, which "reduced Belgium to a state of panic."[52]

Although the responsibility for the Brabant Massacres remained a mystery for many years, evidence later surfaced that they were carried out by a neo-Nazi organization known as Westland New Post (WNP). Michel Libert, a former WNP member, confirmed in 1992 that from 1982 to 1985, it was his job to scout out supermarkets, to see if they had any protection that could interfere with WNP's operations. Libert's orders came from WNP commander Paul Latinus, who was paid by the Pentagon's DIA. A Belgian journalist reported that when he asked Latinus who had asked him to set up the WNP, he said: "American military secret services."[53]

With regard to the motivation behind the massacres, a member of WNP later said that the plan was to "make the population believe that these terrorist attempts were done by the Left."[54] A report issued by the Belgian parliament in 1990 said that the Brabant killings were "part of a conspiracy to destabilize Belgium's democratic regime, possibly to prepare the ground for a right-wing coup."[55]

Reaction to Exposure of US False Flags in Europe

Following the exposure of Operation Gladio in Italy in 1990, the discovery that other NATO countries had similar clandestine units became a major scandal in Europe (although it was scarcely mentioned in the US media). NATO has officially denied the whole story, but in 1990 Secretary General Manfred Wörner reportedly confirmed to the NATO ambassadors that "the military command of the allied forces—Supreme Headquarters Allied Powers Europe (SHAPE)—coordinated the activities of the 'Gladio Network.'"[56]

One member of the European Parliament, speaking about this secret network, was especially incensed by "the fact that it was set up by the CIA and NATO which, while purporting to defend democracy were actually undermining it and using it for their own nefarious purposes." Another member said:

> I should like to protest most strongly against the fact that the American military, whether through SHAPE, NATO or the CIA, think they can interfere in what is our democratic right.[57]

These revelations show the falsity of an assumption widely held by Americans. While recognizing that the US military sometimes does terrible things to its enemies, most Americans have assumed that US military leaders would not order the killing of innocent civilians in allied countries for political purposes. Operation Gladio showed this assumption to be false.

Some Americans, however, might grant even this and still assume that our military leaders would not run false flag operations that would kill fellow Americans. But this assumption was disproved by the discovery of Operation Northwoods.

4. Operation Northwoods

Early in 1962, the Joint Chiefs of Staff presented President John Kennedy with a plan, called Operation Northwoods, describing "pretexts which would provide justification for US military intervention in Cuba." Exemplifying the "strategy of tension" that was being used by the Pentagon in Europe, this document advocated "a period of heightened US-Cuban tensions which place the United States in the position of suffering justifiable grievances." This plan would make the world ready for US intervention "by developing the international image of the Cuban government as rash and irresponsible, and as an alarming and unpredictable threat to the peace of the Western Hemisphere."[58]

The document then suggested several possible actions that would help create this image, such as a "Communist Cuban terror campaign in the Miami area . . . and even in Washington." One of the possibilities was what the Joint Chiefs called a "Remember the Maine" incident: "We could blow up a U.S. ship in Guantánamo Bay and blame Cuba." Accordingly, this false flag operation, devised by the Pentagon's military leaders, would have involved killing American citizens. President Kennedy did not approve this plan, but if a person such as Richard Nixon had been in the White House, the plan for Operation Northwoods may well have been put into effect.

Conclusion

When there is evidence suggesting to some observers that the US government had carried out operations that kill citizens of friendly countries, mainstream (corporate) commentators quickly resist this suggestion, saying that our nation does not do such things. This is all the more the case when evidence suggests to some observers that agents of the US government had targeted American citizens. These commentators declare that any such suggestion is beyond the pale: Agents of our government simply would not do such a thing. However, the history of false flag operations carried out by the American government shows that people have no basis for being so certain.

Endnotes

1 Walter LaFeber, *The Clash: U.S.-Japanese Relations throughout History* (New York: Norton, 1997), 166.

2 On the Mukden incident, see LaFeber, *The Clash,* 164-66; Louise Young, *Japan's Total Empire: Manchuria and the Culture of Wartime Imperialism* (Berkeley: University of California Press, 1999), 40. See "Mukden Incident," *Wikipedia* (http://en.wikipedia.org/wiki/Manchurian_Incident), or "Mukden Incident," *Encyclopedia Britannica*, 2006 (http://www.britannica.com/eb/article-9054193).

3 The question of responsibility for the Reichstag fire had long remained controversial. But the dominant view, that the fire was set by the Nazis themselves, was confirmed in 2001 with the publication of *Der Reichstagbrand: Wie Geschichte Gemacht Wird*, by Alexander Bahar and Wilfried Kugel (Berlin, Edition Q, 2001). This book presents ample evidence of Nazi responsibility, including the testimony of a member of the SA, who said that he was in the subterranean passageway that night and saw other SA members bringing explosive liquids from one building to the other. Accordingly, Bahar and Kugel

substantiated the position contained in William Shirer's *The Rise and Fall of the Third Reich* (New York: Simon and Schuster, 1990), 191-93. This view was also argued by Benjamin Carter Hett in *Burning the Reichstag: An Investigation into the Third Reich's Enduring Mystery* (Oxford, 2014). Writing in the *London Review of Books* (8 May 2014), Richard J. Evans rejected Hett's arguments as well as those of Bahar and Kugel. But Evans' main argument seemed to be that they were "conspiracy theorists" (as suggested by the title of his review, "The Conspiracists").

4 Wilhelm Klein, "The Reichstag Fire, 68 Years On" (review of Alexander Bahar and Wilfried Kugel, *Der Reichstagbrand*), World Socialist Website, 5 July 2001. This review provides a helpful summary of the book.

5 Ibid.

6 See Ian Kershaw, *Hitler: 1936-45: Nemesis* (New York: Norton, 2001), 221; "Nazi Conspiracy and Aggression, Vol. II: Criminality of Groups and Organizations" (http://www.nizkor.org/hweb/imt/nca/nca-02/nca-02-15-criminality-06-05.html); and "Gleiwitz Incident," Wikipedia (http://en.wikipedia.org/wiki/Gleiwitz_incident#References).

7 Howard Zinn, *A People's History of the United States* (1980; New York: HarperPerennial, 1990), 150; Richard Van Alstyne, *The Rising American Empire* (1960; New York, Norton, 1974), 143.

8 Zinn, *A People's History*, 155.

9 Van Alstyne, *The Rising American Empire*, 146.

10 Ibid., 146, 151.

11 Stuart Creighton Miller, *Benevolent Assimilation: The American Conquest of the Philippines, 1899-1903* (New Haven: Yale University Press, 1982), 57-62.

12 Daniele Ganser, *NATO's Secret Armies: Operation Gladio and Terrorism in Western Europe* (New York: Frank Cass, 2005).

13 Paul Williams, *Operation Gladio: The Unholy Alliance between the Vatican, the CIA, and the Mafia* (Amherst: Prometheus Books, 2015).

14 Ibid., 23-24.

15 Ibid., 25.

16 Ganser, *NATO's Secret Armies*, 2, 13, 16, 91-97, 227, 241, 245-46.

17 Williams, *Operation Gladio*, 25.

18 Ibid., 26-27.

19 Ibid., 28.

20 Ganser, *NATO's Secret Armies*, 1.

21 Williams, *Operation Gladio*, 28-29, 61.

22 Ibid., 30-33.

23 Ibid., 40.

24 Ibid., 40 (quoting Jamie Cameron Graham, "The Secret History of the CIA's Involvement in the Narcotics Trade," Doctoral Dissertation, University of Nottingham, 2009).

25 Ganser, *NATO's Secret Armies*, 27-29.

26 Williams, *Operation Gladio*, 62.

27 Ganser, *NATO's Secret Armies*, 53-54.

28 Williams, Operation Gladio, 95.

29 Ganser, *NATO's Secret Armies*, 119.

30 Ibid., 3.

31 Williams, *Operation Gladio*, 103.

32 Ibid., *Operation Gladio*, 108; Ganser, *NATO's Secret Armies*, 5.

33 Ganser, *NATO's Secret Armies*, 3, 119-20.

34 Ibid., 7, quoting Judge Casson on *Newsnight*, BBC1, 4 April 1991.

35 Ibid., quoting the *Observer*, 7 June 1992.

36 Ibid., 9-11.

37 Ibid., 82, 120. On the evidence linking NATO and the United States to the Bologna massacre, see ibid., 25, 81.

38 Ibid., 234-35.

39 Ibid., 234-35.

40 U.S. Department of State, "Misinformation about 'Gladio/Stay Behind' Networks Resurfaces: Thirty Year-Old Soviet Forgery Cited by Researchers," USINFO, Identifying Misinformation, 20 January 2006 (http://usinfo.state.gov/media/Archive/2006/Jan/20-127177.html).

41 Allan Francovich, "Gladio: The Foot Soldiers," BBC2, 24 June 1992, cited in Ganser, *NATO's Secret Armies*, 235.

42 Former CIA agent Philip Agee, describing the CIA's attempt to prevent any participation of Communists in the executive branch of government, wrote: "For the CIA this is evidently the priority of priorities" (Philip Agee and Louis Wolf Louis, *Dirty Work: The CIA in Western Europe* [Secaucus: Lyle Stuart, 1978], 182; quoted in Ganser, *NATO's Secret Armies,* 85).

43 Ganser, *NATO's Secret Armies*, 86.

44 Ibid., 88 (this is Ganser's summary statement).

45 Ibid., 90.

46 Ibid., 98.

47 Ibid., 115-18.

48 Ibid., 225-30.

49 Ibid., 239.

50 Ibid., 241-43.

51 Ibid., 241.

52 Ibid., 138-39.

53 Ibid., 144-47, citing Francovich, "Gladio: The Foot Soldiers."

54 Ibid., 142-43, 146.

55 Ibid., 143, quoting Phil Davison, "A Very Right-Wing Coup Plot Surfaces in Belgium," *Independent*, 24 January 1990.

56 Ibid., 27, quoting the Portuguese newspaper *Expresso*, 24 November 1990. According to the Spanish newspaper *El Pais*, 26 November 1990, Wörner added that SHAPE's coordination of Gladio had been confirmed by US General John Galvin, who was then the Supreme Allied Commander Europe (ibid., 26).

57 Ibid., 21, 22.

58 This memorandum can be found at the National Security Archive, 30 April 2001 (http://www.gwu.edu/~nsarchiv/news/20010430). It was revealed to US readers by James Bamford in *Body of Secrets: Anatomy of the Ultra-secret National Security Agency* (2001: New York: Anchor Books, 2002), 82-91.

| Chapter 12 |

SOME POST-COLD WAR INTERVENTIONS

In 1989, the Soviet Union collapsed. For US imperialists, this development created both an opportunity and a problem. The opportunity was obvious: It meant that the goal to make the American empire universal would no longer be obstructed by another power of comparable strength. "In the two decades that followed the end of the Cold War," reported Walter LaFeber, "the United States carried out more military interventions than it had during the previous forty-five years of waging that war."[1]

The problem was that the disappearance of the Soviet Union meant that "the communist menace" could no longer provide an enemy of global scope to serve as an excuse for American interventions around the world. Moreover, to most Americans, including many in Congress, massive military spending no longer seemed necessary. There was much talk of a "peace dividend," meaning that tax dollars previously used for military spending could be devoted to matters such as health, education, infrastructure, and the environment. This was a serious threat. As Stephen Shalom pointed out in *Imperial Alibis*, a new rationale for continued high levels of military spending was needed.[2]

Equally important, the loss of the Soviet enemy meant that there was no longer any justification for the continued existence of the US-dominated NATO.

This chapter provides three examples of how Washington behaved under the new situation.

1. The Invasion of Panama

The collapse of the Soviet Empire was symbolized by the fall of the Berlin Wall on November 9, 1989. Just a little over a month later, on December 20, 1989, the administration of George H. W. Bush invaded Panama in what was called, with or without a straight face, "Operation Just Cause." This operation was meant to provide at least part of the answer to the question of how the United States could continue overturning governments.

The attack on Panama was massive. Washington originally claimed that only 200 Panamanian civilians were killed, then raised the figure to around 500.[3] But the Central American Human Rights Commission said, as did Catholic and Episcopal Churches, that an estimate of 3,000 would be conservative. The title of the commission's report was "Panama: More than an Invasion, . . . a Massacre."[4] Eyewitnesses reported that US helicopters fired at strictly civilian buildings, that US troops shot at ambulances and bayoneted wounded people to death, and that US tanks ran over dead bodies and even a bus, killing all its passengers.

Especially singled out for attack was El Chorillo neighborhood. At 1:00 AM, while its residents were sleeping, it was attacked by tanks, helicopters, rockets, and flame-throwers. People burned to death in the incinerated buildings or leaped from their windows. People running through the streets in panic were cut down in crossfire and crushed by tanks.[5] This "bloodbath," said a spokesperson for El Chorillo's refugees, killed over 2000 people and created 15,000 refugees.[6]

What was the reason for this massive attack on this tiny, helpless country? What was the "just cause"? One of the reasons given, "to protect American lives," was based on an incident on the night of December 16-17. Four US marines, after approaching a sensitive Panamanian roadblock, were fired at, with one being killed, another wounded. The Pentagon claimed that the soldiers were unarmed and had simply gotten lost. The *Los Angeles Times*, however, revealed that the marines were armed and had provoked the response with obscenities and disobedience to an order to get out of their car.[7] The conclusion that this incident was merely a pretext for the invasion is reinforced by evidence showing that the war had been planned for some time in advance.[8]

That evidence is supported, furthermore, by the fact that the White House, with the aid of the compliant US media, had orchestrated a campaign to demonize Panama's ruler, General Manuel Noriega, months before.[9] This media campaign provided reasons that were later used to justify the invasion—that Noriega had stolen the 1989 election and that he was involved in the drug racket.[10] Still another sign that the invasion occurred for reasons other than the publicly provided ones was that, although in October of 1989, the Panamanian Defense Forces had Noriega in custody and offered to turn him over to the United States, the Bush Administration declined the offer.[11] Furthermore, a European diplomat reported that shortly after the invasion began, he telephoned the US military to tell them that Noriega was in the flat of his mistress's grandmother, but he was told that the military "had other priorities."[12]

As for the real reasons for the invasion, one factor was that the exposure of Noriega's drug dealing, combined with his failure to hew the US line on Nicaragua, made him no longer a useful client. This fact was especially crucial at the time because the administration of the Panama Canal was scheduled to pass back into Panamanian hands on January 1, 1990. The invasion put the government back into the hands of the white-skinned pro-American elite, which had been displaced in 1968.[13]

The Bush administration's original plan, in fact, had been to establish a US military government, but it later decided to install a local man, Guillermo Endara, as president. Of course, said a Pentagon study, Endara's government was "merely a facade."[14] It was a facade to hide the fact that Washington had established direct control over ministries and institutions through which it could, in the words of a Mexican journal, "permanently control all the actions and decisions of the government."

With the establishment of this parallel government, the journal continued, "things have returned to the way they were before 1968."[15] What had happened in 1968 was a coup, led by General Torrijos, which had displaced the rule of the white elite, who constitute about 8 percent of the population. Although Torrijos and his successor, Noriega, were dictators, they were *populist* dictators, and their two decades of rule brought remarkable changes. In Noam Chomsky's words:

> Black, Mestizo, and Indigenous Panamanians gained their first share of power, and economic and land reforms were undertaken. . . . [I]nfant mortality declined from 40 percent to less than 20 percent and life expectancy increased by nine years. . . . Indigenous communities were granted autonomy and protection for their traditional lands, to an extent unmatched in the hemisphere.[16]

Obviously such advances could not be allowed to stand indefinitely. The reversion to the pre-1968 state of things was confirmed by a report in the *Miami Herald* the following June (of 1990), which said:

> Six months after the U.S. invasion, Panama is showing signs of growing prosperity—at least for the largely white-skinned business class that has regained its influence. . . . The upper class and the middle classes are doing great. . . . But the poor are in bad shape. . . . The Catholic Church has begun to denounce what it sees as a lack of government concern for the poor.[17]

The massive attack on El Chorillo was part of this project to aid Panama's elite class. The owners of this neighborhood had wanted "to transform this prime piece of real estate into a posher district," but Noriega had stood in the way, allowing the poor to live there rent-free. US forces removed this obstacle "by bombing the neighborhood into rubble and then leveling the charred ruins with bulldozers."[18] This violent gentrification of El Chorillo was simply part of the economic purpose of the invasion, as suggested by the fact that Bush afterwards announced that $1 billion in aid would be given to rebuild Panama—at least $600 million of which would enrich American banks and corporations.[19]

Still another motive was suggested by a human rights commission report that "the U.S. Army used highly sophisticated weapons—some for the first time in combat—against unarmed civilian populations."[20] Among these weapons were F-117A stealth fighters, which were used to bomb facilities that had no fighter planes or even any radar. An aviation journal, explaining the likely rationale, said:

> By demonstrating the F-117A's capability to operate in low-intensity conflicts, . . . the operation can be used by the Air Force to justify the huge investment made in stealth technology [to] an increasingly skeptical Congress.[21]

The same conclusion was reached by a retired military officer. Saying "100 Special Forces guys" would have sufficed to capture Noriega, he suggested that "this big operation was a Pentagon attempt to impress Congress just when they're starting to cut back on the military."[22]

When President Bush was asked by a reporter, "Was it really worth it to send people to their death for this? To get Noriega?" Bush replied that "every human life is precious, and yet I have to answer yes, it has been worth it."[23] The US House of Representatives, showing no interest in the question of how many Panamanian civilians were killed, passed a resolution 389-26 commending the president for his handling of the invasion and expressing sadness over the loss of 23 American lives.[24] Some human lives are obviously more precious than others.

In light of the interests served by the US invasion of

Panama, the government's justification for it was especially revealing. Article 51 of the UN Charter forbids the use of force by any nation except for self-defense, and only then until there is time for the Security Council to act. But the American Ambassador to the UN informed it, on the day of the invasion, that this article "provides for the use of armed force . . . to defend our interests."[25] With this interpretation, the United States was saying that it had the right to invade any country not simply for "self-defense," as virtually everyone else understood it, but also for the sake of defending any interest whatsoever.

The fact that US leaders now felt free to announce this new doctrine was suggested by the fact that, on the day after the invasion, General Colin Powell, the new Chairman of the Joint Chiefs of Staff, said: "We have to put a shingle outside our door saying, 'Superpower lives here.'"[26]

The people of Latin America, however, did not need this shingle. An article in *El Tiempo*, calling Operation Just Cause an "imperialist invasion of Panama," said: "We live in a climate of aggression and disrespect . . . [in] absolute submission . . . to the service of an implacable superpower." An editorial, denouncing "international totalitarianism in the guise of democracy," said that Bush "declared plainly to Latin America that for the North American government, there is no law—only its will—when imposing its designs on the hemisphere."[27] As the rest of the world would soon come to see, however, this policy was not to be limited to the Western Hemisphere.

That same day—January 5, 1990—a story in the *Boston Globe* said that former assistant secretary of state Elliott Abrams, who had been convicted for his role in the Iran-Contra Scandal, expressed pleasure over the invasion of Panama. Now that developments in Moscow have lessened the prospect for a small operation to escalate into a superpower conflict, Abrams said, "Bush probably is going to be increasingly willing to use force."[28] That prediction would come true a year later in Iraq.

2. The 1991 Attack on Iraq

Although Saddam Hussein's invasion of Kuwait was as illegal as was the US invasion of Panama, he had understandable reasons for it. Kuwait was exceeding its OPEC quota of oil production by 40 percent, thereby driving down the price of oil. This violation was costing Iraq billions of dollars and thereby preventing its economic recovery—a recovery necessary for it to pay back the $90 billion it had borrowed for its war with Iran. Kuwait was also reportedly using slant drilling under the border to steal oil from Iraq's share of the Rumaila oil fields. At the same time, while other creditors were being patient, Kuwait was demanding immediate payment of the billions that Iraq had borrowed from it, hoping to use this as leverage to force a favorable settlement of its long-term border dispute with Iraq.[29]

Saddam explained all this to the US ambassador, April Glaspie, at a meeting he had requested on July 25, 1990, after his troops were already amassed on the Iraq-Kuwait border, ready to attack. He had good reason to expect American support. His Baath Party had come to power through a CIA-engineered coup; Washington had allowed him to slaughter Kurds with impunity; and it supported him during his long war with Iran, even turning a blind eye to his use of poison gas against Kurds and Iranians. Saddam knew, moreover, that the United States had no respect for the United Nations or international law generally. Saddam could well have assumed that he and the Americans had what could be called a "barbarians' agreement."

Besides all this, Ambassador Glaspie told him (the conversation was being tape recorded): "We have no opinion on the Arab-Arab conflicts, like your border disagreement with Kuwait," adding that "[Secretary of State] James Baker has directed our official spokesmen to emphasize this instruction."[30]

On August 1, Saddam sent his forces into Kuwait, evidently having understood Glaspie's statement as a green light to invade the tiny country to his south—as Bush had recently done to a tiny country to *his* south.[31]

The Bush Administration, however, immediately expressed outrage at this violation of international law.[32] The UN General Assembly, ironically, had just condemned Bush's invasion of Panama as a "flagrant violation of international law and of [Panama's] independence, sovereignty, and territorial integrity." But there was no Security Council resolution against the United States because the US representative, of course, vetoed all attempts to pass one.[33] Then the United States, with no apparent sense of shame, used carrot-and-stick tactics to get the Security Council to pass resolutions condemning Iraq, demanding its withdrawal from Kuwait, and authorizing the use of "all necessary means" to compel it to withdraw if it had not done so by January 15, 1991.[34]

The Bush administration was ready to provide those means. First, claiming that Saddam was ready to invade Saudi Arabia next, Bush within days sent troops to Saudi Arabia in what was called Operation Desert Shield. The Bush administration then assembled a coalition of forces that began its attack in January of 1991.

The attack, dubbed Operation Desert Storm, dropped over 100,000 tons of explosives, the equivalent of about 6 Hiroshima atomic bombs.[35] The bombing campaign targeted Iraq's "civilian infrastructure, including power, sewage, and water systems"—targets, points out Chomsky, "having little relation to driving Iraq from Kuwait" but "designed for long-term US political ends."[36]

Late in February, Iraq announced that, having accepted a peace plan offered by Moscow, it was withdrawing from Kuwait immediately and unconditionally. As it was retreating in surrender on February 26, US planes attacked the head and tail of the long convoy, thereby immobilizing it. US forces then began slaughtering the Iraqi troops in what American soldiers called a "Turkey shoot" (thereby using a term US troops had used in the Philippines a century earlier). Evidently 25,000 - 30,000 Iraqis were killed during this 40-hour slaughter.[37]

Another 30,000 Iraqis were killed when, after America had encouraged a popular uprising against Saddam's regime, the Shias responded. Fearing the emergence of an Islamic government in alliance with Iran, American forces gave Saddam a free hand to slaughter the Shias.[38]

Evidence that Saddam Fell into an American Trap

Two months after the attack began, Claude Cheysson, who had formerly been France's foreign minister, said: "The Americans were determined to go to war" and Saddam "walked into a trap."[39] This opinion had already been expressed a month and a half before the attack by the Iraqi ambassador to the United States, who said that Ambassador Glaspie's avowal of US neutrality on the dispute between Iraq and Kuwait was "part and parcel of the setup."[40] Most Americans would, of course, be suspicious of claims made by Iraqi and even French spokespersons. But there is considerable evidence that they were right.

This evidence includes (1) US motives for a war with Iraq, (2) Kuwaiti behavior, (3) US behavior, (4) physical and testimonial evidence of collusion between US and Kuwaiti leaders.

1. US Motives for War with Iraq: There were several reasons why the US government, including the Pentagon, might have wanted a war with Iraq at that time.

First, the attack on Panama had not been sufficient to end the calls for huge cut-backs in military spending, now that the Cold War was over. President Bush was railing against those who would "naïvely cut the muscle out of our defense posture," but news reports said that "the administration and Congress are expecting the most acrimonious hard-fought defense budget battle in recent history" and that "tensions have escalated" between Congress and the Pentagon.[41] Shortly after Iraq's invasion of Kuwait, Bush argued that it, in the words of the *Washington Post*, "underscores the need to go slowly in restructuring U.S. defense forces."[42] After US troops were deployed to Saudi Arabia, Lawrence Korb, former assistant secretary of defense, said this deployment "seems driven . . . by upcoming budget battles on Capitol Hill."[43] If he was right, the plan worked. "Operation Desert Shield," reported the *Los Angeles Times* in October, "forged a major change in the political climate of the negotiations, forcing lawmakers who had been advocating deep cuts on the defensive." As a result, the budget agreement reached in October "would spare much of the funding that has been spent each year to prepare for a major Soviet onslaught on Western Europe."[44]

A second possible motive was provided by the fact that Bush's popularity was declining. Although his approval rating in January, following his invasion of Panama, had been at 80 percent, by July it had dropped to 60 percent. Again, if this was a motive, it worked. After the bombing began, his approval rating rose to 82 percent, his highest ever.[45]

Although these first two motives could have been satisfied by wars in any one of many places, there were also motives related to Iraq in particular. One of these was the fact that the United States was being edged out of its dominating position in the Gulf. The United States had fallen to fourth place among arms suppliers, and many Gulf States, including Saudi Arabia, were refusing to allow a permanent US military presence. This problem was also solved by the Gulf War: The United States sold some $60 billion worth of arms in the ensuing decade and its military presence in the Gulf increased dramatically.[46]

A fourth possible motive reflected the fact that, although the United States had supported Saddam during his war with Iran and had even shielded him from any consequences after his use of poison gas, he was becoming increasingly less subservient. Besides supporting the Palestinian cause, he was becoming a new spokesman for Arab nationalism, warning of the danger that "the Arab Gulf region will be ruled by American will," with the result that the distribution and price of oil would be dictated on the basis of American interests alone.[47] The US attack on Iraq, followed by the brutal sanctions, showed not only Saddam but the leaders of other countries in the region the danger of challenging US hegemony in the region, even verbally.

Finally, as Saddam's statement illustrated, US hegemony in the region was so important because of the region's oil. As the notorious draft of the Pentagon's Defense Planning Guidance document of 1992 stated in a paragraph mentioning Iraq's invasion of Kuwait, "our overall objective is to remain the predominant outside power in the region and preserve US and Western access to the region's oil."[48]

Kuwait's Behavior: That the Bush administration had wanted Iraq to invade Kuwait, thereby providing an excuse for the United States to go to war, is also suggested by Kuwait's behavior leading up to the invasion.

In the first place, Kuwait had taken several actions certain to anger Saddam. As mentioned above, Kuwait was using slant-drill technology to steal oil from Iraq's portion of the Rumaila oil fields; Kuwait was greatly violating OPEC agreements, thereby causing crude oil prices to plummet thereby making it impossible for Iraq to repay the money he had borrowed for its war with Iran; and Kuwait was demanding immediate repayment of the $30 billion it had loaned Iraq.[49]

In addition to behaving in this unreasonable way, Kuwait's leaders rebuffed every attempt by Saddam to enter into negotiations—and did so in a way that one senior US official called "nasty" and "arrogant."[50] When these leaders did respond to Saddam's financial demands, which involved many billions of dollars, they offered "an insulting half-million dollars."[51]

As suggested by several observers—including Jordan's King Hussein and a political science professor at Kuwait University—this behavior by tiny little Kuwait was clearly irrational unless it had been encouraged by a very powerful ally.[52]

US Behavior: The idea that the United States might have encouraged Kuwait's provocative behavior before the invasion by Iraq is suggested not only by the existence of US motives to attack Iraq, discussed above, but also by US behavior, both before and after Iraq's invasion of Kuwait.

Before the invasion, the US military had worked out plans for an attack on Iraq. In the Pentagon's planning in 1990 for possible wars, "the Soviet threat" had been replaced by "the Iraqi threat." War games involved responses to an Iraqi invasion of Kuwait with bombing targets in Iraq.[53] The overall planning for the war against Iraq was under the direction of General Norman Schwarzkopf, who would later be put in charge of the war itself. "After the war," reported professor of international law Francis

Boyle, "Schwarzkopf referred to 18 months of planning for the campaign"[54]—which would mean that planning had begun over a year before Iraq's invasion of Kuwait. Part of this planning involved secretly expanding a network of military-intelligence bases in Saudi Arabia.[55] The planning also involved sending "massive quantities of United States weapons, equipment, and supplies" to these bases in January 1990—eight months before Iraq's invasion of Kuwait.[56]

The Bush administration's behavior after Iraq's invasion of Kuwait provided additional evidence that it was bent on war. In the first place, the Bush administration, in order to justify Operation Desert Shield, falsely claimed that top-secret satellite photographs taken in the middle of September (1990) showed that over a quarter million Iraqi troops and 1500 tanks were in southern Kuwait, ready to invade Saudi Arabia. Jean Heller of the *St. Petersburg Times*, after obtaining photos from Soviet commercial satellites for the same period and having them examined by experts, exposed the lie in a story headlined "Photos Don't Show Buildup."[57] Although this story was published on January 6, 1991, US mainstream news outlets failed to pick it up and the US-led attack went ahead as scheduled ten days later. "To this day," reported a story in the *Christian Science Monitor* in 2002, "the Pentagon's photographs of the [alleged] Iraqi troop build-up remain classified."[58]

Besides lying about the deployment of Iraqi troops in Kuwait, the Bush administration colluded with Kuwait to manufacture a lie about their behavior. This lie—that Iraqi troops had ripped premature babies from incubators in Al Adnan hospital in Kuwait City and "left them on the cold floor to die"—was told to the US Congress by a 15-year-old Kuwaiti girl who testified that she had been working as a volunteer at the hospital at the time. Nurses at this hospital later said not only that this never happened but also that they had never seen the girl before they saw her on CNN. It turned out that she was really Nayirah al-Sabah, the daughter of the Kuwaiti ambassador to the United States. She and six other "witnesses" had been coached by Hill & Knowlton, a public relations firm that had been given a $2 million contract by the Kuwaiti government to make the case for a US war against Iraq. President Bush, who had a long-standing relationship with the al-Sabah family, cited this story at least five times in making the case for going to war.[59]

The president also lied about Saddam's invasion itself, claiming that it was "without provocation," whereas, as we have seen, it had been multiply provoked. Indeed, there is good reason to believe that the Bush administration knew that it would take great provocation to get Saddam to invade Kuwait because a study by the Strategic Studies Institute of the US Army War College issued a report early in 1990 that said:

> Baghdad should not be expected to deliberately provoke military confrontations with anyone. Its interests are best served now and in the immediate future by peace. . . . Force is only likely if the Iraqis feel seriously threatened.[60]

And, indeed, it was only after two years of provocations from Kuwait, which did seriously threaten the Iraqis, that they took action—and only then after they thought they had America's blessing.

Bush's commitment to going to war is also shown by the fact that he greatly exaggerated the seriousness of Iraq's invasion of Kuwait, comparing it with Hitler's invasion of Poland and saying that it threatened another world war. Bush even said that Saddam was "worse than Hitler."[61]

That the Bush administration was chomping at the bit to go to war is shown, furthermore, by the fact that it used not only lies but also threats and what William Blum called "history's most spectacular bribes"—thereby violating the rules of the UN Security Council, the very institution whose rules it claimed to be enforcing. According to Blum's summary statement, based on many reports, about bribes:

> Egypt was forgiven many billions of dollars in debt, while Syria, China, Turkey, the Soviet

> Union, and other countries received military or economic aid and World Bank and IMF loans, had sanctions lifted, not only from the US but, under Washington's pressure, from Germany, Japan and Saudi Arabia. As an added touch, the Bush administration stopped criticizing the human rights record of any coalition member.[62]

According to the UN charter, nations, besides not bribing other members of the Security Council, are also not supposed to punish, or threaten to punish, them. And yet when the delegate from Yemen got some applause from the gallery for his vote against a US-backed resolution to authorize the use force against Iraq, Secretary of State James Baker reportedly told the US delegation: "I hope he enjoyed that applause, because this will turn out to be the most expensive vote he ever cast." Whether or not Baker actually made this comment, Yemen did learn, within a few days, that its US aid was being sharply reduced.[63] Besides losing some $70 million, moreover, John Pilger reported, "Yemen suddenly had problems with the World Bank and the IMF, and 800,000 Yemini workers were expelled from Saudi Arabia." Pilger reported, moreover, that economic threats were used by the US delegation against Ecuador and Zimbabwe.[64]

The Bush administration also showed its desire for war by dismissing out of hand all offers by Saddam to negotiate a withdrawal. In August, shortly after his invasion, Saddam said he would withdraw in return for sole control of the Rumaila oil fields, Kuwait's agreement to abide by OPEC quotas, access to the Persian Gulf, and the lifting of the sanctions that had just been imposed. One Bush administration Middle East specialist called this proposal "serious" and "negotiable," but it was summarily rejected.[65] Saddam got the same response from an offer he made in October and yet another on January 2, in which he made fewer demands.[66] Finally, word was received on January 11 that Saddam was willing to pull out with even fewer conditions, insisting only for guarantees that his troops would not be attacked as they withdrew and that there would be negotiations to address the Iraq-Kuwait disputes and an international conference to address Palestinian grievances. He said only that he needed to wait until January 17 to withdraw so he could save face by showing that he had not been intimidated.[67] The US-led coalition, however, began its attack as soon as the deadline of midnight on January 15 had passed.

Evidence of Collusion: In addition to all this circumstantial evidence suggesting that US and Kuwaiti leaders had colluded to lure Saddam into invading Kuwait so that US forces could come to the rescue, there is actual physical and testimonial evidence of this collusion.

After the invasion, Iraqis found a memo in a Kuwaiti intelligence file about a meeting in November of 1989 between CIA Director William Webster and the head of state security for Kuwait. This memo said, among other things:

> We agreed with the American side that it was important to take advantage of the deteriorating economic situation in Iraq in order to put pressure on that country's government to delineate our common border. The Central Intelligence Agency gave us its view of appropriate means of pressure, saying that broad cooperation should be initiated between us. . . .

Although the CIA declared the document a "total fabrication," it did not, as the *Los Angeles Times* pointed out, *appear* to be a forgery. Its genuineness was suggested, furthermore, by the fact that, when the Kuwaiti foreign minister was confronted with the document, he fainted.[68]

Additional evidence that "the American side" encouraged Kuwait's economic pressure and its refusal to negotiate was provided by Yassar Arafat, who said that at an Arab summit in May of 1990, Saddam had offered to negotiate a mutually acceptable border with Kuwait. However, "The US was encouraging Kuwait not to offer any compromise."[69] We might, of course, be skeptical of such a statement coming from Arafat, an ally of Saddam who himself had been badly treated by the United States.

But we have similar testimony from a long-time US ally, King Hussein of Jordan. He later stated that, just before the invasion, the Kuwaiti foreign minister—the man who later fainted—had said: "We are not going to respond to [Iraq]. . . . [I]f they don't like it, let them occupy our territory. . . . [W]e are going to bring in the Americans." The king also reported that Kuwait's emir—the brother of the foreign minister—had told his military officers that if Iraq invaded, "American and foreign forces would land in Kuwait and expel them."[70]

Michael Emery, whose article "How Mr. Bush Got His War" contained these statements from his interview with King Hussein, further reported that:

> The evidence shows that President George Bush, British prime minister Margaret Thatcher, Egyptian president Hosni Mubarak, and other Arab leaders secretly cooperated on a number of occasions, beginning August 1988 [when the Iran-Iraq war ended], to deny Saddam Hussein the economic help he demanded for the reconstruction of his nation . . . [and that] Washington and London encouraged the Kuwaitis in their intransigent insistence.[71]

Part of the evidence to which Emery referred was a note from Kuwait's emir to his prime minister, prior to the invasion. Pointing out that their policy of intransigence had support from Egypt, Washington, and London, he urged: "Be unwavering in your discussions [with the Iraqis about their financial demands]. . . . We are stronger than they think."

In the light of this evidence, it seems impossible to interpret April Glaspie's statement to Saddam—"We have no opinion on. . . your border disagreement with Kuwait"—as anything other than deliberate deception. This conclusion was reportedly reached, in fact, by Lee Hamilton, then a member of the US House Committee on International Relations. According to former CIA agent John Stockwell, "Hamilton concluded, from hearings on this, that [America] had deliberately given Saddam Hussein the green light to invade Kuwait."[72]

This conclusion was also reached by another member of the House of Representatives, Henry Gonzalez, who wrote:

> CIA representatives in Kuwait . . . encourag[ed] Kuwait to refuse to negotiate its differences with Iraq as required by the United Nations Charter, including Kuwait's failure to abide by OPEC quotas [and] its pumping of Iraqi oil from the Rumaila oil field.[73]

A similar conclusion was drawn by some newspapers. The *New York Daily News* wrote: "State Department officials . . . led Saddam Hussein to think he could get away with grabbing Kuwait. Bush and Co. gave him no reason to think otherwise."[74] Likewise, *The International Herald Tribune* published a story entitled "Setting the American Trap for Hussein."[75] That does seem to be what happened, making what came afterwards all the more despicable.

Crippling Sanctions, Continuing Attacks

Operation Desert Storm resulted, as we have seen, in perhaps 100,000 Iraqi deaths. That, however, was only the beginning. The United Nations, led by the United States, then imposed crippling sanctions, which prevented Iraq from getting enough food but also from receiving things such as vaccines, chemicals for water purification, and parts for sewage pumps, with the result that sewage spilled into the rivers from which most people got their drinking water. One can read the gruesome details in the first chapter of Dilip Hiro's *Iraq*, "Life in Iraq," which is oriented around the difference between what Iraqis called life "before the sanctions" and "after the sanctions."

These sanctions, first imposed during the George H. W. Bush administration, were not lifted by the Clinton Administration. By 1996, as a result, evidently over 500,000 children had died from typhoid, dysentery, and other easily preventable diseases, leading one pair of authors to speak of "sanctions of mass destruction."[76]

When Clinton's ambassador to the UN, Madeleine Albright, was asked whether she thought this price was worth paying, she notoriously replied, similarly to Bush's reply about Panama: "It is a difficult question. But, yes, we think the price is worth it."[77] An event causing a half million American lives would perhaps have been viewed somewhat differently.

In any case, Clinton also continued other policies of the Bush administration, most notably the so-called no-fly zones over both the northern and the southern parts of Iraq. These zones were established unilaterally by the United States, with no authorization from the Security Council—a fact seldom pointed out to the American public by the Fourth Estate.[78]

Clinton's administration also had US planes attack Iraqi targets on a regular basis, compounding the illegality of its flights. The most intense attack was Operation Desert Fox, which occurred in December of 1998, while Clinton was facing impeachment hearings. This attack lasted for 100 hours, during which 415 cruise missiles and 600 laser-guided bombs were sent against Iraqi targets.[79]

Incessantly pounding Iraq had simply become a way of life for the US military. In August of 1999, the Pentagon revealed that over the previous 8 months the Anglo-American air forces had attacked 359 Iraqi targets, firing some 1,100 missiles—over three times the enormous number fired during Desert Fox.[80] It is not surprising, therefore, that after 9/11 the Iraqi foreign minister said: "All Muslim and Arab people consider America the master of terrorism, the terrorist power number one."[81]

3. The Destruction of Yugoslavia

At about the same time as the US Gulf War, the George H.W. Bush administration started wars in Europe. Explaining the main motivation, William Engdahl said that, given the destruction of the Soviet Union,

> Washington faced an entirely new challenge. Suddenly, the rationale for permanent US military and political control over the nations of the EU was under existential threat. Europe was beginning to sense its true independent power in the world as leading circles there contemplated life after NATO—Europeans would no longer have to bow to countless US dictates merely because of a real or imagined threat of the Soviets.[82]

In 1991, the Maastricht Treaty (formally, the Treaty on European Unity) was signed by the heads of the states of the European Union. Forming the basis for a possible United States of Europe, the treaty authorized an independent European NATO, to be run by the EU states, not by the USA. Washington saw this development as a threat to America's global power.[83]

The response of the Bush administration, Engdahl added, "was to covertly trigger events in Yugoslavia that would explode in a violent war in the heart of Europe," thereby shattering the idea that European wars were a thing of the past and that, therefore, the European countries no longer needed a US-led NATO.

Yugoslavia had been established in 1945 as a socialist federal republic consisting of six republics with different religions: Serbia, Macedonia, and Montenegro were primarily Orthodox Christian; Slovenia and Croatia were primarily Roman Catholic; and Bosnia-Herzegovina was primarily Muslim. The Bush administration's plan was to start wars to break up Yugoslavia into independent and non-socialist countries.

The execution of the plan began by using the International

Monetary Fund (IMF), which is controlled by the United States, to destroy Yugoslavia's economy. Predictably, "amid growing economic chaos, each region fought for its own survival against its neighbors."[84]

The Bush administration then made war inevitable by passing a Foreign Operations Appropriations Act, which said that any part of Yugoslavia that failed to declare independence within six months would lose all US financial support. "The Act threw the Yugoslav federal government in Belgrade into existential crisis. It was unable to pay the enormous interest on its foreign debt or even to arrange the purchase of raw materials for industry. Credit collapsed and recriminations broke out on all sides."[85]

Bosnia-Herzegovina

Not relying on the Appropriations Act alone, the Bush administration had its Pentagon fly into Europe thousands of veterans of the Mujahideen operation in Afghanistan, which the US had used to defeat the Soviet Union there. In 1992, these fighters were flown to Bosnia-Herzegovina (situated between Catholic Croatia and Orthodox Serbia), to help Bosnia's Muslims.[86] "Violent political Islamic fundamentalism," said Engdahl, "was suddenly at the heart of Europe and Washington made it happen."[87]

However, a plan was drafted in Lisbon that year to prevent a civil war in Bosnia-Herzegovina between Muslims, Catholics, and Orthodox Christians. The plan, conceived by Britain and Portugal, proposed to partition the country by religious concentration. All three leaders in Bosnia-Herzegovina signed the treaty.

But Secretary of State Lawrence Eagleburger instructed Warren Zimmermann, the US ambassador to Yugoslavia, to convince Alija Izetbegović, the leader of the Bosnian Muslims, to renege on the Lisbon treaty. Zimmerman convinced Izetbegović by promising him political, diplomatic, and military aid if he would renege. The Lisbon Treaty likely could have avoided the Bosnian war. However, "Avoiding such a war was precisely what Washington wanted to prevent from happening. They wanted the Bosnian war for their larger geopolitical strategy in Europe and beyond."[88]

Because the Serbs were the ones most opposed to the breakup of the Yugoslav federation, they were America's main target. By demonizing the Serbs as Nazis, guilty of "ethnic cleansing" comparable to the holocaust and "portraying Bosnian Muslims as the hapless victims of Serb atrocities. . . , the way was clear to blame the Serb forces in Bosnia for every imaginable crime."[89]

> While US propaganda machinery turned out endless fake stories of Serbian bombings of civilian villagers and hospitals, attacks on UN so-called "safe zones," and fabricated accounts of tens of thousands of rapes of Muslim women in what the Western media, led by the *New York Times*, claimed were Serb-run "rape camps," the Muslim jihadist mercenaries working alongside Izetbegović's army created appalling atrocities against Bosnian Serbs that were blacked out of US and Western media.[90]

In that situation, Bill Clinton, who had taken over the presidency from Bush, was able, albeit with difficulty, to persuade allies to endorse an air campaign by NATO to undermine the military capabilities of the Bosnian Serb Army.

The most important demonization of the Serbs involved the "Srebrenica massacre" of innocent Bosnian Muslims in a UN safe zone. Here is what happened: Prior to the massacre, Bosnian Muslim jihadists, under the leadership of one Naser Orić, used the safe haven in Srebrenica as an illegal base for attacks on Serbian villages, in violation of the UN humanitarian rules for safe havens. Orić's soldiers slaughtered over 3,500 Orthodox Christians, including women and children. These killings "created a rage and fury for revenge among the Bosnian Serb soldiers fighting to take control of Srebrenica away from the Bosnians." But when those soldiers entered Srebrenica, they encountered no opposition. After letting the women, children, and elderly go to safety, the Serbs shot the men.[91]

The reason there was no opposition was explained later by Canadian Major General Lewis Mackenzie, who had been in command of Srebrenica. In an op-ed entitled "The Real Story behind Srebrenica," he wrote:

> [T]he man who led the Bosnian Muslim fighters [knew] that the Bosnian Serb army was going to attack Srebrenica to stop him from attacking Serb villages. So he and . . . his fighters slipped out of town. Srebrenica was left undefended with the strategic thought that, if the Serbs attacked an undefended town, surely that would cause NATO and the UN to agree that NATO air strikes against the Serbs were justified.[92]

In other words, said Engdahl, "Washington wanted the Srebrenica massacre as casus belli it could use against the Serb population."[93] This plan worked.

> The Clinton administration got what they wanted—the pretext for NATO to continue its existence as the controlling US-run military organization in Western Europe. It also got a permanent 80,000-man NATO occupation force in Bosnia-Herzegovina to enforce "peace."[94]

The Bosnian War, which took place in Bosnia-Herzegovina between 1992 and 1995, ended up being the most devastating conflict in Europe since World War II, with more than 100,000 people killed and 2.2 million people displaced. But it achieved Clinton's purpose, beginning the breakup of Yugoslavia.[95]

Given Washington's hope that the dissolution of the Yugoslav Federation would "light the fuse to an explosive new series of Balkan wars," it provided finances for the wars:

> Washington's financial support was typically channeled into extreme nationalist or former fascist organizations that would guarantee a violent and bloody dismemberment of Yugoslavia. . . . Right-wing and fascist organizations [which had been maintained in exile by the CIA] were suddenly revived and began receiving covert support.[96]

Sir Alfred Sherman, an adviser to Margaret Thatcher, the British prime minister, said in 1997: "The war in Bosnia was America's war in every sense of the word. The United States administration helped start it, kept it going, and prevented its early end."[97] As for keeping it going, Engdahl wrote: "The longer the war in Bosnia-Herzegovina raged, the better it was for Washington's attempt to revive the role of a US-led NATO in the Balkans and Europe."[98]

But in 1995, America suddenly brought the war to an end. Why? Washington found it far more important to secure a permanent military base in Kosovo, in order to be able to control the entire region, including the Middle East and the Caucasus.[99]

Bombing Kosovo

In 1999, Clinton had NATO launch a second war on Yugoslavia, beginning with Serbia's province of Kosovo, which was composed primarily of ethnic Albanians. The Clinton administration's main reasons for this war centered on Slobodan Milošević, the president of Yugoslavia. Engdahl wrote:

> By 1999, it was clear to Washington that the stubbornly popular Milošević had to go if they were to bring forward their agenda of NATO military domination of post-Soviet Europe. Washington was determined to construct a huge military air base in Kosovo, then an integral part of Serbia, in order to secure their control of the entire region of Southeast Europe and put the vital Russian Black Sea Fleet at Crimea within striking distance of a US air attack.[100]

The fighting in Kosovo occurred primarily between Serbian troops and the Kosovo Liberation Army (KLA), whose fighters were trained by Mujahideen mercenaries recruited by the US. Although originally composed of Kosovars, the KLA was augmented by "former US Pentagon special forces and retired military." In 1998, the KLA escalated its attacks on government officials in Belgrade, the capital of Yugoslavia. At the time, the KLA had only 500 trained fighters. But by providing the KLA with arms and training, Western powers by 1999 built it into a major guerrilla army with perhaps 30,000 members.[101]

Having no interest in ones who might be open to a diplomatic solution with the Serbian government, "Washington deliberately froze out the Kosovo moderates in favor of the jihadists of the KLA mafia, who were guaranteed not to go for peace."[102] As for the term "mafia": Former NSA official Wayne Madsen said that "the KLA was, in fact, a grouping of mafia clans in Kosovo who were known drug traffickers well before working for the US." In 1999, the *Washington Times* reported that the Clinton administration was fully aware of the KLA's heroin trafficking, but the mainstream press ignored this story. In fact, although the US State Department had classified the KLA as a terrorist organization, the Clinton administration and the press began referring to its members as "democratic freedom fighters."[103]

NATO supported these "freedom fighters" by bombing the Serbs. The reason for the US participation in the war in Kosovo, said President Clinton, that it was "necessary to stop ethnic cleansing and bring stability to Eastern Europe." Clinton told the nation that in intervening, "we are *upholding our values*, protecting our interests, and advancing the cause of peace." British Prime Minister Tony Blair called this a new kind of war, in which we are *fighting "for values*," for a "new internationalism where the brutal repression of whole ethnic groups will no longer be tolerated."[104]

Both Clinton and Blair said that NATO was bombing the Serbs in order to stop its ethnic cleansing of Kosovo's Albanians. But as Chomsky emphasized, their claim had the facts backwards.

Although Serb atrocities in Kosovo were quite real, and often ghastly, "the bombing was not undertaken in 'response' to ethnic cleansing and to 'reverse' it, as leaders alleged." Rather, "Clinton and Blair decided in favor of a war that led to a radical escalation of ethnic cleansing."[105]

Defenders of the bombing called it a "humanitarian intervention." The bombing was justified, they said, by the vast crimes that occurred. However, pointed out Chomsky,

> the vast crimes took place after the bombing began: they were not a cause but a consequence. *It requires considerable audacity, therefore, to take the crimes to provide retrospective justification for the actions that contributed to inciting them.*[106]

Moreover, the "vast crimes"—including what the US government called "ethnic cleansing"—were an *anticipated* consequence of the bombing. General Wesley Clark, NATO's Supreme Commander, said that it was "entirely predictable" that the bombing would result in an intensification of Serb terror and violence: "The military authorities fully anticipated the vicious approach that Milošević would adopt, as well as the terrible efficiency with which he would carry it out."[107]

Bombing Belgrade

In addition to bombing Kosovo in support of the KLA, Clinton's NATO began bombing Belgrade, the capital of Serbia and Yugoslavia. Showing disdain for international law, "Clinton's bombing was done in violation of the UN Charter, the UN Security Council, and the NATO Charter itself."[108] This attack, which employed 2,300 missiles as well as 14,000 bombs, lasted 78 days, devastating Belgrade.

> The illegal bombing destroyed and damaged 25,000 homes, 300 miles of roads and close to 400 miles of railways. Many public buildings

> were damaged, including 14 airports, 19 hospitals, 18 kindergartens, 69 schools, 176 cultural monuments and 44 bridges. The attacks killed at least 5,000 people (some sources claim it was closer to 18,000), injured 12,500, and left the area contaminated with depleted uranium.[109]

This devastation of Belgrade had been planned. As the bombing started, General Clark said: "We are going to systematically and progressively attack, disrupt, degrade, devastate, and ultimately . . . destroy [Milosevic's] forces and their facilities." In response, Harold Pinter said that Milosevic's forces and facilities, "as we now know, included television stations, schools, hospitals, theatres, old people's homes."[110]

The Treatment of Milošević

In any case, when the bombing was ended, Milošević withdrew, on the understanding that the UN would enforce order in Kosovo were he to remove Yugoslav troops, ending the decade-long war. Nevertheless, in 2001, the United States pressured the Yugoslav government to extradite Milošević to a specially created International Criminal Tribunal in The Hague, on charges of "war crimes and crimes against humanity committed in Kosovo." The Yugoslav authorities acceded to this pressure because the United States had threatened, if the extradition request was refused, to cut off financial aid from the IMF and World Bank.[111]

At the Hague tribunal, Milošević was indicted for genocide, complicity in genocide, murder, extermination, and torture. The main basis for the genocide charge was the Srebrenica massacre. But in 2004, a 7,000-page report by a team of specialists, headed by Amsterdam University professor Cees Wiebes, concluded that Milošević was innocent of the massacre and genocide. Weibes' team offered their evidence to the Hague tribunal chief prosecutor, but were brushed off.

In 2006, Milošević was found dead in his prison cell. However, in 2016—ten years too late—the Hague Tribunal, in a trial of Bosnian Serb leader Radovan Karadžić, ruled that there was insufficient evidence to declare Milošević guilty of the genocide charge, which had been used to justify "NATO military aggression against the people of Serbia."[112]

To summarize the human results of the plan to destroy Yugoslavia: "a gruesome series of regional, ethnic wars that would last a decade and result in the deaths of more than 133,000 people, with some estimates of over 200,000 dead."[113]

The Western Reaction

Although the true story behind the destruction of Yugoslavia was extremely ugly, the Western governments and media presented it as a highly moral episode. In his 1999 book entitled *The New Military Humanism: Lessons from Kosovo,* Noam Chomsky wrote:

> The crisis in Kosovo has excited passion and visionary exaltation of a kind rarely witnessed. The events have been portrayed as "a landmark in international relations," opening the gates to a stage of world history with no precedent, a new epoch of moral rectitude under the guiding hand of an "idealistic New World bent on ending inhumanity. . . . These new conceptions are to displace the decaying institutions of world order that have proven to be a disastrous failure," hence must be discarded in favor of emerging ideas with "innovative but justifiable" departures from earlier norms. [114]

In these new conceptions of international relations, states act "in the name of principles and values" that are truly humane.[115]

What were the "decaying institutions of world order"? The reference was primarily to international law based on the United Nations, with its principle that each nation is sovereign, in the sense that nation A cannot initiate a war with nation B unless nation A has proof that an attack by nation B is imminent—too imminent to allow time for the UN to intervene. What were the "innovative but justifiable" departures from earlier norms? Primarily the notion of "humanitarian war," according to which the United States could attack another country without any knowledge that it intended to attack America, needing only the claim that that other country is committing war crimes—or at least that that country is planning to do so.

For example, Law Professor Michael Glennon advocated what he called "The New Interventionism," by which he meant a new era in world affairs in which "enlightened states" (meaning mainly the United States and Britain) will at last be able to use force where they "believe it to be just," discarding "the restrictive old rules" and obeying "modern notions of justice" that they fashion. "The crisis in Kosovo illustrates," continued Glennon, "America's new willingness to do what it thinks right—international law not withstanding."[116]

Another example: Anthony Lake, Clinton's national security advisor, advocated the "new Wilsonian view," according to which "the United States uses its monopoly on power to intervene in other countries to promote democracy."[117] This new Wilsonianism of the Clinton administration led some observers to say that American foreign policy had entered a "noble phase" with a "saintly glow."[118]

However, as shown by the above discussion of the destruction of Yugoslavia—which deals with the real motivations of the Bush and Clinton administration, not the propaganda—there was nothing noble or saintly about this operation. America did not suddenly start doing what is right. Rather, it continued doing what it believed to be in its own interest, no matter how many lives it took and countries it destroyed.

Conclusion

As pointed out earlier, many American commentators had assumed that the terrible things done by the American government since 1945 were done in response to threats and actions of the Soviet Union. But after the Soviet Union collapsed, Americans could see that their country's behavior did not change, that American actions have been aggressive not defensive, carrying out a long-time goal of global dominance. The US behavior in Panama, Iraq, and Yugoslavia leaves no doubt.

Endnotes

1 Walter LaFeber, "Illusions of an American Century," in Andrew J. Bacevich, ed., *The Short American Century* (Harvard University Press, 2012), 158-86, at 182.

2 See Stephen Rosskamm Shalom, *Imperial Alibis: Rationalizing U.S. Intervention after the Cold War* (Boston: South End, 1993). The need for this rationale also provided the theme for Noam Chomsky's introduction to his *Deterring Democracy* (see the next note).

3 Noam Chomsky, *Deterring Democracy*, 2nd ed. (New York: Hill and Wang, 1992), 164; William Blum, *Killing Hope: U.S. Military and C.I.A. Interventions Since World War II* (Common Courage, 2008), 305.

4 Chomsky, *Deterring Democracy*, 164-65 (quoting *Brecha*, CODEHUCA, "Report of Joint CODEHUCA-CONADEIP Delegation," January-February 1990, San José).

5 Blum, *Killing Hope*, 305.

6 Chomsky, *Deterring Democracy*, 165.

7 Blum, *Killing Hope*, 310 (citing *The Los Angeles Times*, 22 December 1990).

8 For one thing, when General Max Thurman was appointed the new Commander-in-Chief of the Southern Command, he was reportedly told by Admiral William Crowe, Chairman of the Joint Chiefs of Staff, that Bush would be calling for large-scale military action in Panama in the near future; see Blum, *Killing Hope*, 311 (citing Kevin Buckley, *Panama: The Whole Story* [1991], 193, who in turn cited the *Washington Post National Weekly Edition*, 22-28 January 1990).

9 The success of the campaign was illustrated by ABC's Ted Koppel, who said: "Manuel Noriega belongs to that special fraternity of international villains, men like Qaddafi, Idi Amin, and the Ayatollah Khomeini, whom Americans just love to hate," so that "strong public support for a reprisal was all but guaranteed" (ABC TV, quoted in *The Progressive*, February 1990, and in Chomsky, *Deterring Democracy*, 145).

10 The problem with these reasons is that the US Government had long known about Noriega's involvement with drugs and had supported him

when he stole the election in 1989 (Chomsky, *Deterring Democracy*, 153, 180; Blum, *Killing Hope*, 306-09).

11 Blum, *Killing Hope*, 309.

12 Ibid., 310.

13 Chomsky, *Deterring Democracy*, 159-60.

14 Blum, *Killing Hope*, 313 (citing *The Nation*, 3 October 1994: 346).

15 Chomsky, *Deterring Democracy*, 169 (quoting *Excelsior*, 28 February 1990).

16 Ibid., 168.

17 Andres Oppenheimer, *Miami Herald*, 20 June 1990.

18 Chomsky, *Deterring Democracy*, 169. The first of the two quotations is from an article by Pamela Constable in the *Boston Globe*, 11 July 1990.

19 Ibid., 163.

20 Ibid., 166.

21 Ibid., 166 (quoting *Aviation Week and Space Technology*, 1 January 1990).

22 Ibid., 166.

23 Blum, *Killing Hope*, 305.

24 Chomsky, *Deterring Democracy*, 157.

25 Ibid., 147.

26 *Washington Post*, 21 December 1989.

27 *El Tiempo*, 5 January 1990.

28 Quoted in Stephen Kurkjian and Adam Pertman, "Repairing the Damage in Panama," *Boston Globe*, 5 January 1990.

29 Dilip Hiro, *Iraq: In the Eye of the Storm* (New York: Thunder's Mouth Press/Nation Books, 2002), 33-34; Chomsky, *Deterring Democracy*, 195-96.

30 Quoted in Nafeez Mosaddeq Ahmed, *Behind the War on Terror: Western Secret Strategy and the Struggle for Iraq* (Clairview Books, 2003), 75, from the *New York Times*, 23 September 1990, and 17 July 1991.

31 Hiro, *Iraq*, 34; Noam Chomsky, *Rogue States: The Rule of Force in World Affairs* (South End Press, 2000), 21-22; Ahmed, *Beyond the War on Terror*, 75.

32 Chomsky, *Deterring Democracy*, 185.

33 Chomsky, *Rogue States*, 22; *Deterring Democracy*, 187.

34 This, of course, is only one of hundreds of cases in which, in parallel situations, one violation of international law is condemned by the UN while another is not, due to the veto power held by the leading imperialist states, which they exercise on behalf of themselves and their client states. The fact these states have permanent veto power means that the enforcement of international law is not even close to impartial.

35 Hiro, *Iraq*, 37-39.

36 Chomsky, *Deterring Democracy*, 410.

37 Chomsky, *Deterring Democracy*, 410; Hiro, *Iraq*, 38-39, Joyce Chediac, "Twenty-five Years Ago: The 1991 Iraq Gulf War, America Bombs the 'Highway of Death,'" Global Research, 27 February 2016.

38 Hiro, *Iraq*, 40-43.

39 "Setting the American Trap for Hussein," *International Herald Tribune*, 11 March 1991.

40 *Los Angeles Times*, 1 November 1990, quoted in Blum, *Killing Hope*, 323.

41 *Washington Post*, 13 January, 12 February, and 16 June, 1990; quoted in Blum, *Killing Democracy*, 320.

42 *Washington Post*, 3 August 1990.

43 *Washington Post*, 25 November 1990.

44 *Los Angeles Times*, 18 October 1990.

45 *The Gallup Poll: Public Opinion 1991* (Wilmington, Delaware, 1992).

46 Ahmed, *Beyond the War on Terror*, 67-68, 86, citing Robert Dreyfuss, "The Thirty Year Itch," *Mother Jones*, March/April 2003.

47 Quoted in Ralph Schoenman, *Iraq and Kuwait: A History Suppressed* (Santa Barbara: Veritas Press, 1992), 11-12.

48 This document, authored primarily by Paul Wolfowitz and Lewis Libby, was leaked to the *New York Times*, where it was discussed in Patrick Tyler, "US Strategy Plan Calls for Insuring No Rivals Develop," *New York Times*, 8 March 1992. For the resulting furor because of the document's openly imperialistic language, see Andrew J. Bacevich, *American Empire: The Realities and Consequences of U.S. Diplomacy* (Cambridge: Harvard University Press, 2002), 43-46.

49 Ahmed, *Beyond the War on Terror*, 69-70.

50 Knut Royce, "A Trail of Distortion against Iraq," *Newsday*, 21 January 1991, quoted in Ahmed, *Beyond the War on Terror, 69.*

51 Blum, *Killing Hope*, 323.

52 *San Francisco Chronicle*, 13 March 1991; Milton Viorst, "A Reporter at Large: After the Liberation," *The New Yorker,* 30 September 1991; both cited in Ahmed, *Beyond the War on Terror*, 70, 72.

53 Major James Blackwell, *Thunder in the Desert: The Strategy and Tactics of the Persian Gulf* War (New York: Bantam Books, 1991), 85-86; *Los Angeles Times*, 5 August 1990; *Washington Post*, 23 June 1991; all cited in Blum, *Killing Hope*, 324.

54 Francis A. Boyle, "US War Crimes During the Gulf War," *New Dawn Magazine*, No. 15 (September-October 1992).

55 Gen. Carl E. Vuono, US Army Chief of Staff, "A Strategic Force for the 1990s and Beyond," US Army: January 1990, 1-17, cited in Ahmed, *Beyond the War on Terror*, 65.

56 Boyle, "US War Crimes."

57 Jean Heller, "Photos Don't Show Buildup," *St. Petersburg Times*, 6 January 1991.

58 Scott Peterson, "In War, Some Facts Less Factual," *Christian Science Monitor*, 6 September 2002.

59 See Chalmers Johnson, *The Sorrows of Empire: Militarism, Secrecy, and the End of the Republic* (New York: Henry Holt, 2004), 230; Maggie O'Kane, *The Guardian*, 5 February 2003; and, on the long-standing relationship between Bush and the al-Sabah family, see Craig Unger, *House of Bush, House of Saud: The Secret Relationship between the World's Two Most Powerful Dynasties* (New York & London: Scribner, 2004), 249.

60 Quoted in Glenn Frankel, "Imperialist Legacy: Lines in the Sand," *Washington Post*, 31 August 1990, and in Ahmed, *Beyond the War on Terror*, 70.

61 *Los Angeles Times*, 6 November 1990: 4; quoted in Blum, *Killing Hope,* 27.

62 Blum cited the following sources for the bribery in general: *Wall Street Journal*, 14 January 1991; *Fortune Magazine*, 11 February 1991: 47; and Ramsey Clark, *The Fire This Time*, 153-56. For the IMF and World Bank loans, Blum cited *Washington Post*, 30 January 1991. He also cited these sources for particular countries: Daniel Pipes, *Foreign Affairs*, Fall 1991: 41-42 (Syria); *Los Angeles Times*, 18 June 1992 (Turkey); Elaine Sciolino, *The Outlaw State: Saddam Hussein's Quest for Power and the Gulf Crisis* (New York: John Wiley, 1991), 237-39.

63 Sciolino, *The Outlaw State*, 237-38; quoted in Blum, *Killing Hope*, 327.

64 John Pilger, cited in Norman Solomon and Reese Erlich, *Target Iraq: What the New Media Didn't Tell You* (New York: Context Books, 2003), 69-70.

65 Knut Royce, "Middle East Crisis Secret Offer: Iraq Sent Pullout Deal to US," *Newsday*, 29 August 1990.

66 Ibid.

67 *Guardian,* 12 January 1991: 2; cited in Blum, *Killing Hope*, 329.

68 *Los Angeles Times*, 1 November 1990; *Washington Post*, 19 August 1990; both cited in Blum, *Killing Hope*, 323.

69 *Christian Science Monitor*, 5 February 1991, quoted in Blum, *Killing Hope*, 21.

70 King Hussein's statements are reported in "How Mr. Bush Got His War" by Michael Emery, who interviewed the king on February 19, 1991. Emery's article appeared in Greg Ruggiero and Stuart Sahulka, eds., *Open Fire* (New York: New Press, 1993), and in somewhat different form in *Village Voice*, 5 March 1991.

71 Ibid., quoted (from the *Village Voice* version) by Ahmed, *Beyond the*

War on Freedom, 73.

72 John Stockwell, "The CIA and the Gulf War," a lecture given February 20, 1991 (http://www.serendipity.li/cia/stock2.html).

73 House Resolution 86, 21 February 1991, quoted in Ahmed, *Beyond the War on Terror*, 77-78.

74 *New York Daily News*, 29 September 1991.

75 "Setting the American Trap for Hussein."

76 John Mueller and Karl Mueller, "Sanctions of Mass Destruction," *Foreign Affairs*, May-June 1999: 43-53. They argued that, in addition to the other arguments against them, "economic sanctions may well have been a necessary cause of the deaths of more people in Iraq than have been slain by all so-called weapons of mass destruction throughout history" (51).

77 Hiro, *Iraq*, 18. On the impact of sanctions, including in later years, see Anthony Arnove, ed., *Iraq under Siege: The Deadly Impact of Sanctions and War*, updated ed. (Cambridge: South End, 2002).

78 Ibid., 147-49.

79 Ibid., 130.

80 Ibid., 147.

81 Ibid., 173-74.

82 F. William Engdahl, *Manifest Destiny: Democracy as Cognitive Dissonance* (Wiesbaden: mine.Books, 2018), 90.

83 Ibid., 91.

84 Ibid., 93.

85 Ibid., 94.

86 Professor Cees Wiebes of Amsterdam University later published a book entitled *Intelligence and the War in Bosnia: 1992-1995* (Studies in Intelligence History, 2003), in which he documented the secret alliance between the Pentagon and radical Islamic groups from the Middle East—including Osama bin Laden's Afghan Mujahideen networks—to assist Bosnia's Muslims.

87 Engdahl, *Manifest Destiny*, 96.

88 Ibid., 97.

89 Ibid., 101, 114.

90 Ibid., 105.

91 Ibid., 108-09.

92 Lewis Mackenzie, "The Real Story behind Srebrenica," *Globe and Mail*, 14 July, 2005.

93 Engdahl, *Manifest Destiny*, 109.

94 Ibid., 110.

95 Maria Markovic, "Are the Clintons Serbia's Most Hated Couple?" Telesur, 24 March 2016.

96 Engdahl, *Manifest Destiny*, 95.
97 Ibid., 94.
98 Ibid. 104.
99 Ibid., 109.
100 Engdahl, *Manifest Destiny,* 122.
101 Ibid., 113-14.
102 Ibid., 111.
103 Ibid., 111-12.
104 Noam Chomsky, *The New Military Humanism: Lessons from Kosovo* (Common Courage, 1999), 3.
105 Ibid. 16.
106 Noam Chomsky, "A Review of NATO's War over Kosovo," Z Magazine, April-May, 2001.
107 Chomsky, *The New Military Humanism,* 20-21.
108 Ibid., 114.
109 Markovic, "Are the Clintons Serbia's Most Hated Couple?"
110 Harold Pinter, "Foreword," in Philip Hammond and Edward S. Herman, ed., *Degraded Capability: The Media and the Kosovo Crisis* (Pluto Press, 2000), vii.
111 Engdahl, *Manifest Destiny,* 130.
112 Andy Wilcoxson, "Hague Tribunal Exonerates Slobodan Milosevic Again," Strategic Culture, 12 July 2017.
113 Engdahl, *Manifest Destiny,* 95.
114 Chomsky, *The New Military Humanism*, 1.
115 Ibid., 2.
116 Ibid., 4-5, citing Michael Glennon, "The New Interventionism," *Foreign Affairs,* May/June 1999.
117 Ibid., 14, citing Anthony Lake, *The New York Times,* 23 September 1994.
118 Ibid., 14, citing Sebastian Mallaby, "Uneasy Partners," *NYT* Book Review, 21 September 1997.

| Chapter 13 |

THE DRIVE FOR GLOBAL DOMINANCE

As we have seen, the end of the Cold War presented an opportunity for advocates of an American empire of truly global scope. The empire could now, without facing Soviet-backed resistance, take over counties not open to US economic domination. Within elite members of these promoters, however, there existed a divide over the question of how aggressively America should use its overwhelmingly dominant military power to advance its interests.

One school of thought held the traditional view that this military might should be used as a last resort, only after economic and diplomatic efforts had failed. Even then, military power should not—except within the Americas—-be used unilaterally but only with the cover of a UN resolution or at least with some multilateral alliance. This type of imperialism is ultimately more effective, this school of thought held, because its imperialistic designs can be more effectively disguised—partly through benign language, such as "globalization," so that it can induce cooperation, or at least avoid provoking massive resistance.

The other school of thought held that now that the United States had finally acquired the overwhelming military superiority for which it had long been striving, it should use it, partly because America's relative military strength is now much greater than its relative economic strength, partly because the government needs to keep the corporations who supply military hardware busy, and partly because military victories could now be won more quickly. Furthermore, such victories would have a salutary effect on other countries who might contemplate resistance to US suggestions about restructuring their economies.

With regard to the objection that this approach would be counter-productive because, by being so blatantly imperialistic, it would reveal America's true designs and hence produce resistance, this more militaristic school of thought evidently believed that America's power is now so great that it need not worry about this objection. Be that as it may, the more militaristic approach to carrying out what Richard Falk called "the global domination project"[1] has certainly proved to be revelatory. This chapter traces the rise of this more militaristic approach and the resulting revelation.

1. Early Manifestations of the Militaristic School

Although one might suppose that the Clinton administration used US power in a sufficiently brutal way, in both Iraq and the US-led NATO war against Serbia, there were Americans, some of whom had been in the Reagan and Bush I administrations, who were frustrated that the United States, with its one-and-only-superpower rating, was not using its power more fully. One early expression of this outlook was made by Colin Powell, who in early 1992 told members of Congress that the US requires "sufficient power" to "deter any challenger from ever dreaming of challenging us on the world stage." Powell even said: "I want to be the bully on the block," implanting in the mind of potential opponents that "there is no future in trying to challenge the armed forces of the United States."[2]

A more systematic statement came in the first version of the Pentagon's 1992 "Defense Planning Guidance" (DPG), authored primarily by Paul Wolfowitz, then the undersecretary of defense for policy, and Lewis "Scooter" Libby (who would become Vice-President Cheney's chief of staff in the Bush II administration). Although a secret document, it was leaked to the

New York Times.[3] Among the passages publicly revealed were the following:

> Our first objective is to prevent the re-emergence of a new rival. This . . . requires that we endeavor to prevent any hostile power from dominating a region whose resources would, under consolidated control, be sufficient to generate global power. These regions include Western Europe, East Asia, the territory of the former Soviet Union, and Southwest Asia. . . . [T]he U.S. must . . . establish and protect a new order that . . . convinc[es] potential competitors that they need not aspire to a greater role or pursue a more aggressive posture to protect their legitimate interests. . . . . [W]e must maintain the mechanisms for deterring potential competitors from even aspiring to a regional or global role. . . . We will retain the preeminent responsibility for addressing selectively those wrongs which threaten not only our interests, but those of our allies or friends.[4]

Note that, according to the DPG, it was the United States, not the United Nations, that was to "establish and protect" the new order.

If some people think that the UN functions somewhat as a world government, Washington certainly has never been under this illusion. It knows that, insofar as there is already a world government, the United States is it. This fact is illustrated by the US military's division of the world into six military "commands" (in addition to the Central Command [which covers 20 countries from Afghanistan to Egypt to Syria], there are also Africa, European, Northern, Pacific, and Southern Commands).[5] Also, a 2018 article was entitled "The New US Defense Strategy: All the World Our Battlefield."[6]

In any case, among the "interests" mentioned by the

draft DPG was "access to vital raw materials, primarily Persian Gulf oil," and among the options mentioned for protecting those interests was *preemptive* military action.

Andrew Bacevich said that "the draft DPG was in effect a blueprint for permanent American global hegemony."[7] Writing that "Wolfowitz had been indiscreet" by openly stating that "calculations of power and self-interest rather than altruism and high ideals provided the proper basis for framing strategy," Bacevich called the draft DPG "the Wolfowitz Indiscretion," for which Wolfowitz was "roundly denounced."[8]

Accordingly, the Pentagon distanced itself from this draft, withdrew it, and rewrote it in kinder, gentler language. But the *ideas* remained unchanged. They were expressed in a series of future publications with three major themes: (1) Carrying out preemptive attacks, (2) bringing about regime change in a number of countries, beginning with Iraq, and (3) achieving total global hegemony.

2. Later Developments

In 1996, Richard Perle, who had been in Reagan's Pentagon and would be influential during the Bush II presidency, was the primary author of a document advising Israel that it should work for the removal of Saddam Hussein as a first step to replacing other governments in the area, including those of Syria, Lebanon, and Iran.[9]

In 1997, former National Security Advisor Zbigniew Brzezinski published a book entitled *The Grand Chessboard: American Primacy and its Geostrategic Imperatives*. Portraying the Eurasian landmass as the key to world power, he said that Central Asia, with its vast oil reserves, was the key to the domination of Eurasia. For America to maintain its global primacy, Brzezinski said, it must prevent any possible adversary from controlling that region. Of course, knowing that one should not be as indiscreet as Wolfowitz in public, Brzezinski said:

> The ultimate objective of American policy should be benign and visionary: to shape a truly cooperative global community, in keeping with ... the fundamental interests of humankind.

However, having made this nod to piety, Brzezinski immediately added: "But in the meantime, it is imperative that no Eurasian challenger emerges, capable of dominating Eurasia and thus also of challenging America."[10]

The unexpressed premise was that America is the rightful ruler not only of the Western Hemisphere but of the whole world and its resources, so that although Eurasia is the home of both China and Russia, for either to seek to control its resources would be tantamount to "challenging America."

In any case, Brzezinski then argued that although the present "window of historical opportunity for America's constructive exploitation of its global power could prove to be relatively brief," the American public might be unwilling to use its power for imperial purposes.[11] This is the problem:

> America is too democratic at home to be autocratic abroad. This limits the use of America's power, especially its capacity for military intimidation. . . . [T]he pursuit of power is not a goal that commands popular passion, except in conditions of a sudden threat or challenge to the public's sense of domestic well being.[12]

What *would* make the American public willing would be "a truly massive and widely perceived direct external threat." This passage, near the end of the book, is parallel to an earlier passage in which Brzezinski said that the American public was willing to support "America's engagement in World War II largely because of the shock effect of the Japanese attack on Pearl Harbor."[13] If one reads those two passages together, Brzezinski seemed to be saying that the best thing that could happen would be a new Pearl

Harbor. Only in light of such a "massive and widely perceived direct external threat," he implied, would American taxpayers be willing to foot the bill for the project to maintain and increase American geopolitical primacy.

That same year, 1997, saw the founding of the Project for the New American Century (PNAC), whose members included Donald Rumsfeld, Dick Cheney, Paul Wolfowitz, Richard Perle, William Kristol, Richard Armitage, John Bolton, Robert Kagan, and his father Donald Kagan. In 1998, all these men signed a PNAC letter to President Clinton urging him to take military action for the purpose of "removing Saddam Hussein and his regime from power."

In 2000, PNAC published *Rebuilding America's Defenses*, which is a blueprint for maintaining America's global preeminence, for precluding the rise of a great power rival, and for shaping the world in accord with American interests. While saying that the conflict with Saddam provided the "immediate justification" for military action in Iraq, it added that "the need for a substantial American force presence in the Gulf transcends the issue of the regime of Saddam Hussein." In other words, even if Saddam were not there, America needed to take over Iraq. The report also called for preventing any other countries, even close allies, from attaining more political power. And it advocated "regime change" not only in Iraq but also in China, North Korea, Libya, Syria, and Iran. It is clear, therefore, that the plan to take over Iraq was hatched out of America's imperial designs, not in response to 9/11, which merely provided the pretext.

The apparent hope for a Pearl Harbor type event was expressed even more explicitly in this PNAC document than in Brzezinski's book. Calling for a fulfillment of the "revolution in military affairs," this document said that the needed transformation would probably come about slowly, "absent some catastrophic and catalyzing event—like a new Pearl Harbor."[14] The precedent of Pearl Harbor seemed to be much on the minds of many people in high places. On the night of 9/11, for example, President Bush reportedly wrote in his diary: "The Pearl Harbor of the 21st century took place today."[15]

The US wars in Afghanistan and Iraq have been widely interpreted by critics as wars for oil. Although the Bush Administration has, of course, denied that this was a motive, there was considerable talk about wars for oil during the first year of the Bush presidency. For example, an article in the journal of the Army War College argued not only for the legitimacy of war in the Persian Gulf on behalf of lower gas prices but also for the acceptability of presidential subterfuge in the promotion of a conflict. The author explicitly urged that, in order to mobilize public support for a war, the actual reasons for it would need to be hidden.[16]

In April of 2001, a report commissioned by the Council on Foreign Relations and former Secretary of State James Baker, who played a major role in Bush's election in 2000, argued that Iraq needed to be overthrown so that America could control its oil. Although this report was cited in mainstream newspapers,[17] in some other countries the later discussion about the motives for the war in the American press would occur as if this story had never appeared.

With regard to whether the war in Afghanistan was a response to 9/11, former Pakistani Foreign Secretary Niaz Naik reported that he was told by senior American officials at a meeting on July 21, 2001, that military action to overthrow the Taliban in Afghanistan was planned to "take place before the snows started falling in Afghanistan, by the middle of October at the latest." The goal, he said, was to topple the Taliban regime and install a transitional government in its place. So the war against the Taliban could be billed as a response to the attacks on 9/11 only if the Bush Administration had precognition about those attacks.

That operations against both Afghanistan and Iraq were on the minds of US officials beforehand is suggested by the fact that Secretary of Defense Rumsfeld, on the afternoon of 9/11, reportedly wrote in a note to General Richard Myers—the acting head of the Pentagon's Joint Chiefs of Staff—that he wanted the "best info fast. Judge whether good enough hit S.H. [Saddam Hussein] at same time. Not only UBL [Usama bin Laden]. Go massive. Sweep it all up. Things related and not."[18] The next morning at the Cabinet meeting, according to Bob Woodward's *Bush At War*, Rumsfeld insisted that Saddam's Iraq should be "a principal target of the first round of terrorism."[19] On September 17, President Bush signed a "top secret" document with a plan for going to war in Afghanistan, which also directed the Pentagon to begin planning military options for an invasion of Iraq.[20]

Whether or not the PNAC knew that Bush had already signed this document, on September 20 it published an open letter urging Bush to attack Iraq immediately. On November 21, Bush said:

> Afghanistan is just the beginning on the war against terror. There are other terrorists who threaten America and our friends, and there are other nations willing to sponsor them. We will not be secure as a nation until all of these threats are defeated.[21]

A short time later, *The Guardian* reported that "the US has honed a hit list of countries to target for military action in rogue regions across the globe where it believes terror cells flourish," including Iraq.[22] What was seldom reported was that this "hit list" had been formulated long before 9/11. In any case, in his State of the Union speech in January of 2002, Bush labeled Iraq, Iran, and North Korea an "axis of evil," warning that he would "not wait on events" to prevent them from using weapons of mass destruction against the United States. The doctrine of preemptive warfare was thereby publicly announced, albeit without using the term.

In May of 2002, Rumsfeld's Defense Policy Guidance document was published. It contained all the key elements of the 1992 draft, although preemptive strikes were now called "unwarned attacks." It even spoke of preemptive strikes with earth-penetrating nuclear weapons to attack "hardened and deeply buried targets." Besides the emphasis on preemptive attacks, this new version of the DPG also retained the 1992 draft's motif of global dominance.[23]

The themes in these previous documents were then

synthesized in *The National Security Strategy of the United States of America*, published in September of 2002 (*NSS 2002*). The idea of preemption was prominent, even in the covering letter signed by the president. It said that with regard to "our enemies' efforts to acquire dangerous technologies," America will, in self-defense, "act against such emerging threats before they are fully formed."

The document itself, saying that "our best defense is a good offense,"[24] also stated:

> Given the goals of rogue states and terrorists, the United States can no longer rely on a reactive posture as we have in the past. The inability to deter a potential attacker, the immediacy of today's threats, and the magnitude of potential harm that could be caused by our adversaries' choice of weapons, do not permit that option. We cannot let our enemies strike first."

To justify this doctrine, *NSS 2002* said:

> For centuries, international law recognized that nations need not suffer an attack before they can lawfully take action to defend themselves against forces that present an imminent danger of attack. . . . We must adapt the concept of imminent threat to the capabilities and objectives of today's adversaries. . . . The United States has long maintained the option of preemptive actions to counter a sufficient threat to our national security. The greater the threat, . . . the more compelling the case for taking anticipatory action to defend ourselves, even if uncertainty remains as to the time and place of the enemy's attack. To forestall or prevent such hostile acts by our adversaries, the United States will, if necessary, act preemptively.[25]

One problem with this statement, from the viewpoint of world order, was that the United States thereby arrogated to itself the right to decide which other countries present an "imminent danger of attack." Given the weakness of the United Nations, there is no neutral court in which the case and counter case can be made. There is, to be sure, the "court of public opinion," but Washington, as we have seen, was paying little heed to it. President Bush, in fact, said that to make decisions on the basis of world opinion would be like doing so based on the views of a "focus group" (this from the then-president of the nation whose Declaration of Independence spoke of "a decent respect for the opinions of mankind").

In any case, given the world order at that time, the United States felt itself in a position to be not only prosecutor but also judge, jury, and executioner. Given the fact that "self-defense" was now explicitly extended to include defense of American interests, such as America's interest in controlling most of the world's oil, Washington could justify preemptive attacks for virtually anything it wanted. Because this justification rested on the doctrine that might makes right, America needed to maintain military dominance.

The need for this dominance was emphasized in *NSS 2002*'s final chapter, which said:

> It is time to reaffirm the essential role of American military strength. We must build and maintain our defenses beyond challenge [so that we can] dissuade future military competition. [US forces must be] strong enough to dissuade potential adversaries from pursuing a military build-up in hopes of surpassing, or equaling, the power of the United States.[26]

The United States, in other words, *must* maintain more power than that of all its potential adversaries combined. It is no wonder, therefore, that the United States came to spend almost as much on military matters as the rest of the world's countries combined.

America's long-standing commitment to double standards was expressed in the document's discussion of one potential adversary, China, to which *NSS 2002* gave this patronizing advice:

> In pursuing advanced military capabilities that can threaten its neighbors in the Asia-Pacific region, China is following an outdated path that, in the end, will hamper its own pursuit of national greatness. In time, China will find that social and political freedom is the only source of that greatness.[27]

To become great, in other words, China should pursue exactly the opposite course being taken by the USA.

The US Government's growing conviction that it must be free from any constraints of international law was shown in one of the commitments of *NSS 2002*:

> to ensure that our efforts . . . are not impaired by the potential for investigations, inquiry, or prosecution by the International Criminal Court (ICC), whose jurisdiction does not extend to Americans.[28]

It does not extend to Americans, obviously, because rulers are not judged by their subjects.

The most honest statement of *NSS 2002* said: "The events of September 11, 2001, . . . opened vast, new opportunities."[29] There are some critics of American imperialism who argue that Washington deliberately allowed the attacks of 9/11 to occur, or even directly engineered them. Be that as it may, the Bush Administration certainly *used* the attacks to justify, and get Congressional funding for, plans that had already been formulated—plans to bring about regime change in countries that had not yet been integrated into the American Empire.

The so-called War on Terror began with an attack on

Afghanistan in 2001. By 2018, 76 countries were involved in this conflict. And, according to the Costs of War Project, the War on Terror had cost the United States $5.6 trillion, with interest payments for the borrowed money estimated to add another $7.9 trillion to the national debt.[30]

3. Full Spectrum Dominance

As *NSS 2002* and the documents it synthesizes make clear, Washington's goal was to have such military superiority that America could do whatever it pleased without fear of retaliation from anyone. At the center of this project was the drive for the military control of space.

One might have thought that with the invention of nuclear weapons, the arms race had come to an end. After the "ultimate weapon" had been created, what else was there to do? But as the attacks on Serbia and then on Iraq in 1991 and 2003 showed, there were computerized weapons to be developed and then perfected. When the motives for the first attack on Iraq are discussed, one must include the Pentagon's desire to test in actual combat conditions, in order to be able to improve, these "smart" weapons, which were central to the much-discussed "revolution in military affairs."

Indeed, in the history of warfare, that attack was in some respects the most important war of the modern era, argued intelligence consultant George Friedman, co-author of *The Future of War*.[31] He wrote: "The gulf war was the first space war," which means: "The 500-year history of ballistic warfare has come to an end."[32] Calling it a "space war" means only that the computerized weapons were guided through the use of space satellites, not that there were actually weapons in space. But this was to be next.

Indeed, the aim to weaponize and hence dominate space was the centerpiece of the "revolution in military affairs." The program was spelled out quite explicitly in a document called "Vision for 2020," which began with this mission statement: "U.S. Space Command—dominating the space dimension of military operations to protect US interests and investment." This document engaged in no sentimental propaganda about the need for the United States to dominate space for the sake of promoting democracy or otherwise serving humanity. Rather, it said candidly, if indiscreetly: "The globalization of the world economy . . . will continue with a widening between 'haves' and 'have-nots.'"

In other words, as America's domination of the world economy was to increase, the poor would get still poorer while the rich would get still richer. This increasing gap would make the poor hate America all the more, so it would need to be able to obliterate all of its enemies before they can hurt it. This could be done through what the advocates of this program have called "Global Battlespace Dominance." Because some people found this term too explicit, the term shifted to the one quoted by Bacevich: "Full Spectrum Dominance"—being dominant not only on land, at sea, and in the air, but also having control of space as well. The US Space Command is the new branch of the military in charge of this program.

The only part of this program that has received much public discussion is the defensive aspect of it, which in the Reagan Administration was called the Strategic Defense Initiative but came to be called the Missile Defense Shield. This name was in line with calling what is housed in the Pentagon "the Department of Defense," even though, as Bacevich pointed out, it is really a Department of Power Projection—which *NSS 2002* implicitly admitted in saying that "our best defense is a good offense." Just as changing the name of the Department of War to the Department of Defense in the middle of the 20th century obscured its true function, so does the idea that America's goal in space is to build a defensive shield.

This so-called shield was only one part of a three-part program. The second part was putting surveillance technology in space, with the goal of being able to zero in on any part of the planet with such precision that every enemy of US forces can be identified. The third part of the program was putting actual weapons in space, including laser cannons, which have the offensive potential, as one writer put it, to "make a cruise missile look like a firecracker."[33] With laser weapons on our satellites, the United States would be able to destroy any satellites any adversarial country would try to send up.

The US Space Command could thereby maintain total and permanent dominance. The aggressive purposes of the US Space Command's program were announced in the logos of some of its divisions. One says, "Master of Space"; another says, "In Your Face from Outer space."[34] Wouldn't the Romans be envious! They could not have even dreamed of such power to intimidate.

The course through which America has intended to achieve total global dominance has, to be sure, been bloody. The very first steps, exterminating the Native Americans instead of enslaving them and then bringing in substitutes from Africa, cost, as we saw, some 20 million lives. But, like the first President Bush on the deaths caused by the invasion of Panama and Madeleine Albright on the deaths caused by the sanctions on Iraq, our ancestors thought the price was "worth it," because they were fulfilling America's manifest destiny. This idea of our manifest destiny has not disappeared. Bob Smith, Republican senator from New Hampshire, said in August 2001: "Space is our next manifest destiny."[35]

4. Revelations

As we have seen, at the end of the 19th century, America's unprovoked aggression against Cuba and the Philippines served as a revelation to some Americans as to the true nature of their country's foreign policy. These Americans, such as Mark Twain and William James, saw that America was becoming an empire, and not a benign one. They formed an Anti-Imperialist League, which was quite effective, attracting a big following during the American wars to take Cuba and the Philippines. Many Americans remained negative toward the idea of getting into World War I.

But eventually, uncritical patriotism recovered, especially during World War II and the early years of the Cold War, in which America was able to portray itself as the selfless defender of the free world against fascist and then Communist totalitarianism. In spite of some very serious domestic problems related to foreign policy, such as the McCarthyism of the 1950s, America's foreign policy itself came in for little criticism.

But then the 20th century had its major revelatory event, the American war in Vietnam, through which a large number of Americans, beginning about 1965, started becoming aware that their government had policies that were very different from the public proclamations about promoting freedom, democracy, and human rights. Many of the leading critics of American imperialism today, such as Noam Chomsky and Richard Falk, were awakened in that period. In 1967, Chomsky said: "The war is simply an obscenity, a depraved act by weak and miserable men," adding: "I suppose this is the first time in history that a nation has so openly and publicly exhibited its own war crimes."[36]

Throughout the late 1960s and the '70s, suspicion of the government's motives was widespread, and this suspicion was intensified by the Watergate scandal, which forced President Nixon to resign. In response, many steps were taken to overcome not only the so-called Vietnam Syndrome, meaning the reluctance of Americans to support military intervention abroad, but also a more general suspicion about governmental motives.

These steps included the creation of well-funded conservative think-tanks to shape public opinion in the desired directions. Military policy was altered to engage only in battles that could be won quickly and with the loss of few American lives. Reporters, and especially television cameras, were prevented from witnessing the bloody results of military operations, especially against civilians. The Reagan presidency was heavily devoted to making Americans feel good about being Americans again, especially after the Carter Administration's humiliations in Iran. Reagan labeled the Soviet Union an "evil empire," which meant, by implication, that America was the good empire.

All this worked. Fairly uncritical patriotism became the order of the day. America's designated enemies, such as tiny little Grenada and Manuel Noriega of tiny little Panama, were widely perceived as genuinely evil threats against which US military action was justified. These operations prepared the way for the Gulf War, which although initially opposed by about half of the American people and half of Congress, turned out to be wildly popular. The first President Bush proclaimed: "By God, we've licked the Vietnam syndrome once and for all."[37]

The resulting inclination to trust the official statements about the motives for war was illustrated by the public's attitude toward Slobodan Miloŝević. Although there was little if any evidence to support the crimes with which he had been charged—so little that, as pointed out in the previous chapter, the Hague Tribunal later ruled that there was insufficient evidence to support the charges—the American public at the time seemed largely to accept the idea that Miloŝević was so evil that the Serbians, having accepted his rule, deserved what they got.[38]

An important factor in America's acceptance of the view of Miloŝević as a genocidal monster was the demeanor of the American leaders. Both President Clinton and his secretary of defense, William Cohen, came across to the American public as non-bellicose men simply doing their duty, somewhat reluctantly, to oppose evil.

However, to discerning policy watchers, something very important had occurred. The Cold War, which had been virtually over for some time, was, with the dissolution of the Soviet Union, *officially* over. And yet there was no major shift in US foreign policy or military spending. For a relatively small number of people who had hitherto accepted the official view of the Department of Defense—that its primary mission really was defense—a revelation was occurring. The view that the United States had been amassing its military power merely to defend America and the rest of the "free world" from the menace of Communism was contradicted by the US government's behavior after the Cold War was over.

The post-Cold War attacks on Panama, Iraq, and Serbia, combined with a re-reading of US foreign policy, resulted in a new revelation—but one that, because of the limited circles in which it occurred, must be called merely a proto-revelation, analogous to the one that occurred during the wars against Cuba and the Philippines almost a century earlier.

* * * * * * *

The new full-fledged revelation, analogous to the one produced by the Vietnam War, occurred almost as soon as the 21st century began. It was not long after September 11, 2001, that as Jonathan Freedland put it, "the word of the hour [was] empire," with America suddenly "bearing its name." As we have seen, however, the fact that people were suddenly referring to an American empire and to US imperialism did not mean that something fundamentally new had begun. Rather, the behavior of the Bush-Cheney administration—its arrogance, its bellicose language, its militarism, and its rather transparent rationalizations of its aggressive policies—simply served, for the most part, as a new revelation of what had been true of the American project all along.

The qualification "for the most part" is important. The willingness (not only to flout international law publicly, as the Clinton administration did in destroying Yugoslavia), but even publicly to declare its inapplicability to America, was significantly new, as was the rush to take over the remainder of the world's vital resources and to achieve complete geopolitical control in a matter of years. So was the intensity and extensiveness of the effort to curtail the civil and political rights of American citizens, so that if large numbers of people began to protest, they could be silenced. Accordingly, to understand the Bush-Cheney Administration as representing primarily a revelation of a long-term trajectory, rather than as a change of direction, is not to deny that this administration was the most dangerous one that Washington had thus far had.

The destructiveness of the Bush-Cheney administration was discussed in my 2017 book, *Bush and Cheney: How They Ruined America and the World*[39]—which could be considered the sequel to the present book. The Iraq War, which was engineered by the Bush-Cheney administration by using multiple lies, has provided the strongest revelation yet of the true nature of the American empire since the Vietnam War. But the Bush-Cheney administration was also destructive in many other ways: Giving a false account of the 9/11 attacks; using this false account to justify the wars in Afghanistan and Iraq; greatly increasing military spending; developing a doctrine of preemptive war in order to bring about regime change; using 9/11 to heighten Islamophobia; starting to employ drone warfare; shredding and US constitution; and moving the world closer to either nuclear or ecological holocaust.

That book also described the major imperialistic moves of the Obama administration: greatly increasing the murderous use of drone warfare; using NATO to bring about regime-change in Libya; continuing the efforts of the Bush-Cheney administration to bring about regime change in Syria; engineering regime change in Ukraine; and further shredding the Constitution..

As the public becomes more aware of the truth of those events, the idea that the American empire is divine, working to promote democracy, will be increasingly laughable.

Endnotes

1 "Resisting the Global Domination Project: An Interview with Professor Richard Falk," *Frontline* 20/8 (April 12-25, 2003).

2 Colin Powell, testimony to Congress, 1992.

3 Patrick E. Tyler, "Excerpts From Pentagon's Plan: 'Prevent the Re-Emergence of a New Rival,'" New York Times, 8 March 1992

4 This statement is uncannily similar to a statement made about the Roman Empire by Joseph Schumpeter in 1919. For Rome, he said, "There was no corner of the known world where some interest was not alleged to be in danger or under actual attack. If the interests were not Roman, they were those of Rome's allies; and if Rome had no allies, the allies would be invented. When it was utterly impossible to contrive such an interest—why, then it was the national honor that had been insulted. The fight was always invested with an aura of legality. Rome was always being attacked by evil-minded neighbors. The

whole world was pervaded by a host of enemies, it was manifestly Rome's duty to guard against their indubitably aggressive designs."

5 United Command Plan: Commanders' Area of Responsibility, Department of Defense.

6 Carl Conetta, "The New US Defense Strategy: All the World Our Battlefield," Facebook, 19 January 2018.

7 Bacevich, American Empire, 44.

8 Ibid., 45.

9 Richard Perle et al., The Institute for Advanced Strategic and Political Studies, "A Clean Break: A New Strategy for Securing the Realm," 8 July 1996.

10 Zbigniew Brzezinski, The Grand Chessboard: American Primacy and Its Geostrategic Imperatives (New York: Basic Books, 1997).

11 Ibid., 210.

12 Ibid., 35-36.

13 Ibid., 24-25, 212.

14 *Rebuilding America's Defenses: Strategy, Forces and Resources for a New Century* (A Report of the Project for the New American Century, September 2000), 51.

15 *Washington Post*, 27 January 2002.

16 Reported in the *Sydney Morning Herald*, 26 December 2002.

17 *Sunday Morning Herald*, 5 October 2002; *Sydney Morning Herald*, 26 December 2002.

18 Reported by CBS News, 4 September 2002.

19 Bob Woodward, *Bush at War* (Simon & Shuster, 2002), 49; reported on ABC's Nightline, 5 March 2003.

20 *Washington Post*, 12 December 2002.

21 White House, 21 November 2001.

22 *The Guardian*, 10 December 2001.

23 David Armstrong, "Dick Cheney's Song of America: Drafting a Plan for Global Dominance," *Harper's*, October 2002.

24 *The National Security Strategy of the United States of America*, September 2002: 6.

25 Ibid., 15.

26 Ibid., 29, 30.

27 Ibid., 27.

28 Ibid., 31.

29 Ibid., 28.

30 Tom Engelhardt, "Seventy-Six Countries Are Now Involved in Washington's War on Terror," TomDispatch, 4 January 2018.

31 See George Friedman and Meredith Friedman, *The Future of War: Power, Technology and American World Dominance in the 21st*

Century (New York: St. Martin's, 1998).

32 Jack Hitt, "Battlefield Space," *The New York Times Magazine*, 5 August 2001.

33 Ibid.

34 Ibid.

35 Hitt, "Battlefield Space."

36 Chomsky, *American Power and the New Mandarins: Historical and Political Essays* (1967; New York: Vintage, 1969), 9-10.

37 Maureen Dowd, "White House Memo; War Introduces a Tougher Bush to Nation," *New York Times*, 2 March 1991.

38 Andy Wilcoxson, "Hague Tribunal Exonerates Slobodan Milošović Again," Strategic Culture, 12 July 2017.

39 Interlink Books, 2017.

| Conclusion |

AMERICAN EXCEPTIONALISM

In the light of the chapters in this book, we can see the absurdity of the claims by the Cheneys quoted in the Introduction—that America is "the greatest force for good the world has ever known," that it is "freedom's defender," and that it is "the most . . . honorable nation in the history of mankind."[1]

If, as Ben Wattenberg said, the American empire is an "imperium of values," then interventions in various countries, such as Iran, Guatemala, Greece, and Indonesia, reflect the values of those who have been running US foreign policy—values diametrically opposed to the basic values shared by Christianity, Judaism, Islam, Buddhism, and other religious traditions.

Rather, as this book has argued, agents of American foreign policy have acted so as to deprive people in other countries of basic rights, such as food, health care, and an adequate income; they have stolen their resources; they have supported systems of torture and terror; they have supported the murder of hundreds of thousands of civilians; and they have engaged in massive deceit, claiming to protect freedom and democracy while doing the exact opposite. More generally, they have treated others as mere means or obstacles to their ends, not as ends in themselves, with a legal and moral basis for exercising the full panoply of their human rights. In so acting, they have done to others what they absolutely would not want done to themselves, their loved ones, and their country.

This book has also sought to show that, once people know something about the history of the American empire, they cannot agree with the claim of the Cheneys that "[n]o nation has ever worked so successfully to extend freedom to others."[2] With Ronald Steel's statement (before his change of mind) that when America intervenes, it does so with "the most noble motives and with the most generous impulses."[3] With Michael Ignatieff's statement that America's empire is "the imperialism of . . . good intentions."[4] With Dinesh D'Souza's claim that the American empire is "the most magnanimous imperial power ever."[5] With Robert Kagan's claim in "The Benevolent Empire" that "the identification of the interests of others with its own has been the most striking quality of American foreign and defense policy."[6]

The view of the American Empire as benevolent is, of course, necessary to the idea that the American empire is divine, whereas the view of the American empire as malign, as outlined herein, is compatible with the view of this nation as demonic. The chapters of this book have addressed but a few episodes of American history germane to this issue. That said, everyone agrees that America has done both good and bad things, so it could not sensibly be called purely divine or purely demonic. But the question is whether the *trajectory* of the American Empire has inclined more towards the divine or toward the demonic.

People who believe in God could agree with George W. Bush that American had "a calling from beyond the stars to stand for freedom."[7] With Henry Cabot Lodge that America has "a great mission for the world—a mission of good, a mission of freedom."[8] People might even agree with Albert J. Beveridge that America was divinely marked to "lead in the redemption of the world."[9] But if one accepts the idea that America has such a calling, a review of the trajectory of America's foreign policy shows that it has not even come close to fulfilling it.

Yet in mainstream political culture, American Exceptionalism in the self-congratulatory sense is widely held as if it had never been challenged.

Reaffirmations of American Exceptionalism

The election of Donald Trump resulted in a renewed burst of discussion about American virtue. A chief problem with Trump in the area of foreign policy, his critics have said, concerns whether he will continue to preserve America's long-standing role as an enforcer of international norms and rules to which, they claim, the US has adhered. As an indication of how pervasive this claim about America's traditional adherence to international norms and rules is in multiple primary outlets of established opinion, note that:

- Writing in *Foreign* Policy, two critics said that by failing to "subscribe to the long-held belief that 'American exceptionalism' and U.S. leadership are intertwined," Trump rejected the idea of an "open, rule-based international economy" that previous presidents had nurtured.

- An article in the *Financial Times* complained about Trump's disregard for "international norms that have governed America as the pillar of the liberal economic order."

- A national-security reporter for CNN criticized Trump for failing to endorse "America's traditional role as a global leader and shaper of international norms."

- Still another critic said that Trump rejected the ideal of "the global community under the rule of law," which the United States had upheld for decades.[10]

Andrew Bacevich on American Exceptionalism

The only problem with these comparisons of Trump with previous precedents, wrote Andrew Bacevich, is that they ignore history, such as:

> meddling in foreign elections; coups and assassination plots in Iran, Guatemala, the Congo, Cuba, South Vietnam, Chile, Nicaragua, and elsewhere; indiscriminate aerial bombing campaigns in North Korea and throughout Southeast Asia; a nuclear arms race bringing the world to the brink of Armageddon; support for corrupt, authoritarian regimes in Iran, Turkey, Greece, South Korea, South Vietnam, the Philippines, Brazil, Egypt, Nicaragua, El Salvador, and elsewhere—many of them abandoned when deemed inconvenient; the shielding of illegal activities through the use of the Security Council veto; unlawful wars launched under false pretenses; "extraordinary rendition," torture, and the indefinite imprisonment of persons without any semblance of due process.[11]

These actions and episodes do not, pointed out Bacevich, suggest a nation committed to the rule of law. "What they reveal instead is a pattern of behavior common to all great powers in just about any era: following the rules when it serves their interest to do so; disregarding the rules whenever they become an impediment." In other words, the American Empire is not exceptional. "[I]n reclassifying yesterday's hegemon as today's promulgator and respecter of norms," concluded Bacevich, "members of [the foreign-policy] establishment perpetrate a fraud."[12] Indeed, they perpetuate it.

Given the actual history of the American Empire, it is a fraud to endorse American Exceptionalism in the self-praising sense. Once this point has been made and documented, digested and accepted, the question arises: How can making this point be valuable? There are at least three ways.

First, there is value in simply recognizing truth. It would be good in itself for Americans to realize that the account of our country as exceptional in the self-congratulatory sense—as morally superior to other countries—is false. The description of our country as exceptional is justified only if used, as Seymour Martin Lipset urged, as a "double-edged sword": If there are some senses in which America is the best, there are also senses in which it is the worst.

Second, if Americans come to accept this fact to the extent that it becomes culturally embedded—so that it is expressed by people from presidents and senators to newspaper and television editors, from school teachers and college professors to stock brokers and business leaders, et cetera—then our country's present arrogance could change to humility. America needs to realize that, although it may presently be richer and more powerful than other nations, it is simply one nation among others, Indeed, this pre-eminent standing may even be on its way out, and what then for us from those towards whom we have been so haughty?

Third, in reflection of this humility, whether it be chosen or ultimately forced upon us by changing circumstances,[13] US leaders must recognize that they have no right to act as if the American government were a de facto global government. They therefore have no right to think in terms of American *exemptionalism*, as if America does not need to follow the rules of international law that other countries must obey. We must disavow the arrogant and dangerous attitude, reflected in the Bush Doctrine that America can engage in preemptive attacks on countries that present no imminent threat.

Endnotes

1 Dick Cheney and Liz Cheney, *Exceptional: Why the World Needs a Powerful America* (Threshold Editions, 2015), 1, 5, 257.

2 Ibid., 259.

3 Ronald Steel, *Pax Americana* (New York: Viking Press, 1967), vii.

4 Michael Ignatieff, "The Burden," *The New York Times Magazine*, 5

January 2003: 24, 52.

5 Dinesh D'Souza, "In Praise of an American Empire," *Christian Science Monitor*, 26 April 2002.

6 Robert Kagan, "The Benevolent Empire," *Foreign Policy*, Summer 1998: 24-35.

7 George W. Bush, "Remarks Accepting the Presidential Nomination at the Republican National Convention in New York City," 2 September 2004.

8 Lodge's speech was reprinted in Julia Ward Howe, ed., *Masterpieces of American Eloquence* (Kessinger, 2011).

9 John B. Judis, "The Chosen Nation: The Influence of Religion on U.S. Foreign Policy," *Carnegie Endowment for International Peace*, March 2005.

10 All four quoted in Andrew J. Bacevich, "The 'Global Order' Myth: Teary-eyed Nostalgia as Cover for U.S. Hegemony,"*American Conservative,* 15 June 2017.

11 Ibid.

12 Ibid.

| Epilogue |

THE AMERICAN CENTURY

The notion of American Exceptionalism in the positive sense has been closely related to the idea of the American Century, meaning a century in which America dominated the global economy and international relations. The relation between the two was explained by Andrew Bacevich in these terms. The allure of the American Century

> stems from the conviction that the United States as a great power differs from every other great power in history. It stands apart, unique, singular, *sans pareil.* It that sense, the American Century is American Exceptionalism manifested on a global scale.[1]

As to when the American Century began, David Traxel published a book entitled *1898: The Birth of the American Century*. However, no one would say that America was then dominant economically and politically. Traxel's claim was only that America's wars in 1898 turned it into a world power.[2]

More realistically, the American Century could be said to have begun at the end of World War I. As mentioned in Chapter 2, this war, besides making America "fabulously rich" (G. J. Meyer), has been called "the war that launched the American Century" (*The Telegraph*). According to that idea, the American Century would have begun in 1918. However, the world was still dominated by the British Empire, which it would be until World War II.

Most commonly, the American Century is said to have begun in 1945 at the end of World War II, or in 1941, when Henry Luce, who created several magazines, published an article in his *Life* magazine entitled "The American Century." Urging President Roosevelt to enter the war, Luce said that being "the most powerful and vital nation in the world," it is time for it "to assume the leadership of the world." Luce proclaimed "that if only Americans would think internationally, [and] surge into the world, . . . the next hundred years would be theirs." American leadership would be able to create "an international moral order." Moreover, Luce said, America "must undertake now to be the Good Samaritan of the entire world."[3]

Because Luce was correct about one big thing—the war left the United States in a position of global primacy—his essay evoked an enormous amount of discussion about the American Century. In our day, two of the central questions are: (1) Assuming there has indeed been an American Century, when did or will it end? (2) Did America become a Good Samaritan and bring about an international moral order?

1. The End of the American Century

Here we will look at the answers of Alfred McCoy, Tom Engelhardt, Andrew Bacevich, Walter LaFeber, and Joseph Nye.

Alfred McCoy

In his 2017 book, *In the Shadows of the American Century,* plus some later essays dealing with Trump, historian Alfred McCoy argued that the American Century—the period during which this country had the economic and military power, along with the perceived moral stature, to call the shots—is not over but soon will be.

Although American leaders and pundits have accepted the idea that the American Century will end in 2040 or 2050, McCoy provided reasons to believe that the end may come even sooner. Alluding to the fact that Luce's famous essay advocating an American Century was published in 1941, McCoy said that this period "will be ending well before 2041."[4]

This might seem impossible, given the seemingly entrenched bastions of America's post-war global power, which "fostered an aura of American power so formidable that Washington could re-order significant parts of the world almost at will, enforcing peace, setting the international agenda, and toppling governments on four continents."[5]

However, wrote McCoy, "So delicate is their ecology of power, when things start to go truly wrong, empires regularly unravel with unholy speed."[6] And the American Empire started to go truly wrong with the Bush-Cheney administration's 2003 invasion of Iraq. "[A]fter expending its economic and diplomatic capital in an Iraq war replete with false intelligence and lurid acts of torture, Washington's leadership began to wane."[7] Things started going even worse with the election of Donald Trump, which "is ensuring the accelerated collapse of American global hegemony."[8]

Before the Bush-Cheney and Trump administrations, to be sure, "long-term trends had already started to limit the influence of any American leader on the world stage." For example, America's share of the global economy dropped from 40% in 1960 to 22% in 2014, then to 15% in 2017, and China probably "will surpass the U.S., in absolute terms, as the world's number one economy within a decade."[9] There has also been "an erosion of U.S. technological primacy, an inability to apply its overwhelming military power in a way that achieved expected policy goals."[10]

However, added McCoy, "Trump has accelerated this decline by damaging almost all the key components in the intricate architecture of American global power." For one thing, "great empires require skilled leadership," but in this regard "the Trump administration has failed spectacularly," with nation after nation pulling away from Washington. For example, the new leader of South Korea won the presidency on a campaign to "learn to say no" to America.[11]

Trump has lost more respect by dropping out of the global attempt to slow global warming.[12] Trump is also cutting back on scientific research, including artificial intelligence, which will be crucial to space warfare and cyber-warfare, while China, which is "ramping up its scientific research across the board," is "launching 'a new multi-billion-dollar initiative' linked to building 'military robots.'"[13]

China, in fact, has a grand strategy to challenge Washington's hegemony: "massive infrastructure investments that would bind Europe and Asia into a 'world island,' the future epicenter of global economic power."[14] While China was working on this, the United States was playing war games:

> During the post-9/11 decade when Washington was spilling its blood and treasure onto desert sands, Beijing was investing its trillions of surplus dollars from trade with the United States in the economic integration of the Eurasian landmass.[15]

Moreover, while America had long been in control of the two "axial ends" of the Eurasian continent—NATO and Asian allies—Trump within his first year greatly reduced America's influence at both ends. "The U.S. has lost its leadership role," said an economist at the Asian Development Bank. "And China is quickly replacing it."[16]

Trump's power to continue to make destructive changes may not last long, and some of his changes may be reversed. But it's unlikely that America, regardless of changes in the White House and Congress, will regain the status it lost during Trump's tenure. According to McCoy, "World leadership lost is never readily recovered."[17]

In saying that the United States is not going to remain the global hegemon indefinitely, McCoy was not simply expressing his personal opinion. He backed it up with the 2012 US National Intelligence Council assessment: "By 2030, no country will be a hegemonic power." Within a decade, for example, China will be "ready to contest American dominion over space and cyberspace."[18]

Of course, America's military power, upon which its empire has been primarily based, will not soon be surpassed, or even equaled. Washington's all-powerful military, granted McCoy, would allow it for some time to "remain 'first among equals' among the other great powers in 2030."[19] But even in this regard, America's superiority is not as great as commonly thought. In 2016, the RAND Corporation published a report entitled *War with China,* which said that an American victory could not be assured.[20]

Moreover, America may soon have insufficient money to finance its military at its present level. Various negative trends

> are encouraging ever sharper criticism of the dollar's role as the world's reserve currency. One of the prime benefits of global power is [that] you get to send the nations of the world bundles of brightly colored paper . . . , and they happily hand over goods of actual value like automobiles, minerals, or oil. . . . By 2005, analysts could argue that "the core advantage of the U.S. economy . . . is the peculiar role of the U.S. currency," which allows it "to keep hundreds of thousands of troops stationed all over the world."[21]

But with the world's central banks holding an astronomical amount in US Treasury notes, Russia, China, and other countries are saying that it no longer makes sense to retain the present arrangements.

> Foreigners watching America become the world's biggest debtor nation, without any of the austerity measures it had imposed on others in similar situations, began to see "the IMF, World Bank, World Trade Organization and other Washington surrogates . . . as vestiges of a lost American empire no longer able to rule by economic strength, left only with military domination. If China, Russia and their allies have their way, the U.S. will no longer . . . have the money for unlimited military spending."[22]

Tom Engelhardt

In a 2012 essay entitled "American Empire: A Disaster on Autopilot," Tom Engelhardt wrote even more disparagingly of US military power than McCoy.

> By all the usual measuring sticks, the U.S. should be supreme in a historically unprecedented way. And yet it couldn't be more obvious that it's not, that despite all the bases, elite forces, private armies, drones, aircraft carriers, wars, conflicts, strikes, interventions, and clandestine operations, despite a labyrinthine intelligence bureaucracy that never seems to stop growing and into which we pour a minimum of $80 billion a year, nothing seems to work out in an imperially satisfying way. . . . One thing seems obvious: a superpower military with unparalleled capabilities for one-way destruction no longer has the more basic ability to impose its will anywhere on the planet. Quite the opposite, U.S. military power has been remarkably discredited globally by the most pitiful of forces.

Suggesting that the role of America as the global hegemon may never be replaced, Engelhardt said: "Explain it as you will, it's as if the planet itself, or humanity, had somehow been inoculated against the imposition of imperial power, as if it now rejected it whenever and wherever applied."[23]

Andrew Bacevich

In a 2012 essay entitled "The American Century Is Over," Andrew Bacevich declared: "If an American Century ever did exist, it's now ended." As to when it ended, Bacevich, while acknowledging the difficulty of identifying historical turning points, suggested that it was 2008, "when Bush gave up on victory in Iraq. . . and when the Great Recession brought the U.S. economy to its knees." It was at that time, Bacevich said, when "what remained of the American Century ran out of steam and ground to a halt."[24]

Bacevich realized that US politicians would reject this view. In 2011, Mitt Romney said that we must not "give in to those who assert America's time has passed." The following year, President Obama declared: "America is back. . . . Anyone who tells you otherwise, anyone who tells you that America is in decline or that our influence has waned, doesn't know what they're talking about." Although this is "pure malarkey," Bacevich said, American politicians will continue to "peddle the fiction that with the right cast of characters running Washington, history will once again march to America's drumbeat."[25]

Walter LaFeber

Some American politicians and commentators speak as if the American Century, far from having ended or being close to it, will continue indefinitely. In 2000, neoconservatives started an organization named "Project for the New American Century." This organization folded in 2006, after the failure of the Iraq War. However, it left, said LaFeber, a "notable legacy: it had helped destroy any lingering hopes for an American Century."[26]

But in 2010, President Obama declared: "There's no reason the 21st century is not going to be the American Century just like the 20th century was."[27] By contrast, historian LaFeber enunciated an even more radical view than Bacevich's. With reference to those who fear that the American Century will not last until its hundredth birthday LaFeber wrote:

> [T]he real problem was not that the American Century had reached a premature end—it was, contrary to Obama's pronouncement, that it had never begun. It had never existed except as an illusion.[28]

Joseph S. Nye, Jr.

In 2015, political scientist Joseph Nye of Harvard University, who is famous for his discussion of "soft power," published a book dealing with the question, *Is the American Century Over?*[29] Although his short answer was "no," he qualified it so much that his position is not as different from McCoy's as his short answer suggested.

In 2041, Nye said, the United States will still have "primacy in power resources and play the central role in the global balance of power among states."[30] In other words, "the American Century is not over," but it "will not look like it did in the twentieth century."[31]

Making a big point about the distinction between *absolute power* and *relative power*, Nye opposed the "declinists," who believe that America has declined in terms of absolute power. However, Nye granted that that the American Century "may end simply because of the rise of others."[32] It is difficult to understand why he considers absolute power relevant: The issue of relative power is what is crucial to whether America is the global hegemon and hence to the question of whether there will still be an American Century.

Moreover, Nye cited, as did McCoy, the US National Intelligence Council's assertion that, although the US will likely remain the most powerful nation, it will no longer be the sole superpower or the global hegemon.[33] But if the United States will no longer have hegemony, how can one still speak of an American Century?

In any case, having said that the American Century would end if another nation overtook the United States, Nye said that the "only country capable of such a role is China."[34] But then, referring to economic, military, and soft power, Nye said that "China still lags far behind the United States in all three dimensions of power."[35] With that assertion, Nye seemed to be back to his original position—that the end of the American Century will not come soon.[36]

This is certainly how McCoy understood Nye's book. McCoy described him as typical of Washington insiders who have "missed the significance of the rapid global changes in Eurasia that are in the process of undermining the grand strategy for world dominion that Washington has pursued these past seven decades." Referring to the "stunning insularity" of Nye's worldview, McCoy added:

> Offering a simple list of ways in which he believes U.S. military, economic, and cultural power remains singular and superior, [Nye's *Is the American Century Over?*] argued that there was no force, internal or global, capable of eclipsing America's future as the world's premier power. For those pointing to Beijing's surging economy and proclaiming this "the Chinese century," Nye offered up a roster of negatives: China's per capita income "will take decades to catch up (if ever)" with America's; it has myopically "focused its policies primarily on its region"; and it has "not developed any significant capabilities for global force projection." Above all, Nye claimed, China suffers "geopolitical disadvantages in the internal Asian balance of power, compared to America." Or put it this way (and in this Nye is typical of a whole world of Washington thinking): with more allies, ships, fighters, missiles, money, patents, and blockbuster movies than any other power, Washington wins. Hands down.[37]

This perspective is perhaps comforting in Washington, said McCoy, "at a moment when America's hegemony is visibly crumbling amid a tectonic shift in global power."[38]

2. America and an International Moral Order

In Luce's essay, he suggested that one value of an American Century would be that this country could use its leadership to work to bring about an international moral order. The second question for this epilogue is whether America has used its power to advance such an order. This section looks at the ideas of three thinkers— Richard Stengel, John Dower, and Tom Engelhardt— who have written about this issue.

Richard Stengel

In 2017, Richard Stengel, former managing editor of *Time* magazine, published an essay in the *Atlantic* entitled "The End of the American Century." According to Stengel, Trump was bringing an end to the role of America that had been advocated by Henry Luce in his famous 1941 essay, "The American Century." Crucial to the creation of such a century would be "a passionate devotion to great American ideals," including love of freedom, justice, and charity. The presidents prior to Trump, Stengel contended, had this love. But because Trump has no love for these ideals, his administration "is the death knell of the American Century."[39]

Clarifying how he understands the "American Century," Stengel said that it does not mean "American power or hegemony" but "America as a global model and guarantor of freedom and rule of law and fairness." These qualities, Stengel explained, lay behind America's influence: "Our power and influence with our friends and adversaries came in large part because we were the one nation that did not always put ourselves first."[40]

There can be no doubt about Stengel's portrayal of Trump. But his portrayal of previous presidents is questionable. Bacevich would certainly question it. Whereas Stengel said that America was one nation that did not always put itself first, Bacevich spoke of America's "unflagging self-interest."[41]

John Dower

In 2017, John Dower published a little book entitled *The Violent American Century.* Unlike Stengel, Dower used "American Century" in the standard sense, referring to America's military and hegemonic power. Not endorsing the view of some that the American Century is over, or soon will be, Dower said that, in spite of the military failures in Vietnam, Korea, Afghanistan, and Iraq, he still considered the label useful:

> For good or evil, America bestrides the globe without truly close competitors. Its economy is second to none. Its prosperity and professed ideals are still beacons to many. However one may evaluate its success in warfighting (or peacekeeping), its reach remains impressive. The world has never seen a state with so many military garrisons in so many far-flung countries. . . . America's annual military spending is greater than much of the rest of the world combined. When it comes to maintaining and ceaselessly updating the most sophisticated instruments of destruction imaginable . . . , the United States simply has no peer.[42]

However, Dower's book differs from most books on the American Century by virtue of the fact that he inserted the term "violent" in the title. In his introduction, he explained:

> [America's] military preeminence, with all its fault lines and failures, is a cardinal aspect of the American century that emerged after World War II. Side by side with this . . . is the violence that runs like a ground bass through these long

> postwar decades. . . . America has engaged in violence abroad far more frequently than most Americans realize or perhaps care to know.[43]

Dower added that "particular attention is given to the generally taboo subject of state terror as practiced by the United States and its allies."[44]

Tom Engelhardt

Equally critical of American violence since World War II was Tom Engelhardt in a 2016 essay asking, "Where Did the American Century Go?" For several decades after America entered World War II, the world seemed to follow Luce's script (except for a few failures, most notably in Vietnam and Korea). Not only did the war leave the United States as the wealthiest, most powerful, and most influential country in the world; but in 1991, the Soviet Union collapsed, leaving America as the only superpower, so that it would seemingly be able to create "a planetary Pax Americana."[45]

However, things did not work out as those crowing about a unipolar world had expected. Who could have imagined, asked Engelhardt, that a single superpower could have utterly failed "to bring the world to anything approximating heel?" Moreover:

> Who would have believed a movie or novel in which that same power, without national enemies of any significance in any of the regions where the fighting was taking place, would struggle unsuccessfully, year after year, to subdue scattered, lightly armed insurgents (aka "terrorists") across a disintegrating region? Who could have imagined that every measure Washington took to assert its might only seemed to blow back (or blow somewhere, anyway)? Who would have believed that its full-scale invasion of one weak Middle Eastern country, its "mission accomplished" moment, would in the

> end prove a trip through "the gates of hell"? Who would have imagined that such an invasion could punch a hole in the oil heartlands of the region that, 13 years later, is still a bleeding wound, now seemingly beyond repair, or that it would set loose a principle of chaos and disintegration that seems to be spreading like a planetary Brexit?[46]

Continuing, Engelhardt said:

> If you were to do a little tabulation of the results of [the] years of American Century-ism across the Greater Middle East, you would discover a signature kind of chaos. . . . Most of the places where the U.S. has let its military and its air power loose—Afghanistan, Iraq, Yemen, Libya, Somalia, and Syria—are now either failed or failing states. . . . Moreover, in the stunted imagination of present-day Washington, the only policies imaginable in response to all this are highly militarized and call for more of the same: more air power in the skies over distant battlefields, more boots on the ground, more private contractors and hired guns, more munitions and weaponry. . . . For such a world, a new term is needed. Perhaps something like *failed region*. This, it seems, is one thing that the American Century has come to mean 75 years after Henry Luce urged it into existence.

An even stronger term might be needed for the American Century, suggested Engelhardt: *failed world.*[47]

* * * * * * *

In the Conclusion, I suggested that America should come

to regard itself as simply one nation among others. At the outset of the 21st century, however, the American government did the opposite, stepping up the drive for global dominance discussed in Chapter 13. But if Alfred McCoy is correct, the American Century will end in the not-too-distant future, so there will be no choice but for America to quit regarding itself as in a class by itself.

As for this epilogue's second question, this book as a whole shows that Luce's dreams for an American Century—that this country would be a Good Samaritan for unfortunate countries and would promote a moral international order—were naive. Instead of fulfilling Luce's dream, the American Century has been, as Dower said, terribly violent and, as Engelhardt added, it ended up leading to a failed world-largely because the American Empire, as Engelhardt said in a later essay, became "an empire of chaos," which is "incapable of producing any results other than destruction and further fragmentation across staggeringly large parts of the planet".[48]

In light of this history, many Americans will likely, with Bacevich, be "more than content to consign the American Century to the past." Indeed, after reviewing the statements of several thinkers who charged that Trump was contributing to the decline of U.S. hegemony, Paul Street asked: "What would be so awful about the end of 'the American Era?'" Reviewing some of the episodes discussed in the present book plus some more (such as the coup in Chile that overthrew the government of Salvador Allende and murdered him), Street asked: "Why should the world mourn the 'premature' end of the 'American Century'?"[49]

Bacevich also hoped that "the United States will accept the outcome gracefully," which I interpret to mean: be willing to begin regarding itself as simply one nation among others. Bacevich also expressed hope that "American policy makers will attend to the looming challenges of multipolarity."[50]

While endorsing these hopes, I would add my own hope that policy makers would rethink the United Nations, finally accepting the vision that the USA and the USSR rejected, according to which no members of the Security Council would be able to veto the will of the majority, so the Council would be able to prevent wars. The Security Council should also have the power to enforce other policies needed to save civilization, such as the power to bring carbon emissions down to virtually zero.

It would be best, moreover, if China, Russia, America, and other countries would agree that the United Nations should be transformed into a global democratic government. Joseph Schwartzberg has shown one way in which this could be done.[51]

Endnotes

1 Andrew J. Bacevich, *The Short American Century* (Harvard University Press, 2012), 231.
2 David Traxel, *1898: The Birth of the American Century* (Vintage, 1999).
3 Henry R. Luce, "The American Century," *Life* magazine, 17 February 1941.
4 Alfred W. McCoy, *In the Shadows of the American Century* (Haymarket Books, 2017), 24.
5 Alfred W. McCoy, "The Demolition of U.S. Global Power: Donald Trump's Road to Debacle in the Greater Middle East," TomDispatch, 16 July 2017.
6 McCoy, *In the Shadows*, 227.
7 Ibid., 231.
8 McCoy, "The Demolition of U.S. Global Power."
9 Alfred W. McCoy, "The World According to Trump: Or How to Build a Wall and Lose an Empire," Information Clearing House, 16 January 2018.
10 McCoy, "The Demolition of U.S. Global Power."
11 McCoy, "The World According to Trump."
12 McCoy, *In the Shadows,* 250.
13 McCoy, "The Demolition of U.S. Global Power."
14 McCoy, *In the Shadows,* 23.
15 Ibid., 207.
16 McCoy, "The World According to Trump"; "The Demolition of U.S. Global Power."
17 McCoy, "The World According to Trump."
18 McCoy, *In the Shadows*, 23, 58.
19 Ibid., 228.

20 Ibid., 220; citing David C. Gompert et al., *War with China: Thinking through the Unthinkable* (Santa Monica: RAND Corporation, 2016), iii-iv. On this point, see Andrei Martyanov, *Losing Military Supremacy : The Myopia of American Strategic Planning* (Atlanta: Clarity Press, 2018).

21 McCoy, *In the Shadows*, 238.

22 Ibid.

23 Tom Engelhardt, "American Empire: A Disaster on Autopilot," Tom Dispatch, 9 October 2012.

24 Andrew Bacevich, "The American Century Is Over," *The Chronicle of Higher Education,* 25 February 2012.

25 Ibid.

26 Walter LaFeber, "Illusions of an American Century," in Andrew J. Bacevich, ed., *The Short American Century* (Harvard University Press, 2012), 158-86, at 184.

27 Quoted in ibid., 158.

28 Ibid., 159.

29 Joseph S. Nye, Jr., *Is The American Century Over?* (Polity Press, 2015).

30 Ibid., 14.

31 Ibid., 125.

32 Ibid., 23.

33 Ibid., 97

34 Ibid., 44.

35 Ibid., 47.

36 In 2018, Nye published a little essay reporting that a Gallup poll of 134 countries showed that the favorable view of the United States had dropped 20 points since the end of Obama's presidency, and also that an index on soft power showed America dropping from first to third place (Joseph S. Nye, "Donald Trump and the Decline of US Soft Power," 6 February, 2018). Given how important Nye considers soft power, one might suspect that he would reconsider his opinion about the continuation of the American Century. However, he simply said that "there is every reason to hope that the US will recover its soft power after Trump."

37 McCoy, *In the Shadows,* 27, referring to Nye, *Is the American Century Over?* 50, 57, 114, 125-26.

38 Ibid., 28.

39 Richard Stengel, "The End of the American Century," *The Atlantic*, 26 January 2017.

40 Ibid.

41 Andrew J. Bacevich, *American Empire: The Realities and Consequences of U.S. Diplomacy* (Cambridge: Harvard University Press, 2002), 4.

42 John W. Dower, *The Violent American Century: War and Terror since World War II* (Haymarket Books, 2017), xi.

43 Ibid., x-xi.

44 Ibid.

45 Tom Engelhardt, "Where Did the American Century Go?" Tomgram, 7 July 2016.

46 Ibid.

47 Ibid.

48 Mark Karlin, "The United States Is a Force for Chaos Across the Planet" (interview of Tom Engelhardt), Truthout, 27 May 2018.

49 Bacevich, "The American Century Is Over." Paul Street, "The World Will Not Mourn the Decline of U.S. Hegemony," TruthDig, 20 February 2018.

50 Bacevich, "The American Century Is Over."

51 Joseph E. Schwartzberg, *Transforming the United Nations System: Design for a Workable World* (United Nations University Press, 2013).

INDEX